As he laye unravelling in the agonie of death, the Standers-by could hear him say softly, I have seen the Glories of the world.

C16 80

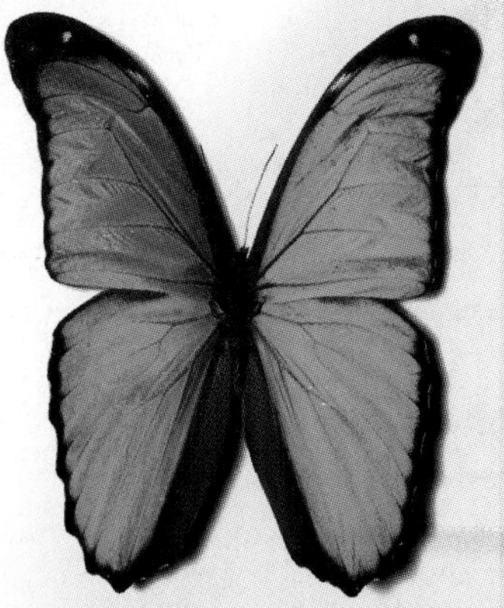

john aubrey

the minutes of lives

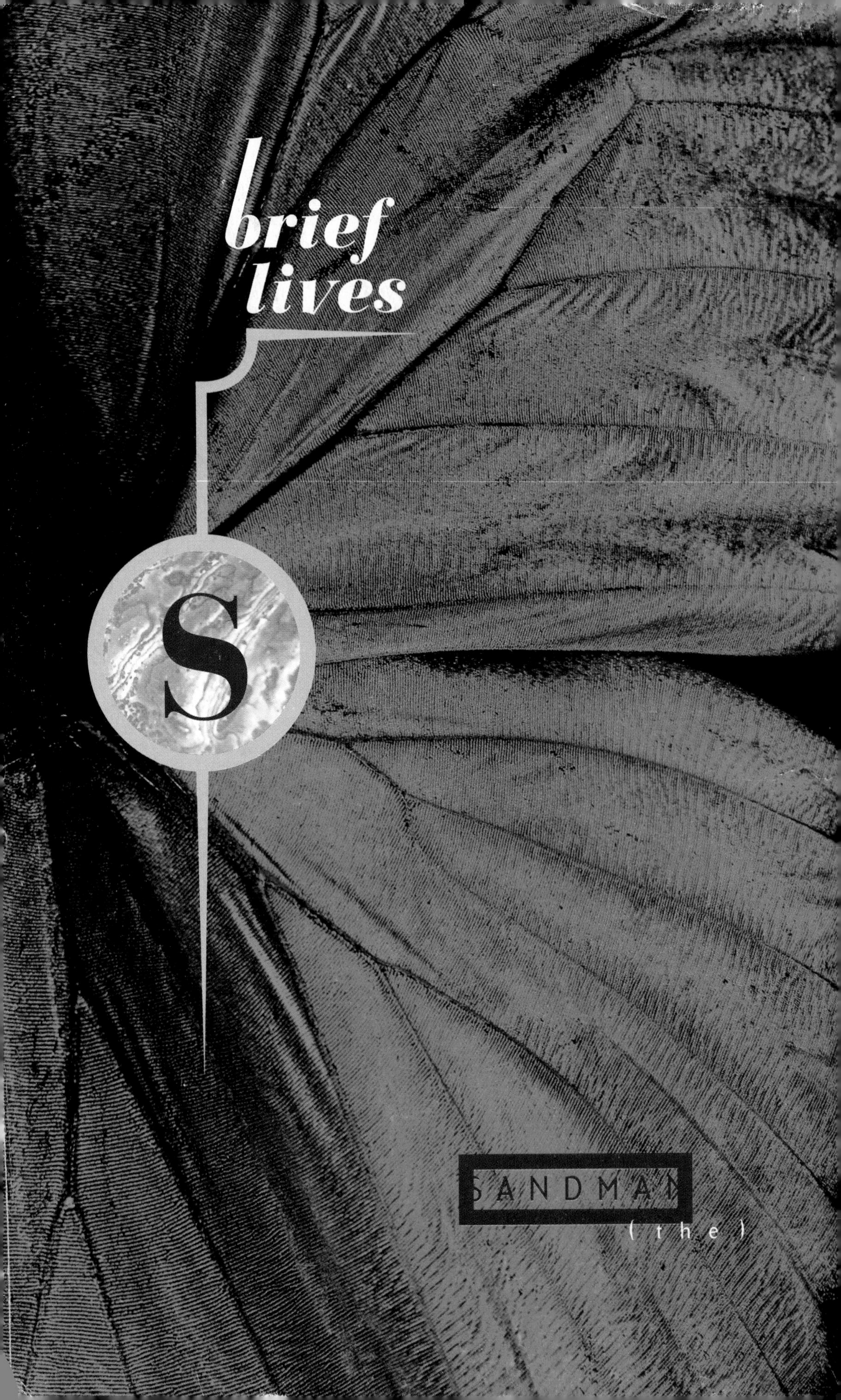
brief
lives
S
SANDMAN
(the)

neil gaiman
writer

penciller jill thompson

vince locke
inker
dick giordano
inker

todd klein
letterer
danny vozzo
colorist
dave mckean
covers and design

foreword by
neil gaiman

afterword by
peter straub

featuring characters created by
gaiman, kieth and dringenberg

SANDMAN

(the) *brief*

lives

Published by DC Comics.
Cover and
compilation copyright © 20 11
DC Comics.
(All Rights Reserved.)
Foreword and Afterword
Copyright © 1994 DC Comics
(All Rights Reserved.)
Originally published in single magazine form as
THE SANDMAN 41-49.
Copyright © 1992, 1993 DC Comics.
All Rights Reserved.

Hi Tori.

DC Comics,
1700 w New Broadway, York, NY 10019,

ISBN
978-1-4012-3263-4

2nd printing.

Cover art, interior illustrations and publication design by Dave McKean

A Warner Bros.
Entertainment
Company

Printed in the USA.

Cover design by Richard Bruning.

Library of Congress Cataloging-in-Publication Data
Gaiman, Neil.
The sandman. Vol. 7, Brief lives / Neil Gaiman, Jill Thompson, Vince Locke.
p. cm.
"Originally published in single magazine form as The Sandman 41-49."
ISBN 978-1-4012-3263-4 (alk. paper)
1. Graphic novels. I. Thompson, Jill, 1966- II. Locke, Vince. III. Title. IV. Title:
Brief lives.
PN6728.S26G457 2012
741.5'973—dc23

2012027193

karen berger
senior vp - executive editor, vertigo & editor - original series

lisa aufenanger, shelly roeberg
assistant editors - original series

bob kahan, scott nybakken
editors

robbin brosterman
design director - books

bob harras
vp - editor-in-chief

diane nelson
president

dan didio & jim lee
co-publishers

geoff johns
chief creative officer

john rood
executive vp - sales, marketing & business development

amy genkins
senior vp - business & legal affairs

nairi gardiner
senior vp - finance

jeff boison
vp - publishing operations

mark chiarello
vp - art direction & design

john cunningham
vp - marketing

terri cunningham
vp - talent relations & services

alison gill
senior vp - manufacturing & operations

hank kanalz
senior vp - digital

jay kogan
vp - business & legal affairs, publishing

jack mahan
vp - business affairs, talent

nick napolitano
vp - manufacturing administration

sue pohja
vp - book sales

courtney simmons
senior vp - publicity

bob wayne
senior vp - sales

not (an introduction)

a few words.

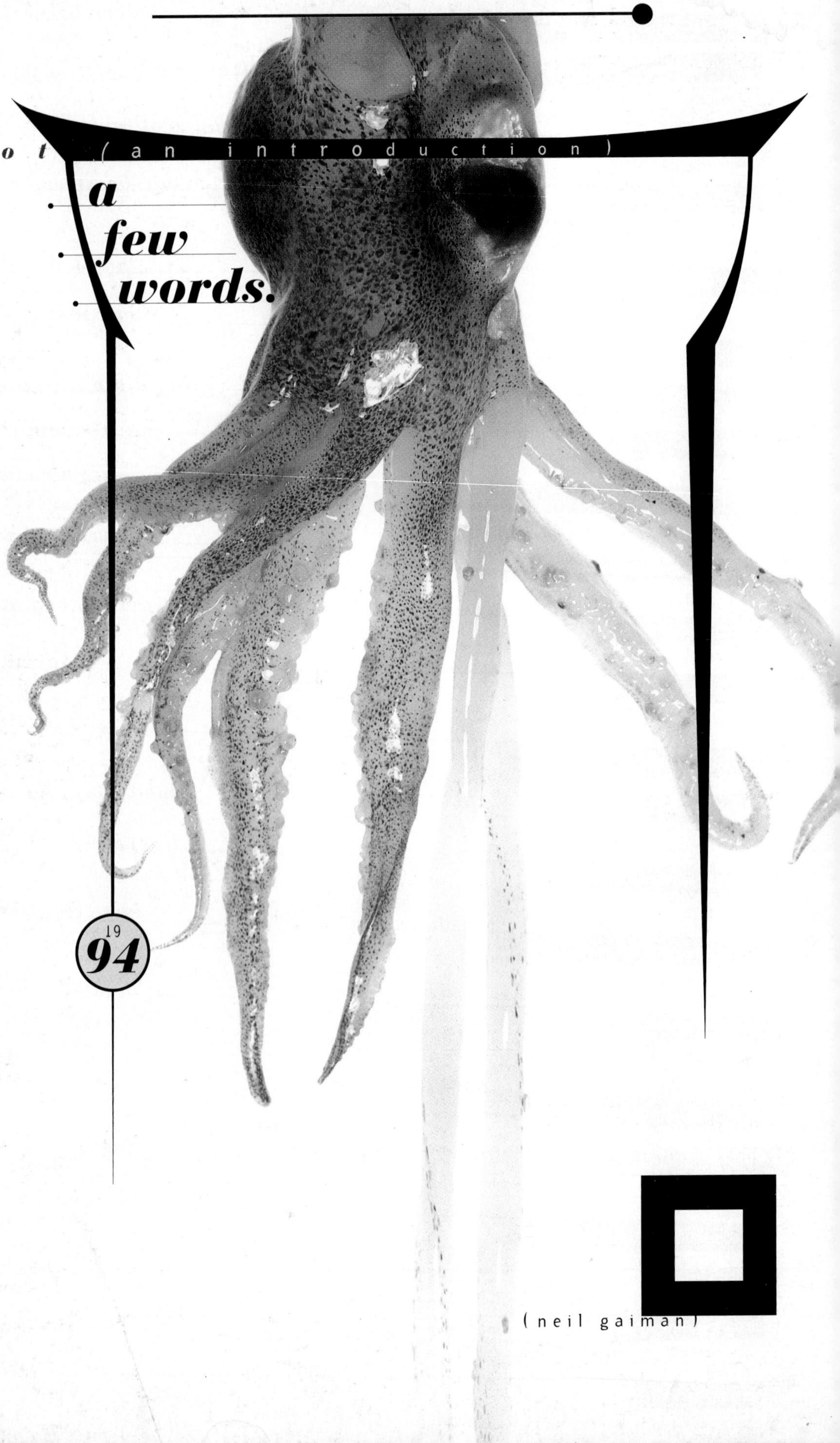

1994

(neil gaiman)

Peter Straub has done a real, honest-to-goodness introduction to the book, which, for reasons of not wanting to give too much away up front, we placed at the end of the book, after the story's over.

You can go and read it now, if you like: it's a very wise and wonderful introduction. Or you can wait until the end, in which case it will be a similarly wise and wonderful conclusion.

But that's the introduction, not this. This is just a few words at the beginning, to say hello, and tell you what you need to know before you start.

Hello.

What you need to know before you start: there are seven beings that aren't gods, who existed before humanity dreamed of gods and will exist after the last god is dead. They are called The Endless. They are embodiments of (in order of age) Destiny, Death, Dream, Destruction, Desire, Despair and Delirium.

Approximately three hundred years ago, Destruction abandoned his realm.

That's all you need.

The artist is always an important force in comics, and, for a writer, a vital collaborator; but I'd like to take this opportunity to extend my particular thanks to Jill Thompson for her contribution to this book, and to both Jill and Vince for their professionalism and skill. I couldn't have done it without you.

And thank you: to Danny Vozzo for all the colors; to Todd Klein, letterer's letterer; to Lisa Aufenanger; to Dick Giordano (for bailing us out); to Karen Berger, the very best editor a boy could wish for; and to Shelly Roeberg, small miracle.

Once again, Bob Kahan has turned a group of comics into a book with persnickety panache.

For Dave McKean, my friend and collaborator and my hardest critic, who, in seven years, hasn't stopped surprising me with the covers or design, thanks seem somewhat inadequate. But thanks, Dave.

This story was written in England and Australia and Waikiki and all over North America. My thanks to all my hosts and friends for permitting me to intrude upon their lives, however briefly.

neil gaiman february 1994

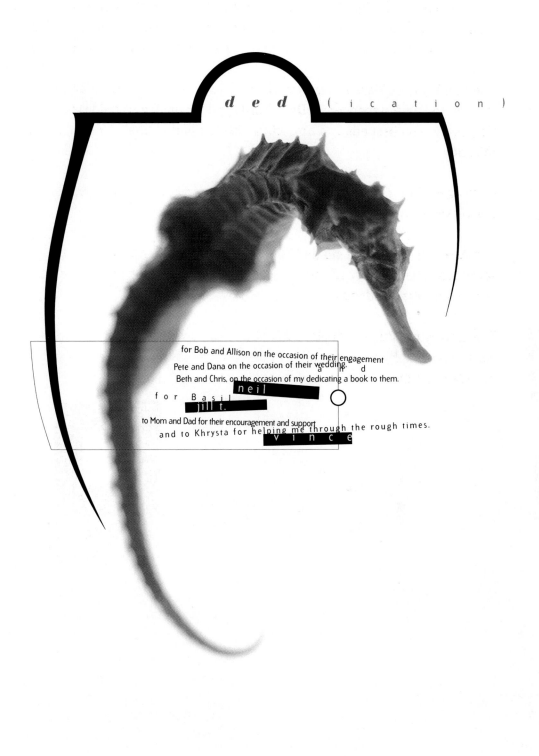

d e d (i c a t i o n)

for Bob and Allison on the occasion of their engagement
Pete and Dana on the occasion of their wedding.
and
Beth and Chris, on the occasion of my dedicating a book to them.

neil

for Basil

jill t.

to Mom and Dad for their encouragement and support
and to Khrysta for helping me through the rough times.

vince

chapter 1

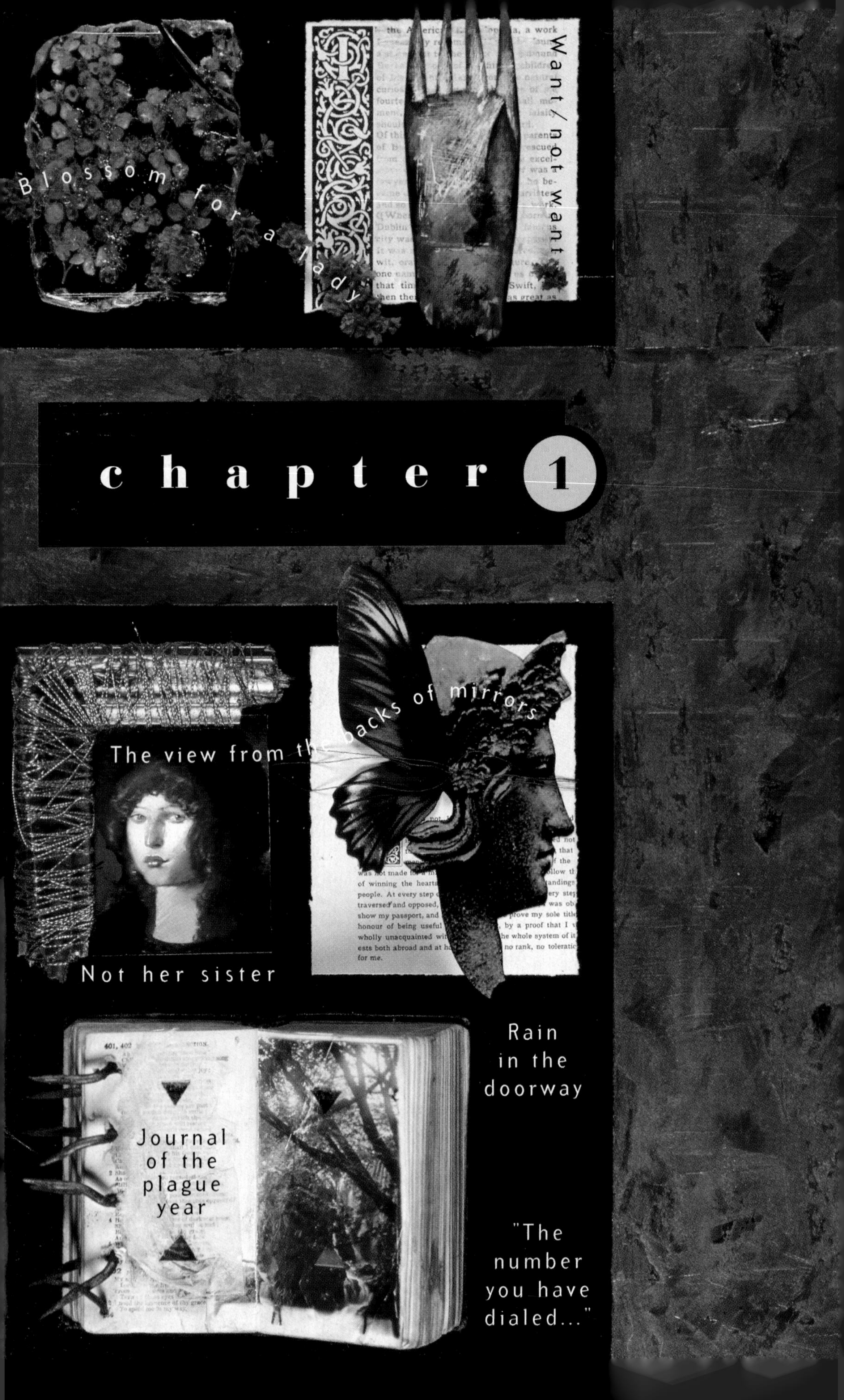
Blossom for a lady
Want/not want
The view from the backs of mirrors
Not her sister
Rain in the doorway
Journal of the plague year
"The number you have dialed..."

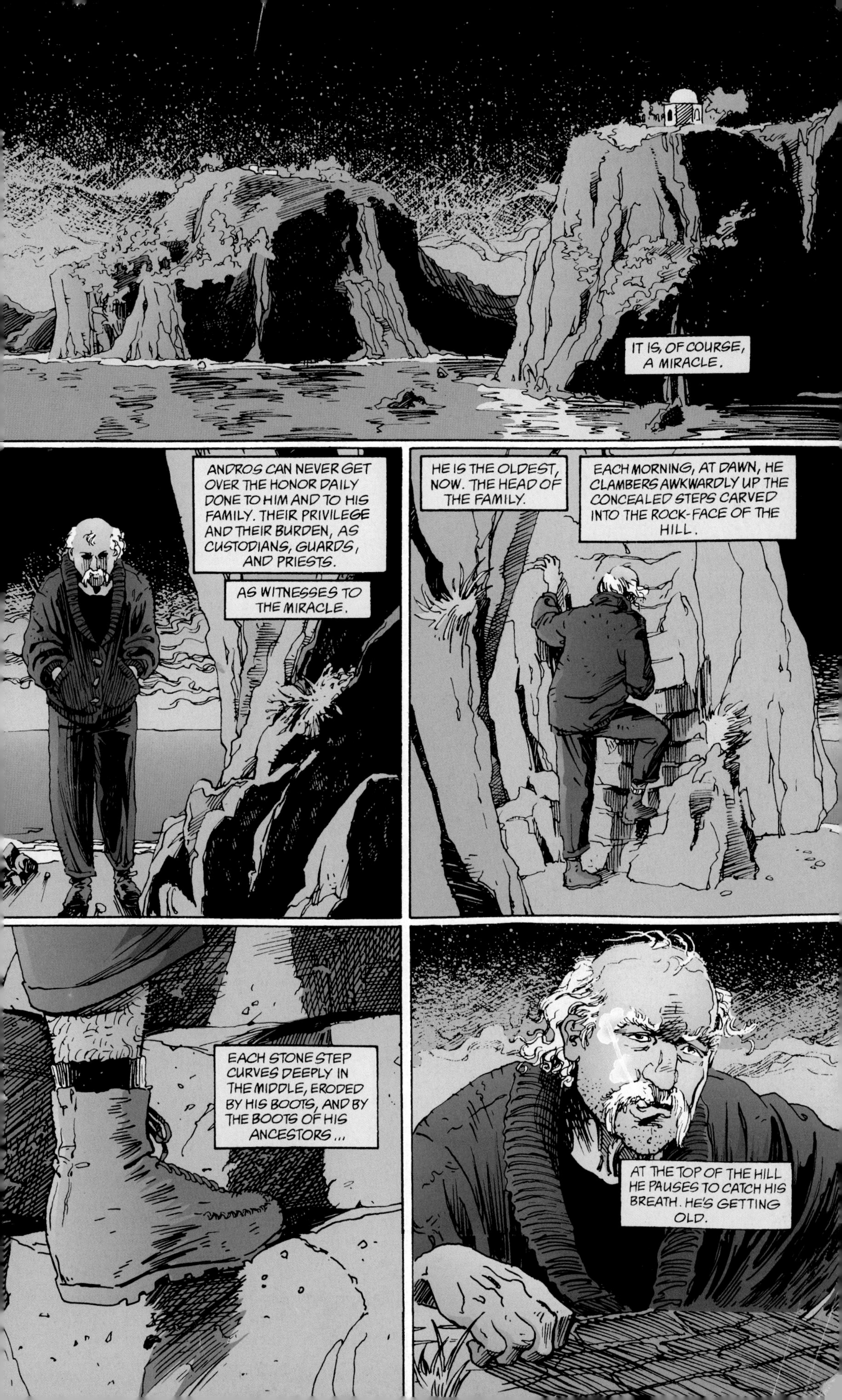
IT IS, OF COURSE, A MIRACLE.
ANDROS CAN NEVER GET OVER THE HONOR DAILY DONE TO HIM AND TO HIS FAMILY. THEIR PRIVILEGE AND THEIR BURDEN, AS CUSTODIANS, GUARDS, AND PRIESTS.
AS WITNESSES TO THE MIRACLE.
HE IS THE OLDEST, NOW. THE HEAD OF THE FAMILY.
EACH MORNING, AT DAWN, HE CLAMBERS AWKWARDLY UP THE CONCEALED STEPS CARVED INTO THE ROCK-FACE OF THE HILL.
EACH STONE STEP CURVES DEEPLY IN THE MIDDLE, ERODED BY HIS BOOTS, AND BY THE BOOTS OF HIS ANCESTORS...
AT THE TOP OF THE HILL HE PAUSES TO CATCH HIS BREATH. HE'S GETTING OLD.

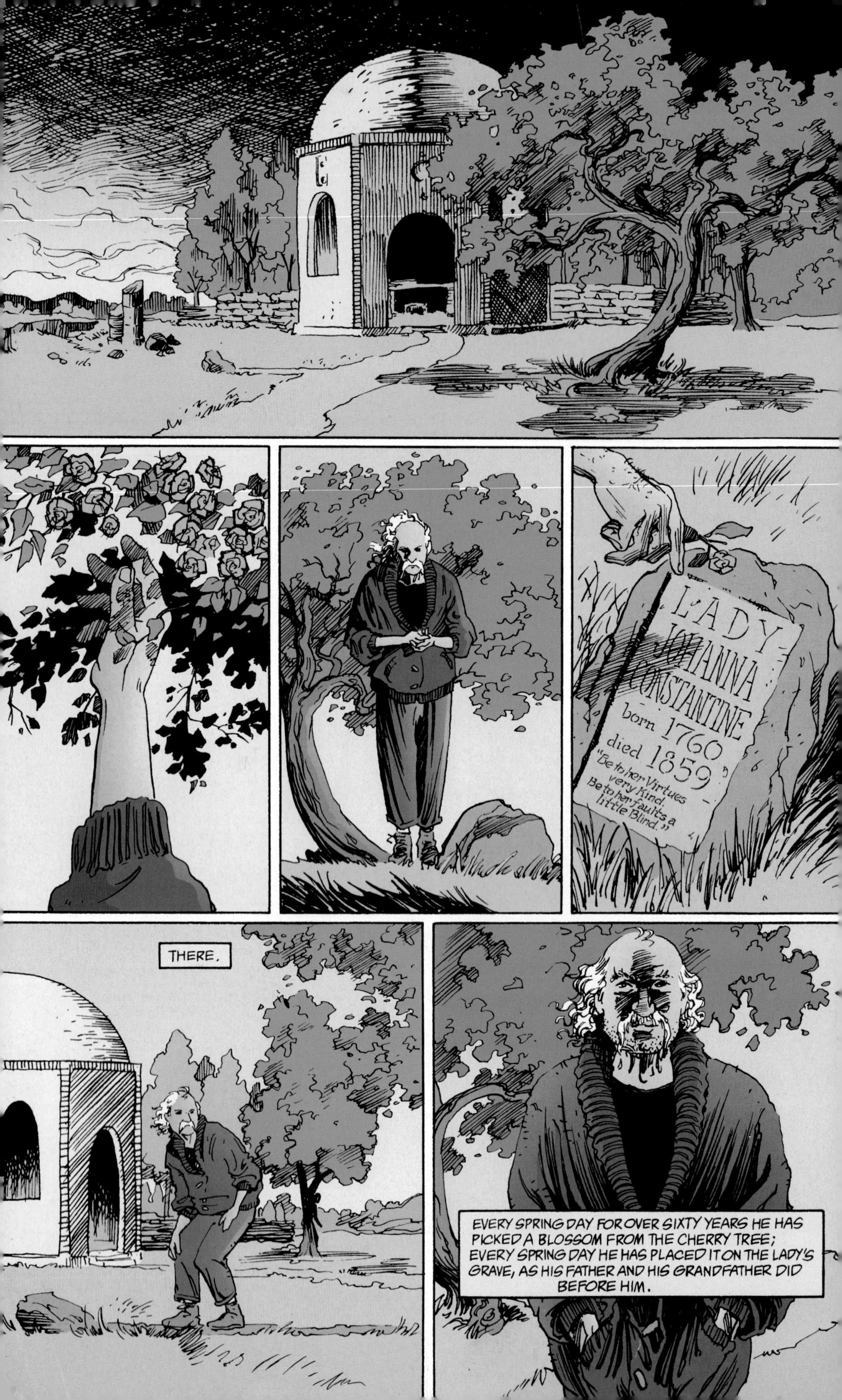
L'ADY
JOHANNA
CONSTANTINE
born 1760
died 1859
"Be to her Virtues
very Kind.
Be to her faults a
little Blind."
THERE.
EVERY SPRING DAY FOR OVER SIXTY YEARS HE HAS PICKED A BLOSSOM FROM THE CHERRY TREE; EVERY SPRING DAY HE HAS PLACED IT ON THE LADY'S GRAVE, AS HIS FATHER AND HIS GRANDFATHER DID BEFORE HIM.

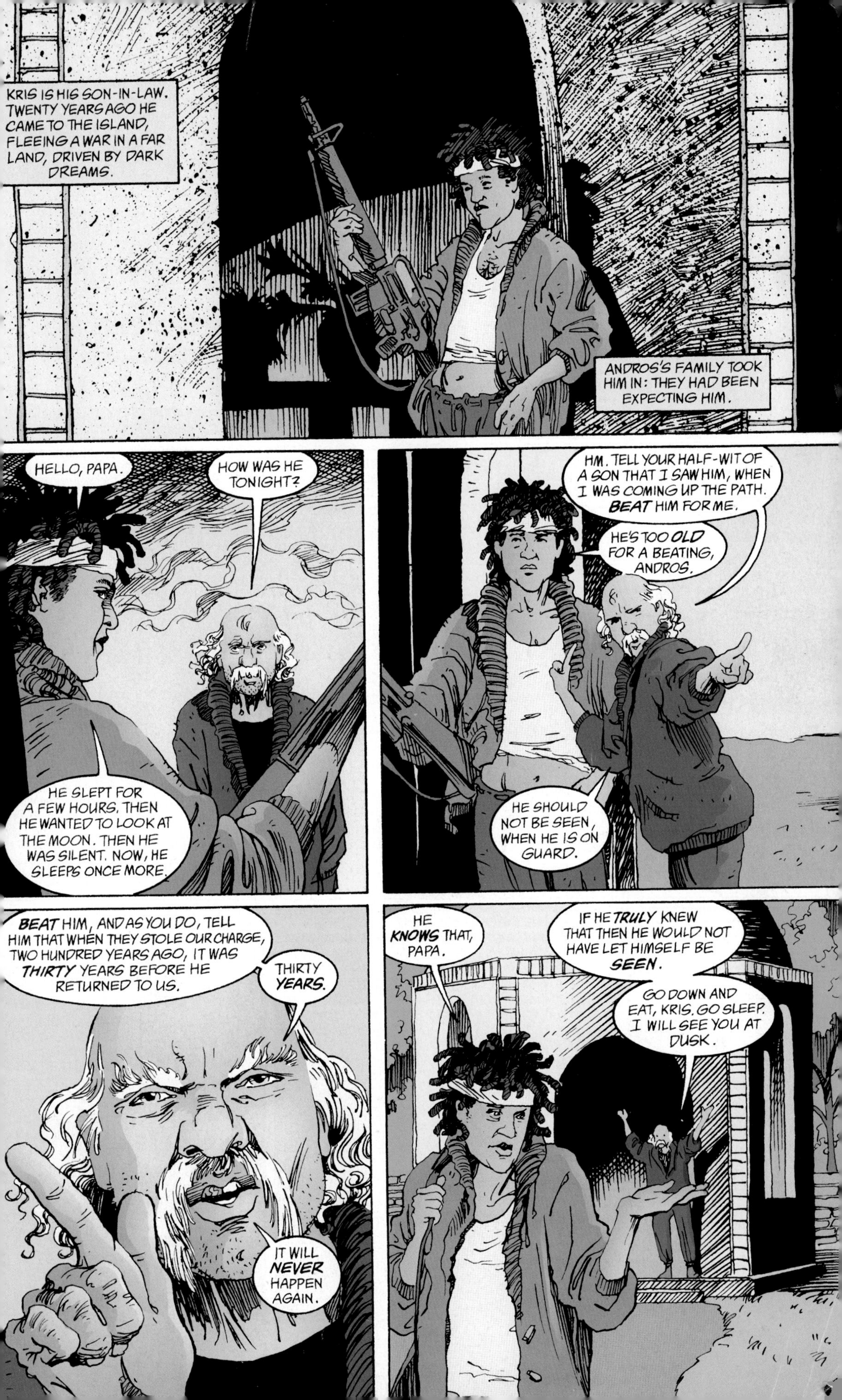
KRIS IS HIS SON-IN-LAW. TWENTY YEARS AGO HE CAME TO THE ISLAND, FLEEING A WAR IN A FAR LAND, DRIVEN BY DARK DREAMS.
ANDROS'S FAMILY TOOK HIM IN: THEY HAD BEEN EXPECTING HIM.
HELLO, PAPA.
HOW WAS HE TONIGHT?
HE SLEPT FOR A FEW HOURS. THEN HE WANTED TO LOOK AT THE MOON. THEN HE WAS SILENT. NOW, HE SLEEPS ONCE MORE.
HM. TELL YOUR HALF-WIT OF A SON THAT I SAW HIM, WHEN I WAS COMING UP THE PATH. **BEAT** HIM FOR ME.
HE'S TOO **OLD** FOR A BEATING, ANDROS.
HE SHOULD NOT BE SEEN, WHEN HE IS ON GUARD.
BEAT HIM, AND AS YOU DO, TELL HIM THAT WHEN THEY STOLE OUR CHARGE, TWO HUNDRED YEARS AGO, IT WAS **THIRTY** YEARS BEFORE HE RETURNED TO US.
THIRTY **YEARS**.
IT WILL **NEVER** HAPPEN AGAIN.
HE **KNOWS** THAT, PAPA.
IF HE **TRULY** KNEW THAT THEN HE WOULD NOT HAVE LET HIMSELF BE **SEEN**.
GO DOWN AND EAT, KRIS. GO SLEEP. I WILL SEE YOU AT DUSK.

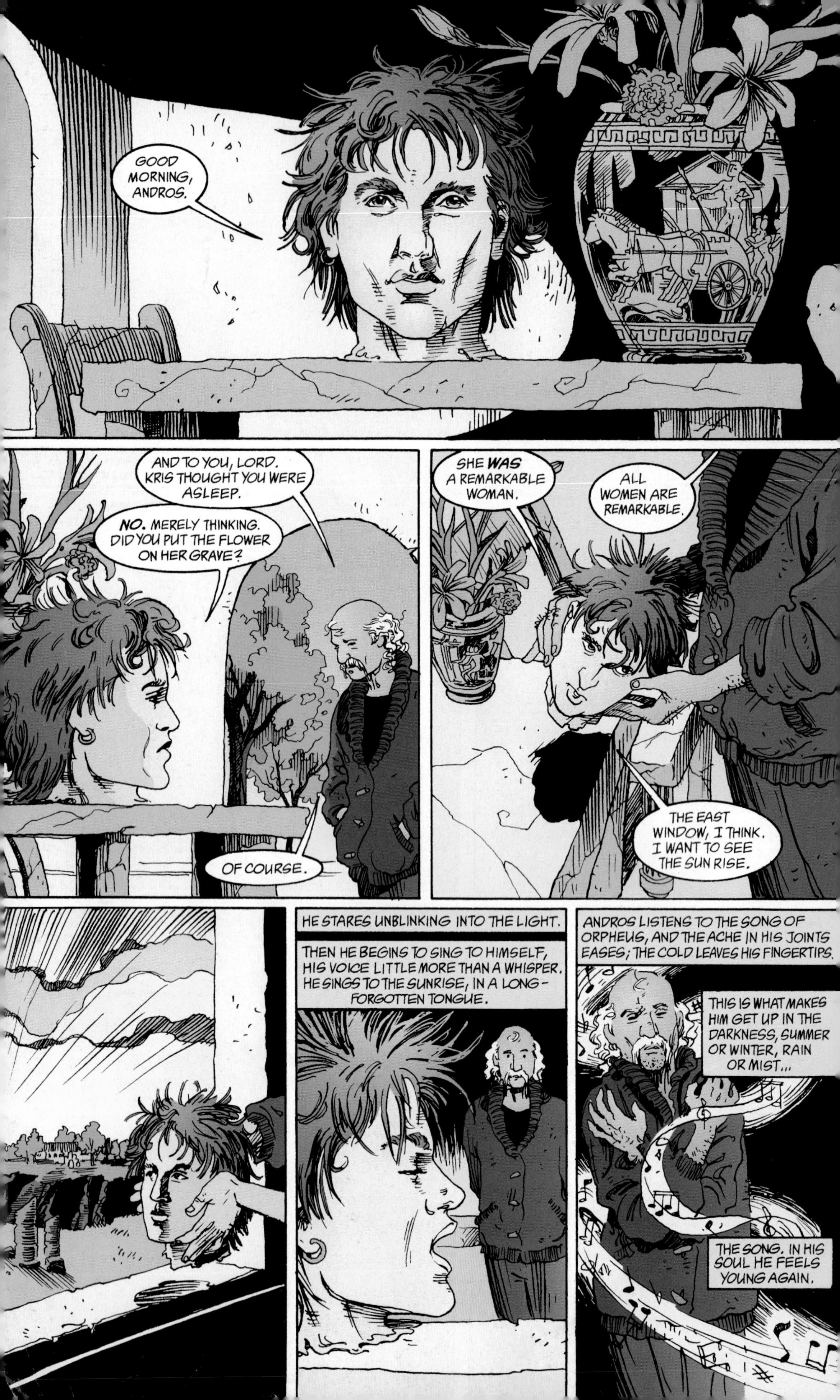
GOOD MORNING, ANDROS.
AND TO YOU, LORD. KRIS THOUGHT YOU WERE ASLEEP.
NO. MERELY THINKING. DID YOU PUT THE FLOWER ON HER GRAVE?
OF COURSE.
SHE WAS A REMARKABLE WOMAN.
ALL WOMEN ARE REMARKABLE.
THE EAST WINDOW, I THINK. I WANT TO SEE THE SUN RISE.
HE STARES UNBLINKING INTO THE LIGHT.
THEN HE BEGINS TO SING TO HIMSELF, HIS VOICE LITTLE MORE THAN A WHISPER. HE SINGS TO THE SUNRISE, IN A LONG-FORGOTTEN TONGUE.
ANDROS LISTENS TO THE SONG OF ORPHEUS, AND THE ACHE IN HIS JOINTS EASES; THE COLD LEAVES HIS FINGERTIPS.
THIS IS WHAT MAKES HIM GET UP IN THE DARKNESS, SUMMER OR WINTER, RAIN OR MIST...
THE SONG. IN HIS SOUL HE FEELS YOUNG AGAIN.

FROM THE EAST WINDOW ONE CAN LOOK ACROSS THE BAY.

THERE IS A HOUSE, ON THE HILL ACROSS THE BAY, AND OCCASIONALLY ANDROS (WHOSE EYES HAVE LOST NONE OF THEIR KEENNESS, IN THEIR SEVENTY YEARS ON THIS EARTH) SPIES TINY FIGURES THERE. TOURISTS, PERHAPS, OR VISITORS TO THE ISLAND.

HE WONDERS WHAT THEY SEE, FROM THEIR VILLA.

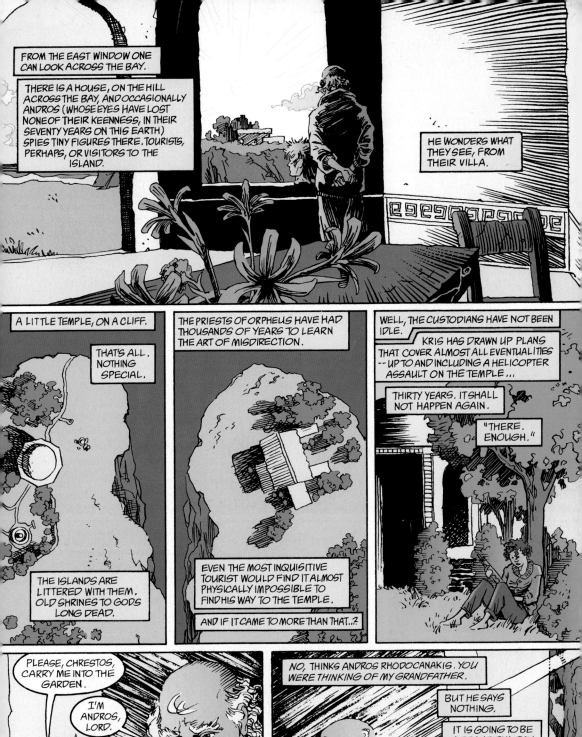

A LITTLE TEMPLE, ON A CLIFF.

THAT'S ALL. NOTHING SPECIAL.

THE ISLANDS ARE LITTERED WITH THEM. OLD SHRINES TO GODS LONG DEAD.

THE PRIESTS OF ORPHEUS HAVE HAD THOUSANDS OF YEARS TO LEARN THE ART OF MISDIRECTION.

EVEN THE MOST INQUISITIVE TOURIST WOULD FIND IT ALMOST PHYSICALLY IMPOSSIBLE TO FIND HIS WAY TO THE TEMPLE.

AND IF IT CAME TO MORE THAN THAT..?

WELL, THE CUSTODIANS HAVE NOT BEEN IDLE. KRIS HAS DRAWN UP PLANS THAT COVER ALMOST ALL EVENTUALITIES -- UP TO AND INCLUDING A HELICOPTER ASSAULT ON THE TEMPLE...

THIRTY YEARS. IT SHALL NOT HAPPEN AGAIN.

"THERE. ENOUGH."

PLEASE, CHRESTOS, CARRY ME INTO THE GARDEN.

I'M ANDROS, LORD.

DID I SAY CHRE...? I'M SORRY. I WAS THINKING OF YOUR FATHER.

NO, THINKS ANDROS RHODOCANAKIS. YOU WERE THINKING OF MY GRANDFATHER.

BUT HE SAYS NOTHING.

IT IS GOING TO BE A BEAUTIFUL DAY.

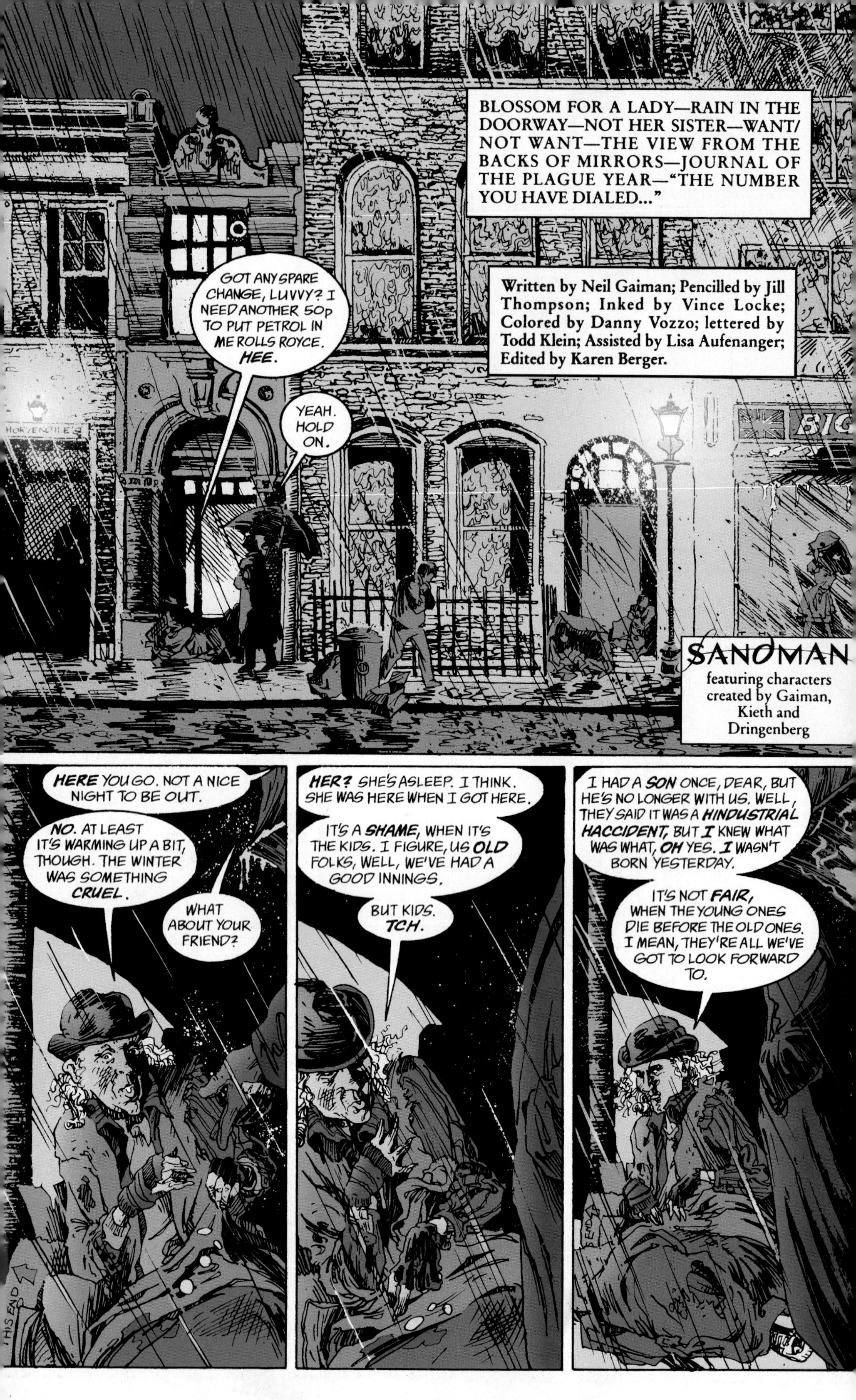

BLOSSOM FOR A LADY—RAIN IN THE DOORWAY—NOT HER SISTER—WANT/NOT WANT—THE VIEW FROM THE BACKS OF MIRRORS—JOURNAL OF THE PLAGUE YEAR—"THE NUMBER YOU HAVE DIALED..."
Written by Neil Gaiman; Pencilled by Jill Thompson; Inked by Vince Locke; Colored by Danny Vozzo; lettered by Todd Klein; Assisted by Lisa Aufenanger; Edited by Karen Berger.
GOT ANY SPARE CHANGE, LUVVY? I NEED ANOTHER 50p TO PUT PETROL IN ME ROLLS ROYCE. HEE.
YEAH. HOLD ON.
SANDMAN
featuring characters created by Gaiman, Kieth and Dringenberg
HERE YOU GO. NOT A NICE NIGHT TO BE OUT.
NO. AT LEAST IT'S WARMING UP A BIT, THOUGH. THE WINTER WAS SOMETHING CRUEL.
WHAT ABOUT YOUR FRIEND?
HER? SHE'S ASLEEP. I THINK. SHE WAS HERE WHEN I GOT HERE.
IT'S A SHAME, WHEN IT'S THE KIDS. I FIGURE, US OLD FOLKS, WELL, WE'VE HAD A GOOD INNINGS.
BUT KIDS. TCH.
I HAD A SON ONCE, DEAR, BUT HE'S NO LONGER WITH US. WELL, THEY SAID IT WAS A HINDUSTRIAL HACCIDENT, BUT I KNEW WHAT WAS WHAT, OH YES. I WASN'T BORN YESTERDAY.
IT'S NOT FAIR, WHEN THE YOUNG ONES DIE BEFORE THE OLD ONES. I MEAN, THEY'RE ALL WE'VE GOT TO LOOK FORWARD TO.

YEAH. WELL. GOOD LUCK.

IT'LL TAKE MORE THAN LUCK TO HELP *ME*, DEARIO. YOU'VE A GOOD HEART.

THERE, NOW, LOVE. THAT WAS ONE THER NICE ONES.

THIRTY PEE AND A BIT OF A NATTER, AND *I* DUNNO, SOMETIMES I THINK A KIND WORD'S BETTER THAN THE RHINO...

YOU SHOULD MOVE *UP* A BIT THERE, LOVE. YOU'LL GET POSITIVELY *SOAKED*.

I'VE BEEN. WET. BEFORE. I THINK.

OH. YOU'RE AWAKE. FEELING BETTER?

I FEEL LIKE... I DON'T KNOW. SOMEPLACE NOBODY EVER *GOES* ANY MORE.

I DON'T KNOW.

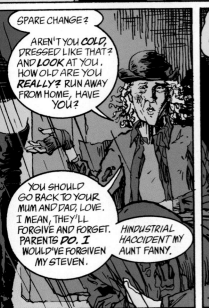

SPARE CHANGE?

AREN'T YOU *COLD*, DRESSED LIKE THAT? AND *LOOK* AT YOU, HOW OLD ARE YOU *REALLY*? RUN AWAY FROM HOME, HAVE YOU?

YOU SHOULD GO BACK TO YOUR *MUM* AND *DAD*, LOVE. I MEAN, THEY'LL FORGIVE AND FORGET. PARENTS *DO*. I WOULD'VE FORGIVEN MY STEVEN.

I HAVEN'T GOT *ANY* PARENTS. THERE WAS A *BIG* FLOOD ONCE AND I GOT *REALLY* WET IN *THAT*, ONLY IT WASN'T RAIN, IT WAS THE GUNKY STUFF INSIDE PEOPLE'S EYES.

I WISH I COULD REMEMBER WHAT IT'S CALLED...

HINDUSTRIAL HACCIDENT MY AUNT FANNY.

YOU LOST *BOTH* PARENTS? *TSK*. POOR DEAR.

I DIDN'T *LOSE* MY PARENTS.

I LOST MY *BROTHER*...

WHAT A *SHAME*. MY *STEVEN* DIED. THEY SAID IT WAS A *HACCIDENT*. BUT *I'VE* GOT PAPERS. *OH* YES. I WASN'T BORN YESTERDAY.

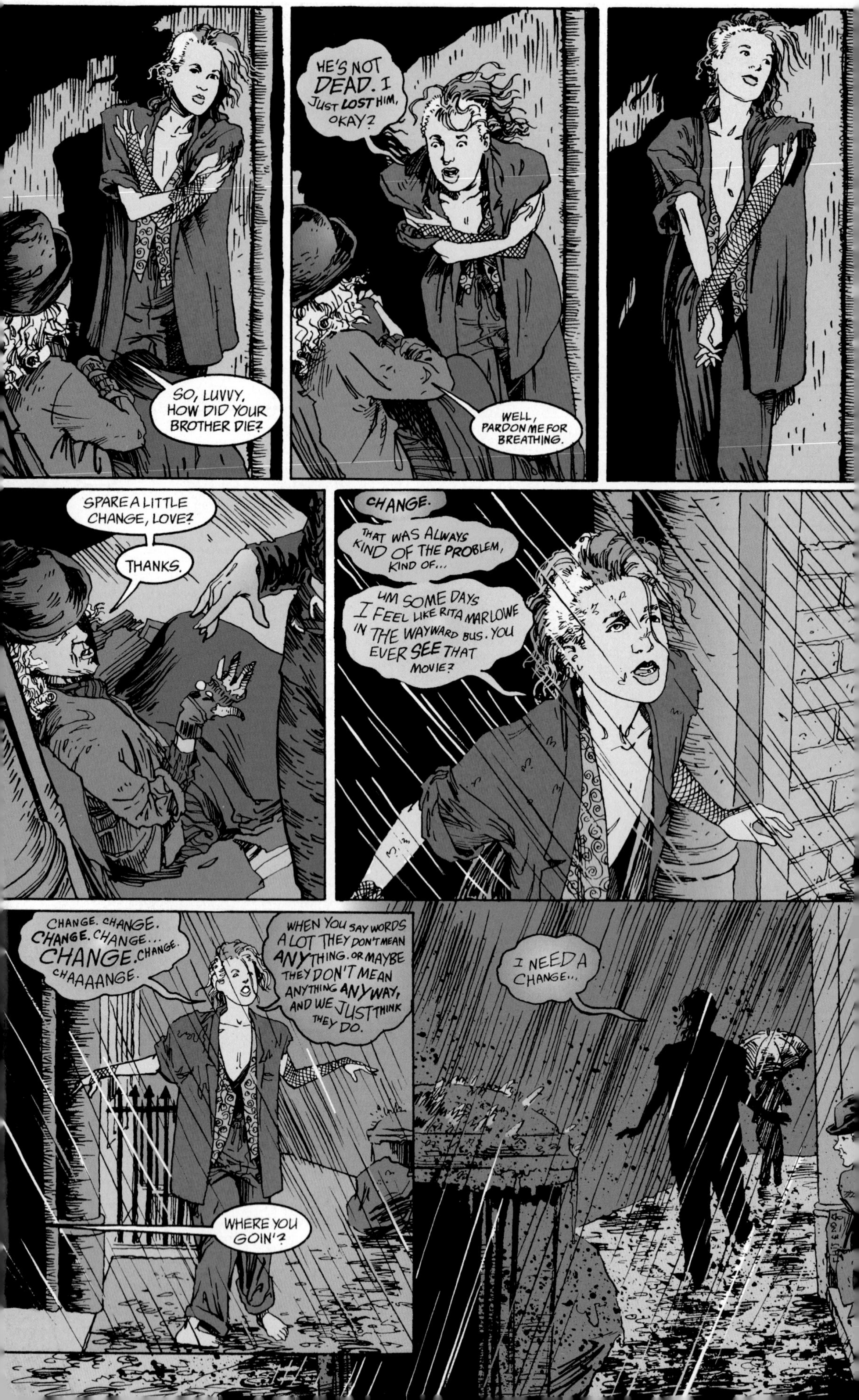
SO, LUVVY, HOW DID YOUR BROTHER DIE?
HE'S NOT DEAD. I JUST LOST HIM, OKAY?
WELL, PARDON ME FOR BREATHING.
SPARE A LITTLE CHANGE, LOVE?
THANKS.
CHANGE.
THAT WAS ALWAYS KIND OF THE PROBLEM, KIND OF...
UM SOME DAYS I FEEL LIKE RITA MARLOWE IN THE WAYWARD BUS. YOU EVER SEE THAT MOVIE?
CHANGE. CHANGE. CHANGE. CHANGE... CHANGE. CHANGE. CHAAAAANGE.
WHEN YOU SAY WORDS A LOT THEY DON'T MEAN ANYTHING. OR MAYBE THEY DON'T MEAN ANYTHING ANYWAY, AND WE JUST THINK THEY DO.
WHERE YOU GOIN'?
I NEED A CHANGE...

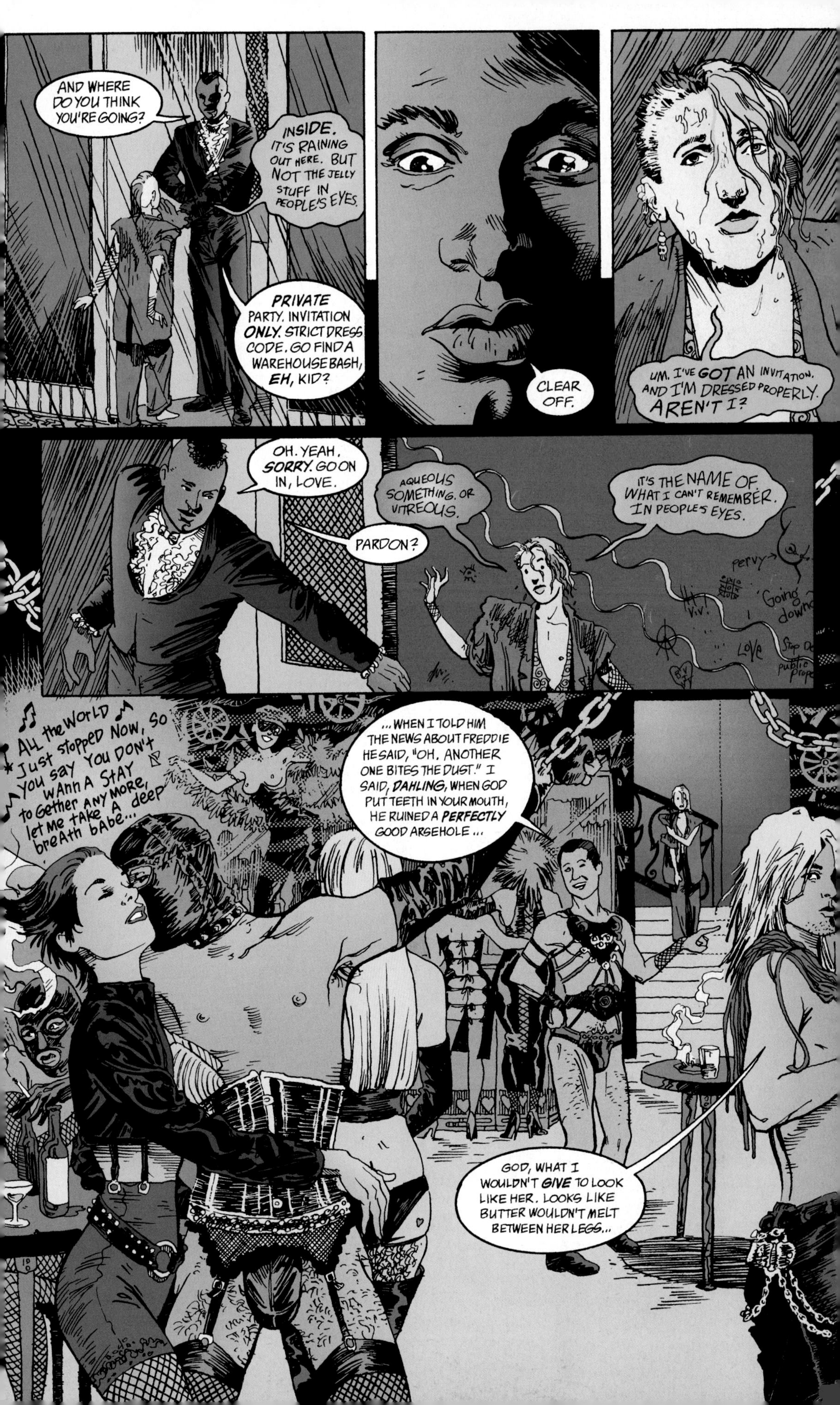
AND WHERE DO YOU THINK YOU'RE GOING?
INSIDE. IT'S RAINING OUT HERE. BUT NOT THE JELLY STUFF IN PEOPLE'S EYES.
PRIVATE PARTY. INVITATION ONLY. STRICT DRESS CODE. GO FIND A WAREHOUSE BASH, EH, KID?
CLEAR OFF.
UM. I'VE GOT AN INVITATION. AND I'M DRESSED PROPERLY. AREN'T I?
OH. YEAH. SORRY. GO ON IN, LOVE.
PARDON?
AQUEOUS SOMETHING. OR VITREOUS.
IT'S THE NAME OF WHAT I CAN'T REMEMBER. IN PEOPLE'S EYES.
pervy
Viv!
Love
All the World Just stopped Now, so You say You Don't wAnnA StAY to Gether Any More, let me take A deep breAth babe...
...WHEN I TOLD HIM THE NEWS ABOUT FREDDIE HE SAID, "OH, ANOTHER ONE BITES THE DUST." I SAID, DAHLING, WHEN GOD PUT TEETH IN YOUR MOUTH, HE RUINED A PERFECTLY GOOD ARSEHOLE...
GOD, WHAT I WOULDN'T GIVE TO LOOK LIKE HER. LOOKS LIKE BUTTER WOULDN'T MELT BETWEEN HER LEGS...

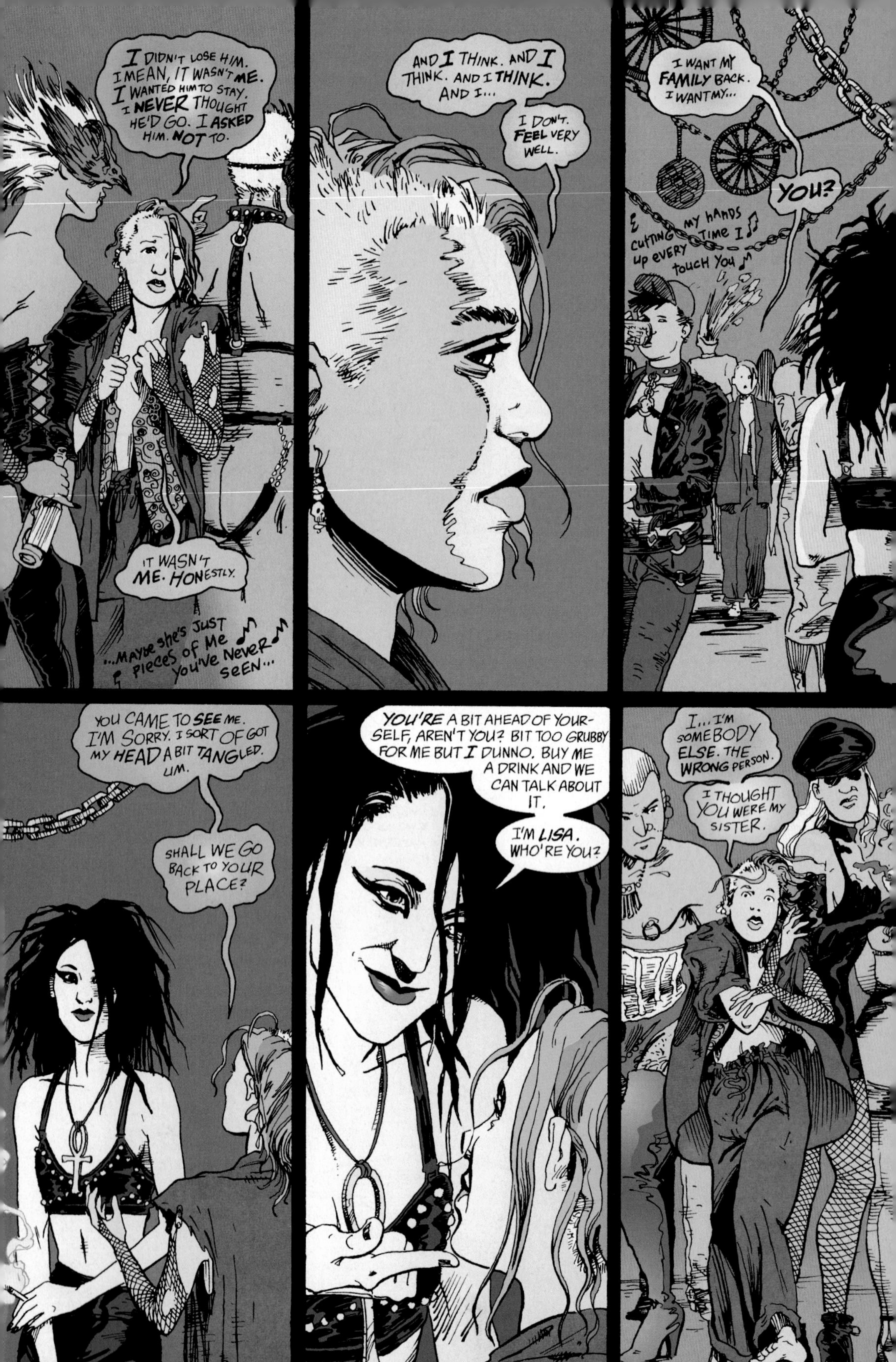
I DIDN'T LOSE HIM. I MEAN, IT WASN'T ME. I WANTED HIM TO STAY. I NEVER THOUGHT HE'D GO. I ASKED HIM. NOT TO.
IT WASN'T ME. HONESTLY.
...MAYBE SHE'S JUST PIECES OF ME YOU'VE NEVER SEEN...
AND I THINK. AND I THINK. AND I THINK. AND I...
I DON'T. FEEL VERY WELL.
I WANT MY FAMILY BACK. I WANT MY...
YOU?
CUTTING MY HANDS UP EVERY TIME I TOUCH YOU
YOU CAME TO SEE ME. I'M SORRY. I SORT OF GOT MY HEAD A BIT TANGLED. UM.
SHALL WE GO BACK TO YOUR PLACE?
YOU'RE A BIT AHEAD OF YOURSELF, AREN'T YOU? BIT TOO GRUBBY FOR ME BUT I DUNNO. BUY ME A DRINK AND WE CAN TALK ABOUT IT.
I'M LISA. WHO'RE YOU?
I... I'M SOMEBODY ELSE. THE WRONG PERSON.
I THOUGHT YOU WERE MY SISTER.

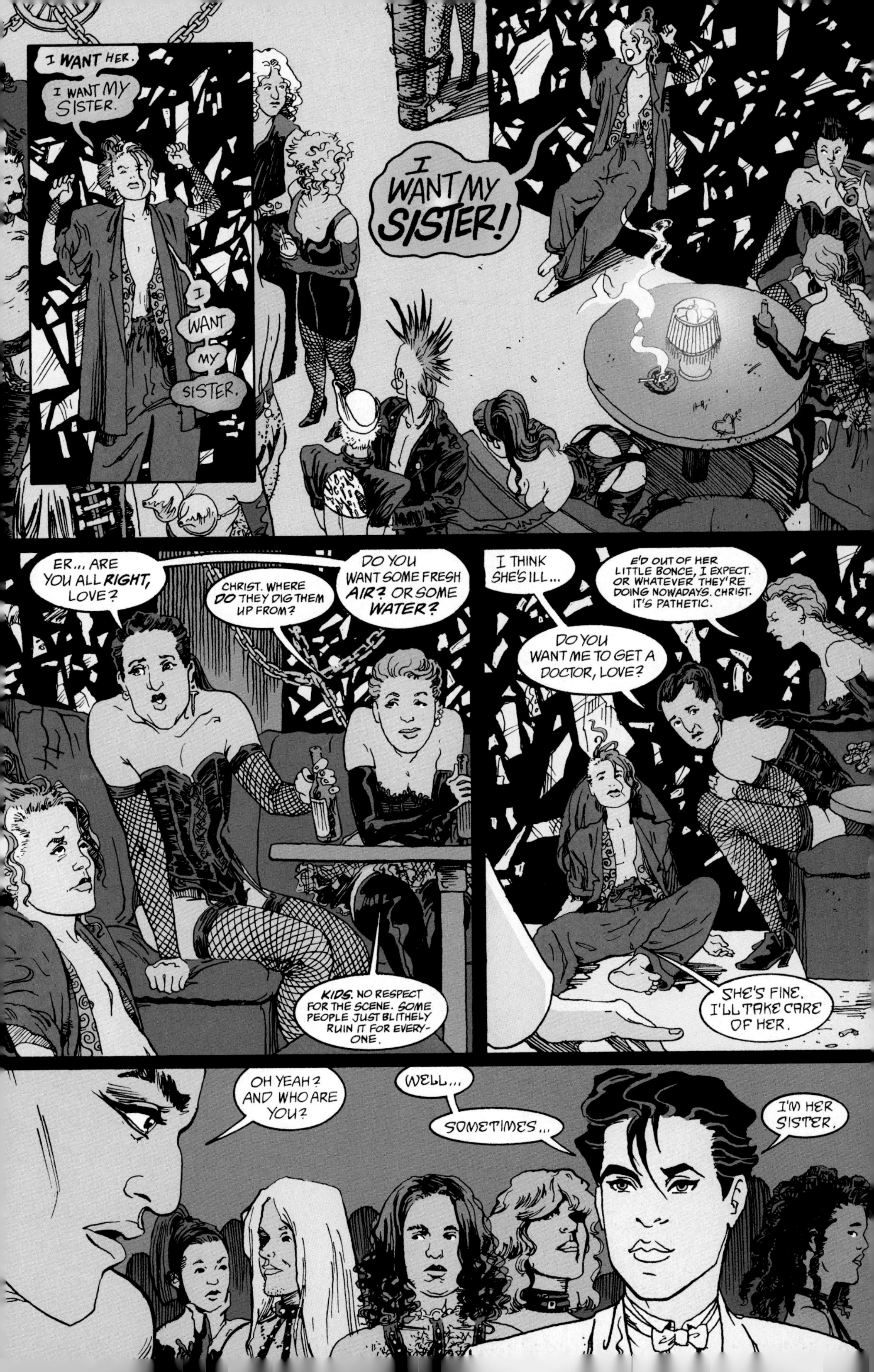

I WANT HER.
I WANT MY SISTER.
I WANT MY SISTER.
I WANT MY SISTER!
ER... ARE YOU ALL RIGHT, LOVE?
CHRIST. WHERE DO THEY DIG THEM UP FROM?
DO YOU WANT SOME FRESH AIR? OR SOME WATER?
KIDS. NO RESPECT FOR THE SCENE. SOME PEOPLE JUST BLITHELY RUIN IT FOR EVERY-ONE.
I THINK SHE'S ILL...
E'D OUT OF HER LITTLE BONCE, I EXPECT. OR WHATEVER THEY'RE DOING NOWADAYS. CHRIST. IT'S PATHETIC.
DO YOU WANT ME TO GET A DOCTOR, LOVE?
SHE'S FINE. I'LL TAKE CARE OF HER.
OH YEAH? AND WHO ARE YOU?
WELL...
SOMETIMES...
I'M HER SISTER.

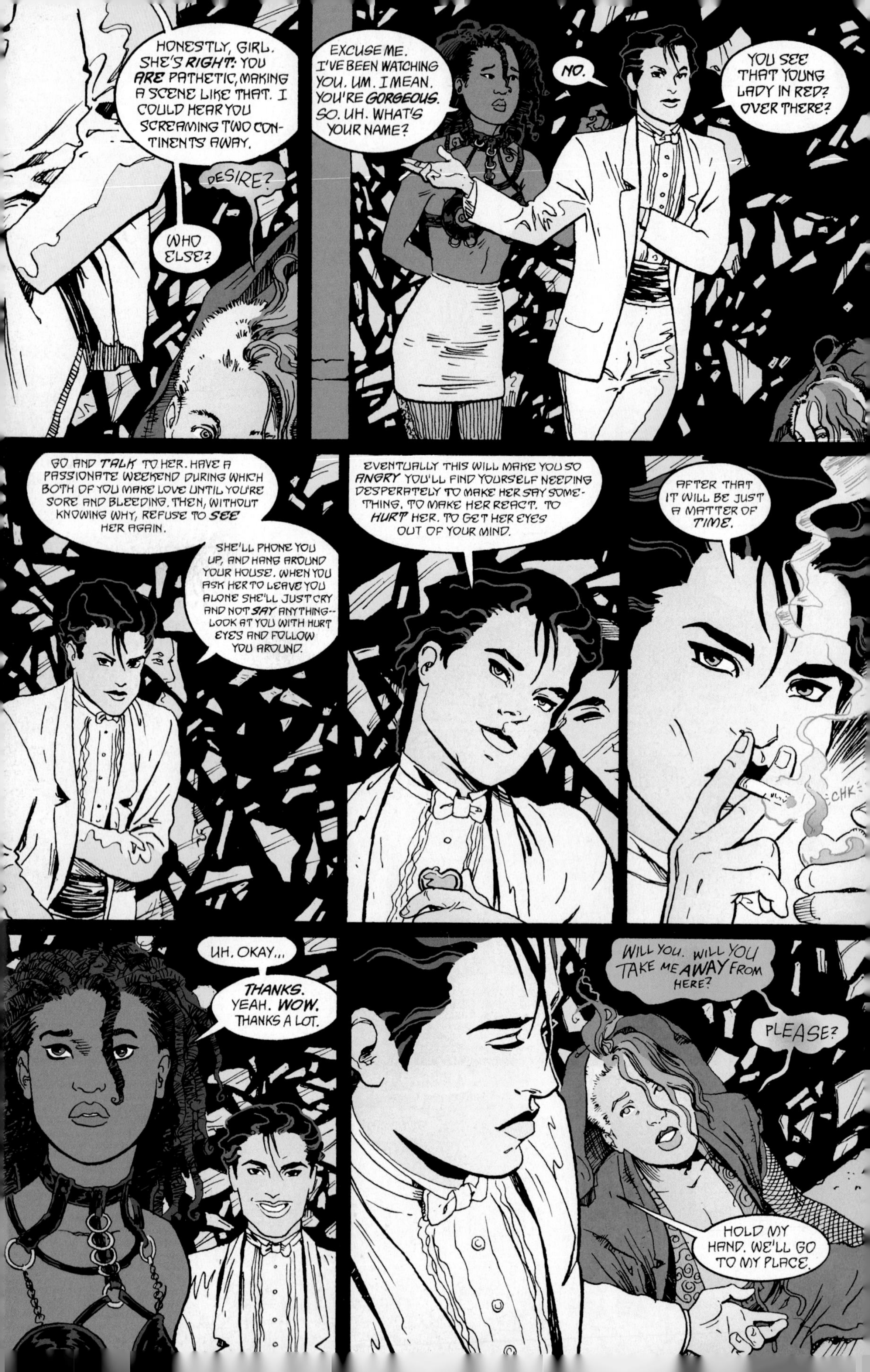
HONESTLY, GIRL. SHE'S RIGHT: YOU ARE PATHETIC, MAKING A SCENE LIKE THAT. I COULD HEAR YOU SCREAMING TWO CONTINENTS AWAY.
DESIRE?
WHO ELSE?
EXCUSE ME. I'VE BEEN WATCHING YOU. UM. I MEAN. YOU'RE GORGEOUS. SO. UH. WHAT'S YOUR NAME?
NO.
YOU SEE THAT YOUNG LADY IN RED? OVER THERE?
GO AND TALK TO HER. HAVE A PASSIONATE WEEKEND DURING WHICH BOTH OF YOU MAKE LOVE UNTIL YOU'RE SORE AND BLEEDING. THEN, WITHOUT KNOWING WHY, REFUSE TO SEE HER AGAIN.
SHE'LL PHONE YOU UP, AND HANG AROUND YOUR HOUSE. WHEN YOU ASK HER TO LEAVE YOU ALONE SHE'LL JUST CRY AND NOT SAY ANYTHING-- LOOK AT YOU WITH HURT EYES AND FOLLOW YOU AROUND.
EVENTUALLY THIS WILL MAKE YOU SO ANGRY YOU'LL FIND YOURSELF NEEDING DESPERATELY TO MAKE HER SAY SOMETHING, TO MAKE HER REACT. TO HURT HER. TO GET HER EYES OUT OF YOUR MIND.
AFTER THAT IT WILL BE JUST A MATTER OF TIME.
CHK
UH. OKAY...
THANKS. YEAH. WOW. THANKS A LOT.
WILL YOU. WILL YOU TAKE ME AWAY FROM HERE?
PLEASE?
HOLD MY HAND. WE'LL GO TO MY PLACE.

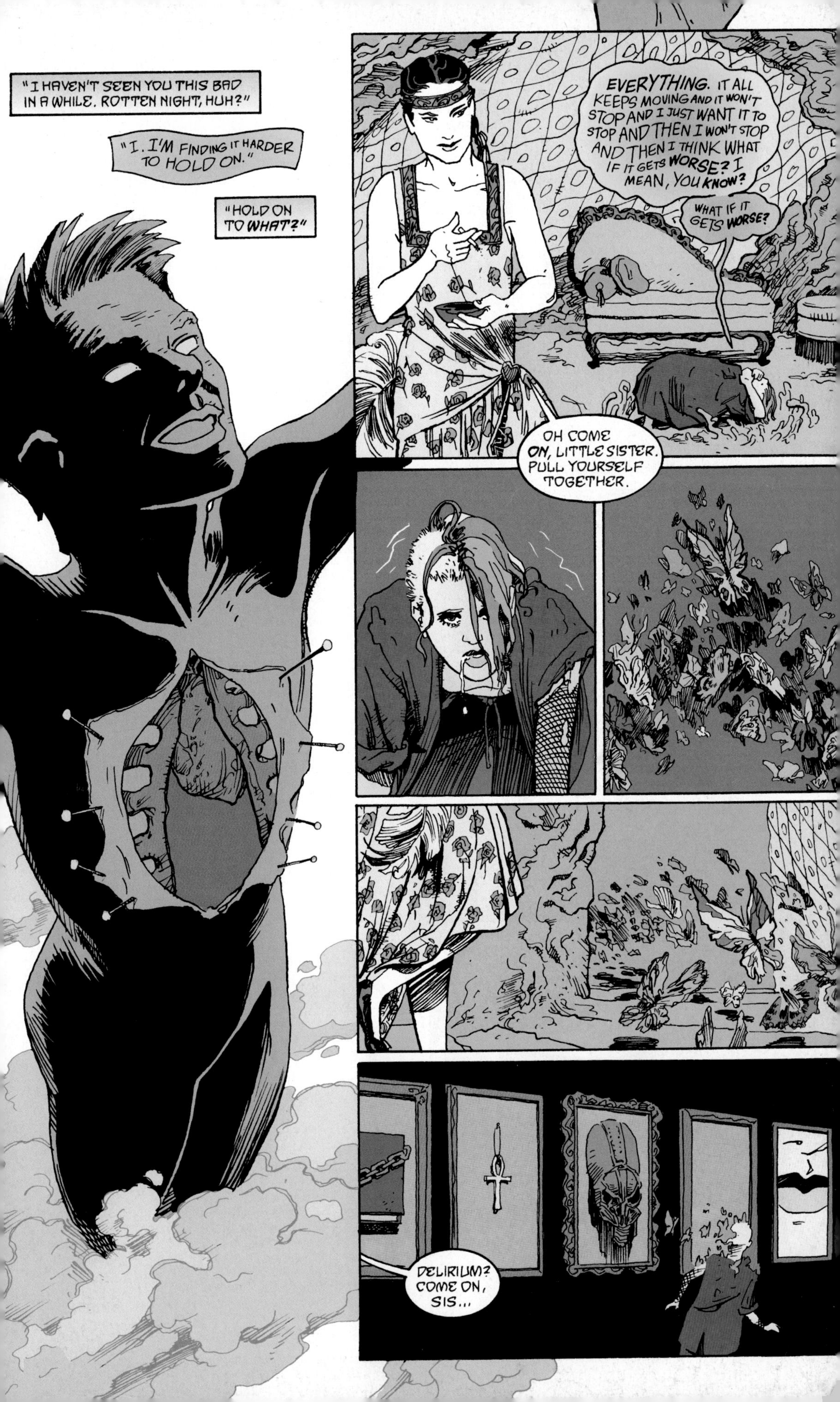
"I HAVEN'T SEEN YOU THIS BAD IN A WHILE. ROTTEN NIGHT, HUH?"
"I. I'M FINDING IT HARDER TO HOLD ON."
"HOLD ON TO WHAT?"
EVERYTHING. IT ALL KEEPS MOVING AND IT WON'T STOP AND I JUST WANT IT TO STOP AND THEN I WON'T STOP AND THEN I THINK WHAT IF IT GETS WORSE? I MEAN, YOU KNOW?
WHAT IF IT GETS WORSE?
OH COME ON, LITTLE SISTER. PULL YOURSELF TOGETHER.
DELIRIUM? COME ON, SIS...

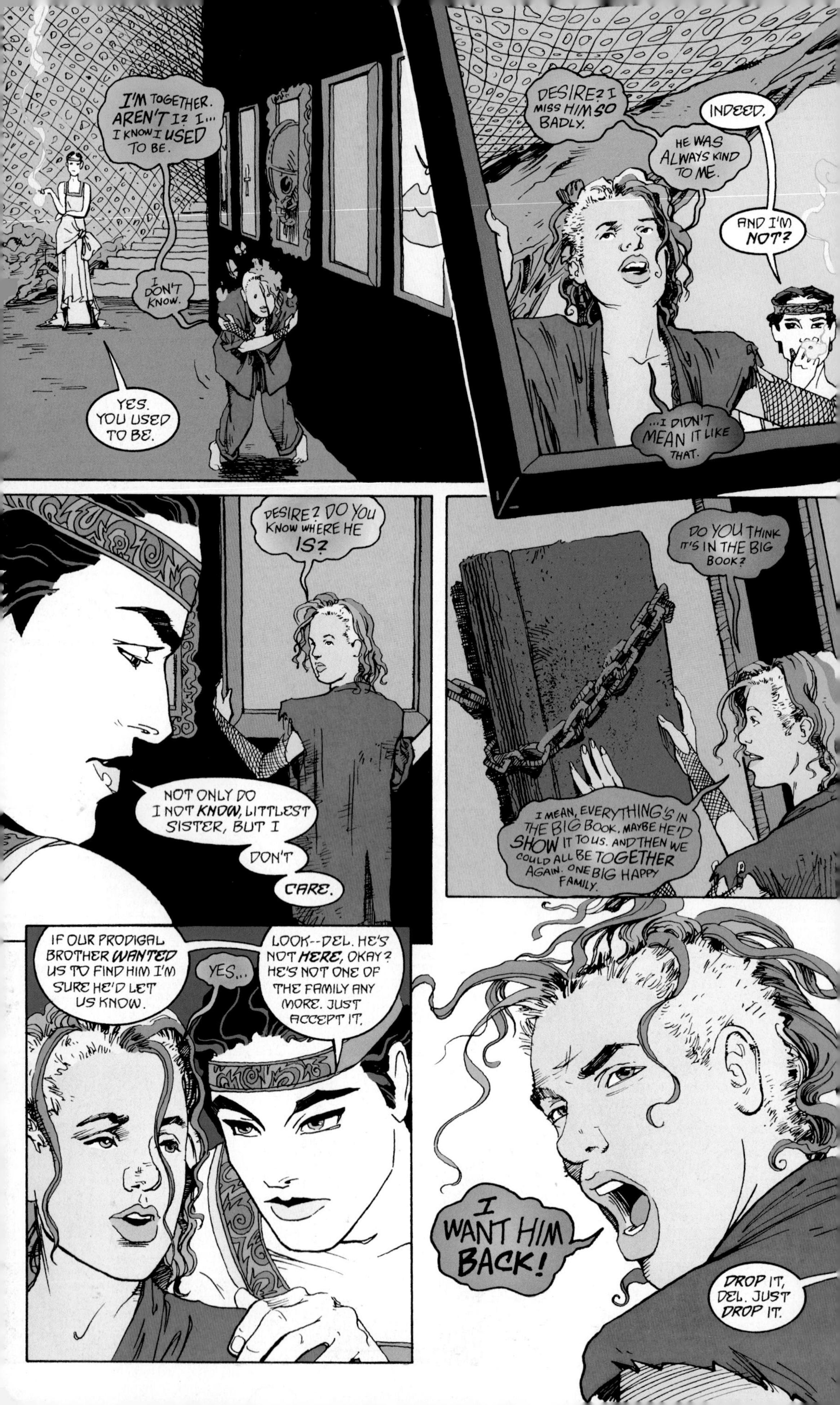
I'M TOGETHER. AREN'T I? I... I KNOW I USED TO BE.
I DON'T KNOW.
YES. YOU USED TO BE.
DESIRE? I MISS HIM SO BADLY.
HE WAS ALWAYS KIND TO ME.
INDEED.
AND I'M NOT?
...I DIDN'T MEAN IT LIKE THAT.
DESIRE? DO YOU KNOW WHERE HE IS?
NOT ONLY DO I NOT KNOW, LITTLEST SISTER, BUT I
DON'T
CARE.
DO YOU THINK IT'S IN THE BIG BOOK?
I MEAN, EVERYTHING'S IN THE BIG BOOK. MAYBE HE'D SHOW IT TO US. AND THEN WE COULD ALL BE TOGETHER AGAIN. ONE BIG HAPPY FAMILY.
IF OUR PRODIGAL BROTHER WANTED US TO FIND HIM I'M SURE HE'D LET US KNOW.
YES...
LOOK--DEL. HE'S NOT HERE, OKAY? HE'S NOT ONE OF THE FAMILY ANY MORE. JUST ACCEPT IT.
I WANT HIM BACK!
DROP IT, DEL. JUST DROP IT.

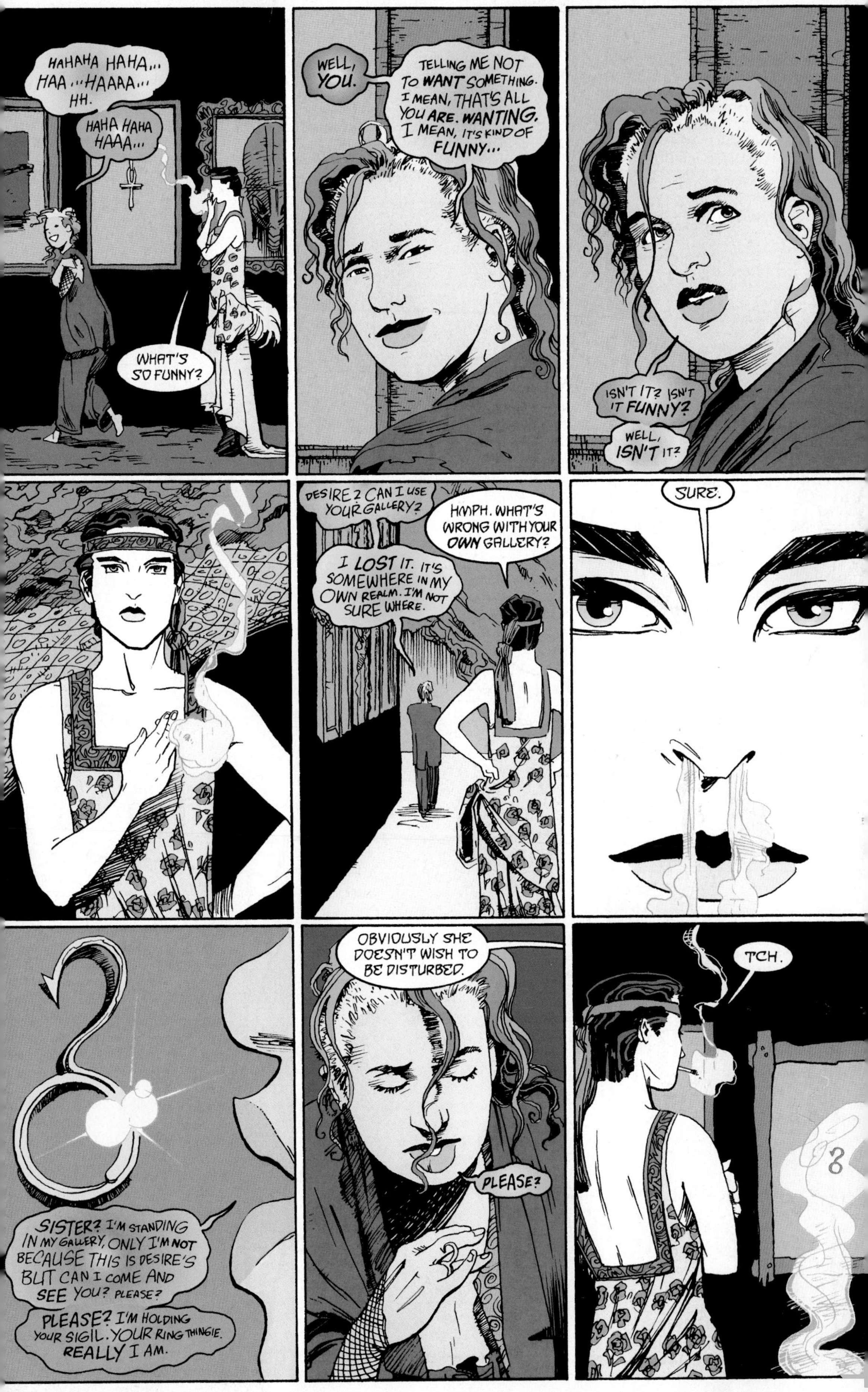
HAHAHA HAHA... HAA...HAAAA... HH.
HAHA HAHA HAAA...
WHAT'S SO FUNNY?
WELL, YOU.
TELLING ME NOT TO WANT SOMETHING. I MEAN, THAT'S ALL YOU ARE. WANTING. I MEAN, IT'S KIND OF FUNNY...
ISN'T IT? ISN'T IT FUNNY?
WELL, ISN'T IT?
DESIRE? CAN I USE YOUR GALLERY?
HMPH. WHAT'S WRONG WITH YOUR OWN GALLERY?
I LOST IT. IT'S SOMEWHERE IN MY OWN REALM. I'M NOT SURE WHERE.
SURE.
SISTER? I'M STANDING IN MY GALLERY, ONLY I'M NOT BECAUSE THIS IS DESIRE'S BUT CAN I COME AND SEE YOU? PLEASE?
PLEASE? I'M HOLDING YOUR SIGIL. YOUR RING THINGIE. REALLY I AM.
OBVIOUSLY SHE DOESN'T WISH TO BE DISTURBED.
PLEASE?
TCH.

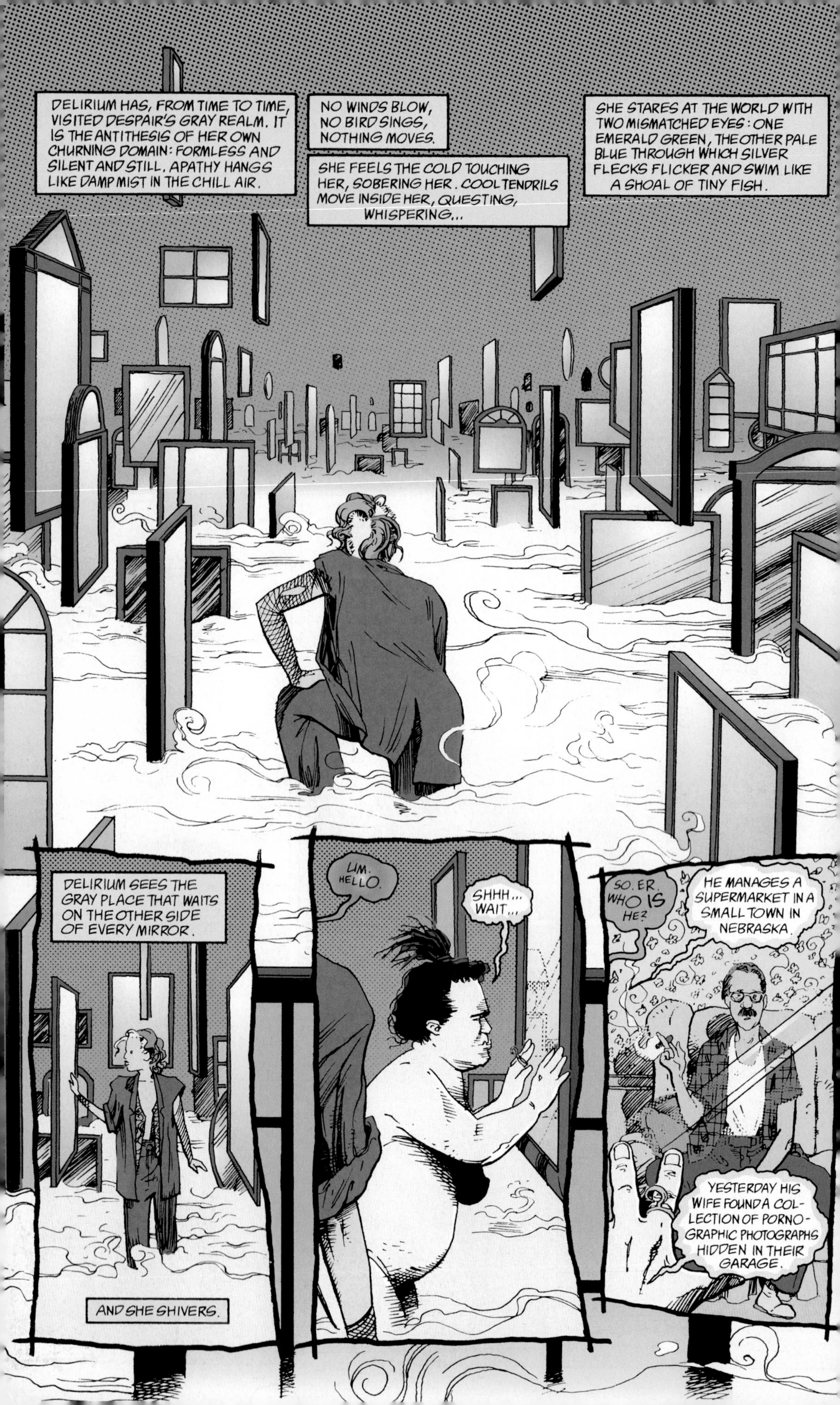
DELIRIUM HAS, FROM TIME TO TIME, VISITED DESPAIR'S GRAY REALM. IT IS THE ANTITHESIS OF HER OWN CHURNING DOMAIN: FORMLESS AND SILENT AND STILL. APATHY HANGS LIKE DAMP MIST IN THE CHILL AIR.
NO WINDS BLOW, NO BIRD SINGS, NOTHING MOVES.
SHE FEELS THE COLD TOUCHING HER, SOBERING HER. COOL TENDRILS MOVE INSIDE HER, QUESTING, WHISPERING...
SHE STARES AT THE WORLD WITH TWO MISMATCHED EYES: ONE EMERALD GREEN, THE OTHER PALE BLUE THROUGH WHICH SILVER FLECKS FLICKER AND SWIM LIKE A SHOAL OF TINY FISH.
DELIRIUM SEES THE GRAY PLACE THAT WAITS ON THE OTHER SIDE OF EVERY MIRROR.
AND SHE SHIVERS.
UM. HELLO.
SHHH... WAIT...
SO. ER WHO IS HE?
HE MANAGES A SUPERMARKET IN A SMALL TOWN IN NEBRASKA.
YESTERDAY HIS WIFE FOUND A COL-LECTION OF PORNO-GRAPHIC PHOTOGRAPHS HIDDEN IN THEIR GARAGE.

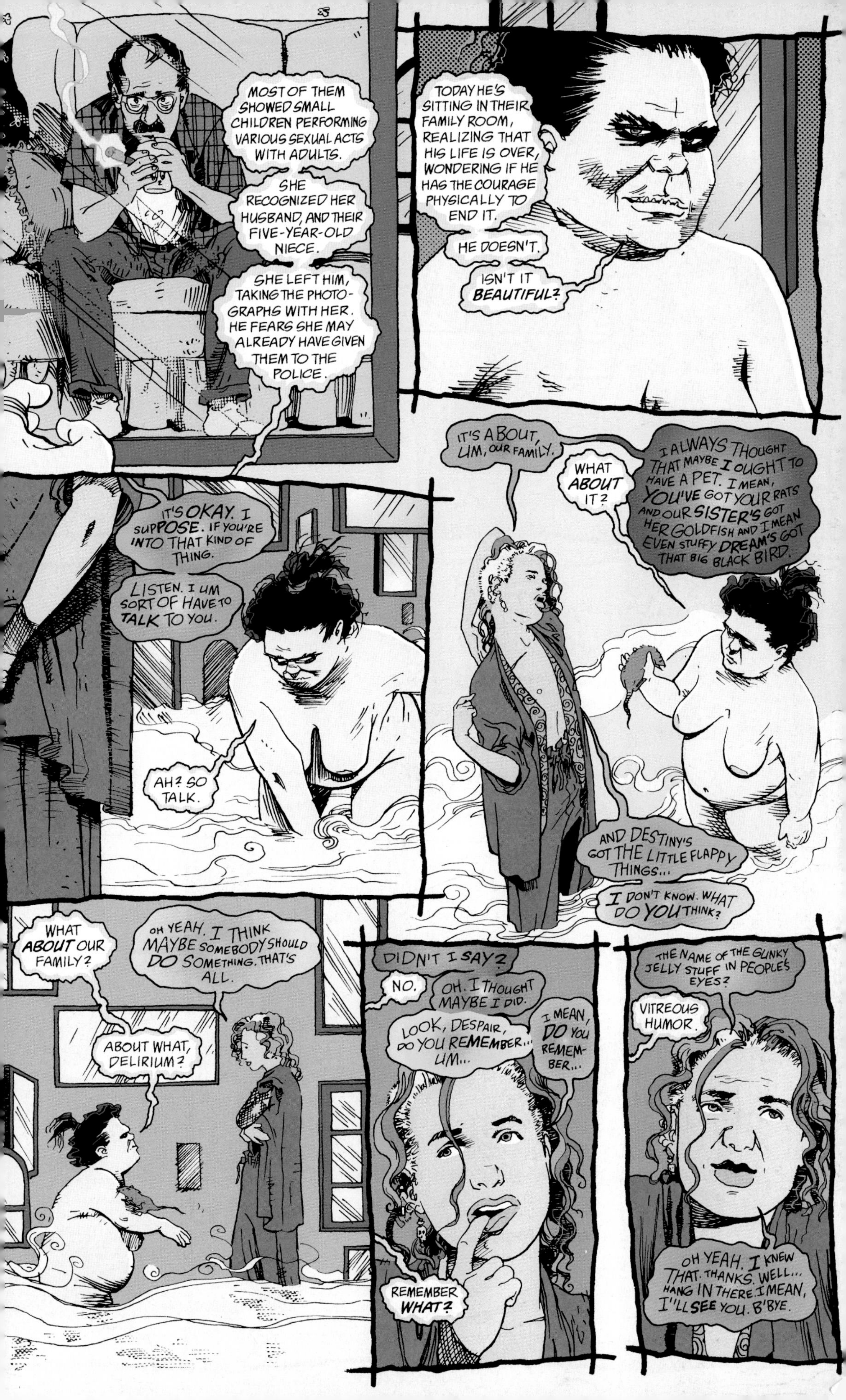
MOST OF THEM SHOWED SMALL CHILDREN PERFORMING VARIOUS SEXUAL ACTS WITH ADULTS.
SHE RECOGNIZED HER HUSBAND, AND THEIR FIVE-YEAR-OLD NIECE.
SHE LEFT HIM, TAKING THE PHOTO-GRAPHS WITH HER. HE FEARS SHE MAY ALREADY HAVE GIVEN THEM TO THE POLICE.
TODAY HE'S SITTING IN THEIR FAMILY ROOM, REALIZING THAT HIS LIFE IS OVER, WONDERING IF HE HAS THE COURAGE PHYSICALLY TO END IT.
HE DOESN'T.
ISN'T IT BEAUTIFUL?
IT'S OKAY. I SUPPOSE. IF YOU'RE INTO THAT KIND OF THING.
LISTEN. I UM SORT OF HAVE TO TALK TO YOU.
AH? SO TALK.
IT'S ABOUT, UM, OUR FAMILY.
WHAT ABOUT IT?
I ALWAYS THOUGHT THAT MAYBE I OUGHT TO HAVE A PET. I MEAN, YOU'VE GOT YOUR RATS AND OUR SISTER'S GOT HER GOLDFISH AND I MEAN EVEN STUFFY DREAM'S GOT THAT BIG BLACK BIRD.
AND DESTINY'S GOT THE LITTLE FLAPPY THINGS...
I DON'T KNOW. WHAT DO YOU THINK?
WHAT ABOUT OUR FAMILY?
OH YEAH. I THINK MAYBE SOMEBODY SHOULD DO SOMETHING. THAT'S ALL.
ABOUT WHAT, DELIRIUM?
DIDN'T I SAY?
NO.
OH. I THOUGHT MAYBE I DID.
LOOK, DESPAIR, DO YOU REMEMBER... UM...
I MEAN, DO YOU REMEMBER...
REMEMBER WHAT?
THE NAME OF THE GUNKY JELLY STUFF IN PEOPLE'S EYES?
VITREOUS HUMOR.
OH YEAH. I KNEW THAT. THANKS. WELL... HANG IN THERE. I MEAN, I'LL SEE YOU. B'BYE.

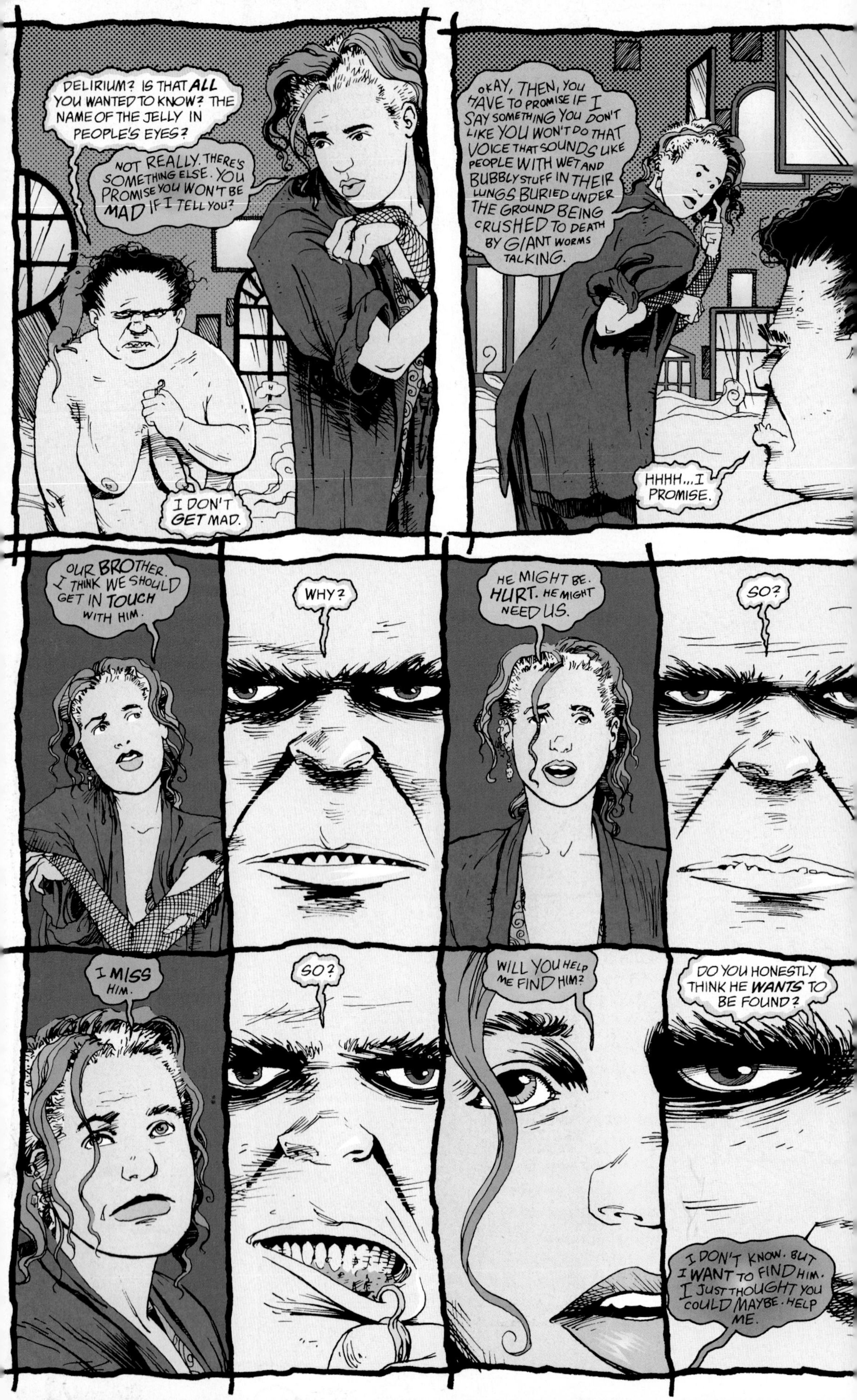
DELIRIUM? IS THAT ALL YOU WANTED TO KNOW? THE NAME OF THE JELLY IN PEOPLE'S EYES?
NOT REALLY. THERE'S SOMETHING ELSE. YOU PROMISE YOU WON'T BE MAD IF I TELL YOU?
I DON'T GET MAD.
OKAY, THEN, YOU HAVE TO PROMISE IF I SAY SOMETHING YOU DON'T LIKE YOU WON'T DO THAT VOICE THAT SOUNDS LIKE PEOPLE WITH WET AND BUBBLY STUFF IN THEIR LUNGS BURIED UNDER THE GROUND BEING CRUSHED TO DEATH BY GIANT WORMS TALKING.
HHHH...I PROMISE.
OUR BROTHER. I THINK WE SHOULD GET IN TOUCH WITH HIM.
WHY?
HE MIGHT BE. HURT. HE MIGHT NEED US.
SO?
I MISS HIM.
SO?
WILL YOU HELP ME FIND HIM?
DO YOU HONESTLY THINK HE WANTS TO BE FOUND?
I DON'T KNOW. BUT I WANT TO FIND HIM. I JUST THOUGHT YOU COULD MAYBE. HELP ME.

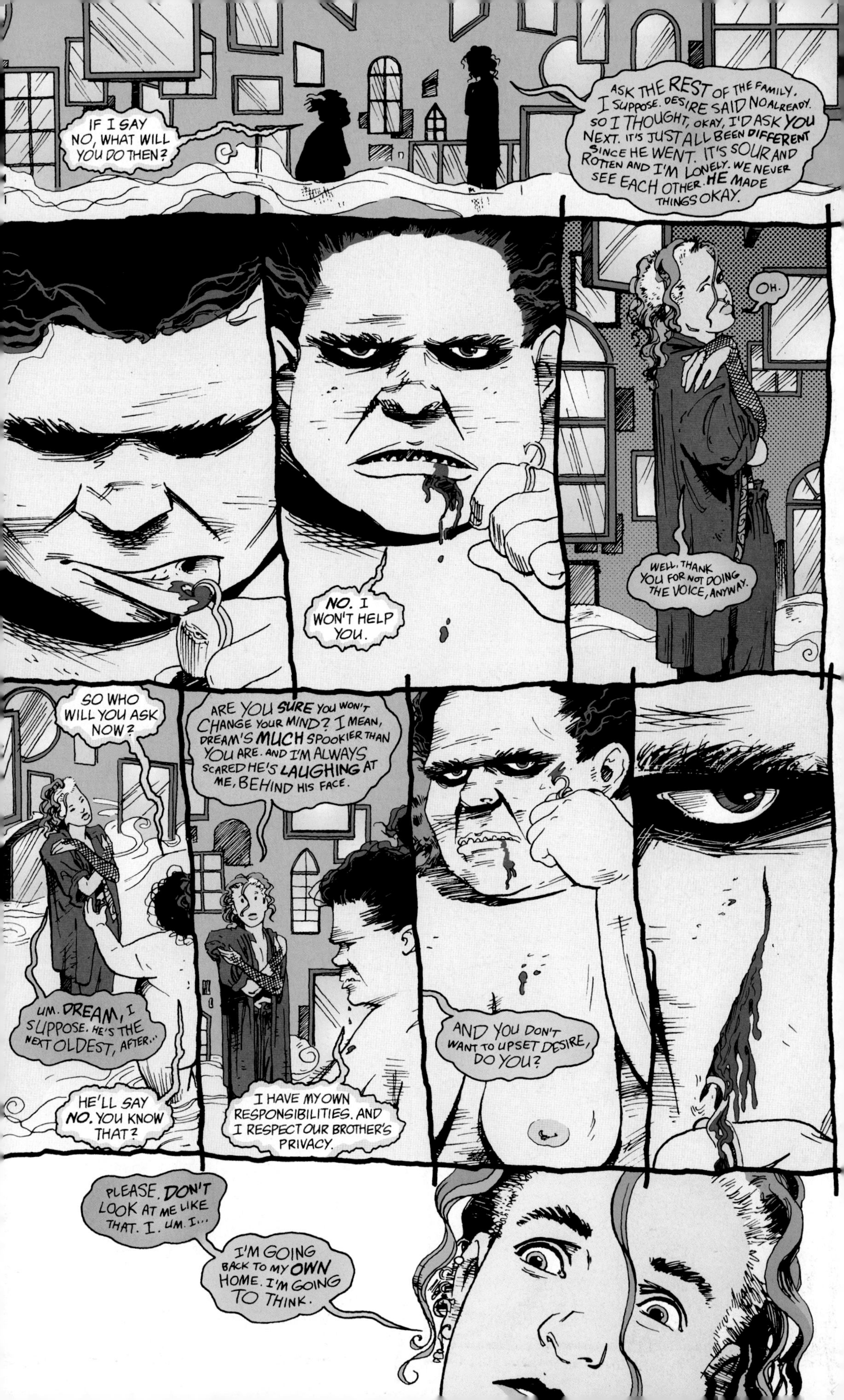
IF I SAY NO, WHAT WILL YOU DO THEN?
ASK THE REST OF THE FAMILY, I SUPPOSE. DESIRE SAID NO ALREADY. SO I THOUGHT, OKAY, I'D ASK YOU NEXT. IT'S JUST ALL BEEN DIFFERENT SINCE HE WENT. IT'S SOUR AND ROTTEN AND I'M LONELY. WE NEVER SEE EACH OTHER. HE MADE THINGS OKAY.
NO. I WON'T HELP YOU.
OH.
WELL, THANK YOU FOR NOT DOING THE VOICE, ANYWAY.
SO WHO WILL YOU ASK NOW?
UM. DREAM, I SUPPOSE. HE'S THE NEXT OLDEST, AFTER...
HE'LL SAY NO. YOU KNOW THAT?
ARE YOU SURE YOU WON'T CHANGE YOUR MIND? I MEAN, DREAM'S MUCH SPOOKIER THAN YOU ARE. AND I'M ALWAYS SCARED HE'S LAUGHING AT ME, BEHIND HIS FACE.
I HAVE MY OWN RESPONSIBILITIES. AND I RESPECT OUR BROTHER'S PRIVACY.
AND YOU DON'T WANT TO UPSET DESIRE, DO YOU?
PLEASE. DON'T LOOK AT ME LIKE THAT. I. UM. I...
I'M GOING BACK TO MY OWN HOME. I'M GOING TO THINK.

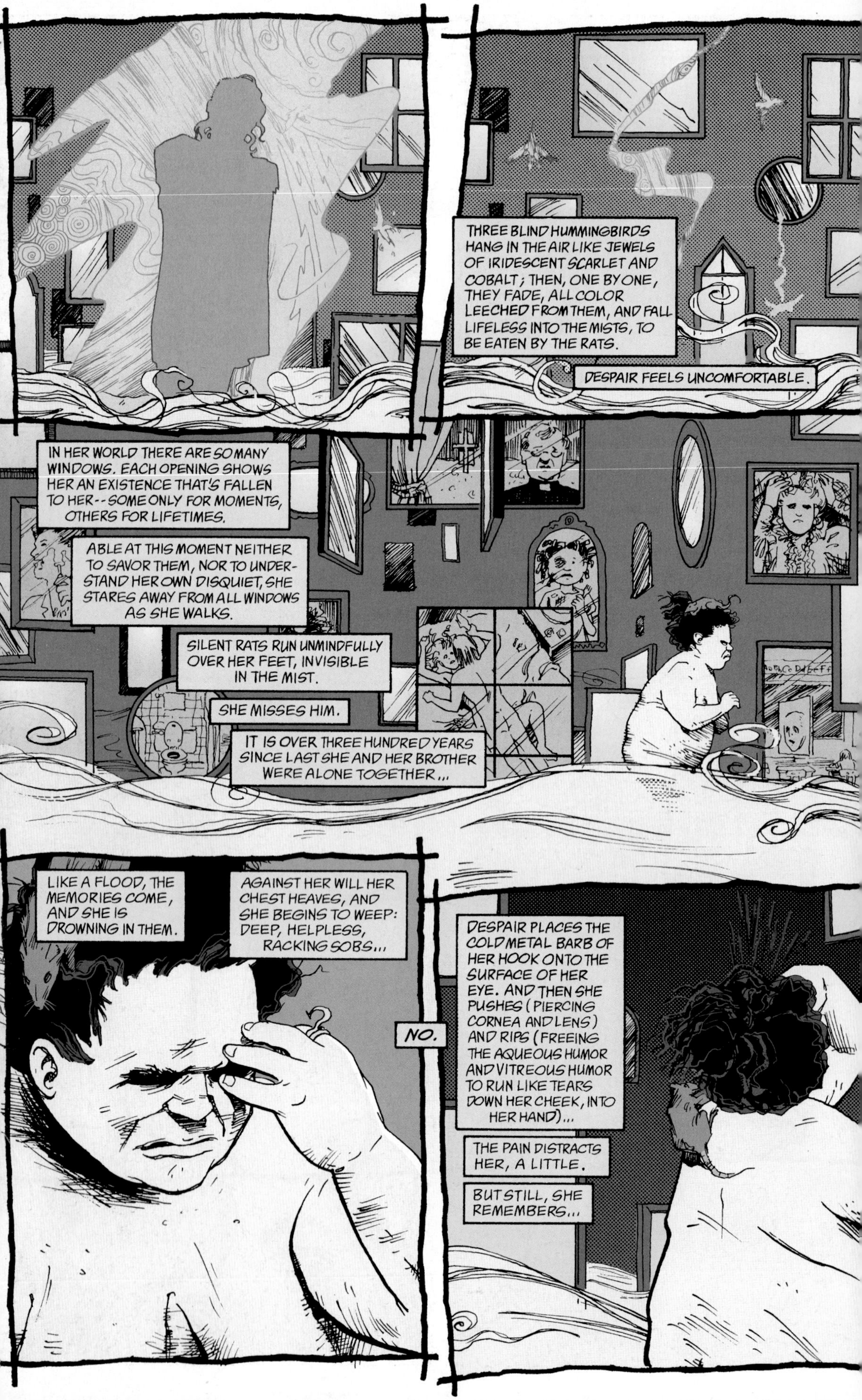
THREE BLIND HUMMINGBIRDS HANG IN THE AIR LIKE JEWELS OF IRIDESCENT SCARLET AND COBALT; THEN, ONE BY ONE, THEY FADE, ALL COLOR LEECHED FROM THEM, AND FALL LIFELESS INTO THE MISTS, TO BE EATEN BY THE RATS.
DESPAIR FEELS UNCOMFORTABLE.
IN HER WORLD THERE ARE SO MANY WINDOWS. EACH OPENING SHOWS HER AN EXISTENCE THAT'S FALLEN TO HER--SOME ONLY FOR MOMENTS, OTHERS FOR LIFETIMES.
ABLE AT THIS MOMENT NEITHER TO SAVOR THEM, NOR TO UNDERSTAND HER OWN DISQUIET, SHE STARES AWAY FROM ALL WINDOWS AS SHE WALKS.
SILENT RATS RUN UNMINDFULLY OVER HER FEET, INVISIBLE IN THE MIST.
SHE MISSES HIM.
IT IS OVER THREE HUNDRED YEARS SINCE LAST SHE AND HER BROTHER WERE ALONE TOGETHER...
LIKE A FLOOD, THE MEMORIES COME, AND SHE IS DROWNING IN THEM.
AGAINST HER WILL HER CHEST HEAVES, AND SHE BEGINS TO WEEP: DEEP, HELPLESS, RACKING SOBS...
NO.
DESPAIR PLACES THE COLD METAL BARB OF HER HOOK ONTO THE SURFACE OF HER EYE. AND THEN SHE PUSHES (PIERCING CORNEA AND LENS) AND RIPS (FREEING THE AQUEOUS HUMOR AND VITREOUS HUMOR TO RUN LIKE TEARS DOWN HER CHEEK, INTO HER HAND)...
THE PAIN DISTRACTS HER, A LITTLE.
BUT STILL, SHE REMEMBERS...

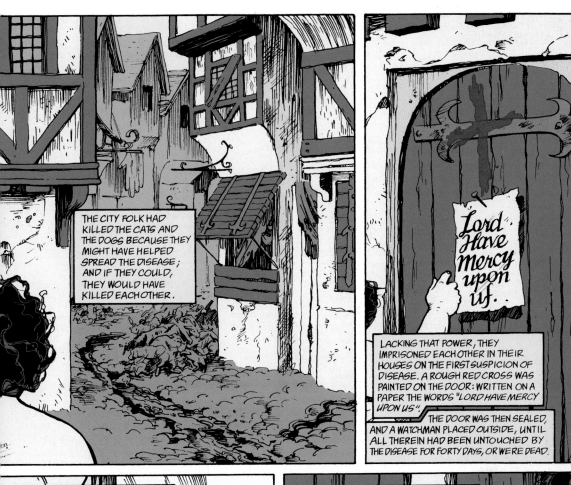

THE CITY FOLK HAD KILLED THE CATS AND THE DOGS BECAUSE THEY MIGHT HAVE HELPED SPREAD THE DISEASE; AND IF THEY COULD, THEY WOULD HAVE KILLED EACH OTHER.

Lord Have mercy upon uf.

LACKING THAT POWER, THEY IMPRISONED EACH OTHER IN THEIR HOUSES ON THE FIRST SUSPICION OF DISEASE. A ROUGH RED CROSS WAS PAINTED ON THE DOOR: WRITTEN ON A PAPER THE WORDS *"LORD HAVE MERCY UPON US"*.

THE DOOR WAS THEN SEALED, AND A WATCHMAN PLACED OUTSIDE, UNTIL ALL THEREIN HAD BEEN UNTOUCHED BY THE DISEASE FOR FORTY DAYS, OR WERE DEAD.

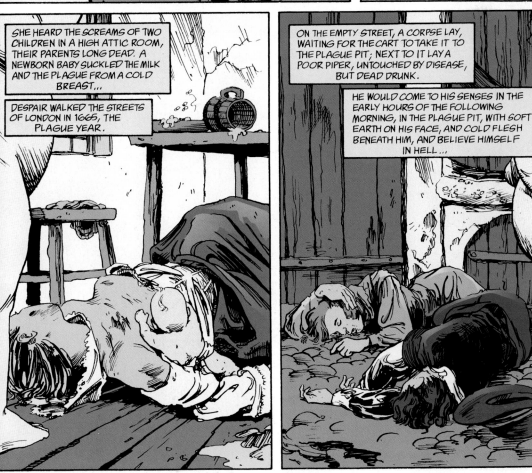

SHE HEARD THE SCREAMS OF TWO CHILDREN IN A HIGH ATTIC ROOM, THEIR PARENTS LONG DEAD. A NEWBORN BABY SUCKLED THE MILK AND THE PLAGUE FROM A COLD BREAST...

DESPAIR WALKED THE STREETS OF LONDON IN 1665, THE PLAGUE YEAR.

ON THE EMPTY STREET, A CORPSE LAY, WAITING FOR THE CART TO TAKE IT TO THE PLAGUE PIT; NEXT TO IT LAY A POOR PIPER, UNTOUCHED BY DISEASE, BUT DEAD DRUNK.

HE WOULD COME TO HIS SENSES IN THE EARLY HOURS OF THE FOLLOWING MORNING, IN THE PLAGUE PIT, WITH SOFT EARTH ON HIS FACE, AND COLD FLESH BENEATH HIM, AND BELIEVE HIMSELF IN HELL...

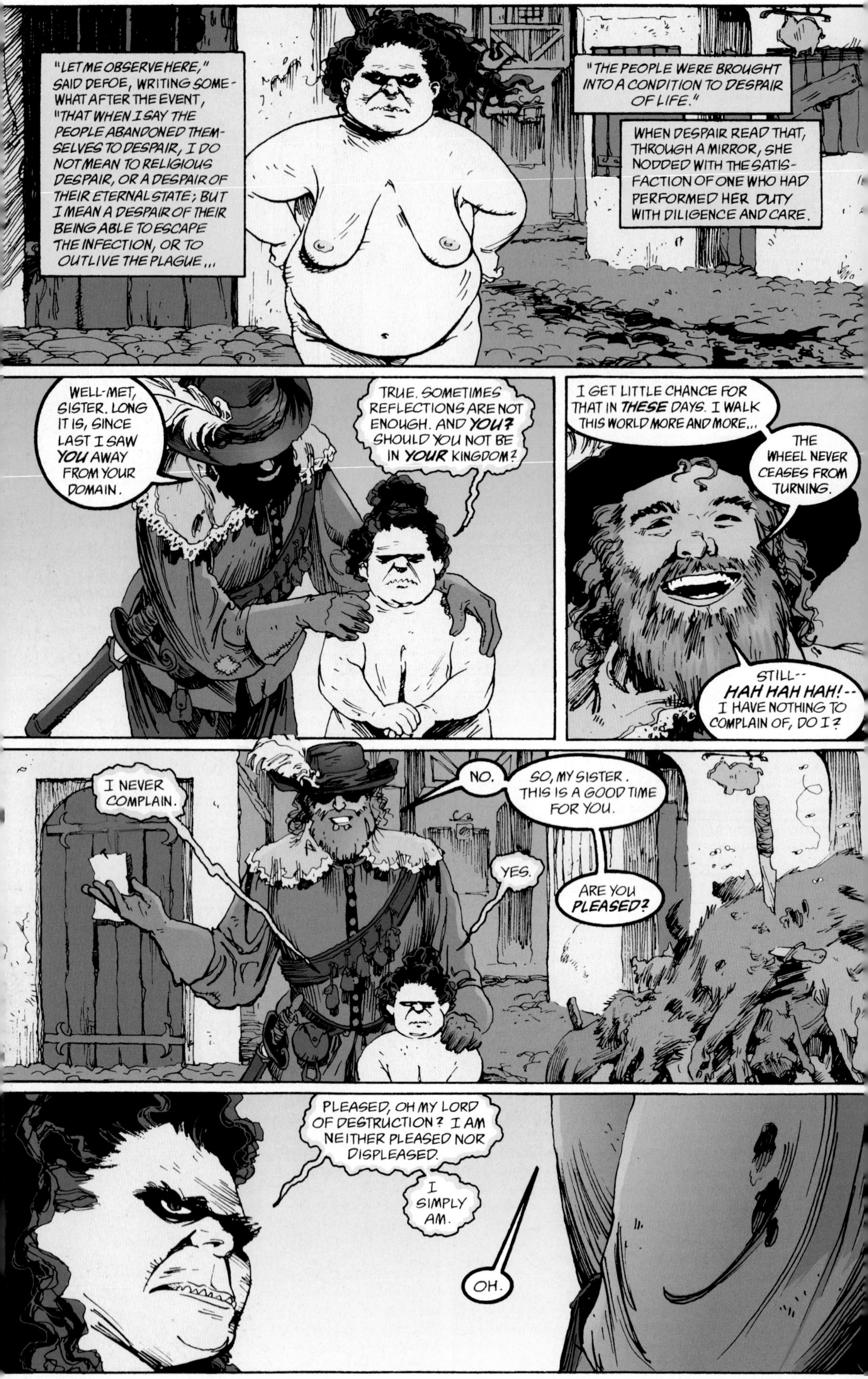
"LET ME OBSERVE HERE," SAID DEFOE, WRITING SOMEWHAT AFTER THE EVENT, "THAT WHEN I SAY THE PEOPLE ABANDONED THEMSELVES TO DESPAIR, I DO NOT MEAN TO RELIGIOUS DESPAIR, OR A DESPAIR OF THEIR ETERNAL STATE; BUT I MEAN A DESPAIR OF THEIR BEING ABLE TO ESCAPE THE INFECTION, OR TO OUTLIVE THE PLAGUE...
"THE PEOPLE WERE BROUGHT INTO A CONDITION TO DESPAIR OF LIFE."
WHEN DESPAIR READ THAT, THROUGH A MIRROR, SHE NODDED WITH THE SATISFACTION OF ONE WHO HAD PERFORMED HER DUTY WITH DILIGENCE AND CARE.
WELL-MET, SISTER. LONG IT IS, SINCE LAST I SAW YOU AWAY FROM YOUR DOMAIN.
TRUE. SOMETIMES REFLECTIONS ARE NOT ENOUGH. AND YOU? SHOULD YOU NOT BE IN YOUR KINGDOM?
I GET LITTLE CHANCE FOR THAT IN THESE DAYS. I WALK THIS WORLD MORE AND MORE...
THE WHEEL NEVER CEASES FROM TURNING.
STILL-- HAH HAH HAH!-- I HAVE NOTHING TO COMPLAIN OF, DO I?
I NEVER COMPLAIN.
NO.
SO, MY SISTER. THIS IS A GOOD TIME FOR YOU.
YES.
ARE YOU PLEASED?
PLEASED, OH MY LORD OF DESTRUCTION? I AM NEITHER PLEASED NOR DISPLEASED.
I SIMPLY AM.
OH.

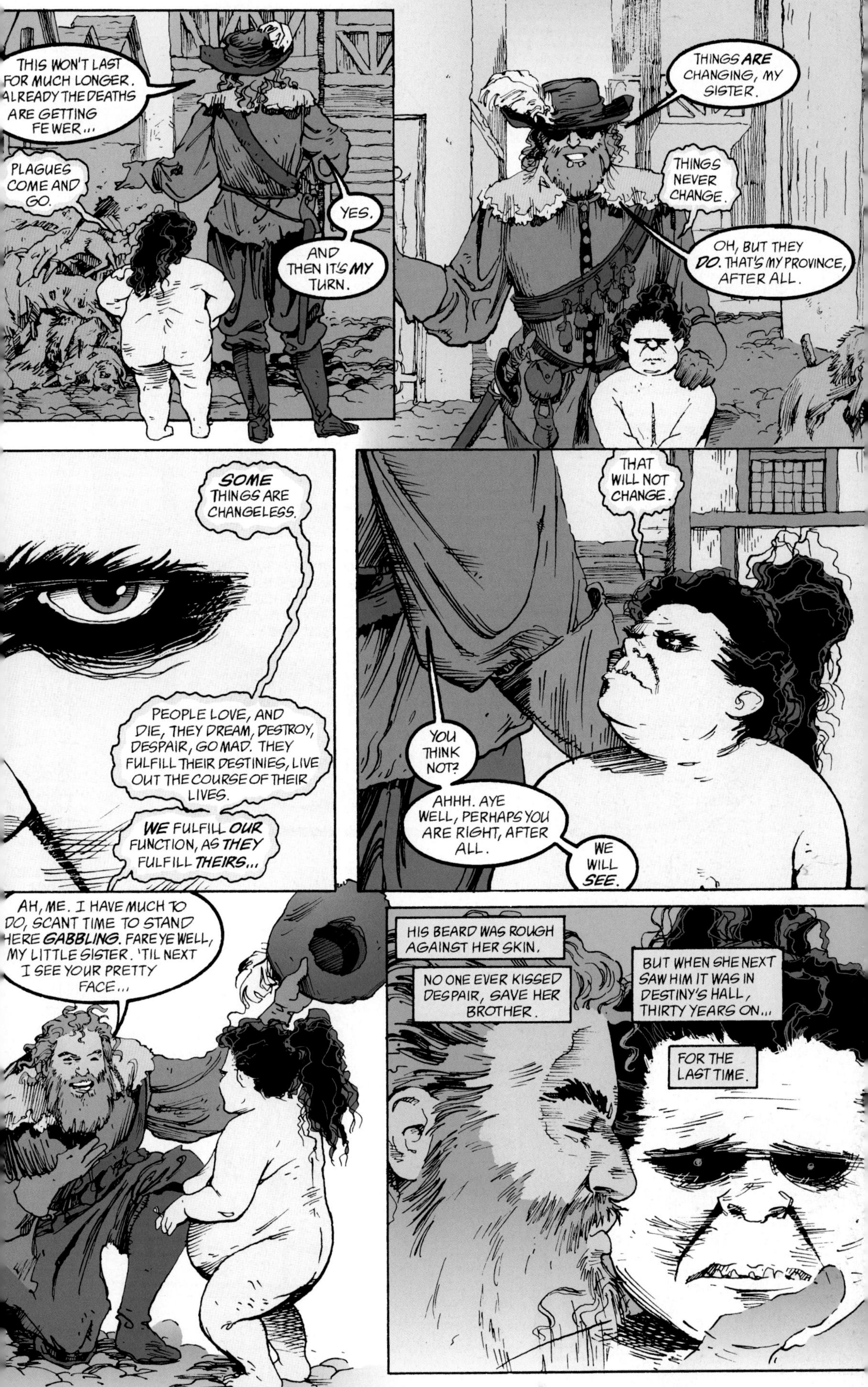
THIS WON'T LAST FOR MUCH LONGER. ALREADY THE DEATHS ARE GETTING FEWER...
PLAGUES COME AND GO.
YES.
AND THEN IT'S MY TURN.
THINGS ARE CHANGING, MY SISTER.
THINGS NEVER CHANGE.
OH, BUT THEY DO. THAT'S MY PROVINCE, AFTER ALL.
SOME THINGS ARE CHANGELESS.
PEOPLE LOVE, AND DIE, THEY DREAM, DESTROY, DESPAIR, GO MAD. THEY FULFILL THEIR DESTINIES, LIVE OUT THE COURSE OF THEIR LIVES.
WE FULFILL OUR FUNCTION, AS THEY FULFILL THEIRS...
THAT WILL NOT CHANGE.
YOU THINK NOT?
AHHH. AYE WELL, PERHAPS YOU ARE RIGHT, AFTER ALL.
WE WILL SEE.
AH, ME. I HAVE MUCH TO DO, SCANT TIME TO STAND HERE GABBLING. FARE YE WELL, MY LITTLE SISTER. 'TIL NEXT I SEE YOUR PRETTY FACE...
HIS BEARD WAS ROUGH AGAINST HER SKIN.
NO ONE EVER KISSED DESPAIR, SAVE HER BROTHER.
BUT WHEN SHE NEXT SAW HIM IT WAS IN DESTINY'S HALL, THIRTY YEARS ON...
FOR THE LAST TIME.

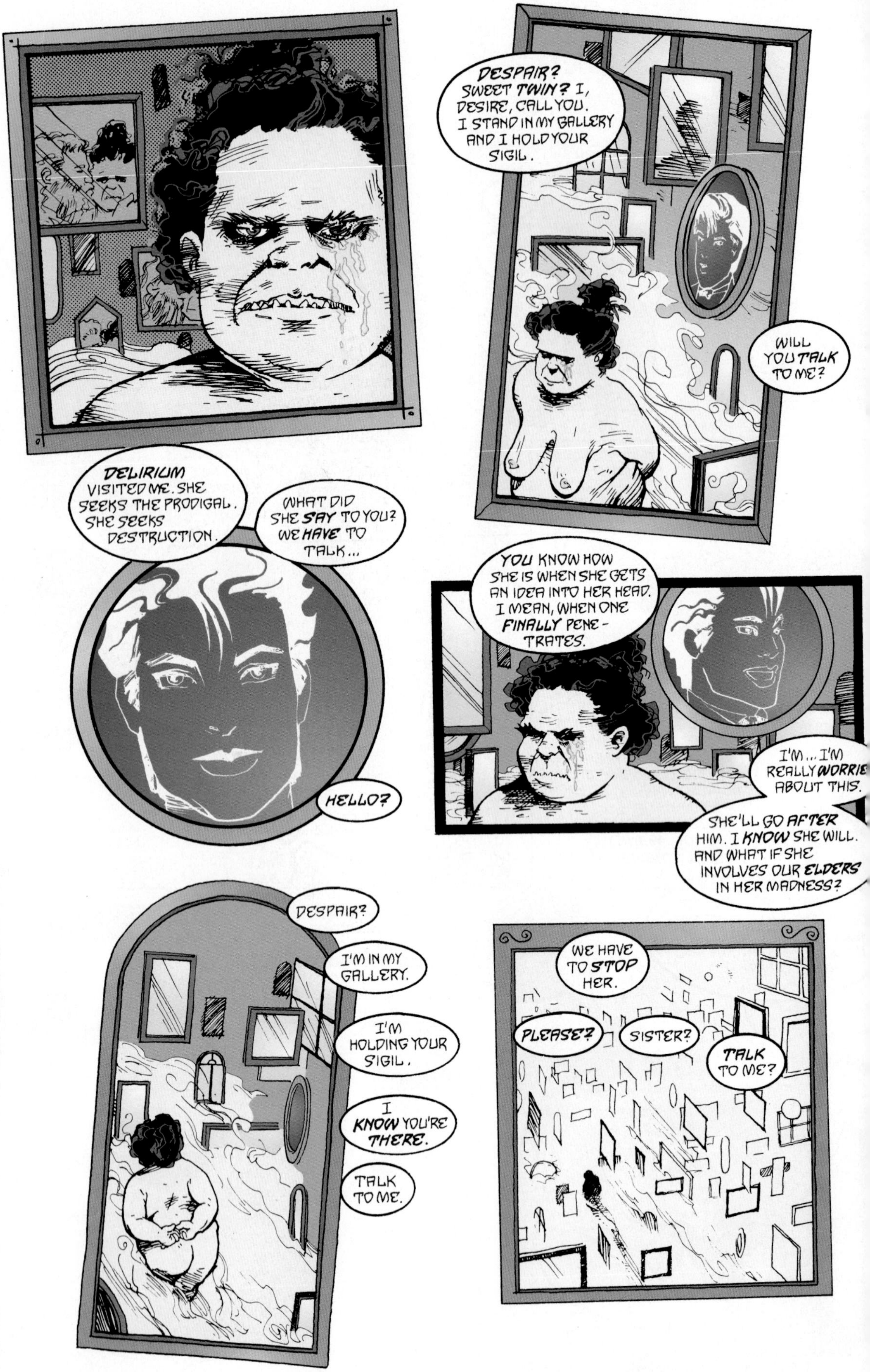
DESPAIR? SWEET TWIN? I, DESIRE, CALL YOU. I STAND IN MY GALLERY AND I HOLD YOUR SIGIL.
WILL YOU TALK TO ME?
DELIRIUM VISITED ME. SHE SEEKS THE PRODIGAL. SHE SEEKS DESTRUCTION.
WHAT DID SHE SAY TO YOU? WE HAVE TO TALK...
HELLO?
YOU KNOW HOW SHE IS WHEN SHE GETS AN IDEA INTO HER HEAD. I MEAN, WHEN ONE FINALLY PENE-TRATES.
I'M... I'M REALLY WORRIE ABOUT THIS.
SHE'LL GO AFTER HIM. I KNOW SHE WILL. AND WHAT IF SHE INVOLVES OUR ELDERS IN HER MADNESS?
DESPAIR?
I'M IN MY GALLERY.
I'M HOLDING YOUR SIGIL.
I KNOW YOU'RE THERE.
TALK TO ME.
WE HAVE TO STOP HER.
PLEASE?
SISTER?
TALK TO ME?

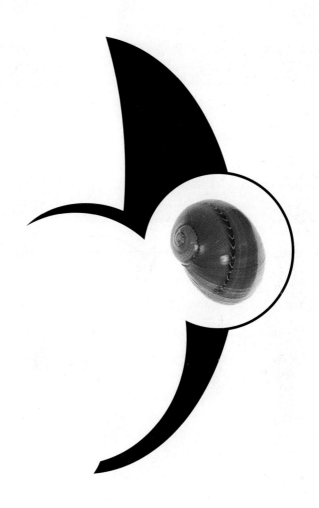

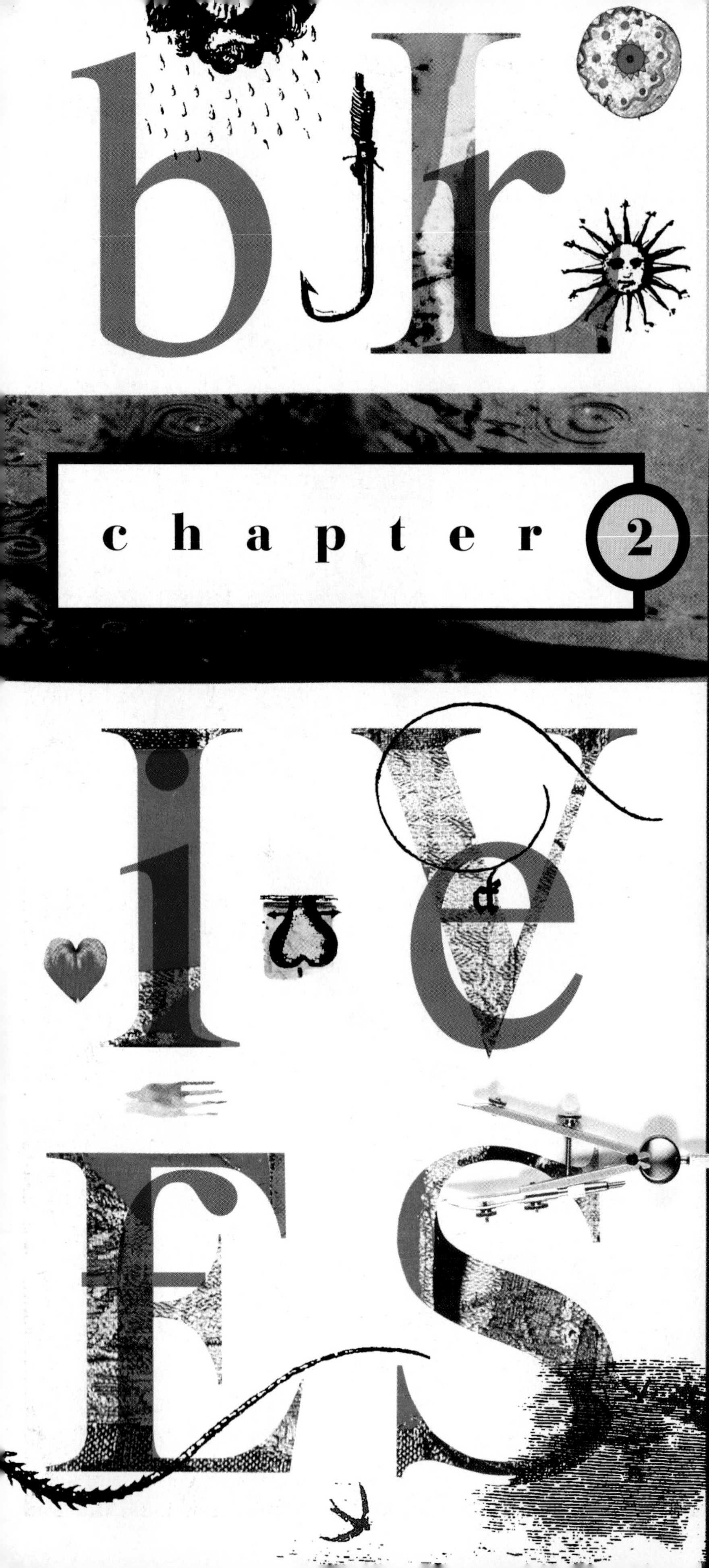

Brief Lives

chapter 2

It always rains on the unlo
Wet dreams
A fishing expedition
She kisses Wyverns
(the Disneyland analogy
Dinner etiquette and chocolate
Desire swears by the first ci
"Things are changing"
What can possibly go wror

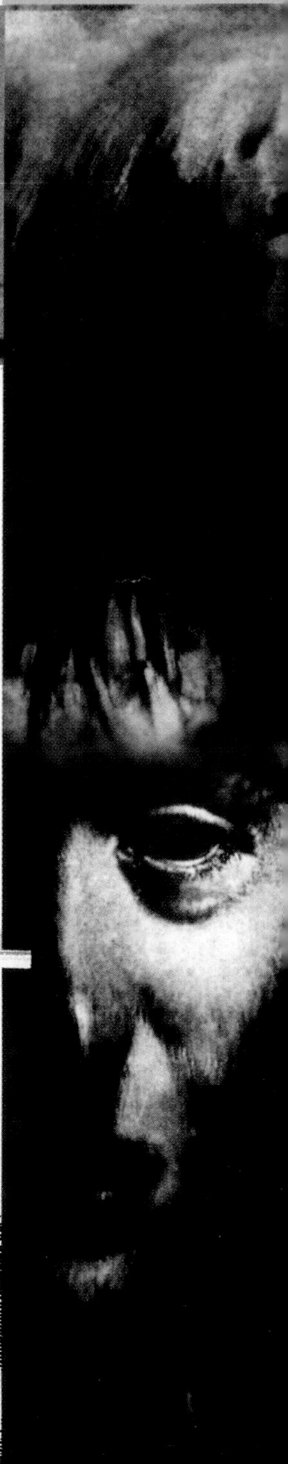

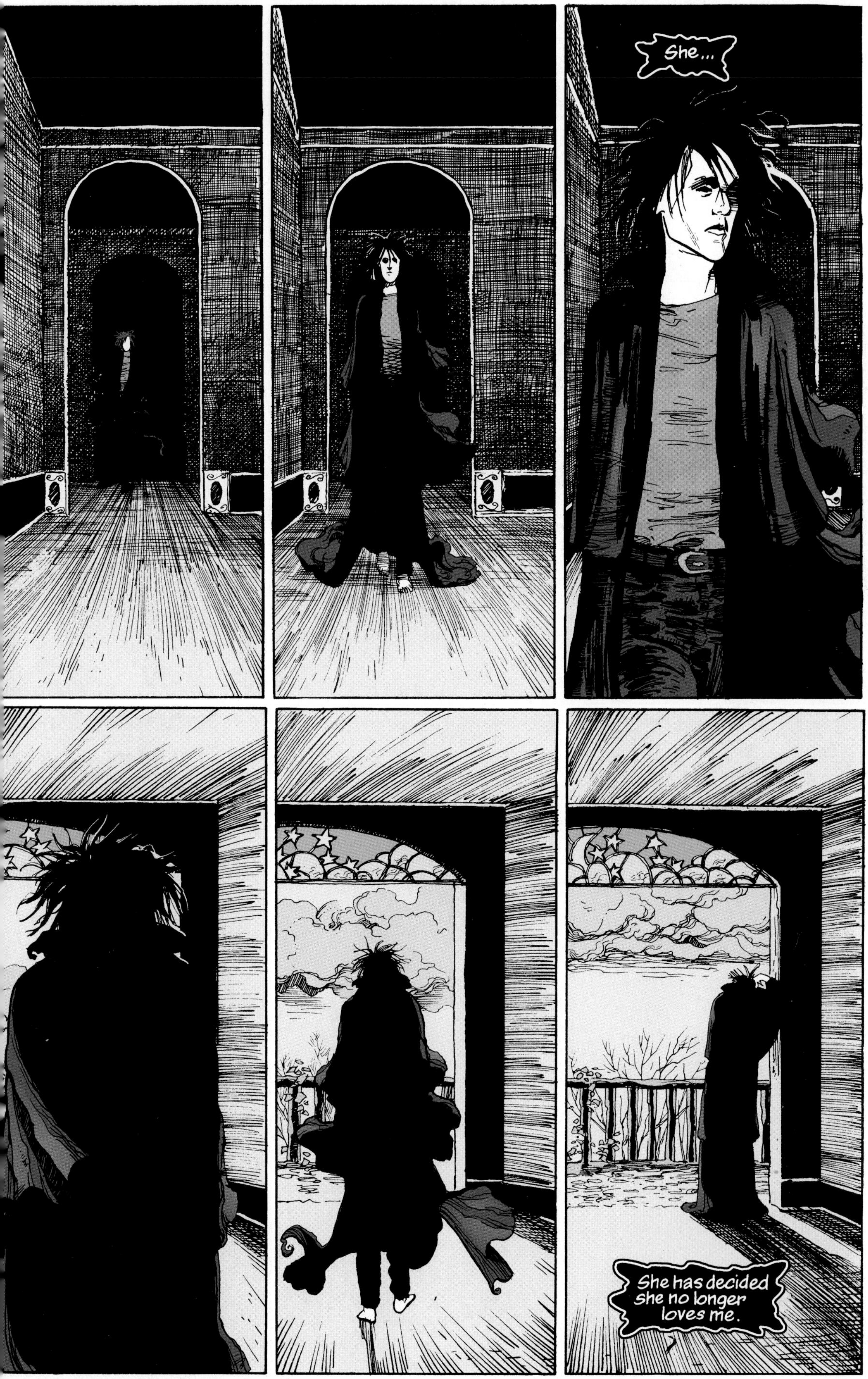
She...
She has decided
she no longer
loves me.

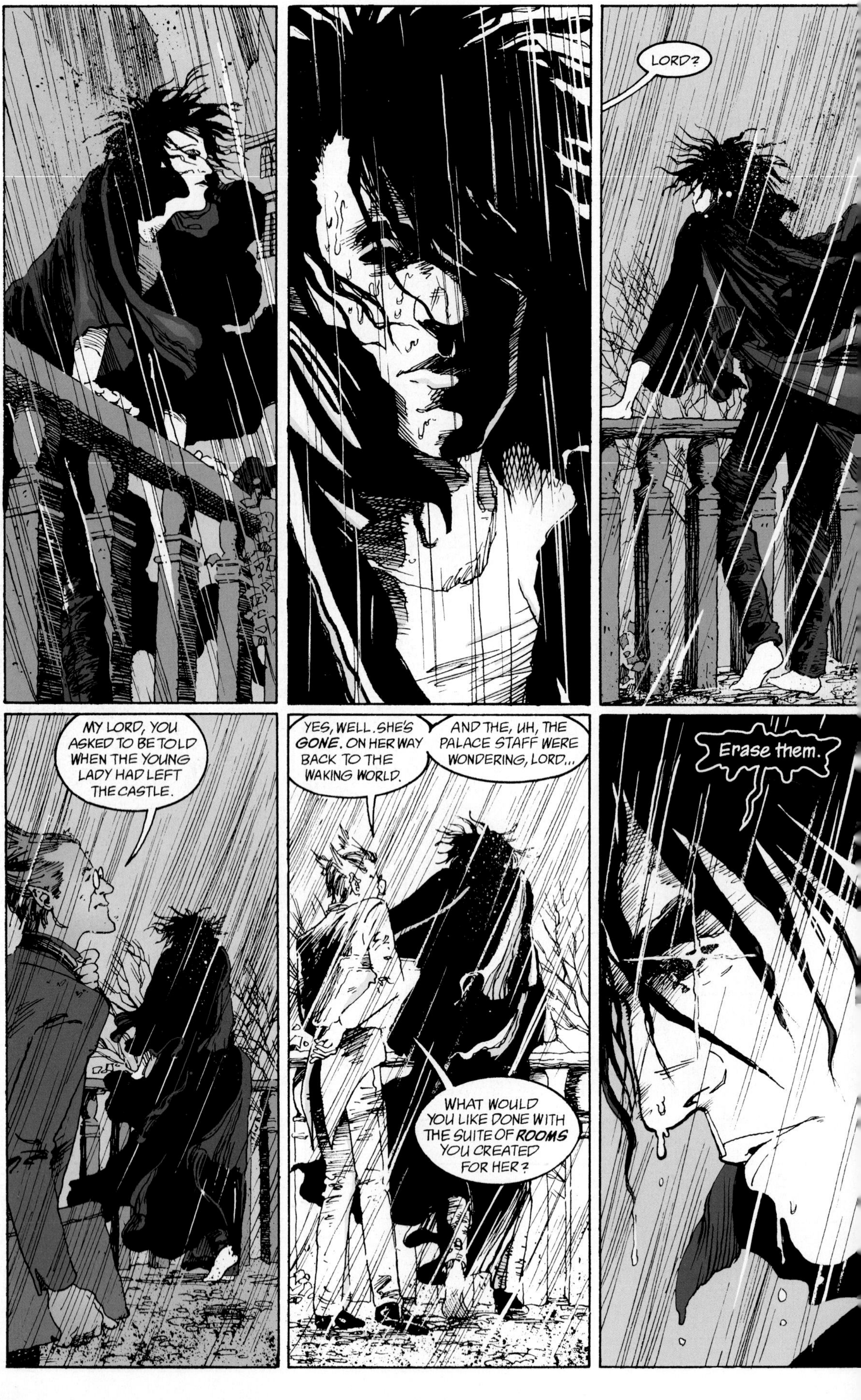
LORD?
MY LORD, YOU ASKED TO BE TOLD WHEN THE YOUNG LADY HAD LEFT THE CASTLE.
YES, WELL. SHE'S GONE. ON HER WAY BACK TO THE WAKING WORLD.
AND THE, UH, THE PALACE STAFF WERE WONDERING, LORD...
WHAT WOULD YOU LIKE DONE WITH THE SUITE OF ROOMS YOU CREATED FOR HER?
Erase them.

TWO: IT ALWAYS RAINS ON THE UNLOVED—WET DREAMS—A FISHING EXPEDITION—SHE KISSES WYVERNS (THE DISNEY-LAND ANALOGY)—DINNER ETIQUETTE AND CHOCOLATE LOVERS—DESIRE SWEARS BY THE FIRST CIRCLE—"THINGS ARE CHANGING"—WHAT CAN POSSIBLY GO WRONG?

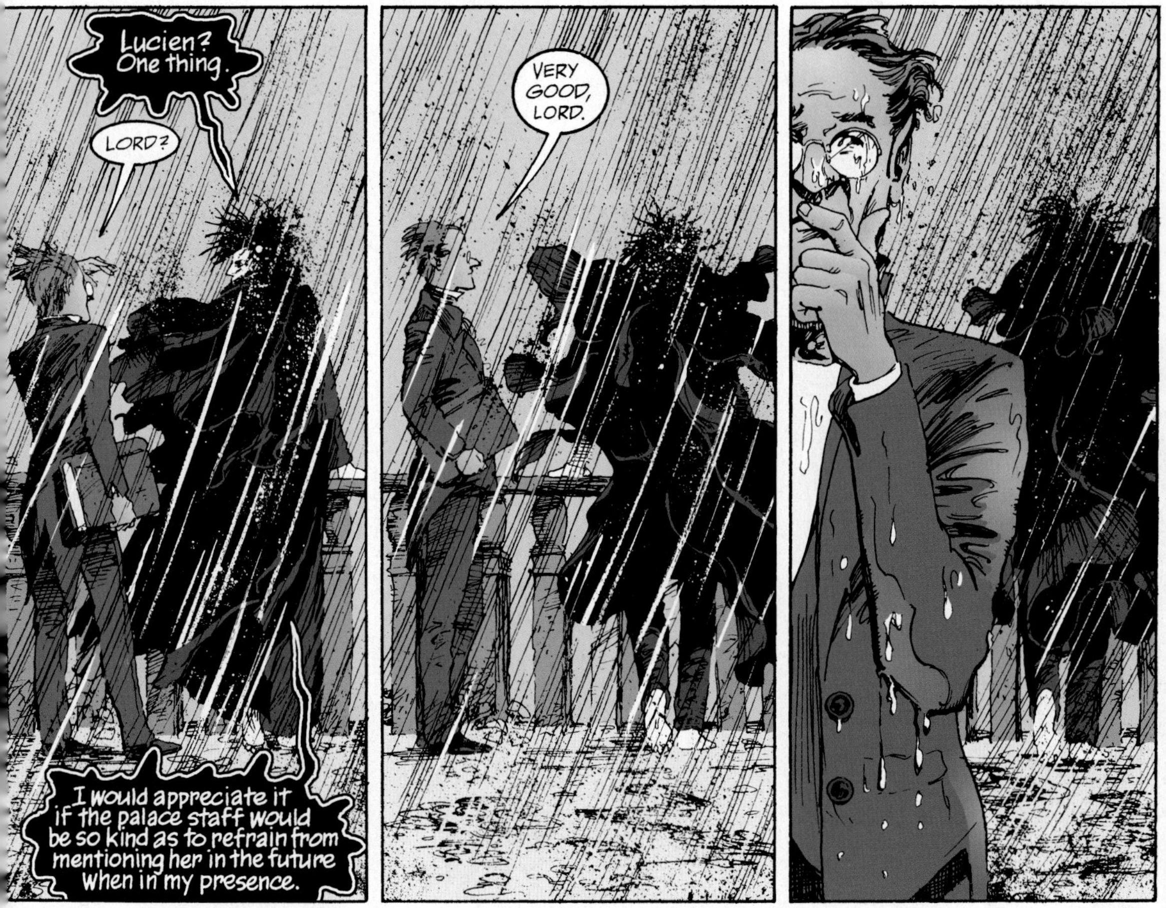

Lucien? One thing.
LORD?
I would appreciate it if the palace staff would be so kind as to refrain from mentioning her in the future when in my presence.
VERY GOOD, LORD.

THE SANDMAN

featuring characters created by Gaiman, Kieth and Dringenberg

Neil Gaiman, writer; Jill Thompson and Vince Locke, artists; Danny Vozzo, colors; Todd Klein, lettering; Karen Berger, editor; and introducing Lisa Aufenanger, assistant editor.

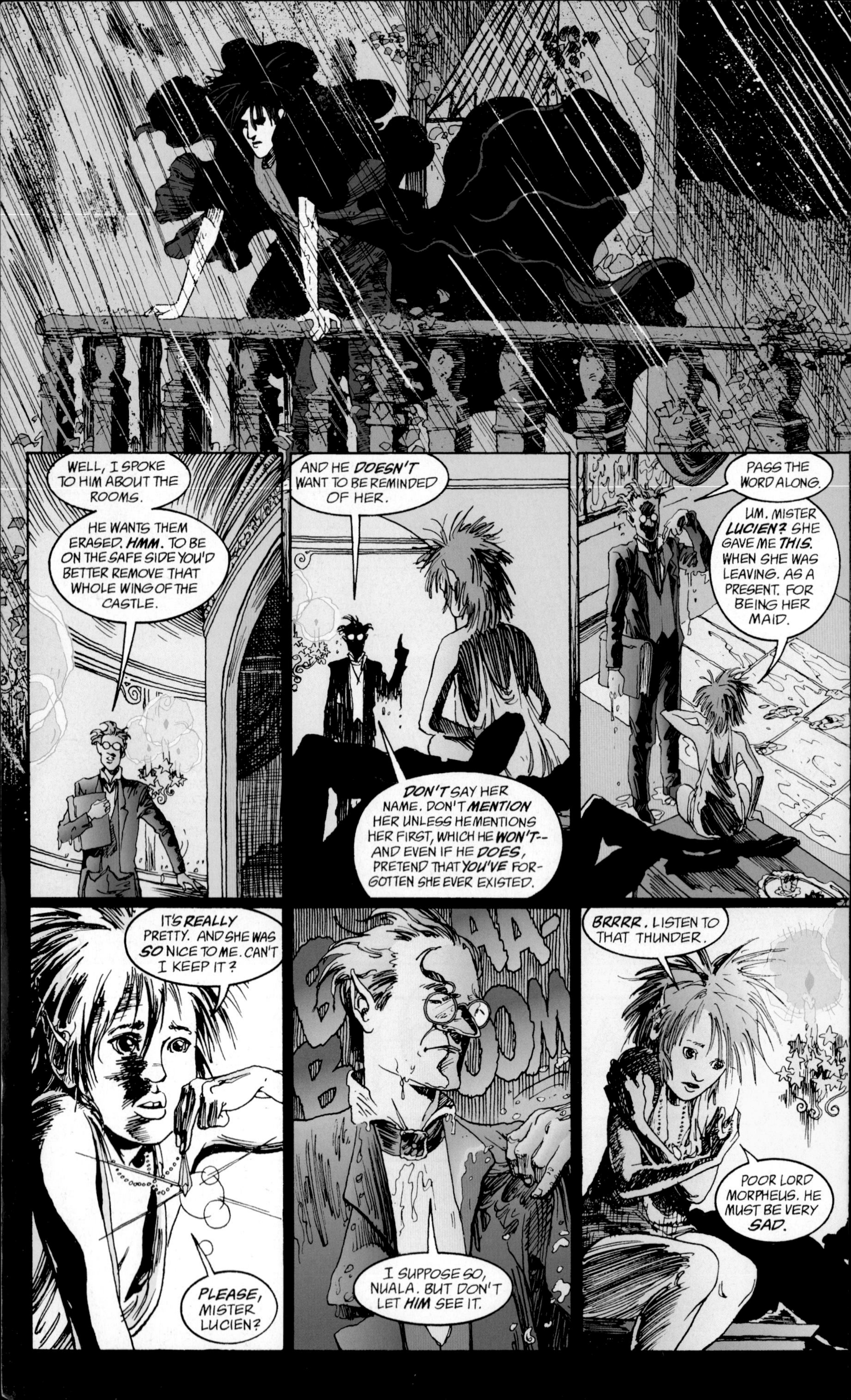
WELL, I SPOKE TO HIM ABOUT THE ROOMS.
HE WANTS THEM ERASED. HMM. TO BE ON THE SAFE SIDE YOU'D BETTER REMOVE THAT WHOLE WING OF THE CASTLE.
AND HE DOESN'T WANT TO BE REMINDED OF HER.
DON'T SAY HER NAME. DON'T MENTION HER UNLESS HE MENTIONS HER FIRST, WHICH HE WON'T-- AND EVEN IF HE DOES, PRETEND THAT YOU'VE FOR-GOTTEN SHE EVER EXISTED.
PASS THE WORD ALONG.
UM. MISTER LUCIEN? SHE GAVE ME THIS. WHEN SHE WAS LEAVING. AS A PRESENT. FOR BEING HER MAID.
IT'S REALLY PRETTY. AND SHE WAS SO NICE TO ME. CAN'T I KEEP IT?
PLEASE, MISTER LUCIEN?
AA-BOOM
I SUPPOSE SO, NUALA. BUT DON'T LET HIM SEE IT.
BRRRR. LISTEN TO THAT THUNDER.
POOR LORD MORPHEUS. HE MUST BE VERY SAD.

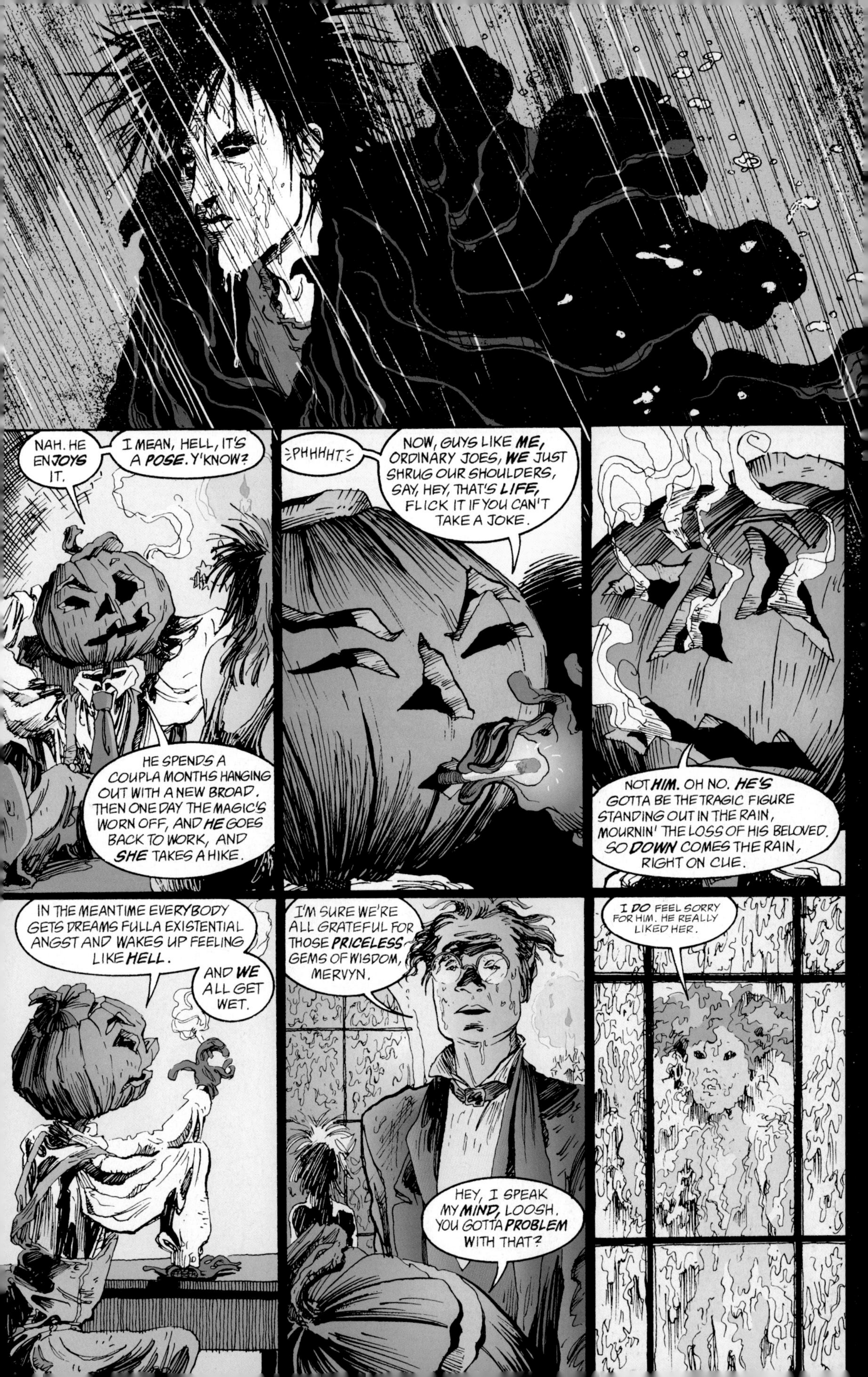

NAH. HE ENJOYS IT.
I MEAN, HELL, IT'S A POSE. Y'KNOW?
HE SPENDS A COUPLA MONTHS HANGING OUT WITH A NEW BROAD. THEN ONE DAY THE MAGIC'S WORN OFF, AND HE GOES BACK TO WORK, AND SHE TAKES A HIKE.
PHHHHT.
NOW, GUYS LIKE ME, ORDINARY JOES, WE JUST SHRUG OUR SHOULDERS, SAY, HEY, THAT'S LIFE, FLICK IT IF YOU CAN'T TAKE A JOKE.
NOT HIM. OH NO. HE'S GOTTA BE THE TRAGIC FIGURE STANDING OUT IN THE RAIN, MOURNIN' THE LOSS OF HIS BELOVED. SO DOWN COMES THE RAIN, RIGHT ON CUE.
IN THE MEANTIME EVERYBODY GETS DREAMS FULLA EXISTENTIAL ANGST AND WAKES UP FEELING LIKE HELL.
AND WE ALL GET WET.
I'M SURE WE'RE ALL GRATEFUL FOR THOSE PRICELESS GEMS OF WISDOM, MERVYN.
HEY, I SPEAK MY MIND, LOOSH. YOU GOTTA PROBLEM WITH THAT?
I DO FEEL SORRY FOR HIM. HE REALLY LIKED HER.

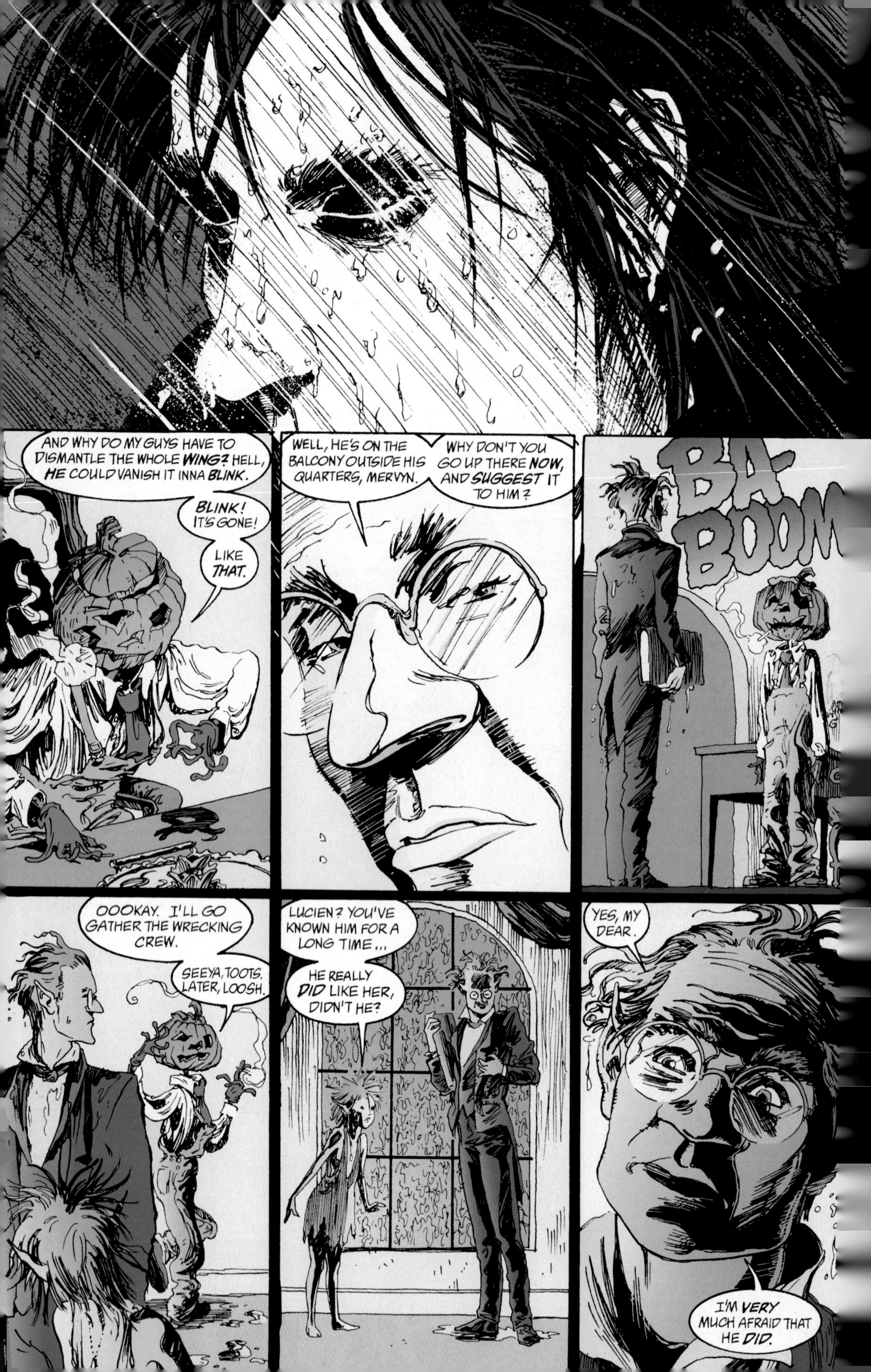

AND WHY DO MY GUYS HAVE TO DISMANTLE THE WHOLE WING? HELL, HE COULD VANISH IT INNA BLINK.
BLINK! IT'S GONE!
LIKE THAT.
WELL, HE'S ON THE BALCONY OUTSIDE HIS QUARTERS, MERVYN.
WHY DON'T YOU GO UP THERE NOW, AND SUGGEST IT TO HIM?
BA-BOOM
OOOKAY. I'LL GO GATHER THE WRECKING CREW.
SEEYA, TOOTS. LATER, LOOSH.
LUCIEN? YOU'VE KNOWN HIM FOR A LONG TIME...
HE REALLY DID LIKE HER, DIDN'T HE?
YES, MY DEAR.
I'M VERY MUCH AFRAID THAT HE DID.

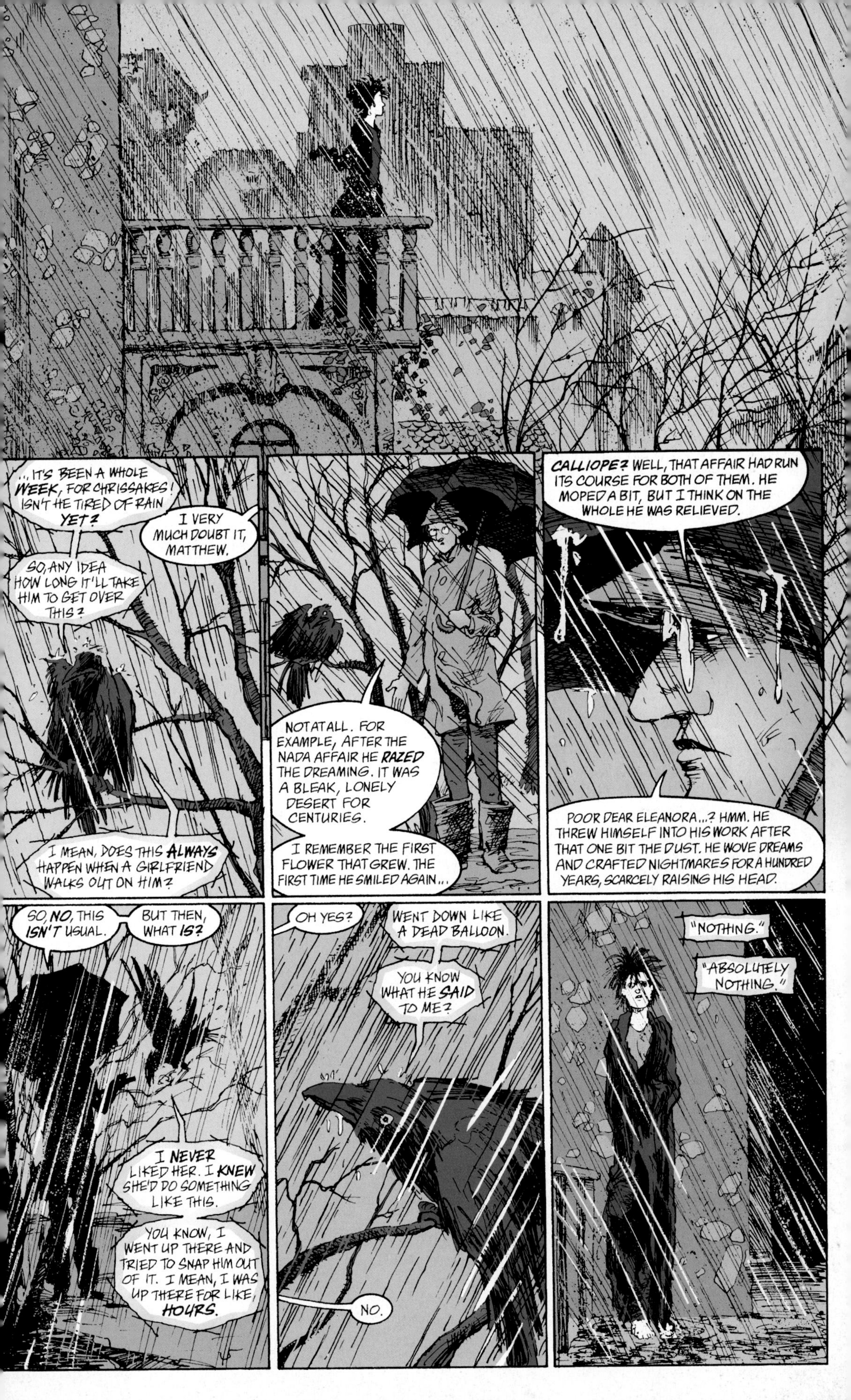
...IT'S BEEN A WHOLE WEEK, FOR CHRISSAKES! ISN'T HE TIRED OF RAIN YET?
I VERY MUCH DOUBT IT, MATTHEW.
SO, ANY IDEA HOW LONG IT'LL TAKE HIM TO GET OVER THIS?
I MEAN, DOES THIS ALWAYS HAPPEN WHEN A GIRLFRIEND WALKS OUT ON HIM?
NOT AT ALL. FOR EXAMPLE, AFTER THE NADA AFFAIR HE RAZED THE DREAMING. IT WAS A BLEAK, LONELY DESERT FOR CENTURIES.
I REMEMBER THE FIRST FLOWER THAT GREW. THE FIRST TIME HE SMILED AGAIN...
CALLIOPE? WELL, THAT AFFAIR HAD RUN ITS COURSE FOR BOTH OF THEM. HE MOPED A BIT, BUT I THINK ON THE WHOLE HE WAS RELIEVED.
POOR DEAR ELEANORA...? HMM. HE THREW HIMSELF INTO HIS WORK AFTER THAT ONE BIT THE DUST. HE WOVE DREAMS AND CRAFTED NIGHTMARES FOR A HUNDRED YEARS, SCARCELY RAISING HIS HEAD.
SO, NO, THIS ISN'T USUAL.
BUT THEN, WHAT IS?
I NEVER LIKED HER. I KNEW SHE'D DO SOMETHING LIKE THIS.
YOU KNOW, I WENT UP THERE AND TRIED TO SNAP HIM OUT OF IT. I MEAN, I WAS UP THERE FOR LIKE, HOURS.
OH YES?
WENT DOWN LIKE A DEAD BALLOON.
YOU KNOW WHAT HE SAID TO ME?
NO.
"NOTHING."
"ABSOLUTELY NOTHING."

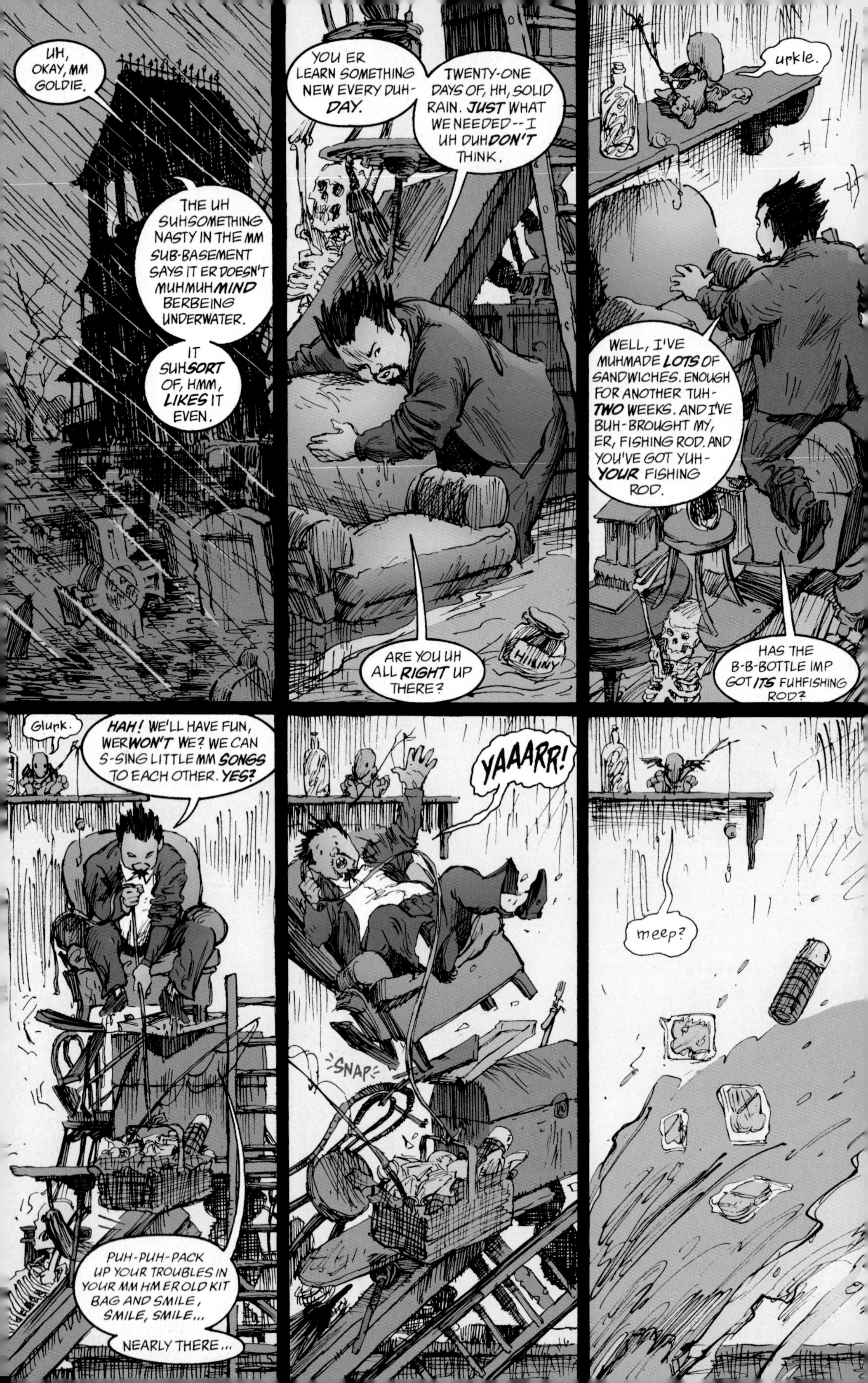
UH, OKAY, MM GOLDIE.
THE UH SUHSOMETHING NASTY IN THE MM SUB-BASEMENT SAYS IT ER DOESN'T MUHMUH MIND BERBEING UNDERWATER.
IT SUHSORT OF, HMM, LIKES IT EVEN.
YOU ER LEARN SOMETHING NEW EVERY DUH- DAY.
TWENTY-ONE DAYS OF, HH, SOLID RAIN. JUST WHAT WE NEEDED--I UH DUHDON'T THINK.
ARE YOU UH ALL RIGHT UP THERE?
urkle.
WELL, I'VE MUHMADE LOTS OF SANDWICHES. ENOUGH FOR ANOTHER TUH- TWO WEEKS. AND I'VE BUH-BROUGHT MY, ER, FISHING ROD. AND YOU'VE GOT YUH- YOUR FISHING ROD.
HAS THE B-B-BOTTLE IMP GOT ITS FUHFISHING ROD?
Glurk.
HAH! WE'LL HAVE FUN, WERWON'T WE? WE CAN S-SING LITTLE MM SONGS TO EACH OTHER. YES?
PUH-PUH-PACK UP YOUR TROUBLES IN YOUR MM HM ER OLD KIT BAG AND SMILE, SMILE, SMILE...
NEARLY THERE...
YAAARR!
SNAP
meep?

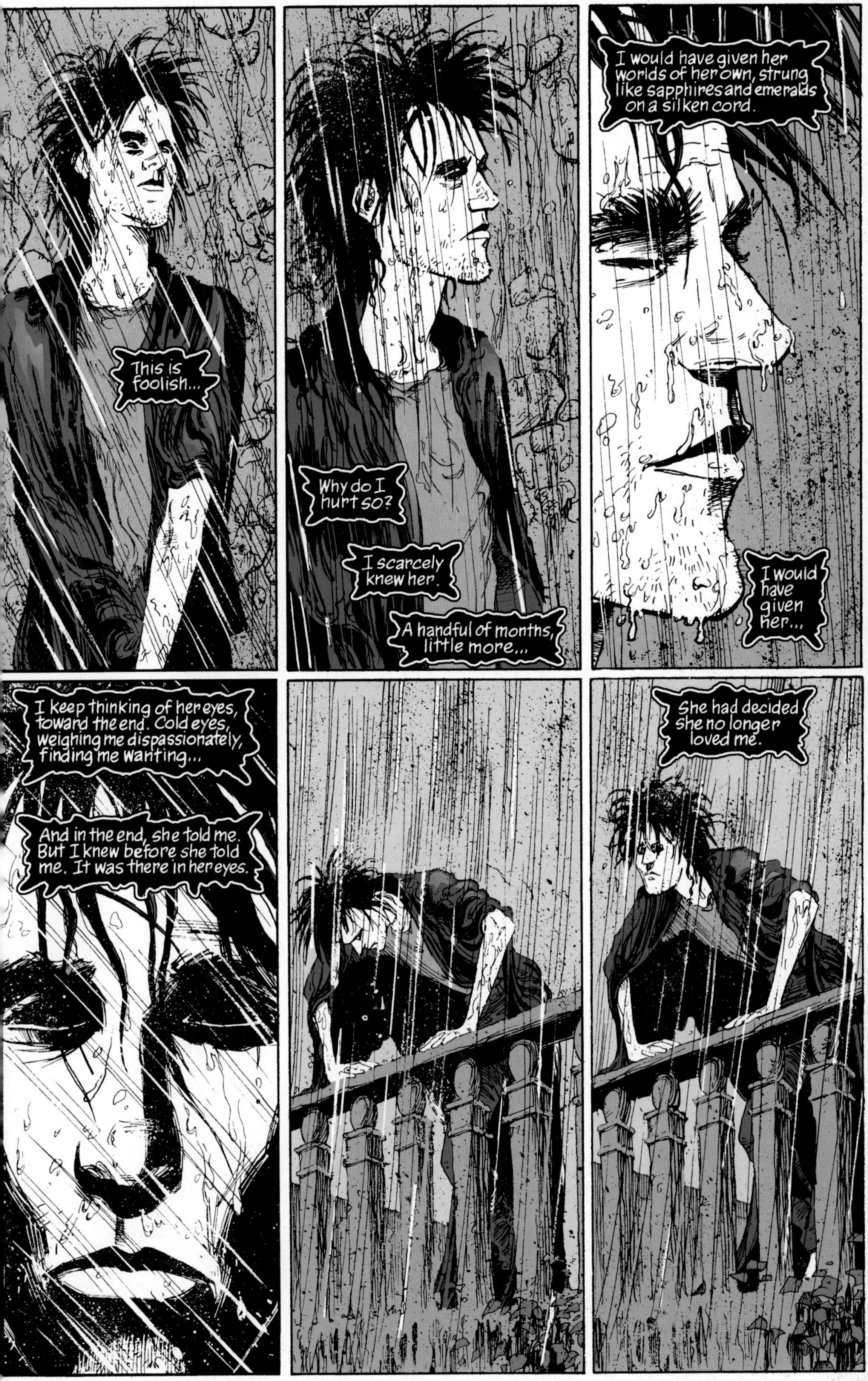
This is foolish...
Why do I hurt so?
I scarcely knew her.
A handful of months, little more...
I would have given her worlds of her own, strung like sapphires and emeralds on a silken cord.
I would have given her...
I keep thinking of her eyes, toward the end. Cold eyes, weighing me dispassionately, finding me wanting...
And in the end, she told me. But I knew before she told me. It was there in her eyes.
She had decided she no longer loved me.

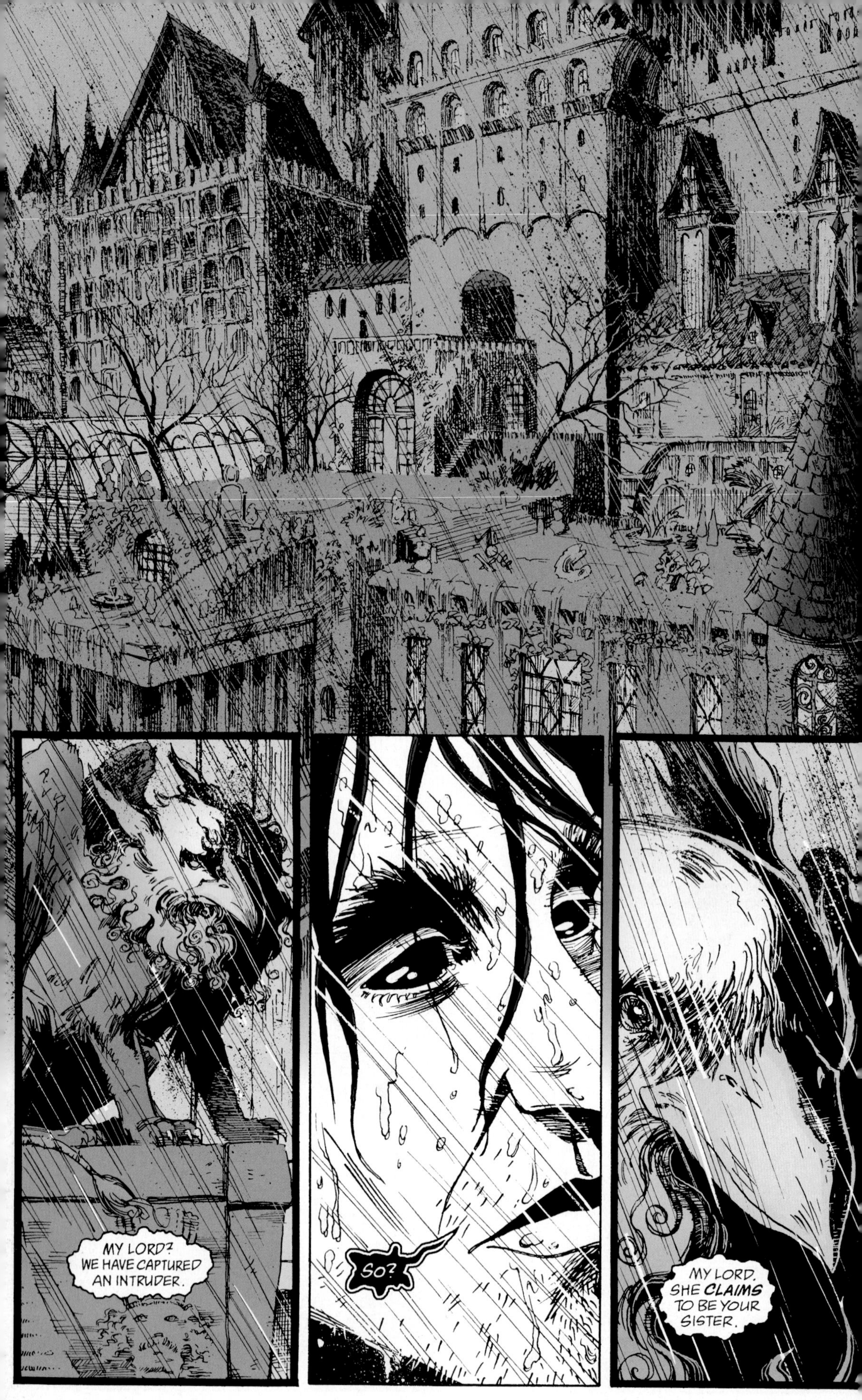
MY LORD?
WE HAVE CAPTURED
AN INTRUDER.
SO?
MY LORD.
SHE **CLAIMS**
TO BE YOUR
SISTER.

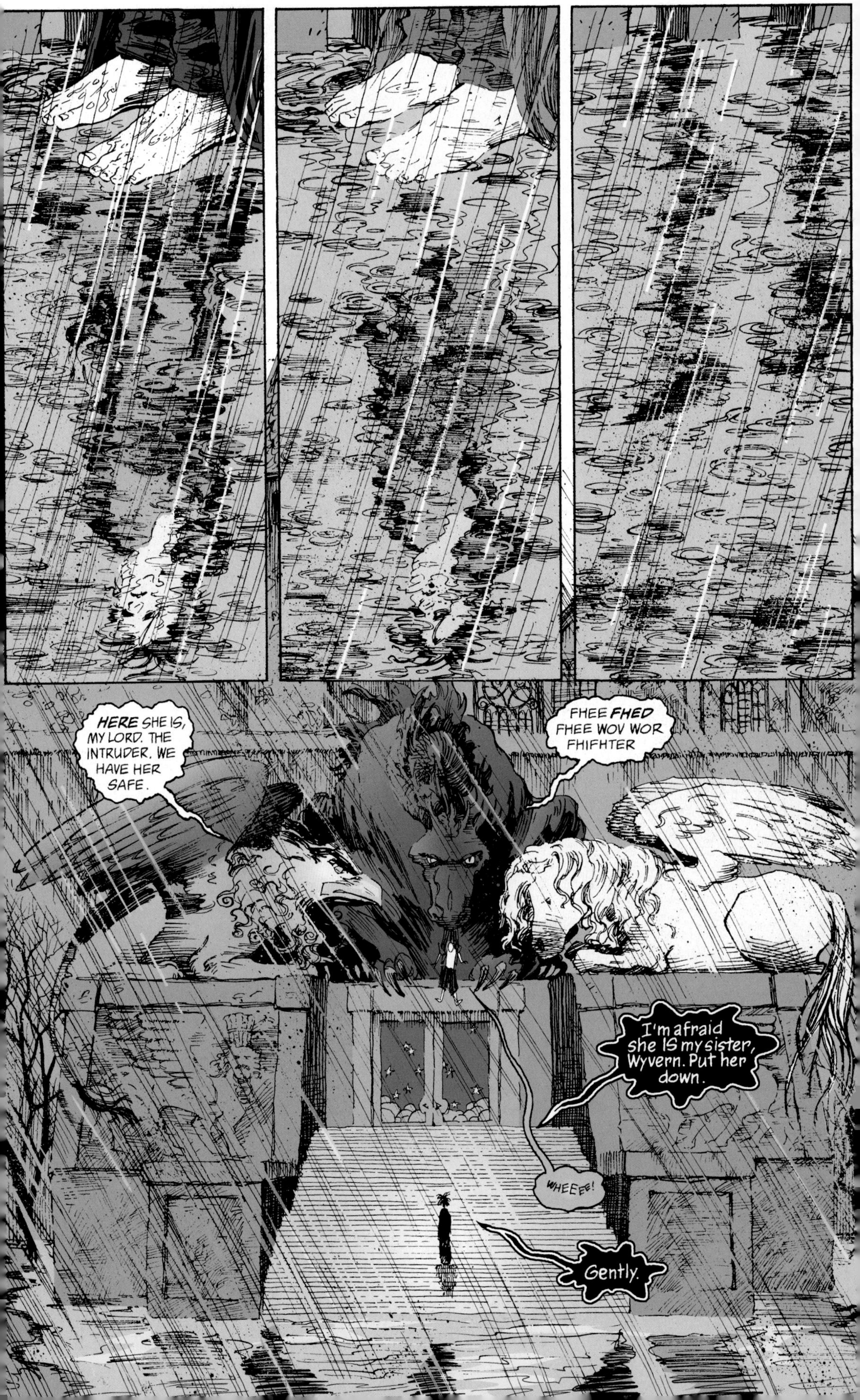
HERE SHE IS, MY LORD. THE INTRUDER. WE HAVE HER SAFE.
FHEE FHED FHEE WOV WOR FHIFHTER
I'm afraid she IS my sister, Wyvern. Put her down.
WHEEEE!
Gently.

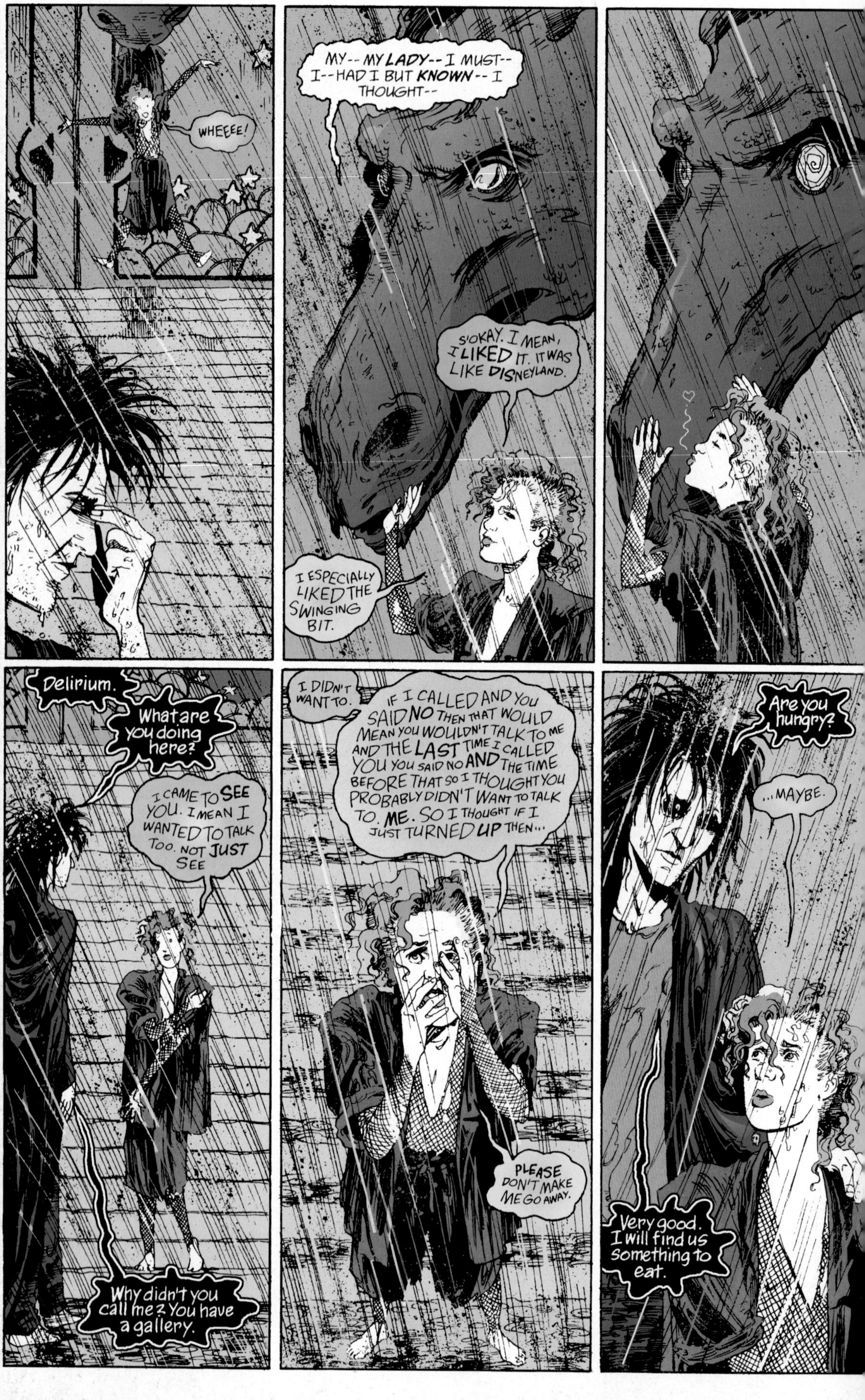
WHEEEE!
MY-- MY LADY-- I MUST-- I--HAD I BUT KNOWN-- I THOUGHT--
S'OKAY. I MEAN, I LIKED IT. IT WAS LIKE DISNEYLAND.
I ESPECIALLY LIKED THE SWINGING BIT.
Delirium.
What are you doing here?
I CAME TO SEE YOU. I MEAN I WANTED TO TALK TOO. NOT JUST SEE
Why didn't you call me? You have a gallery.
I DIDN'T WANT TO.
IF I CALLED AND YOU SAID NO THEN THAT WOULD MEAN YOU WOULDN'T TALK TO ME AND THE LAST TIME I CALLED YOU YOU SAID NO AND THE TIME BEFORE THAT SO I THOUGHT YOU PROBABLY DIDN'T WANT TO TALK TO. ME. SO I THOUGHT IF I JUST TURNED UP THEN...
PLEASE DON'T MAKE ME GO AWAY.
Are you hungry?
...MAYBE.
Very good. I will find us something to eat.

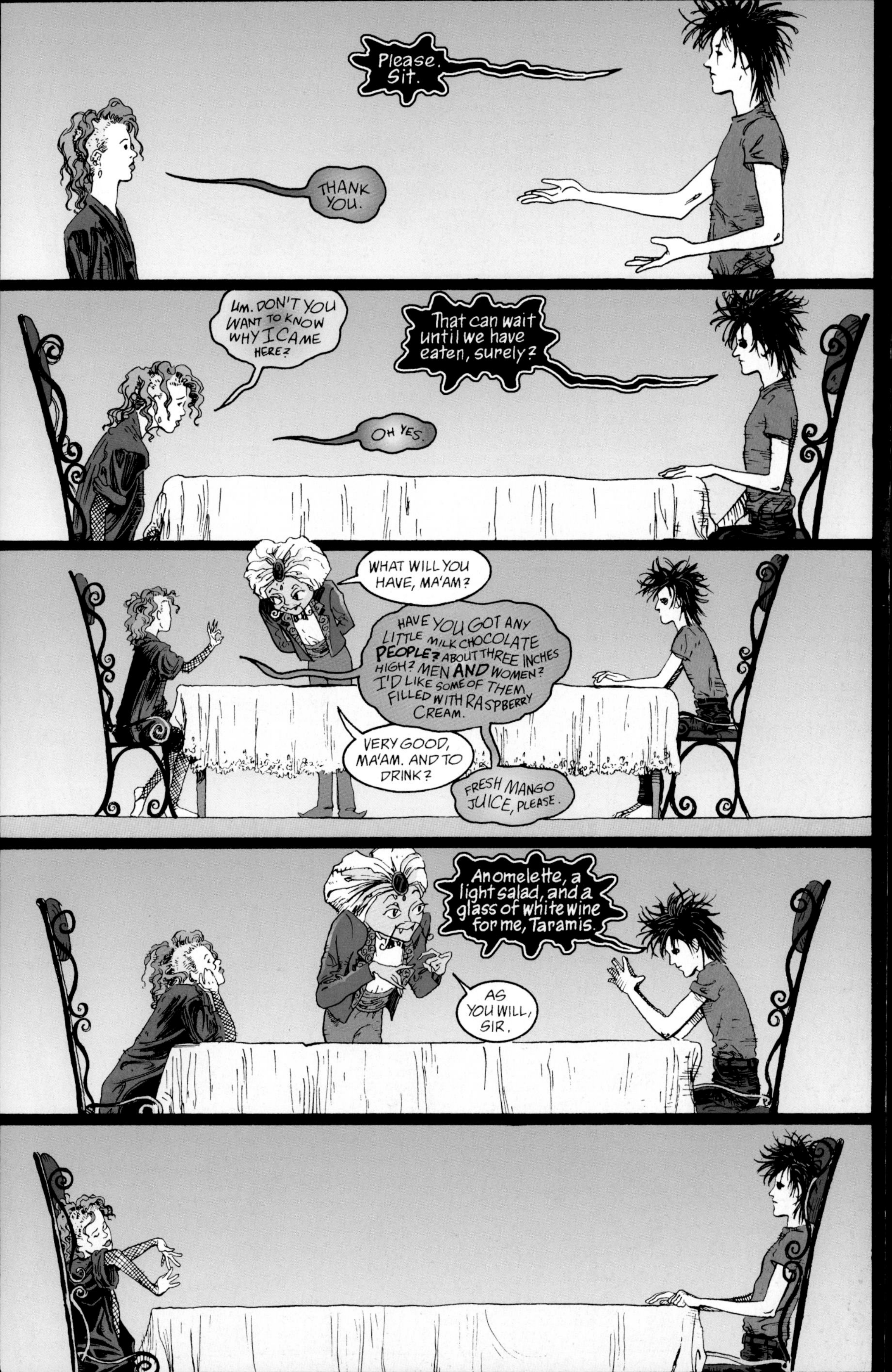
Please. Sit.
THANK YOU.
UM. DON'T YOU WANT TO KNOW WHY I CAME HERE?
That can wait until we have eaten, surely?
OH YES.
WHAT WILL YOU HAVE, MA'AM?
HAVE YOU GOT ANY LITTLE MILK CHOCOLATE PEOPLE? ABOUT THREE INCHES HIGH? MEN AND WOMEN? I'D LIKE SOME OF THEM FILLED WITH RASPBERRY CREAM.
VERY GOOD, MA'AM. AND TO DRINK?
FRESH MANGO JUICE, PLEASE.
An omelette, a light salad, and a glass of white wine for me, Taramis.
AS YOU WILL, SIR.

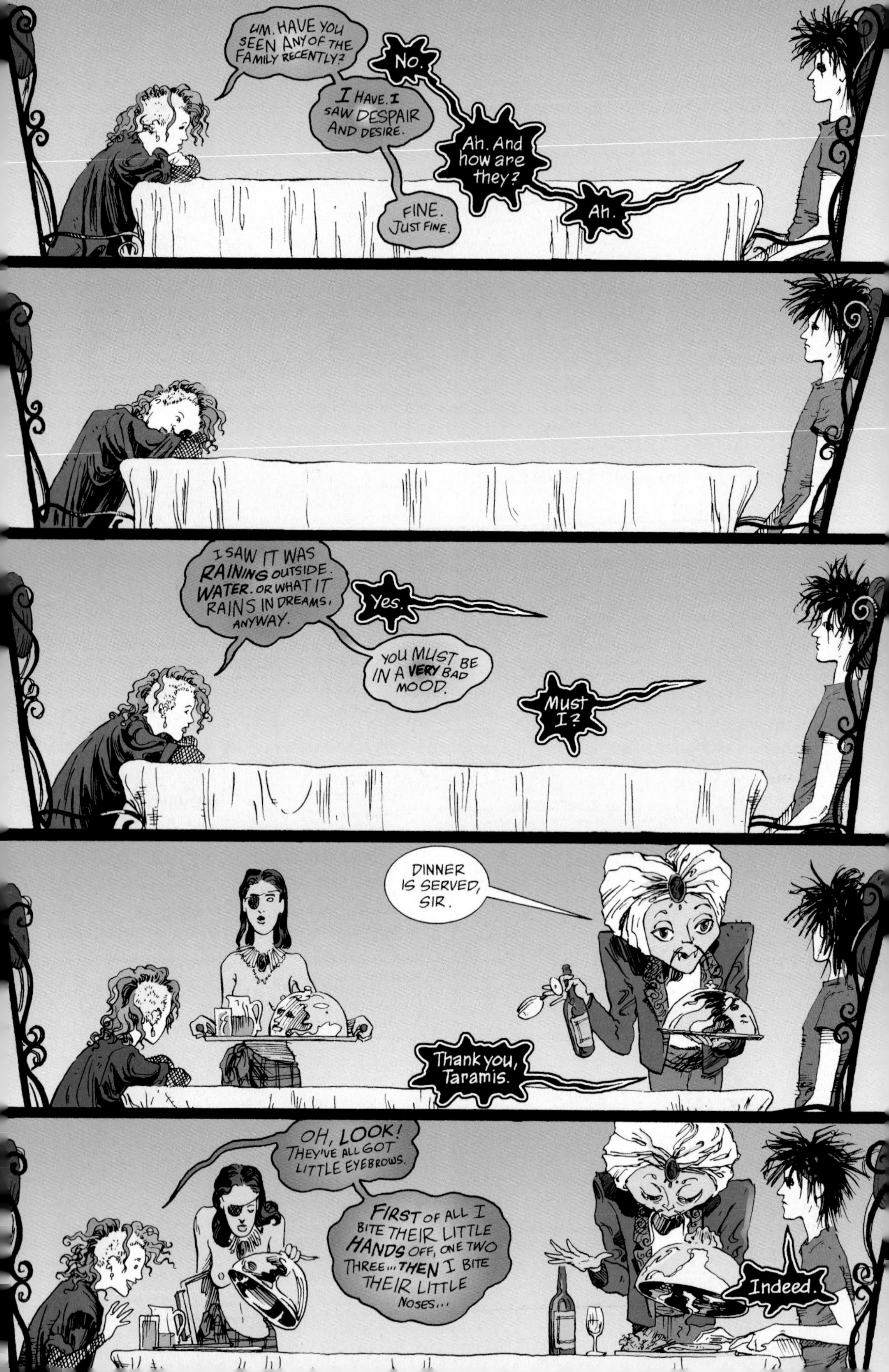
UM. HAVE YOU SEEN ANY OF THE FAMILY RECENTLY?
No.
I HAVE. I SAW DESPAIR AND DESIRE.
Ah. And how are they?
FINE. JUST FINE.
Ah.
I SAW IT WAS RAINING OUTSIDE. WATER. OR WHAT IT RAINS IN DREAMS, ANYWAY.
Yes.
YOU MUST BE IN A VERY BAD MOOD.
Must I?
DINNER IS SERVED, SIR.
Thank you, Taramis.
OH, LOOK! THEY'VE ALL GOT LITTLE EYEBROWS.
FIRST OF ALL I BITE THEIR LITTLE HANDS OFF, ONE TWO THREE... THEN I BITE THEIR LITTLE NOSES...
Indeed.

THERE ARE NOT MANY OF THEM, ALL THINGS CONSIDERED: THE TRULY OLD.

EVEN ON THIS PLANET, IN THIS AGE, WHEN PEOPLE CONSIDER A MERE HUNDRED YEARS, OR A THOUSAND, TO BE AN UNUSUAL SPAN.

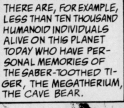

THERE ARE, FOR EXAMPLE, LESS THAN TEN THOUSAND HUMANOID INDIVIDUALS ALIVE ON THIS PLANET TODAY WHO HAVE PERSONAL MEMORIES OF THE SABER-TOOTHED TIGER, THE MEGATHERIUM, THE CAVE BEAR.

THERE ARE TODAY LESS THAN A THOUSAND WHO WALKED THE STREETS OF ATLANTIS (THE FIRST ATLANTIS. THE OTHER LANDS THAT BORE THAT NAME WERE SHADOWS, ECHO-ATLANTISES, MYTH LANDS, AND THEY CAME LATER).

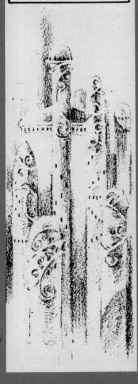

THERE ARE LESS THAN FIVE HUNDRED LIVING HUMANS WHO REMEMBER THE HUMAN CIVILIZATIONS THAT PREDATED THE GREAT LIZARDS. (THERE WERE A FEW; FOSSIL RECORDS ARE UNRELIABLE. SEVERAL OF THEM LASTED FOR MILLIONS OF YEARS.)

THERE ARE ROUGHLY SEVENTY PEOPLE WALKING THE EARTH, HUMAN TO ALL APPEARANCES (AND IN A FEW CASES, TO ALL MEDICAL TESTS CURRENTLY AVAILABLE), WHO WERE ALIVE BEFORE THE EARTH HAD BEGUN TO CONGEAL FROM GAS AND DUST.

HOW WELL DO YOU KNOW YOUR NEIGHBORS? YOUR FRIENDS? YOUR LOVERS?

WALK THE STREETS OF ANY CITY, AND STARE CAREFULLY AT THE PEOPLE WHO PASS YOU, AND WONDER, AND KNOW THIS:

THEY ARE THERE TOO. THE OLD ONES.

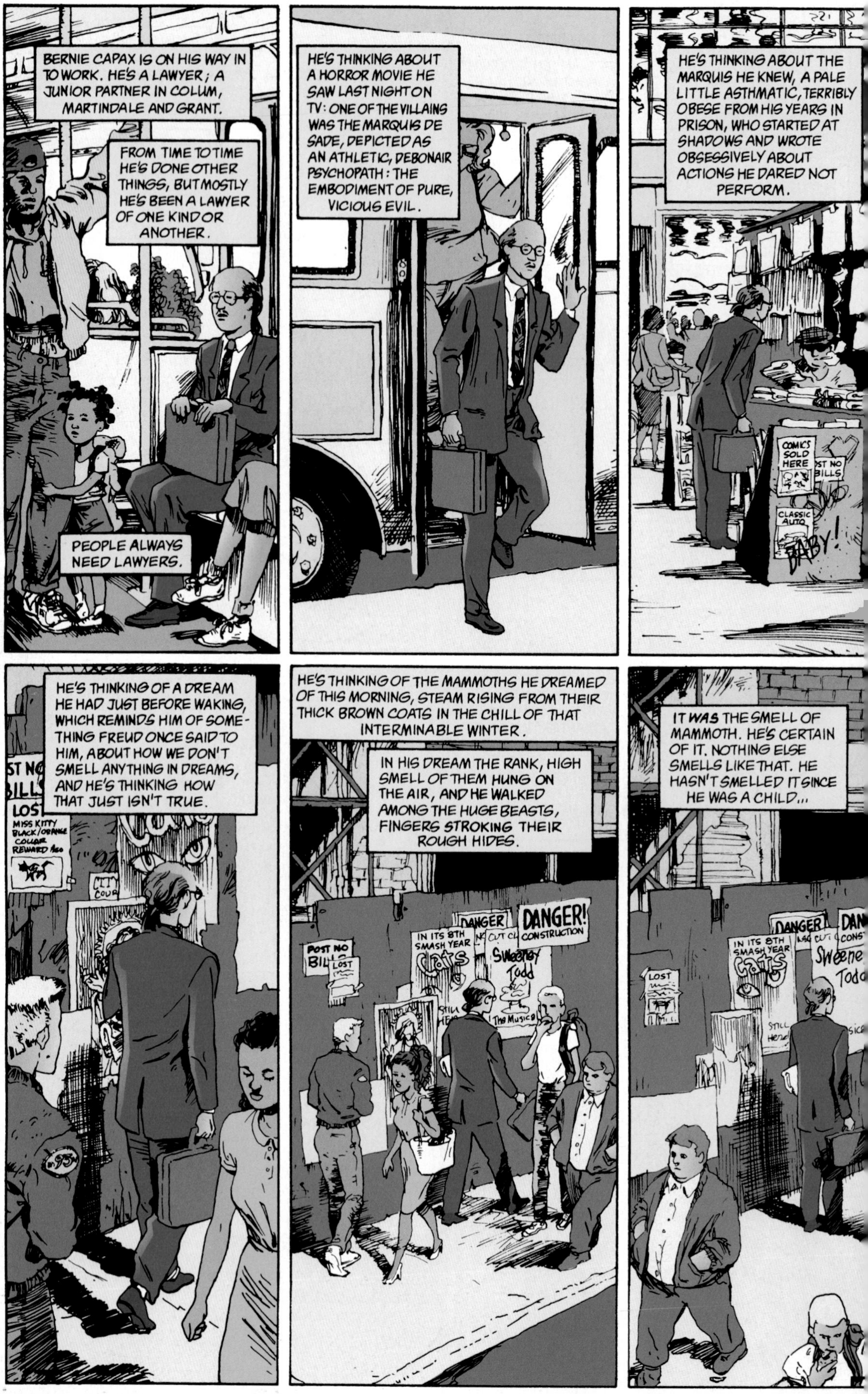
BERNIE CAPAX IS ON HIS WAY IN TO WORK. HE'S A LAWYER; A JUNIOR PARTNER IN COLUM, MARTINDALE AND GRANT.
FROM TIME TO TIME HE'S DONE OTHER THINGS, BUT MOSTLY HE'S BEEN A LAWYER OF ONE KIND OR ANOTHER.
PEOPLE ALWAYS NEED LAWYERS.
HE'S THINKING ABOUT A HORROR MOVIE HE SAW LAST NIGHT ON TV: ONE OF THE VILLAINS WAS THE MARQUIS DE SADE, DEPICTED AS AN ATHLETIC, DEBONAIR PSYCHOPATH: THE EMBODIMENT OF PURE, VICIOUS EVIL.
HE'S THINKING ABOUT THE MARQUIS HE KNEW, A PALE LITTLE ASTHMATIC, TERRIBLY OBESE FROM HIS YEARS IN PRISON, WHO STARTED AT SHADOWS AND WROTE OBSESSIVELY ABOUT ACTIONS HE DARED NOT PERFORM.
COMICS SOLD HERE
CLASSIC AUTO
BABY!
HE'S THINKING OF A DREAM HE HAD JUST BEFORE WAKING, WHICH REMINDS HIM OF SOMETHING FREUD ONCE SAID TO HIM, ABOUT HOW WE DON'T SMELL ANYTHING IN DREAMS, AND HE'S THINKING HOW THAT JUST ISN'T TRUE.
LOST
MISS KITTY
BLACK/ORANGE
COLLAR
HE'S THINKING OF THE MAMMOTHS HE DREAMED OF THIS MORNING, STEAM RISING FROM THEIR THICK BROWN COATS IN THE CHILL OF THAT INTERMINABLE WINTER.
IN HIS DREAM THE RANK, HIGH SMELL OF THEM HUNG ON THE AIR, AND HE WALKED AMONG THE HUGE BEASTS, FINGERS STROKING THEIR ROUGH HIDES.
POST NO BILLS
LOST
DANGER
DANGER! CONSTRUCTION
IN ITS 8TH SMASH YEAR
CATS
Sweeney Todd
IT WAS THE SMELL OF MAMMOTH. HE'S CERTAIN OF IT. NOTHING ELSE SMELLS LIKE THAT. HE HASN'T SMELLED IT SINCE HE WAS A CHILD...
DANGER
IN ITS 8TH SMASH YEAR
CATS
LOST

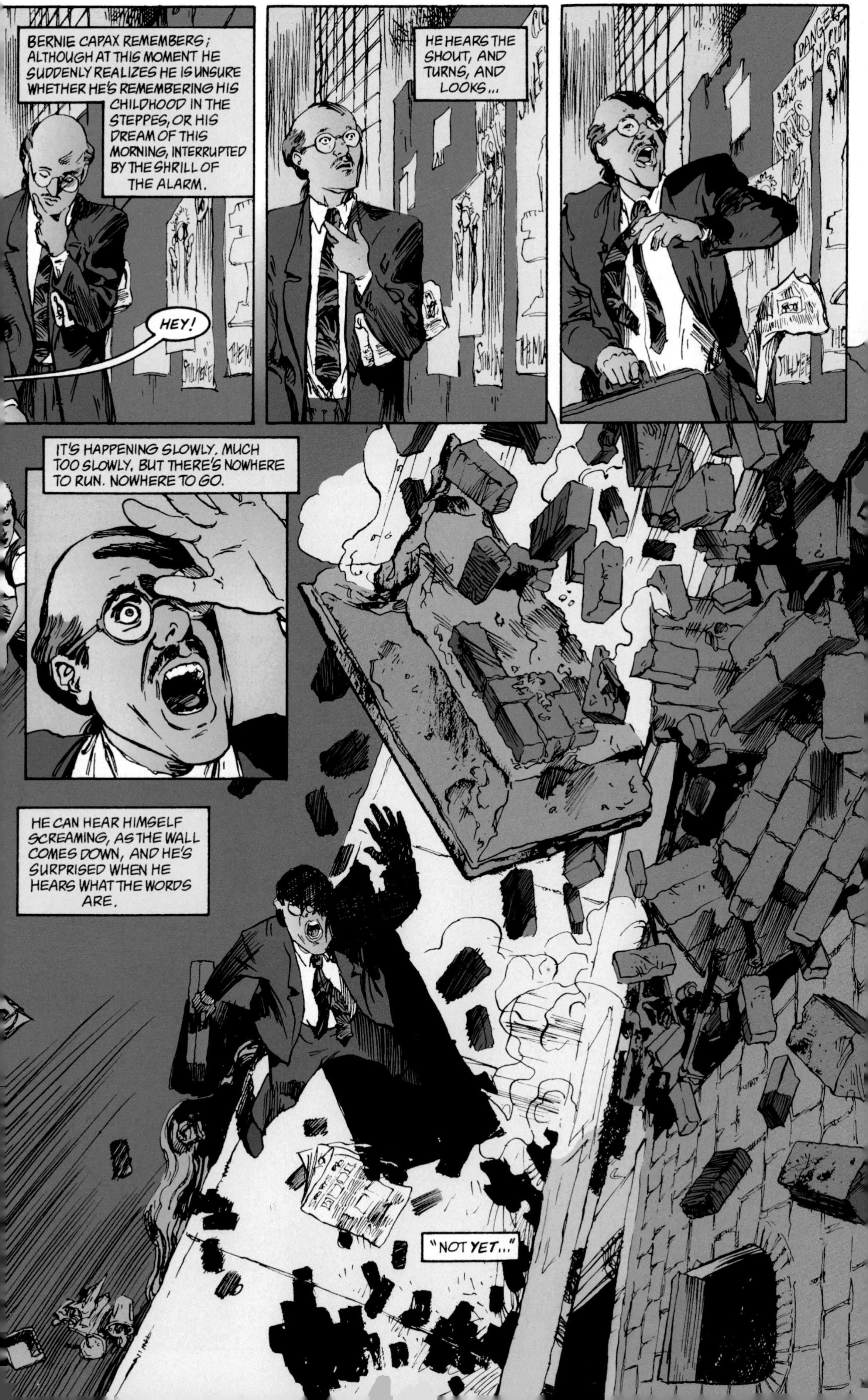
BERNIE CAPAX REMEMBERS; ALTHOUGH AT THIS MOMENT HE SUDDENLY REALIZES HE IS UNSURE WHETHER HE'S REMEMBERING HIS CHILDHOOD IN THE STEPPES, OR HIS DREAM OF THIS MORNING, INTERRUPTED BY THE SHRILL OF THE ALARM.
HEY!
HE HEARS THE SHOUT, AND TURNS, AND LOOKS...
IT'S HAPPENING SLOWLY. MUCH TOO SLOWLY. BUT THERE'S NOWHERE TO RUN. NOWHERE TO GO.
HE CAN HEAR HIMSELF SCREAMING, AS THE WALL COMES DOWN, AND HE'S SURPRISED WHEN HE HEARS WHAT THE WORDS ARE.
"NOT YET..."

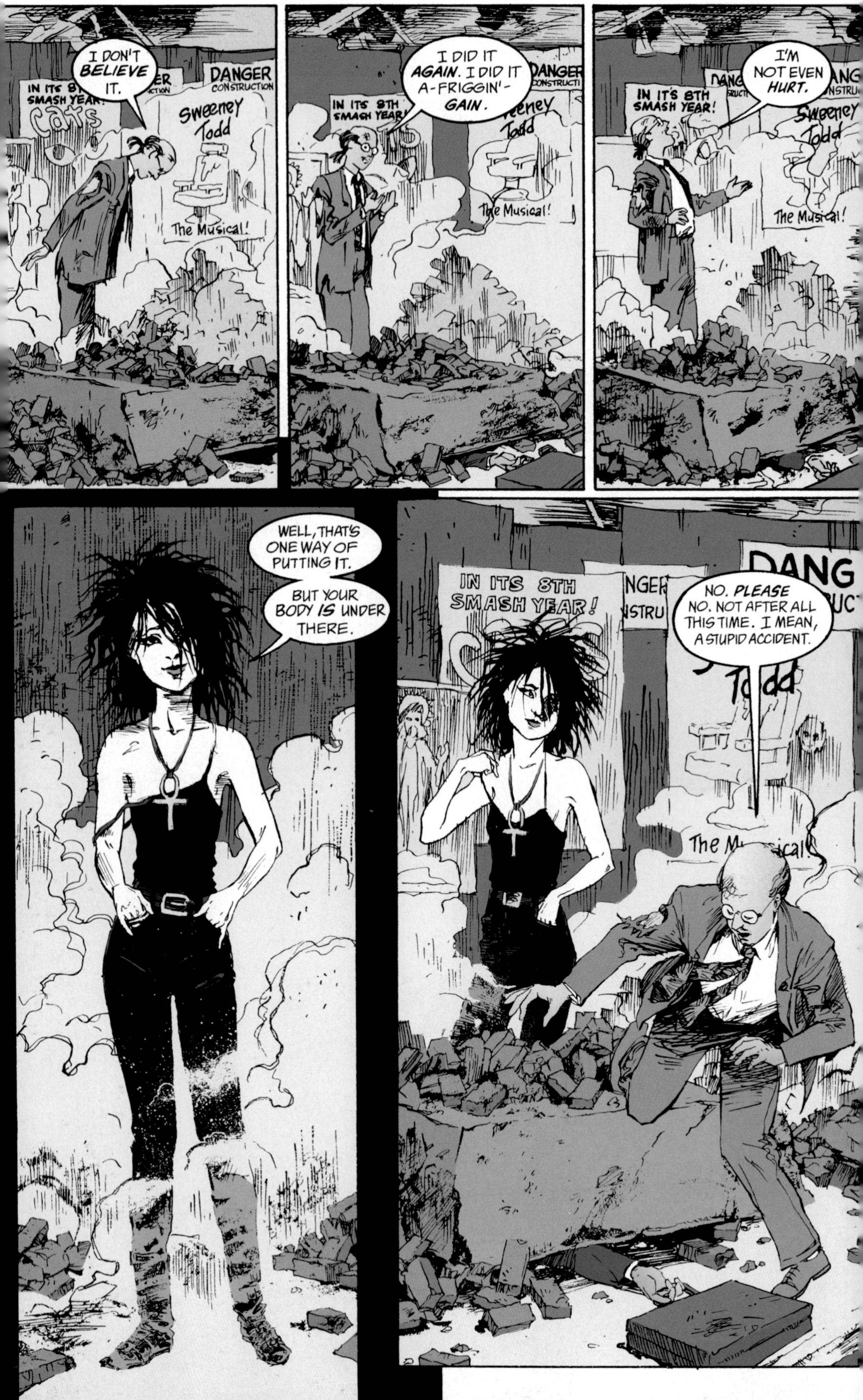
I DON'T BELIEVE IT.
DANGER CONSTRUCTION
IN ITS 8TH SMASH YEAR!
Sweeney Todd
The Musical!
I DID IT AGAIN. I DID IT A-FRIGGIN'-GAIN.
I'M NOT EVEN HURT.
WELL, THAT'S ONE WAY OF PUTTING IT.
BUT YOUR BODY IS UNDER THERE.
IN ITS 8TH SMASH YEAR!
NO. PLEASE NO. NOT AFTER ALL THIS TIME. I MEAN, A STUPID ACCIDENT.

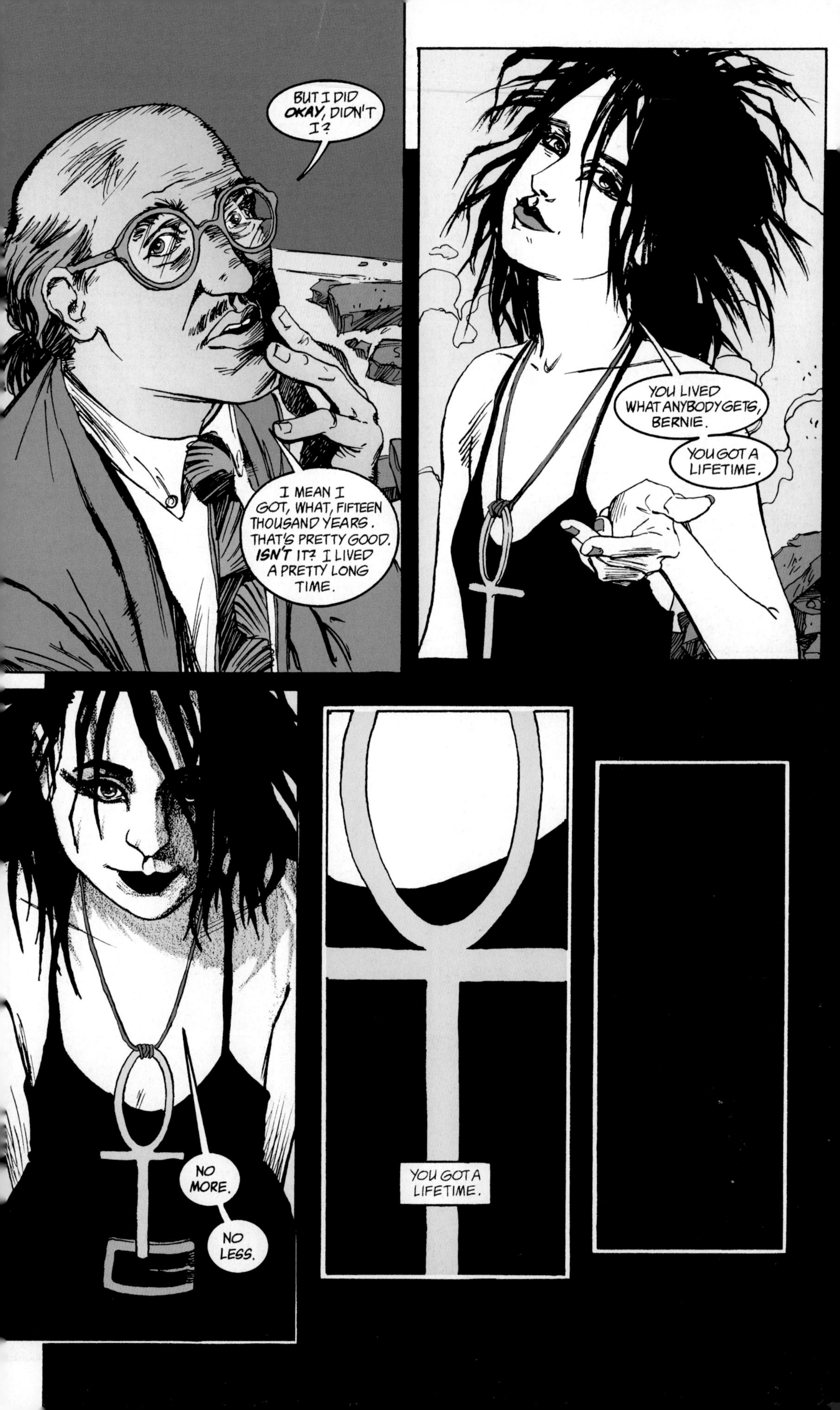

BUT I DID OKAY, DIDN'T I?
I MEAN I GOT, WHAT, FIFTEEN THOUSAND YEARS. THAT'S PRETTY GOOD. ISN'T IT? I LIVED A PRETTY LONG TIME.
YOU LIVED WHAT ANYBODY GETS, BERNIE.
YOU GOT A LIFETIME.
NO MORE.
NO LESS.
YOU GOT A LIFETIME.

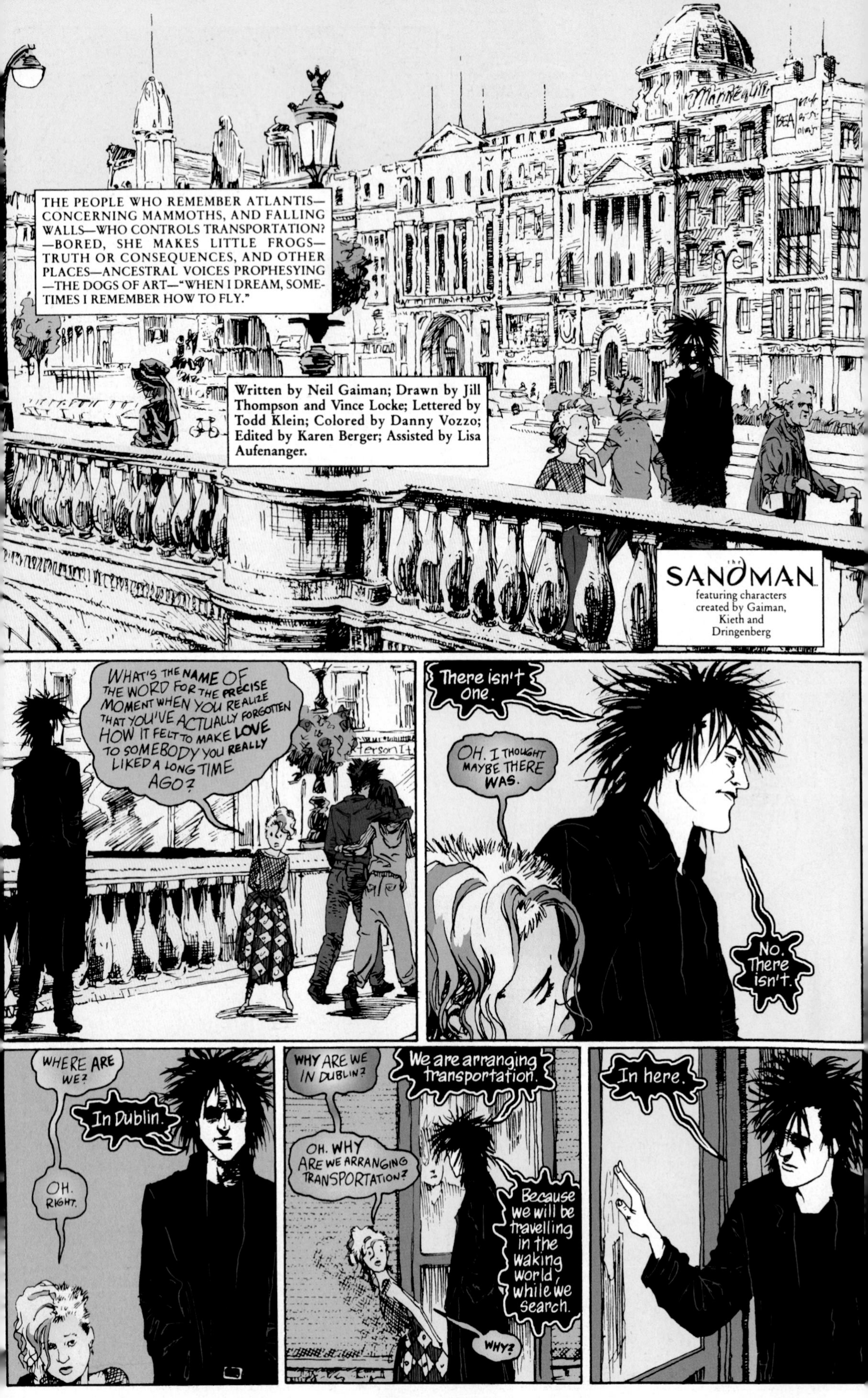

THE PEOPLE WHO REMEMBER ATLANTIS—CONCERNING MAMMOTHS, AND FALLING WALLS—WHO CONTROLS TRANSPORTATION? —BORED, SHE MAKES LITTLE FROGS—TRUTH OR CONSEQUENCES, AND OTHER PLACES—ANCESTRAL VOICES PROPHESYING—THE DOGS OF ART—"WHEN I DREAM, SOMETIMES I REMEMBER HOW TO FLY."
Written by Neil Gaiman; Drawn by Jill Thompson and Vince Locke; Lettered by Todd Klein; Colored by Danny Vozzo; Edited by Karen Berger; Assisted by Lisa Aufenanger.
the SANDMAN featuring characters created by Gaiman, Kieth and Dringenberg
WHAT'S THE NAME OF THE WORD FOR THE PRECISE MOMENT WHEN YOU REALIZE THAT YOU'VE ACTUALLY FORGOTTEN HOW IT FELT TO MAKE LOVE TO SOMEBODY YOU REALLY LIKED A LONG TIME AGO?
There isn't one.
OH. I THOUGHT MAYBE THERE WAS.
No. There isn't.
WHERE ARE WE?
In Dublin.
OH. RIGHT.
WHY ARE WE IN DUBLIN?
We are arranging transportation.
OH. WHY ARE WE ARRANGING TRANSPORTATION?
Because we will be travelling in the waking world, while we search.
WHY?
In here.

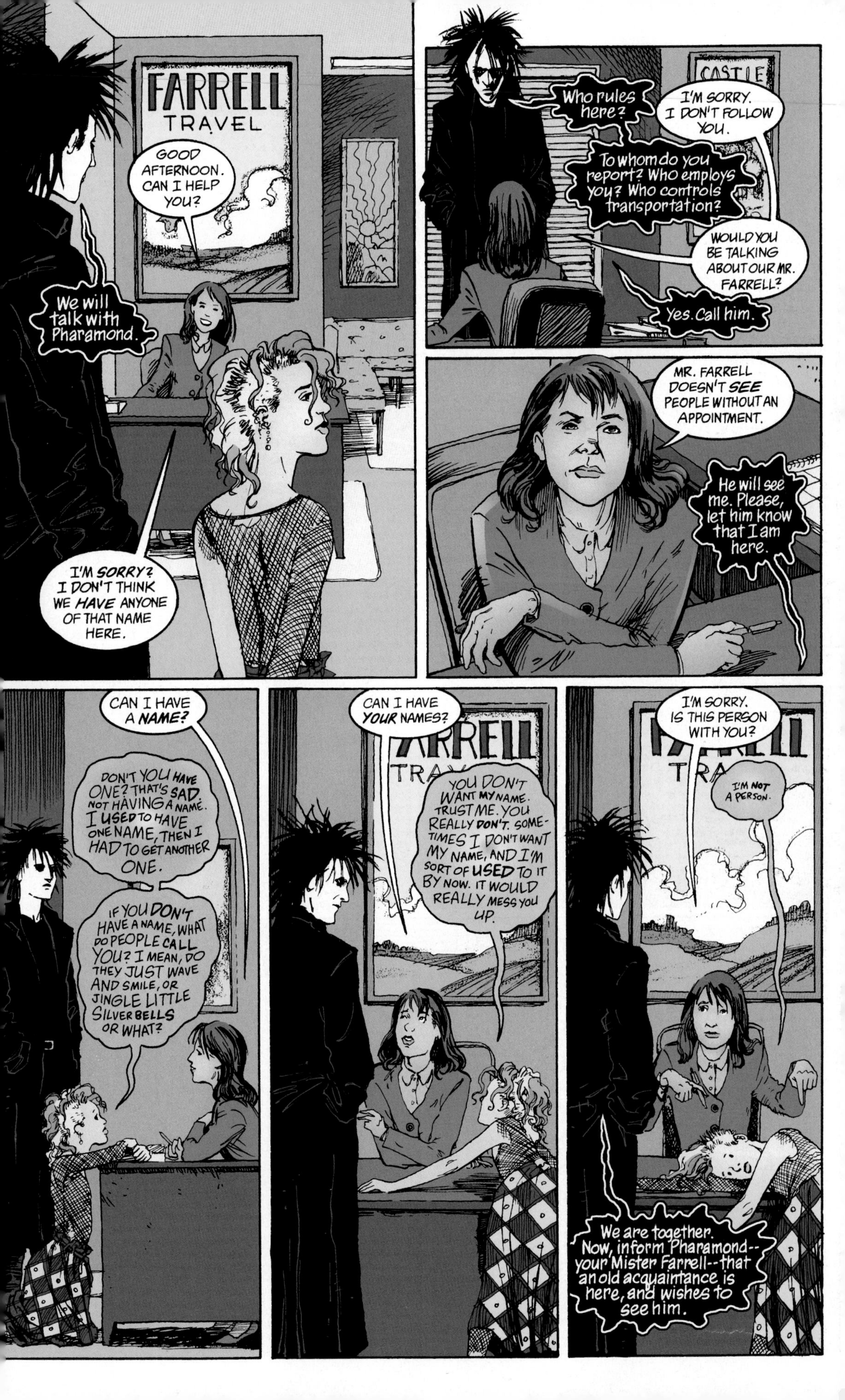
FARRELL
TRAVEL
GOOD AFTERNOON. CAN I HELP YOU?
We will talk with Pharamond.
I'M SORRY? I DON'T THINK WE HAVE ANYONE OF THAT NAME HERE.
CASTLE
Who rules here?
I'M SORRY. I DON'T FOLLOW YOU.
To whom do you report? Who employs you? Who controls transportation?
WOULD YOU BE TALKING ABOUT OUR MR. FARRELL?
Yes. Call him.
MR. FARRELL DOESN'T SEE PEOPLE WITHOUT AN APPOINTMENT.
He will see me. Please, let him know that I am here.
CAN I HAVE A NAME?
DON'T YOU HAVE ONE? THAT'S SAD NOT HAVING A NAME. I USED TO HAVE ONE NAME, THEN I HAD TO GET ANOTHER ONE.
IF YOU DON'T HAVE A NAME, WHAT DO PEOPLE CALL YOU? I MEAN, DO THEY JUST WAVE AND SMILE, OR JINGLE LITTLE SILVER BELLS OR WHAT?
CAN I HAVE YOUR NAMES?
YOU DON'T WANT MY NAME. TRUST ME. YOU REALLY DON'T. SOMETIMES I DON'T WANT MY NAME, AND I'M SORT OF USED TO IT BY NOW. IT WOULD REALLY MESS YOU UP.
I'M SORRY. IS THIS PERSON WITH YOU?
I'M NOT A PERSON.
We are together. Now, inform Pharamond-- your Mister Farrell--that an old acquaintance is here, and wishes to see him.

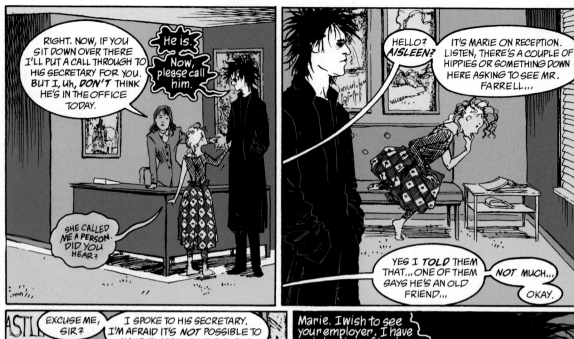

RIGHT. NOW, IF YOU SIT DOWN OVER THERE I'LL PUT A CALL THROUGH TO HIS SECRETARY FOR YOU. BUT I, uh, *DON'T* THINK HE'S IN THE OFFICE TODAY.

He is. Now, please call him.

SHE CALLED ME A PERSON. DID YOU HEAR?

HELLO? *AISLEEN?*

IT'S MARIE ON RECEPTION. LISTEN, THERE'S A COUPLE OF HIPPIES OR SOMETHING DOWN HERE ASKING TO SEE MR. FARRELL...

YES I *TOLD* THEM THAT...ONE OF THEM SAYS HE'S AN OLD FRIEND...

NOT MUCH... OKAY.

EXCUSE ME, SIR?

I SPOKE TO HIS SECRETARY. I'M AFRAID IT'S *NOT* POSSIBLE TO MAKE AN APPOINTMENT TODAY.

BUT IF YOU CAN LEAVE YOUR NAME AND YOUR BUSINESS WITH ME, AND A TELEPHONE NUMBER WE CAN GET YOU ON, I'M *SURE* MISTER FARRELL WILL GET BACK TO YOU.

ASTLE TOURS

Marie. I wish to see your employer. I have no intention of leaving, nor, indeed, of waiting longer.

Call back, and have the following message given to him. Tell him that we drank wine in Babylon together.

I *CAN'T* JUST...

Tell him.

AISLEEN? IT'S MARIE AGAIN... YES....WELL, THOSE PEOPLE ARE *STILL* HERE ...UHUH... WELL, NO... HE'S *VERY* INSISTENT...

HE SAYS CAN YOU *TELL* MR. FARRELL THAT THEY DRANK WINE IN BABYLON TOGETHER. THAT'S RIGHT. *BABYLON.*

SHE'LL TELL HIM, SIR.

Visit beau Tahiti

Thank you.

IS THERE A WORD FOR FORGETTING THE NAME OF SOMEONE WHEN YOU WANT TO INTRODUCE THEM TO SOMEONE ELSE AT THE SAME TIME YOU REALIZE YOU'VE FORGOTTEN THE NAME OF THE PERSON YOU'RE *INTRODUCING* THEM TO AS WELL?

NO.

SO FAR THIS HAS BEEN A ROTTEN DAY FOR FARRELL.

LAST NIGHT AN ORGY IN ROME HAD ENDED BADLY: A YOUNG FEMALE PROSTITUTE CHOKED TO DEATH ON HUMAN SEMEN. HER BODY WAS THROWN INTO THE STREET BY AN AIDE TO THE MINISTER OF CULTURE. TWO OF FARRELL'S CHAUFFERS WERE ARRESTED IN THE POLICE ROUND-UP THAT FOLLOWED.

LOOK, I DON'T *CARE*, LEANDRO. I WANT THEM *OUT*. TODAY.

CAN WE FLY SOMEONE IN FROM NAPLES?

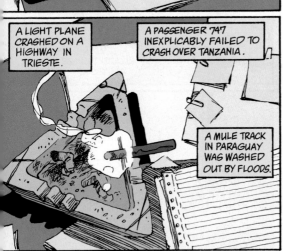

A LIGHT PLANE CRASHED ON A HIGHWAY IN *TRIESTE*.

A PASSENGER 747 INEXPLICABLY FAILED TO CRASH OVER TANZANIA.

A MULE TRACK IN PARAGUAY WAS WASHED OUT BY FLOODS.

...I *SUPPOSE* WE COULD ROUTE IT TO DELHI, KHATMANDU, BANGKOK. BUT I'D STILL RATHER IT WENT BOMBAY-SINGAPORE...

THEN *PAY* THE BLOODY *BRIBE*, FOR CHRISSAKES, KARIN, THAT'S WHAT YOU'RE *THERE* FOR!

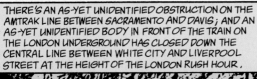

THERE'S AN AS-YET UNIDENTIFIED OBSTRUCTION ON THE AMTRAK LINE BETWEEN *SACRAMENTO* AND *DAVIS*; AND AN AS-YET UNIDENTIFIED BODY IN FRONT OF THE TRAIN ON THE LONDON UNDERGROUND HAS CLOSED DOWN THE CENTRAL LINE BETWEEN WHITE CITY AND LIVERPOOL STREET AT THE HEIGHT OF THE LONDON RUSH HOUR.

AISLEEN! WHERE THE HELL'S THE MEMO FROM *OSLO*?

ON YOUR DESK, UNDER YOUR COFFEE MUG.

OH. YEAH. SORRY.

HIS PERSONAL ASSISTANT TOOK YESTERDAY OFF FOR ROOT-CANAL WORK, AND THE TEMP SEEMS TO HAVE MISFILED FAXES FROM HIS PEOPLE IN SHANGHAI (CHINA), PANAMA CITY (PANAMANIAN REPUBLIC), AND TRUTH OR CONSEQUENCES (NEW MEXICO).

IN ADDITION TO WHICH...

IT'S RECEPTION AGAIN, MR. FARRELL. THEY SAY THOSE PEOPLE WON'T GO AWAY.

WELL, TELL THEM TO CALL *SECURITY*, BODY AND *BLOOD*, AISLEEN, WHAT DO THEY THINK WE *PAY* THEM FOR?

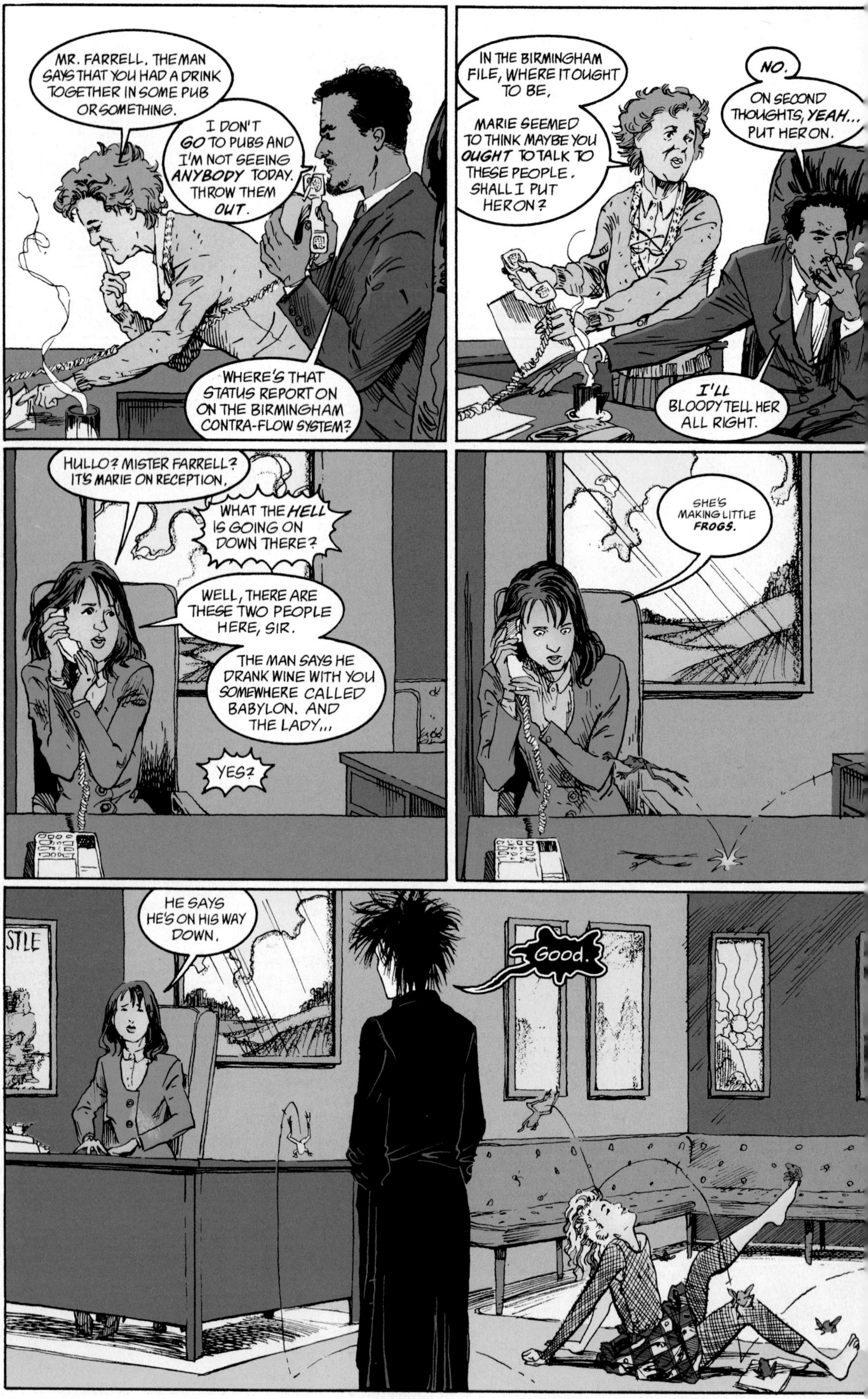

MR. FARRELL. THE MAN SAYS THAT YOU HAD A DRINK TOGETHER IN SOME PUB OR SOMETHING.
I DON'T *GO* TO PUBS AND I'M NOT SEEING *ANYBODY* TODAY. THROW THEM *OUT*.
WHERE'S THAT STATUS REPORT ON ON THE BIRMINGHAM CONTRA-FLOW SYSTEM?
IN THE BIRMINGHAM FILE, WHERE IT OUGHT TO BE.
MARIE SEEMED TO THINK MAYBE YOU *OUGHT* TO TALK TO THESE PEOPLE. SHALL I PUT HER ON?
NO.
ON SECOND THOUGHTS, *YEAH*... PUT HER ON.
I'LL BLOODY TELL HER ALL RIGHT.
HULLO? MISTER FARRELL? IT'S MARIE ON RECEPTION.
WHAT THE *HELL* IS GOING ON DOWN THERE?
WELL, THERE ARE THESE TWO PEOPLE HERE, SIR.
THE MAN *SAYS* HE DRANK WINE WITH YOU SOMEWHERE CALLED BABYLON. AND THE LADY...
YES?
SHE'S MAKING LITTLE *FROGS*.
HE SAYS HE'S ON HIS WAY DOWN.
Good.

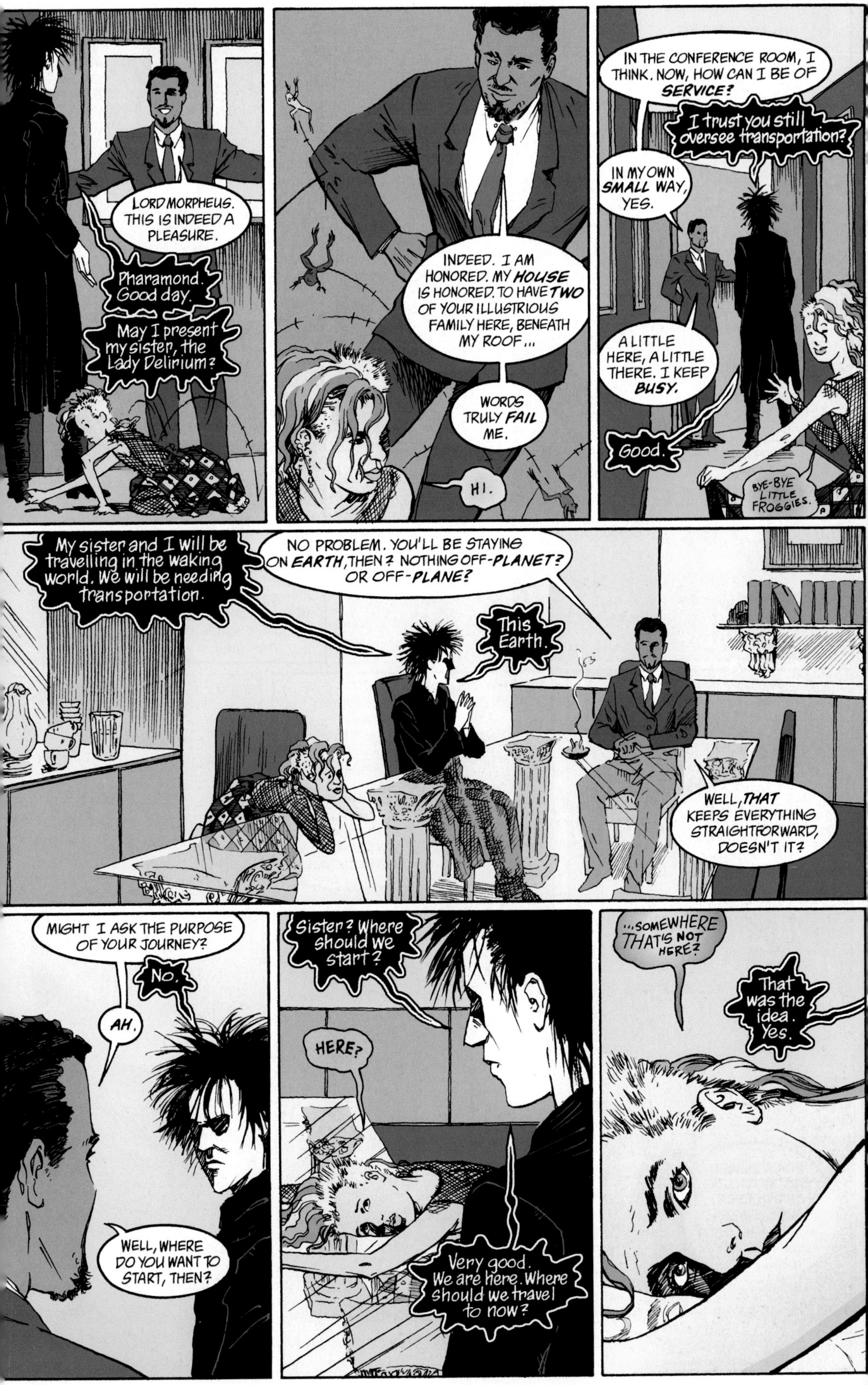
LORD MORPHEUS. THIS IS INDEED A PLEASURE.
Pharamond. Good day.
May I present my sister, the Lady Delirium?
INDEED. I AM HONORED. MY HOUSE IS HONORED. TO HAVE TWO OF YOUR ILLUSTRIOUS FAMILY HERE, BENEATH MY ROOF...
WORDS TRULY FAIL ME.
HI.
IN THE CONFERENCE ROOM, I THINK. NOW, HOW CAN I BE OF SERVICE?
I trust you still oversee transportation?
IN MY OWN SMALL WAY, YES.
A LITTLE HERE, A LITTLE THERE. I KEEP BUSY.
Good.
BYE-BYE LITTLE FROGGIES.
My sister and I will be travelling in the waking world. We will be needing transportation.
NO PROBLEM. YOU'LL BE STAYING ON EARTH, THEN? NOTHING OFF-PLANET? OR OFF-PLANE?
This Earth.
WELL, THAT KEEPS EVERYTHING STRAIGHTFORWARD, DOESN'T IT?
MIGHT I ASK THE PURPOSE OF YOUR JOURNEY?
No.
AH.
WELL, WHERE DO YOU WANT TO START, THEN?
Sister? Where should we start?
HERE?
Very good. We are here. Where should we travel to now?
...SOMEWHERE THAT'S NOT HERE?
That was the idea. Yes.

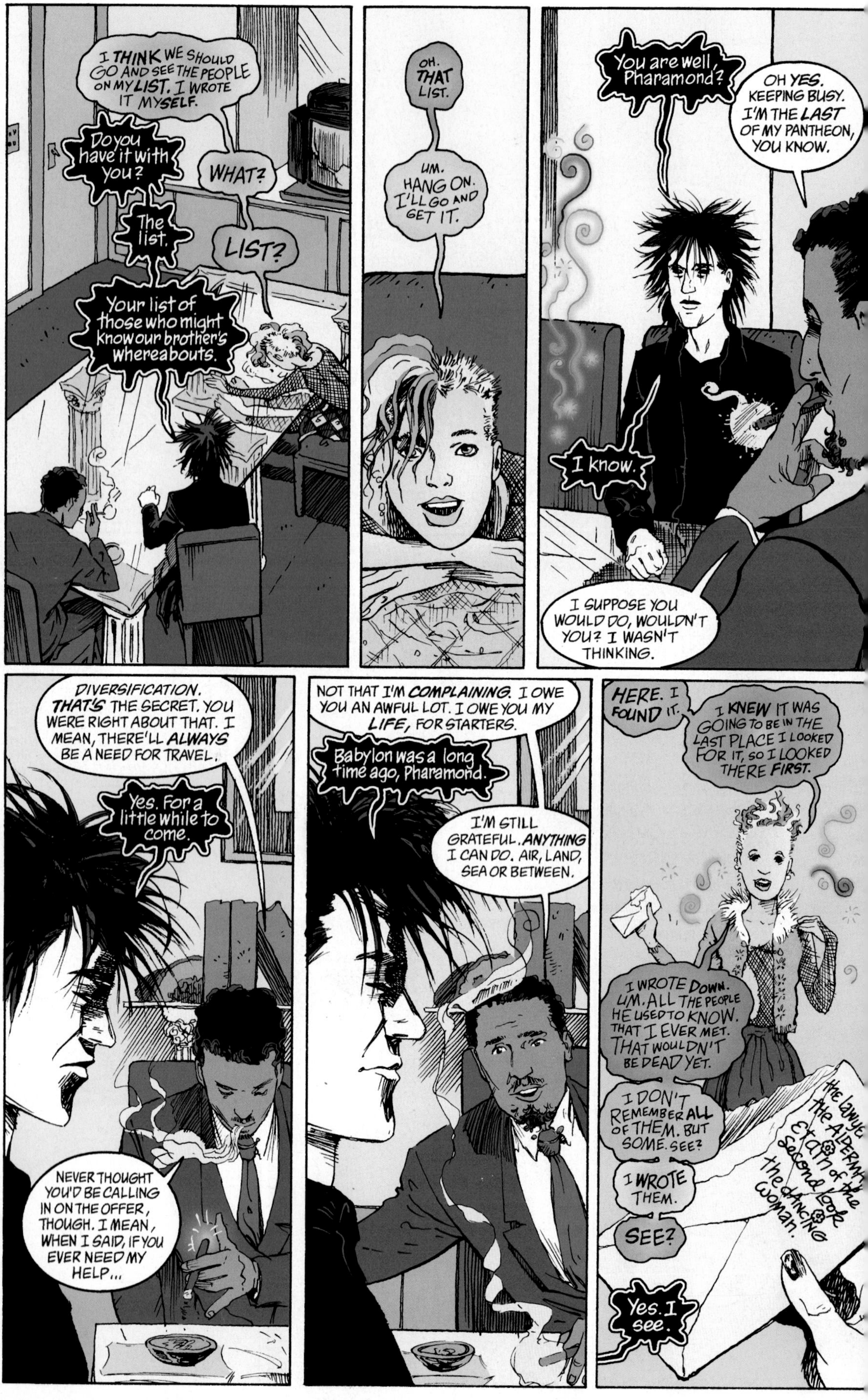
I THINK WE SHOULD GO AND SEE THE PEOPLE ON MY LIST. I WROTE IT MYSELF.
Do you have it with you?
WHAT?
The list.
LIST?
Your list of those who might know our brother's whereabouts.
OH. THAT LIST.
UM. HANG ON. I'LL GO AND GET IT.
You are well, Pharamond?
OH YES. KEEPING BUSY. I'M THE LAST OF MY PANTHEON, YOU KNOW.
I know.
I SUPPOSE YOU WOULD DO, WOULDN'T YOU? I WASN'T THINKING.
DIVERSIFICATION. THAT'S THE SECRET. YOU WERE RIGHT ABOUT THAT. I MEAN, THERE'LL ALWAYS BE A NEED FOR TRAVEL.
Yes. For a little while to come.
NEVER THOUGHT YOU'D BE CALLING IN ON THE OFFER, THOUGH. I MEAN, WHEN I SAID, IF YOU EVER NEED MY HELP...
NOT THAT I'M COMPLAINING. I OWE YOU AN AWFUL LOT. I OWE YOU MY LIFE, FOR STARTERS.
Babylon was a long time ago, Pharamond.
I'M STILL GRATEFUL. ANYTHING I CAN DO. AIR, LAND, SEA OR BETWEEN.
HERE. I FOUND IT.
I KNEW IT WAS GOING TO BE IN THE LAST PLACE I LOOKED FOR IT, SO I LOOKED THERE FIRST.
I WROTE DOWN. UM. ALL THE PEOPLE HE USED TO KNOW. THAT I EVER MET. THAT WOULDN'T BE DEAD YET.
I DON'T REMEMBER ALL OF THEM. BUT SOME. SEE?
I WROTE THEM.
SEE?
the lawye
the ALDERM
Etain of the
second look
the dancing
woman.
Yes. I see.

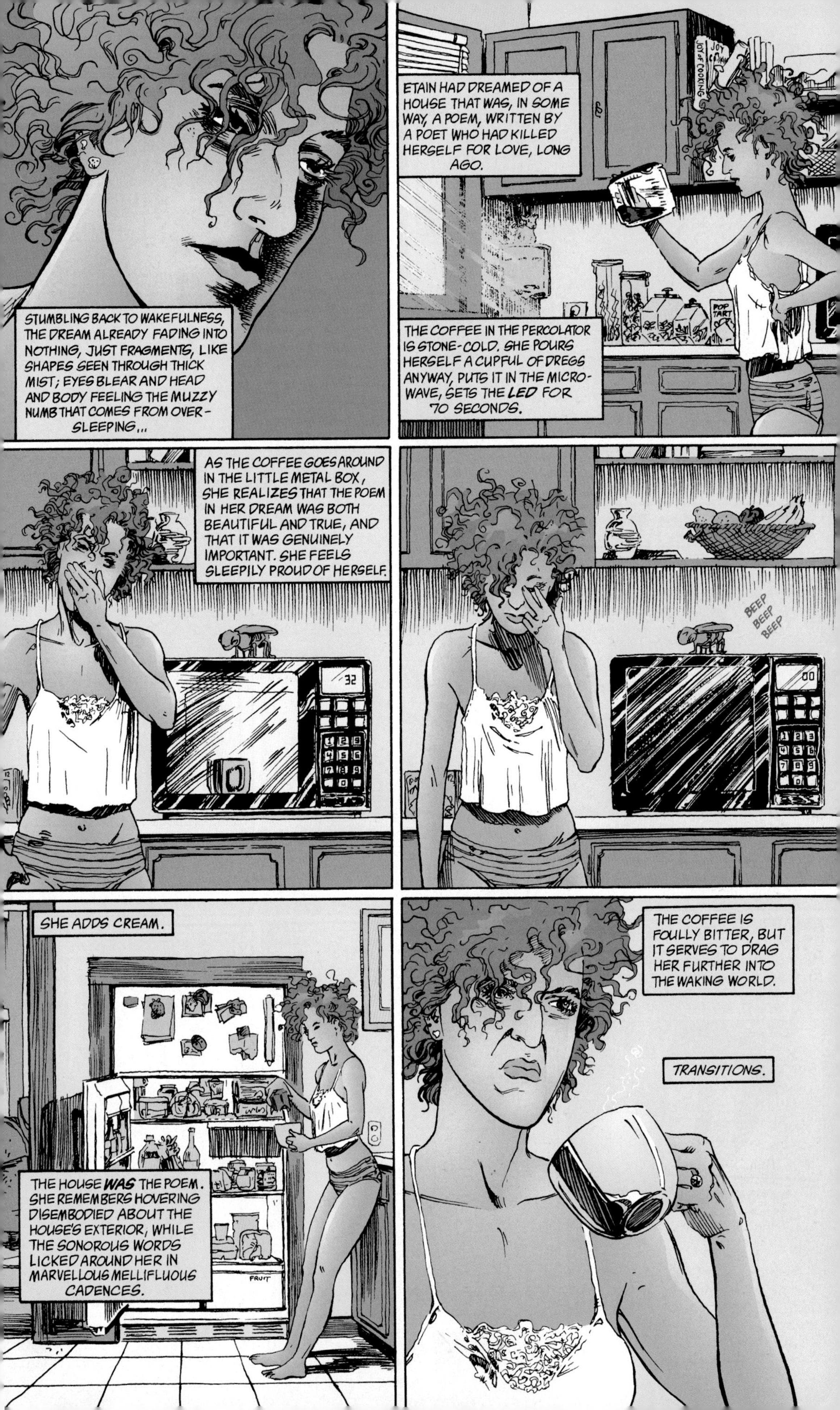
ETAIN HAD DREAMED OF A HOUSE THAT WAS, IN SOME WAY, A POEM, WRITTEN BY A POET WHO HAD KILLED HERSELF FOR LOVE, LONG AGO.
STUMBLING BACK TO WAKEFULNESS, THE DREAM ALREADY FADING INTO NOTHING, JUST FRAGMENTS, LIKE SHAPES SEEN THROUGH THICK MIST; EYES BLEAR AND HEAD AND BODY FEELING THE MUZZY NUMB THAT COMES FROM OVER-SLEEPING...
JOY OF COOKING
THE COFFEE IN THE PERCOLATOR IS STONE-COLD. SHE POURS HERSELF A CUPFUL OF DREGS ANYWAY, PUTS IT IN THE MICRO-WAVE, SETS THE *LED* FOR 70 SECONDS.
AS THE COFFEE GOES AROUND IN THE LITTLE METAL BOX, SHE REALIZES THAT THE POEM IN HER DREAM WAS BOTH BEAUTIFUL AND TRUE, AND THAT IT WAS GENUINELY IMPORTANT. SHE FEELS SLEEPILY PROUD OF HERSELF.
32
BEEP BEEP BEEP
00
SHE ADDS CREAM.
THE HOUSE *WAS* THE POEM. SHE REMEMBERS HOVERING DISEMBODIED ABOUT THE HOUSE'S EXTERIOR, WHILE THE SONOROUS WORDS LICKED AROUND HER IN MARVELLOUS MELLIFLUOUS CADENCES.
FRUIT
THE COFFEE IS FOULLY BITTER, BUT IT SERVES TO DRAG HER FURTHER INTO THE WAKING WORLD.
TRANSITIONS.

OH WELL, EASY COME, EASY GO.

SHE DOESN'T KNOW WHY SAM COLERIDGE BITCHED SO MUCH ABOUT HIS MAN FROM PORLOCK: HE GOT FIFTY-FIVE KILLER LINES DOWN ON PAPER BEFORE HE GOT DISTRACTED, DIDN'T HE?

SHE IS ABOUT TO FIND A PENCIL AND SCRIBBLE THE POEM DOWN, WHEN IT OCCURS TO HER THAT SHE'S LOST THE WORDS.

SHE DOESN'T EVEN KNOW WHAT IT WAS ABOUT.

OH....

AND THE STUFF YOU BRING BACK FROM DREAMS IS FREE.

"AND 'MID THIS TUMULT KUBLA HEARD FROM FAR ANCESTRAL VOICES PROPHESYING WAR..."

LATER, ETAIN WAS UNABLE TO CATEGORIZE THE EVENTS THAT FOLLOWED.

CERTAINLY SHE SMELLED GAS. BUT BY THE TIME SHE SMELLED THE GAS SHE WAS ALREADY RUNNING THROUGH THE BEDROOM, TOWARD THE FIRE ESCAPE.

A SUDDEN FEELING OF SHEER DISBELIEF AS SHE REALIZED THAT SHE HAD GRABBED HER PURSE FROM THE CHAIR, AND THAT SHE WAS ALREADY SHIELDING HER FACE WITH IT, AS SHE JUMPED...

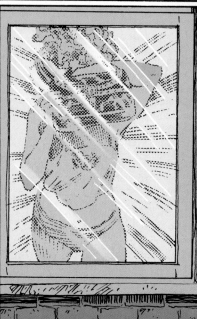

A SHATTERING OF GLASS.

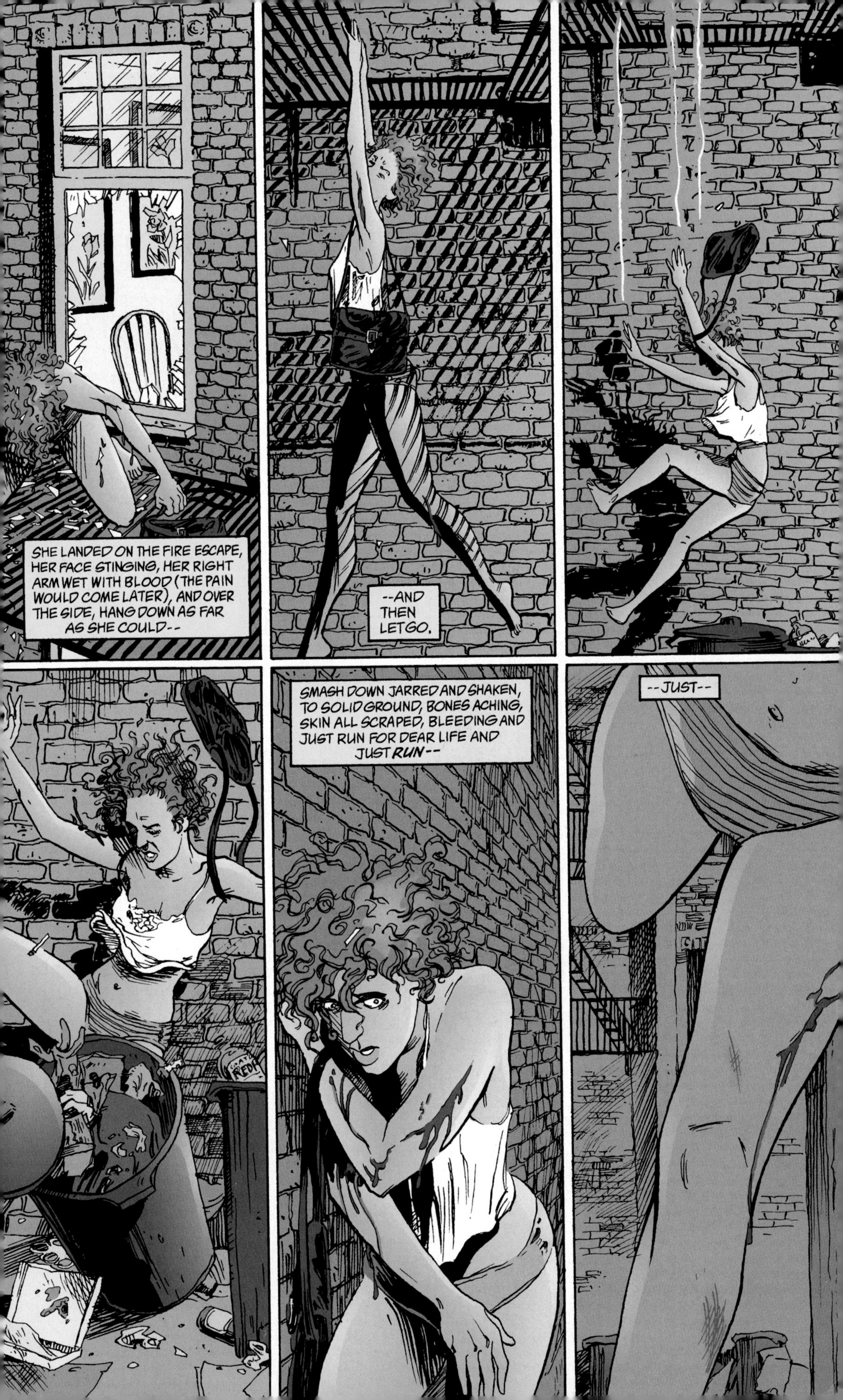
SHE LANDED ON THE FIRE ESCAPE, HER FACE STINGING, HER RIGHT ARM WET WITH BLOOD (THE PAIN WOULD COME LATER), AND OVER THE SIDE, HANG DOWN AS FAR AS SHE COULD--
--AND THEN LETGO.
SMASH DOWN JARRED AND SHAKEN, TO SOLID GROUND, BONES ACHING, SKIN ALL SCRAPED, BLEEDING AND JUST RUN FOR DEAR LIFE AND JUST RUN--
--JUST--

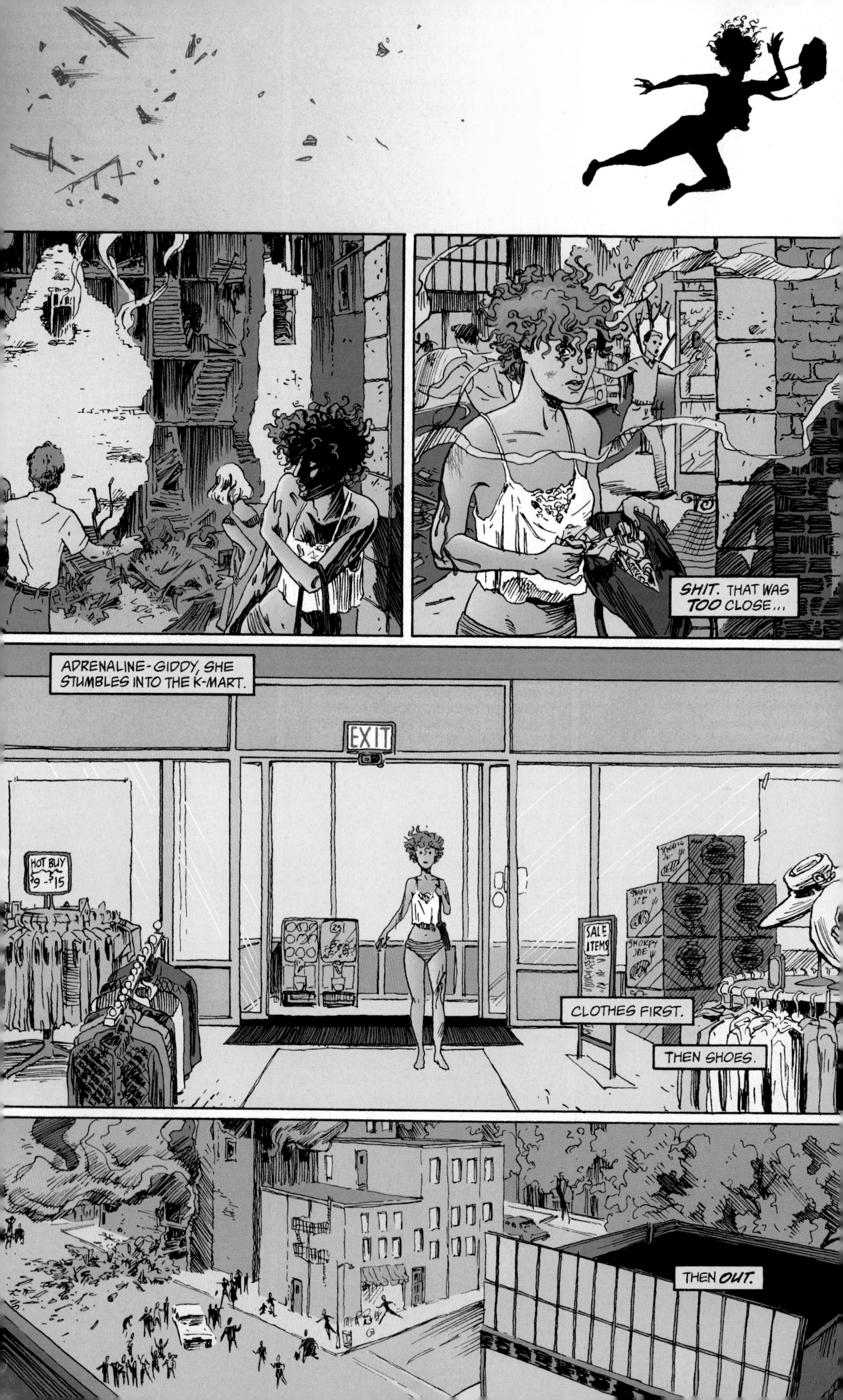
SHIT. THAT WAS TOO CLOSE...
ADRENALINE-GIDDY, SHE STUMBLES INTO THE K-MART.
EXIT
HOT BUY
SALE ITEMS
CLOTHES FIRST.
THEN SHOES.
THEN OUT.

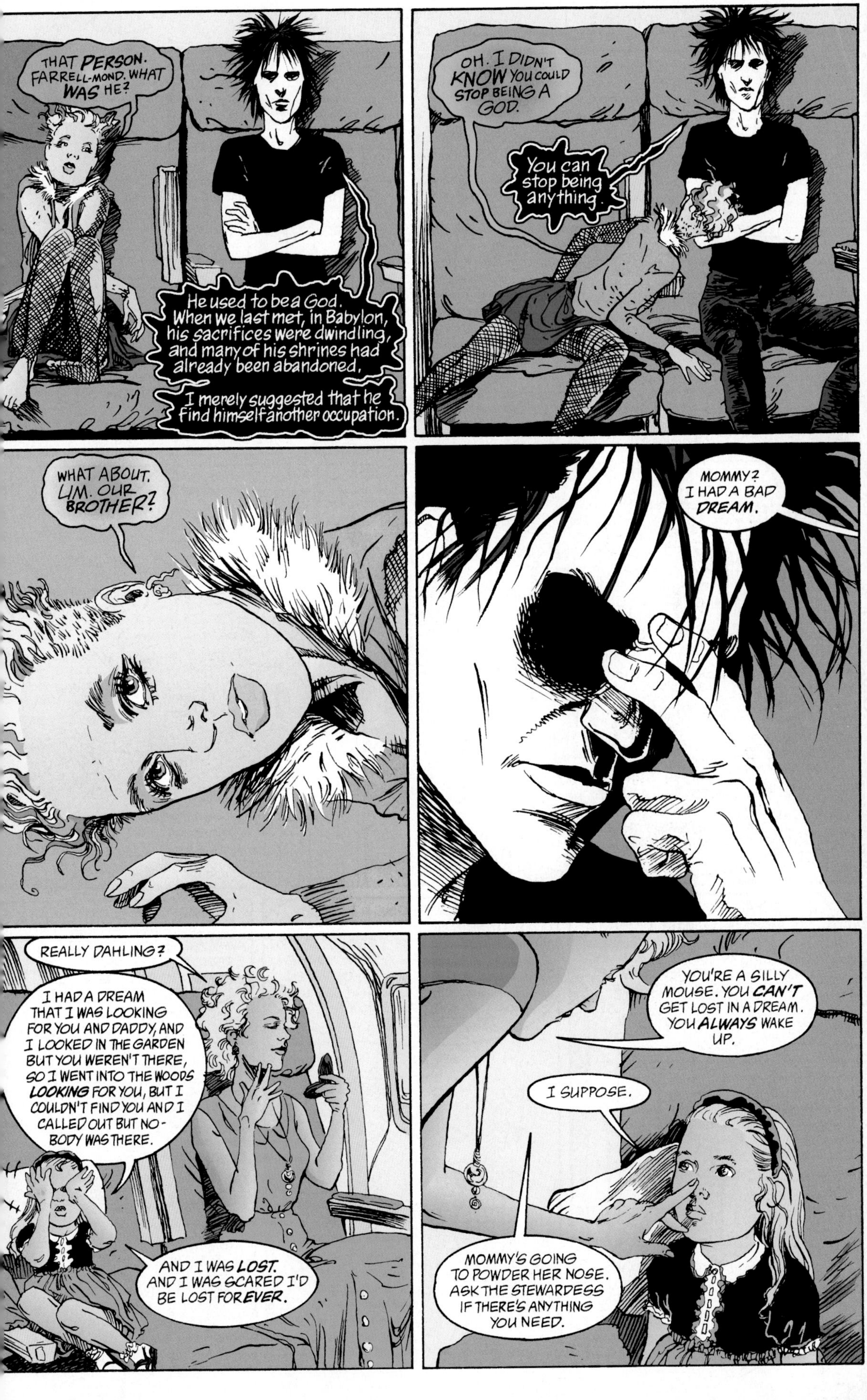

THAT PERSON. FARRELL-MOND. WHAT WAS HE?
He used to be a God. When we last met, in Babylon, his sacrifices were dwindling, and many of his shrines had already been abandoned.
I merely suggested that he find himself another occupation.
OH. I DIDN'T KNOW YOU COULD STOP BEING A GOD.
You can stop being anything.
WHAT ABOUT. UM. OUR BROTHER?
MOMMY? I HAD A BAD DREAM.
REALLY DAHLING?
I HAD A DREAM THAT I WAS LOOKING FOR YOU AND DADDY, AND I LOOKED IN THE GARDEN BUT YOU WEREN'T THERE, SO I WENT INTO THE WOODS LOOKING FOR YOU, BUT I COULDN'T FIND YOU AND I CALLED OUT BUT NO-BODY WAS THERE.
AND I WAS LOST. AND I WAS SCARED I'D BE LOST FOREVER.
YOU'RE A SILLY MOUSE. YOU CAN'T GET LOST IN A DREAM. YOU ALWAYS WAKE UP.
I SUPPOSE.
MOMMY'S GOING TO POWDER HER NOSE. ASK THE STEWARDESS IF THERE'S ANYTHING YOU NEED.

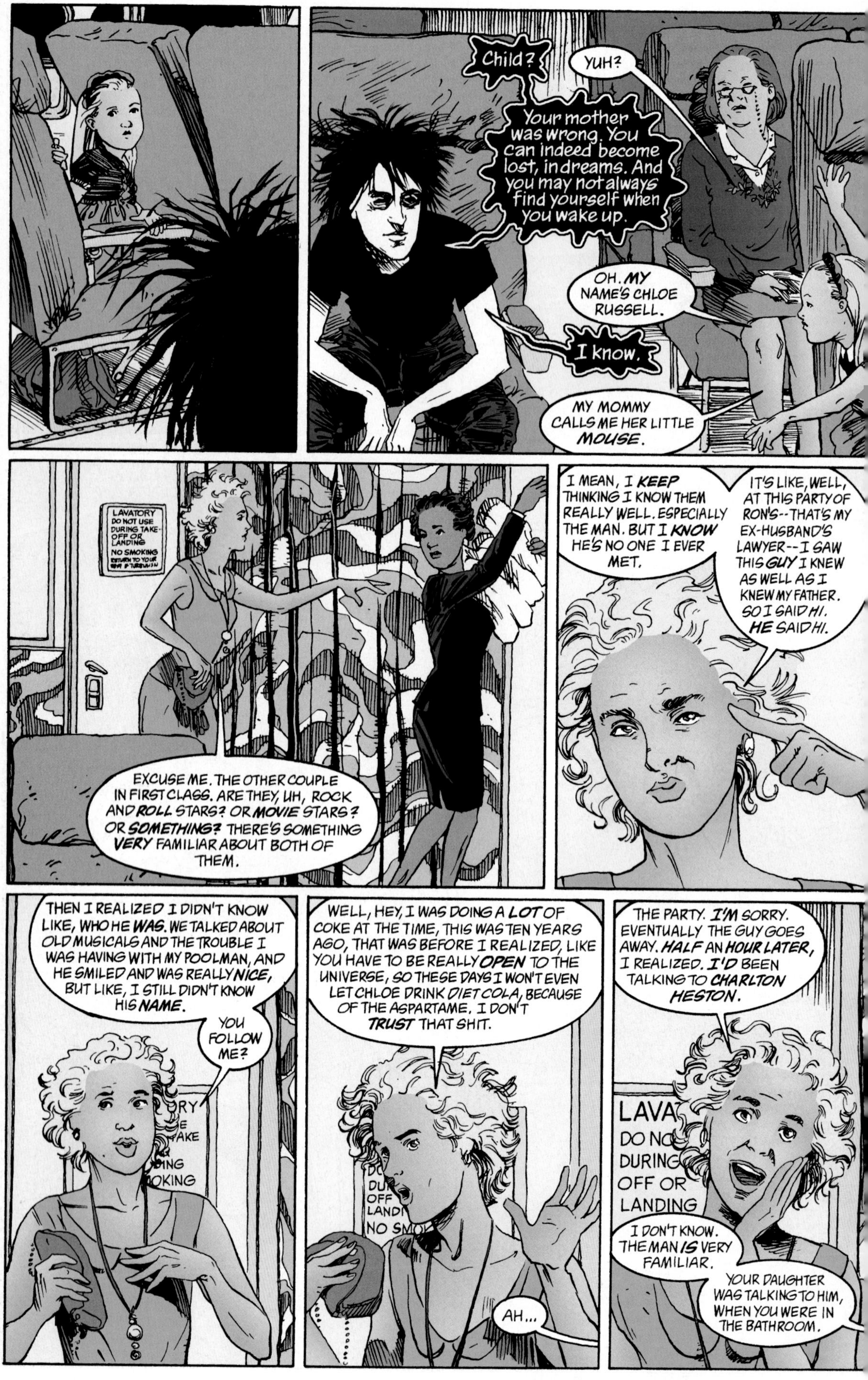
Child?
YUH?
Your mother was wrong. You can indeed become lost, in dreams. And you may not always find yourself when you wake up.
OH. MY NAME'S CHLOE RUSSELL.
I know.
MY MOMMY CALLS ME HER LITTLE MOUSE.
LAVATORY DO NOT USE DURING TAKE-OFF OR LANDING NO SMOKING
EXCUSE ME. THE OTHER COUPLE IN FIRST CLASS. ARE THEY, UH, ROCK AND ROLL STARS? OR MOVIE STARS? OR SOMETHING? THERE'S SOMETHING VERY FAMILIAR ABOUT BOTH OF THEM.
I MEAN, I KEEP THINKING I KNOW THEM REALLY WELL. ESPECIALLY THE MAN. BUT I KNOW HE'S NO ONE I EVER MET.
IT'S LIKE, WELL, AT THIS PARTY OF RON'S--THAT'S MY EX-HUSBAND'S LAWYER--I SAW THIS GUY I KNEW AS WELL AS I KNEW MY FATHER. SO I SAID HI. HE SAID HI.
THEN I REALIZED I DIDN'T KNOW LIKE, WHO HE WAS. WE TALKED ABOUT OLD MUSICALS AND THE TROUBLE I WAS HAVING WITH MY POOLMAN, AND HE SMILED AND WAS REALLY NICE, BUT LIKE, I STILL DIDN'T KNOW HIS NAME.
YOU FOLLOW ME?
WELL, HEY, I WAS DOING A LOT OF COKE AT THE TIME, THIS WAS TEN YEARS AGO, THAT WAS BEFORE I REALIZED, LIKE YOU HAVE TO BE REALLY OPEN TO THE UNIVERSE, SO THESE DAYS I WON'T EVEN LET CHLOE DRINK DIET COLA, BECAUSE OF THE ASPARTAME. I DON'T TRUST THAT SHIT.
AH...
THE PARTY. I'M SORRY. EVENTUALLY THE GUY GOES AWAY. HALF AN HOUR LATER, I REALIZED. I'D BEEN TALKING TO CHARLTON HESTON.
LAVA DO NO DURING OFF OR LANDING
I DON'T KNOW. THE MAN IS VERY FAMILIAR.
YOUR DAUGHTER WAS TALKING TO HIM, WHEN YOU WERE IN THE BATHROOM.

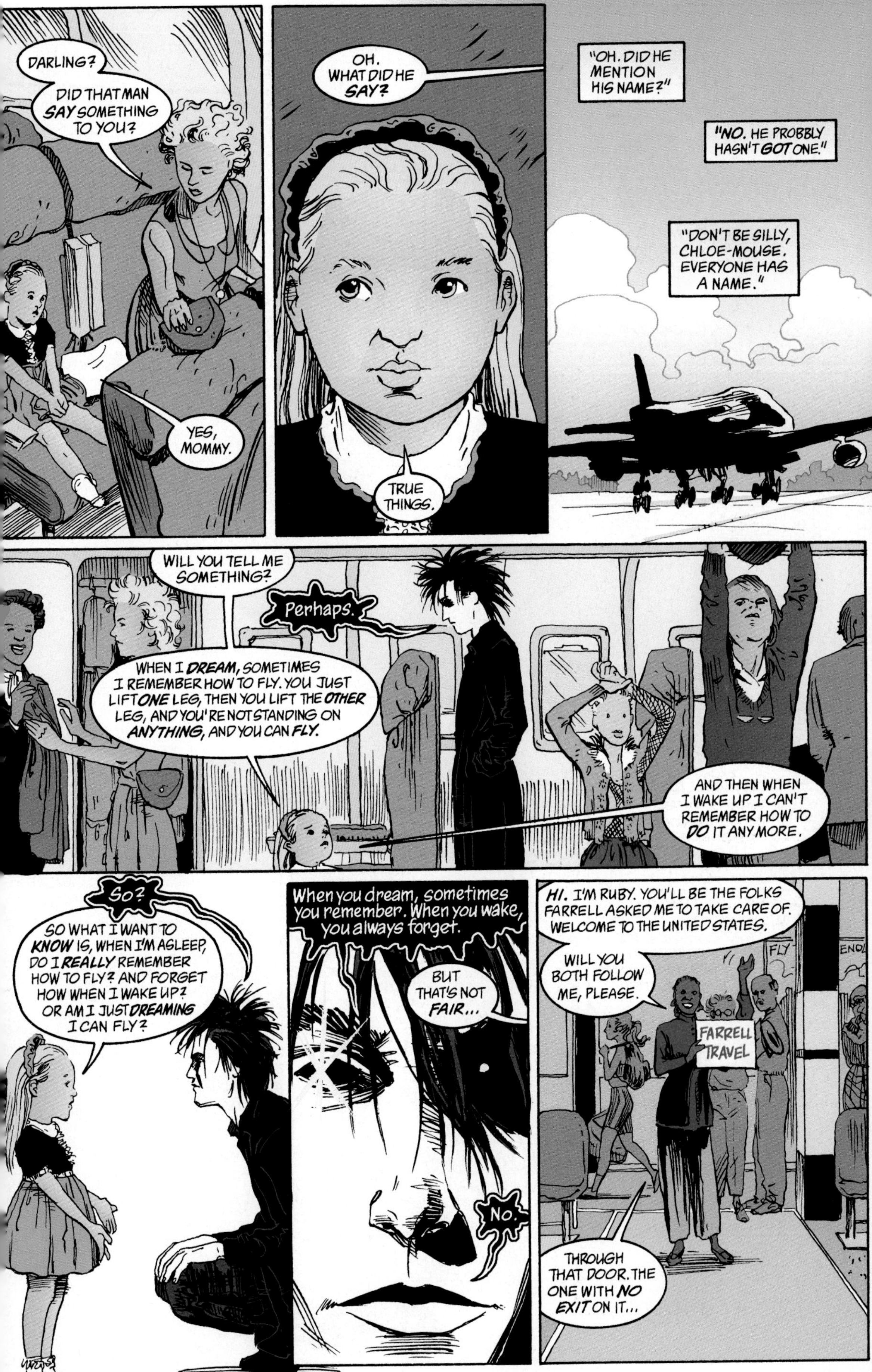

DARLING?
DID THAT MAN SAY SOMETHING TO YOU?
YES, MOMMY.
OH. WHAT DID HE SAY?
TRUE THINGS.
"OH. DID HE MENTION HIS NAME?"
"NO. HE PROBBLY HASN'T GOT ONE."
"DON'T BE SILLY, CHLOE-MOUSE. EVERYONE HAS A NAME."
WILL YOU TELL ME SOMETHING?
Perhaps.
WHEN I DREAM, SOMETIMES I REMEMBER HOW TO FLY. YOU JUST LIFT ONE LEG, THEN YOU LIFT THE OTHER LEG, AND YOU'RE NOT STANDING ON ANYTHING, AND YOU CAN FLY.
AND THEN WHEN I WAKE UP I CAN'T REMEMBER HOW TO DO IT ANY MORE.
So?
SO WHAT I WANT TO KNOW IS, WHEN I'M ASLEEP, DO I REALLY REMEMBER HOW TO FLY? AND FORGET HOW WHEN I WAKE UP? OR AM I JUST DREAMING I CAN FLY?
When you dream, sometimes you remember. When you wake, you always forget.
BUT THAT'S NOT FAIR...
No.
HI. I'M RUBY. YOU'LL BE THE FOLKS FARRELL ASKED ME TO TAKE CARE OF. WELCOME TO THE UNITED STATES.
WILL YOU BOTH FOLLOW ME, PLEASE.
FARRELL TRAVEL
THROUGH THAT DOOR. THE ONE WITH NO EXIT ON IT...

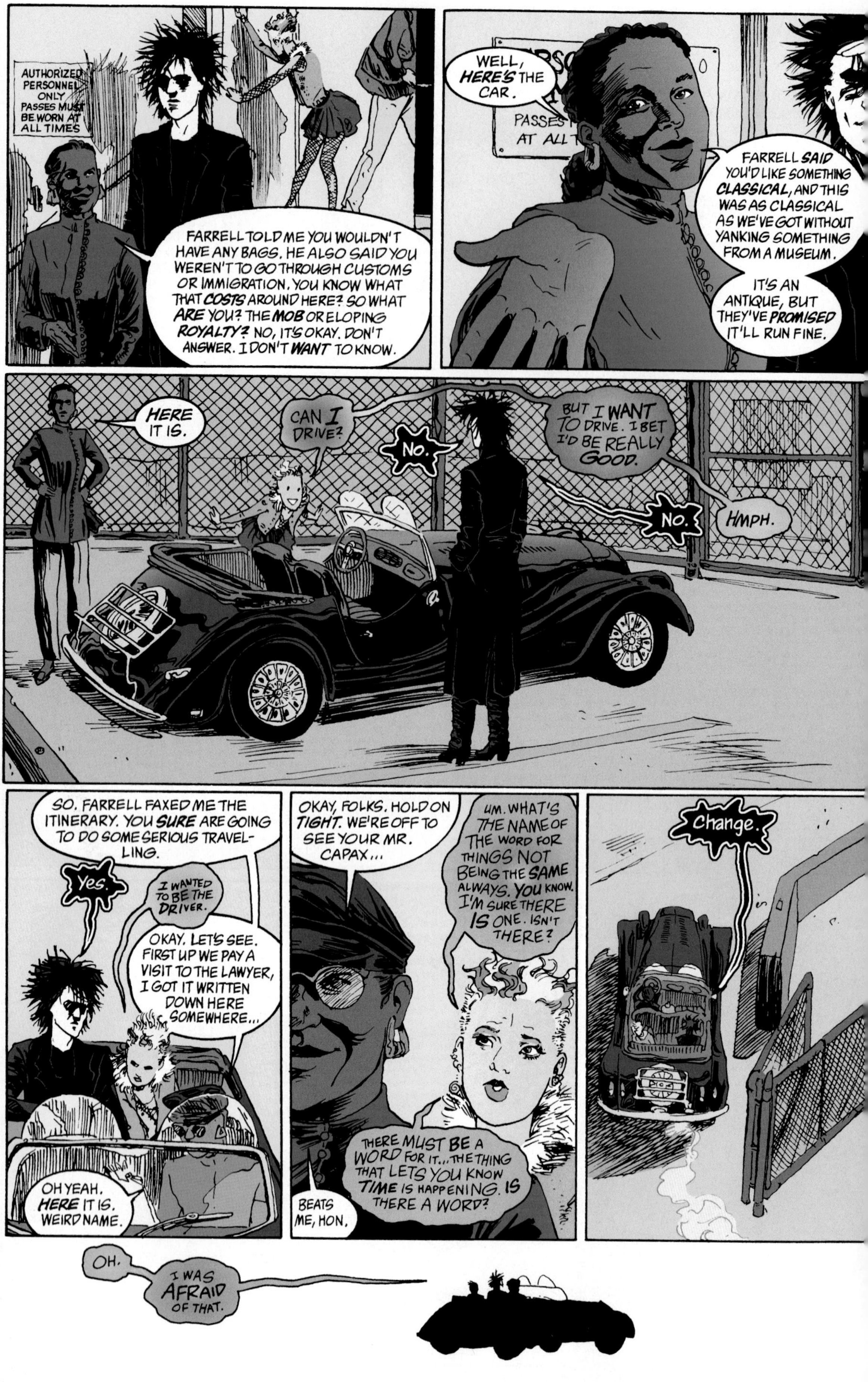
AUTHORIZED PERSONNEL ONLY PASSES MUST BE WORN AT ALL TIMES
FARRELL TOLD ME YOU WOULDN'T HAVE ANY BAGS. HE ALSO SAID YOU WEREN'T TO GO THROUGH CUSTOMS OR IMMIGRATION. YOU KNOW WHAT THAT COSTS AROUND HERE? SO WHAT ARE YOU? THE MOB OR ELOPING ROYALTY? NO, IT'S OKAY. DON'T ANSWER. I DON'T WANT TO KNOW.
WELL, HERE'S THE CAR.
FARRELL SAID YOU'D LIKE SOMETHING CLASSICAL, AND THIS WAS AS CLASSICAL AS WE'VE GOT WITHOUT YANKING SOMETHING FROM A MUSEUM.
IT'S AN ANTIQUE, BUT THEY'VE PROMISED IT'LL RUN FINE.
HERE IT IS.
CAN I DRIVE?
No.
BUT I WANT TO DRIVE. I BET I'D BE REALLY GOOD.
No.
HMPH.
SO. FARRELL FAXED ME THE ITINERARY. YOU SURE ARE GOING TO DO SOME SERIOUS TRAVEL-LING.
Yes.
I WANTED TO BE THE DRIVER.
OKAY. LET'S SEE. FIRST UP WE PAY A VISIT TO THE LAWYER, I GOT IT WRITTEN DOWN HERE SOMEWHERE...
OH YEAH. HERE IT IS. WEIRD NAME.
OKAY, FOLKS. HOLD ON TIGHT. WE'RE OFF TO SEE YOUR MR. CAPAX...
UM. WHAT'S THE NAME OF THE WORD FOR THINGS NOT BEING THE SAME ALWAYS. YOU KNOW. I'M SURE THERE IS ONE. ISN'T THERE?
THERE MUST BE A WORD FOR IT... THE THING THAT LETS YOU KNOW TIME IS HAPPENING. IS THERE A WORD?
BEATS ME, HON.
Change.
OH.
I WAS AFRAID OF THAT.

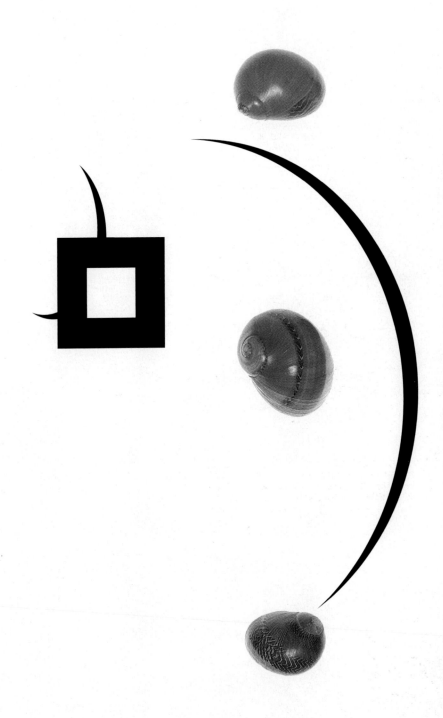

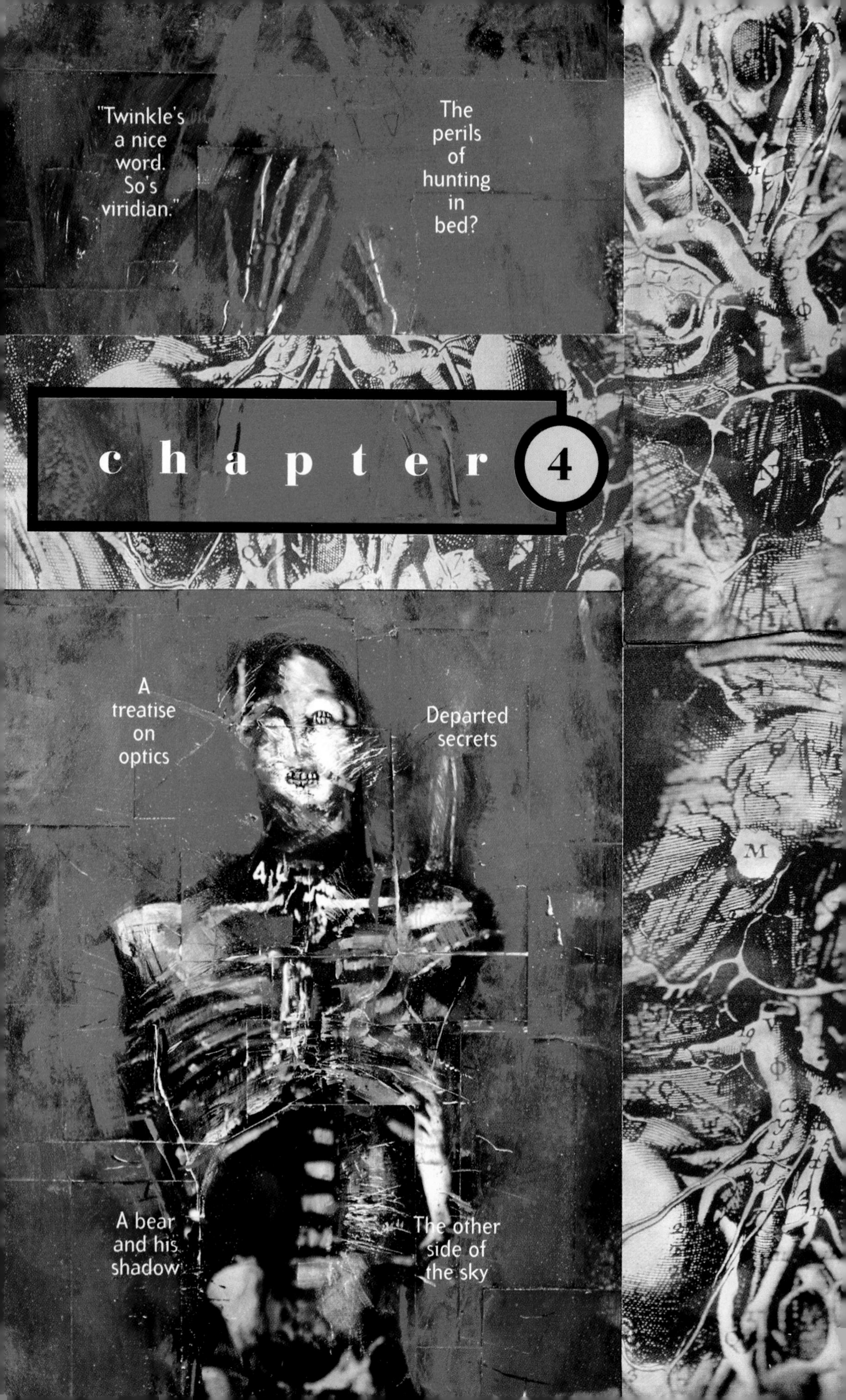
"Twinkle's a nice word. So's viridian."
The perils of hunting in bed?
chapter 4
A treatise on optics
Departed secrets
A bear and his shadow
The other side of the sky

THE LONG DAY IN THE NORTH LANDS.

THE SUN HAS NOT SET FOR OVER A MONTH; EVEN NOW, AT MIDNIGHT, IT HANGS PALE AND SILVER AND COLD ABOVE THE HORIZON.

ON THE OTHER SIDE OF THE SKY, THE LIGHTS OF THE BOREALIS FLICKER AND EXPLODE AND SWIRL IN SURGES OF PLASMA, OF RETINAL PURPLE, FIREWORK YELLOW, *VDU* GREEN.

THE MIDNIGHT SUN.

THIS IS A MIDWINTER DISPLAY, THINKS THE ALDER MAN.

THERE IS SOMETHING DEEPLY UNNATURAL ABOUT SEEING THE NORTHERN LIGHTS IN MIDSUMMER.

THE LAPPS BELIEVE THAT IT IS UNWISE IN ANY WAY TO ATTRACT THE ATTENTION OF THE DANCING NORTHERN LIGHTS, OR THEY WILL CARRY YOU OFF INTO THE SKY, TO BE ONE WITH THEM FOREVER.

THE ALDER MAN IS OLD ENOUGH TO KNOW HOW RARELY THIS HAPPENS. STILL AND ALL, HE IS UNEASY.

HE STAYS AWAKE THROUGH THE NIGHT THAT NEVER COMES, STARING SADLY AT THE LIGHTS IN THE SKY.

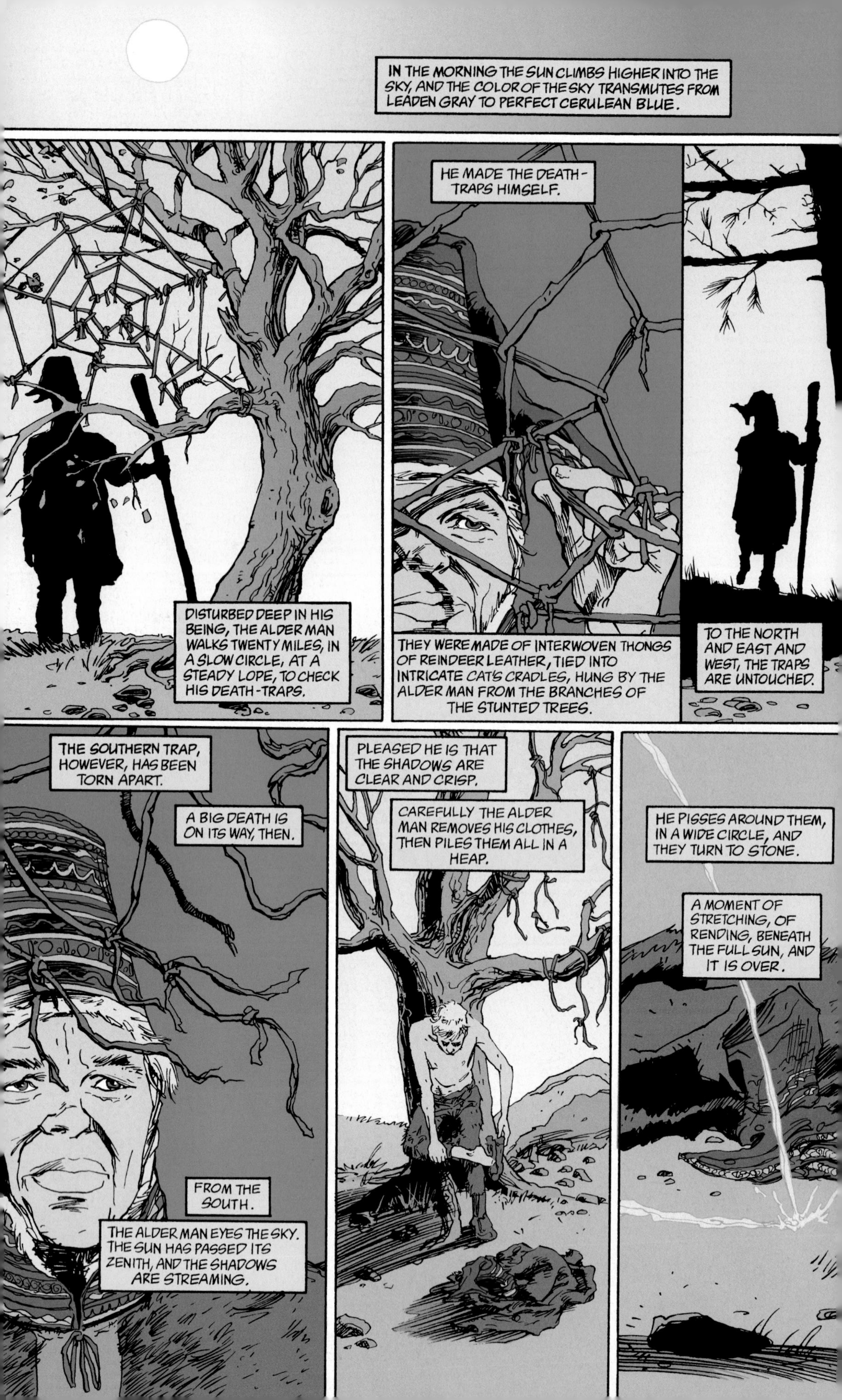

IN THE MORNING THE SUN CLIMBS HIGHER INTO THE SKY, AND THE COLOR OF THE SKY TRANSMUTES FROM LEADEN GRAY TO PERFECT CERULEAN BLUE.
DISTURBED DEEP IN HIS BEING, THE ALDER MAN WALKS TWENTY MILES, IN A SLOW CIRCLE, AT A STEADY LOPE, TO CHECK HIS DEATH-TRAPS.
HE MADE THE DEATH-TRAPS HIMSELF.
THEY WERE MADE OF INTERWOVEN THONGS OF REINDEER LEATHER, TIED INTO INTRICATE CAT'S CRADLES, HUNG BY THE ALDER MAN FROM THE BRANCHES OF THE STUNTED TREES.
TO THE NORTH AND EAST AND WEST, THE TRAPS ARE UNTOUCHED.
THE SOUTHERN TRAP, HOWEVER, HAS BEEN TORN APART.
A BIG DEATH IS ON ITS WAY, THEN.
FROM THE SOUTH.
THE ALDER MAN EYES THE SKY. THE SUN HAS PASSED ITS ZENITH, AND THE SHADOWS ARE STREAMING.
PLEASED HE IS THAT THE SHADOWS ARE CLEAR AND CRISP.
CAREFULLY THE ALDER MAN REMOVES HIS CLOTHES, THEN PILES THEM ALL IN A HEAP.
HE PISSES AROUND THEM, IN A WIDE CIRCLE, AND THEY TURN TO STONE.
A MOMENT OF STRETCHING, OF RENDING, BENEATH THE FULL SUN, AND IT IS OVER.

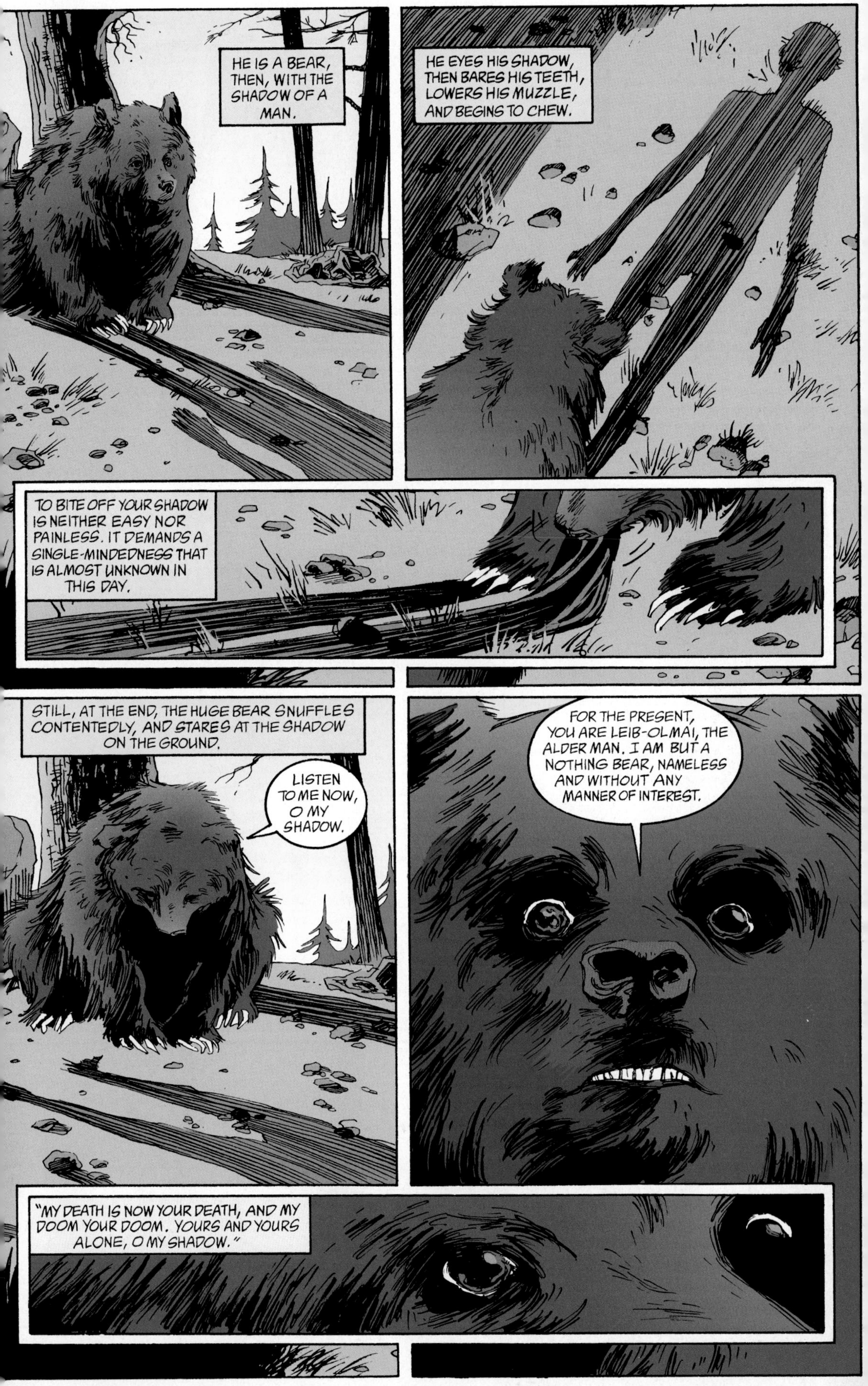
HE IS A BEAR, THEN, WITH THE SHADOW OF A MAN.
HE EYES HIS SHADOW, THEN BARES HIS TEETH, LOWERS HIS MUZZLE, AND BEGINS TO CHEW.
TO BITE OFF YOUR SHADOW IS NEITHER EASY NOR PAINLESS. IT DEMANDS A SINGLE-MINDEDNESS THAT IS ALMOST UNKNOWN IN THIS DAY.
STILL, AT THE END, THE HUGE BEAR SNUFFLES CONTENTEDLY, AND STARES AT THE SHADOW ON THE GROUND.
LISTEN TO ME NOW, O MY SHADOW.
FOR THE PRESENT, YOU ARE LEIB-OLMAI, THE ALDER MAN. I AM BUT A NOTHING BEAR, NAMELESS AND WITHOUT ANY MANNER OF INTEREST.
"MY DEATH IS NOW YOUR DEATH, AND MY DOOM YOUR DOOM. YOURS AND YOURS ALONE, O MY SHADOW."

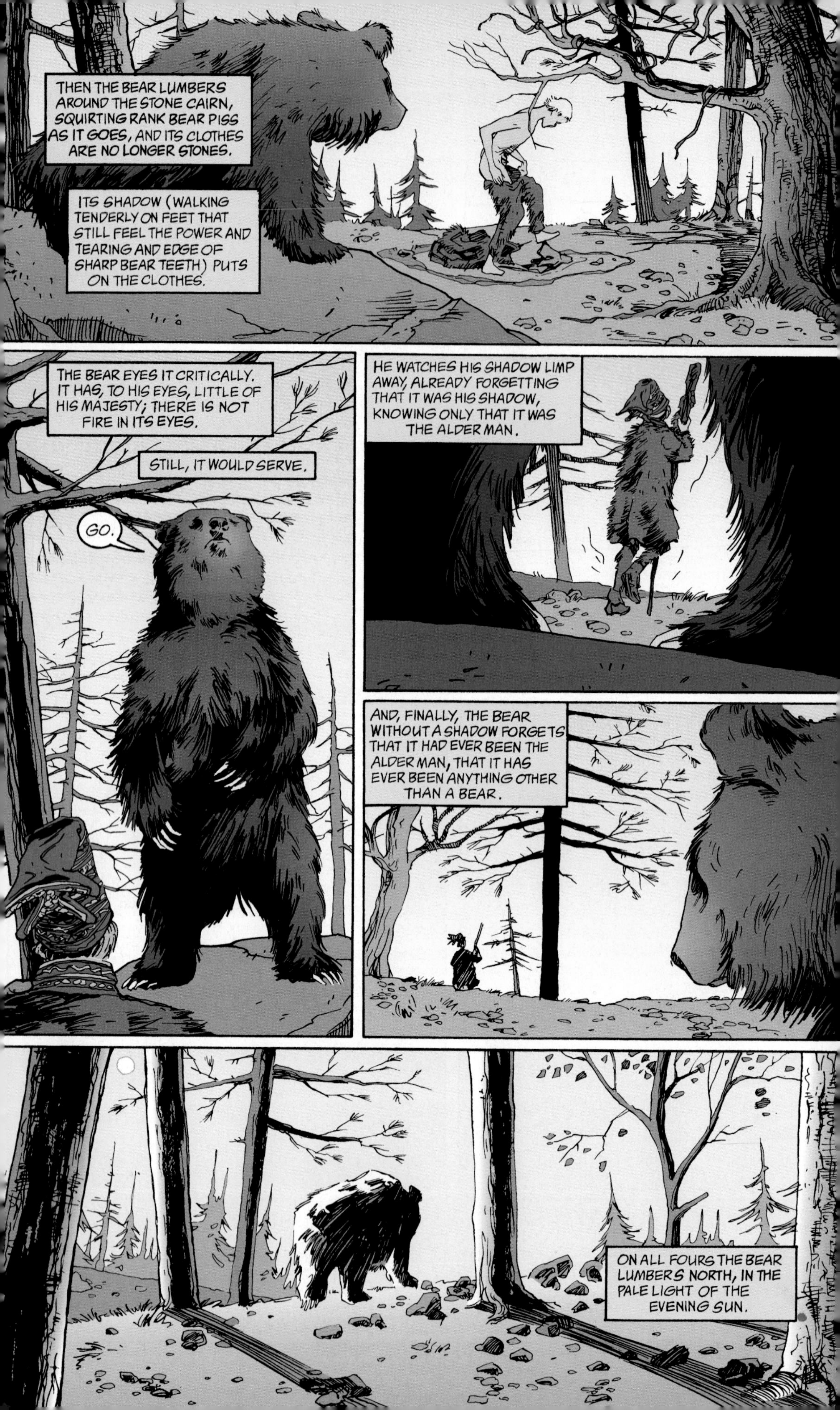
THEN THE BEAR LUMBERS AROUND THE STONE CAIRN, SQUIRTING RANK BEAR PISS AS IT GOES, AND ITS CLOTHES ARE NO LONGER STONES.
ITS SHADOW (WALKING TENDERLY ON FEET THAT STILL FEEL THE POWER AND TEARING AND EDGE OF SHARP BEAR TEETH) PUTS ON THE CLOTHES.
THE BEAR EYES IT CRITICALLY. IT HAS, TO HIS EYES, LITTLE OF HIS MAJESTY; THERE IS NOT FIRE IN ITS EYES.
STILL, IT WOULD SERVE.
GO.
HE WATCHES HIS SHADOW LIMP AWAY, ALREADY FORGETTING THAT IT WAS HIS SHADOW, KNOWING ONLY THAT IT WAS THE ALDER MAN.
AND, FINALLY, THE BEAR WITHOUT A SHADOW FORGETS THAT IT HAD EVER BEEN THE ALDER MAN, THAT IT HAS EVER BEEN ANYTHING OTHER THAN A BEAR.
ON ALL FOURS THE BEAR LUMBERS NORTH, IN THE PALE LIGHT OF THE EVENING SUN.

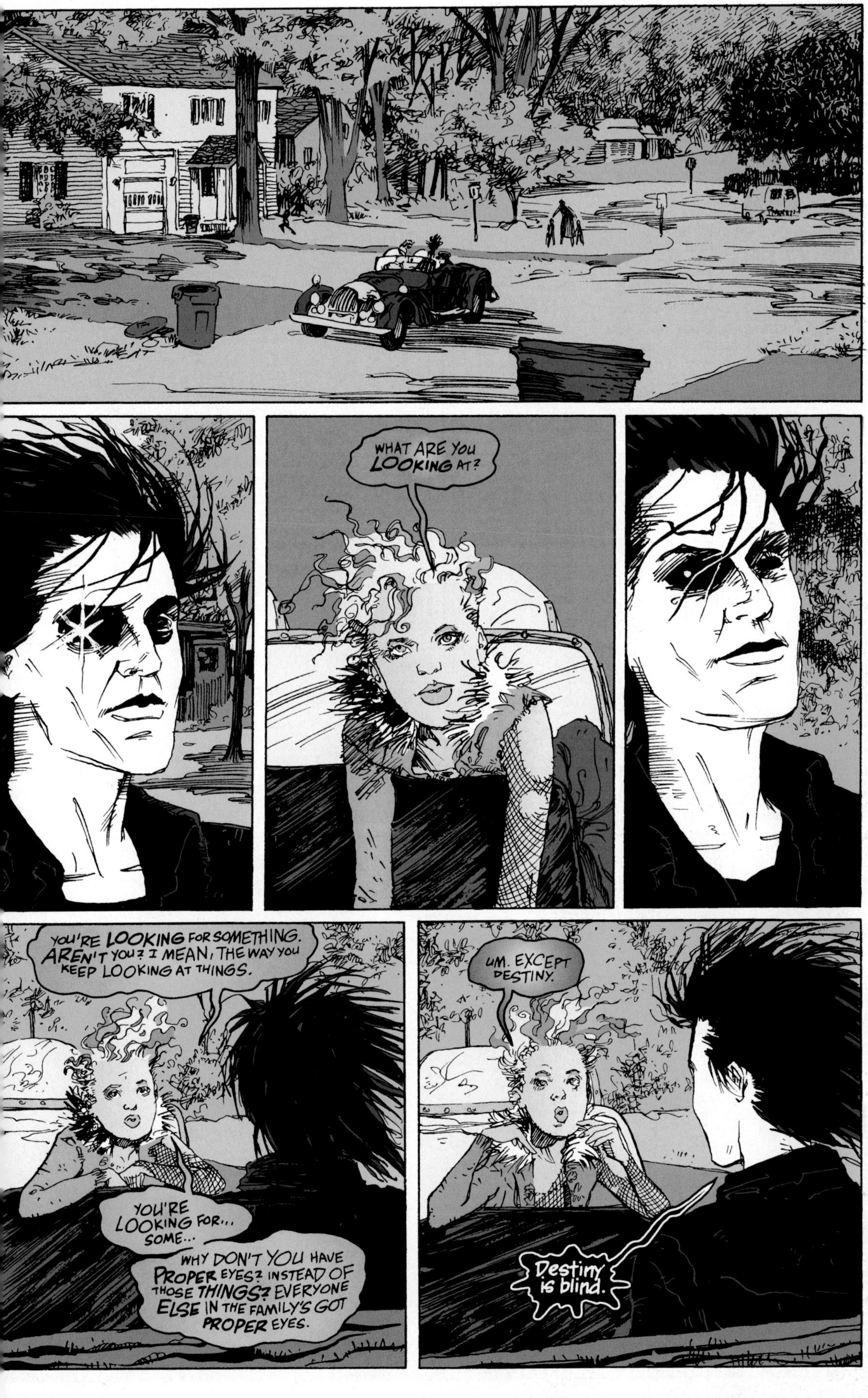
WHAT ARE YOU LOOKING AT?
YOU'RE LOOKING FOR SOMETHING. AREN'T YOU? I MEAN, THE WAY YOU KEEP LOOKING AT THINGS.
YOU'RE LOOKING FOR... SOME...
WHY DON'T YOU HAVE PROPER EYES? INSTEAD OF THOSE THINGS? EVERYONE ELSE IN THE FAMILY'S GOT PROPER EYES.
UM. EXCEPT DESTINY.
Destiny is blind.

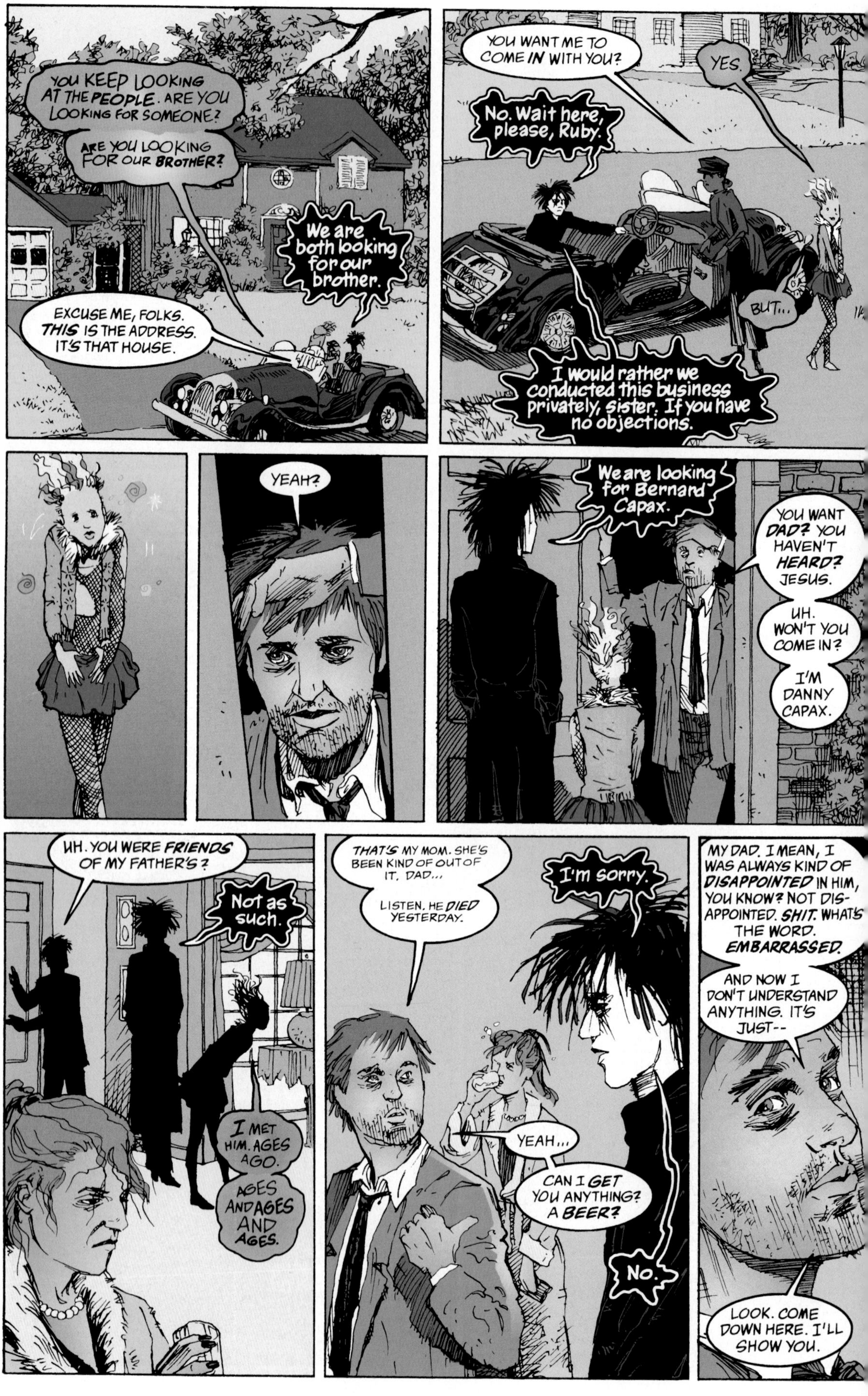
YOU KEEP LOOKING AT THE PEOPLE. ARE YOU LOOKING FOR SOMEONE?
ARE YOU LOOKING FOR OUR BROTHER?
We are both looking for our brother.
EXCUSE ME, FOLKS. THIS IS THE ADDRESS. IT'S THAT HOUSE.
YOU WANT ME TO COME IN WITH YOU?
YES.
No. Wait here, please, Ruby.
BUT...
I would rather we conducted this business privately, sister. If you have no objections.
YEAH?
We are looking for Bernard Capax.
YOU WANT DAD? YOU HAVEN'T HEARD? JESUS.
UH. WON'T YOU COME IN?
I'M DANNY CAPAX.
UH. YOU WERE FRIENDS OF MY FATHER'S?
Not as such.
I MET HIM. AGES AGO.
AGES AND AGES AND AGES.
THAT'S MY MOM. SHE'S BEEN KIND OF OUT OF IT. DAD...
LISTEN. HE DIED YESTERDAY.
I'm sorry.
YEAH...
CAN I GET YOU ANYTHING? A BEER?
No.
MY DAD. I MEAN, I WAS ALWAYS KIND OF DISAPPOINTED IN HIM, YOU KNOW? NOT DIS-APPOINTED. SHIT. WHAT'S THE WORD. EMBARRASSED.
AND NOW I DON'T UNDERSTAND ANYTHING. IT'S JUST--
LOOK. COME DOWN HERE. I'LL SHOW YOU.

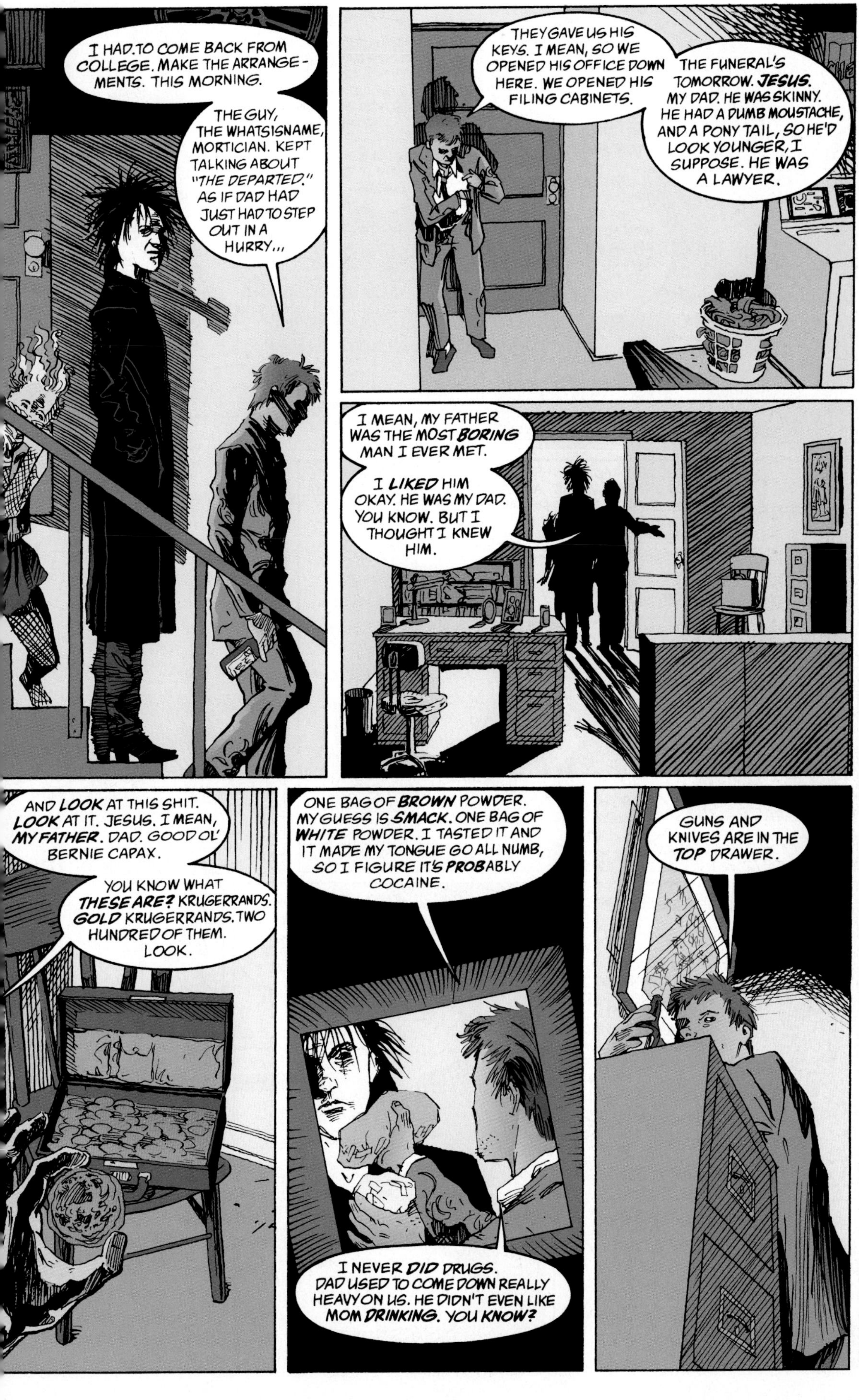
I HAD TO COME BACK FROM COLLEGE. MAKE THE ARRANGE-MENTS. THIS MORNING.
THE GUY, THE WHATSISNAME, MORTICIAN. KEPT TALKING ABOUT "THE DEPARTED." AS IF DAD HAD JUST HAD TO STEP OUT IN A HURRY...
THEY GAVE US HIS KEYS. I MEAN, SO WE OPENED HIS OFFICE DOWN HERE. WE OPENED HIS FILING CABINETS.
THE FUNERAL'S TOMORROW. **JESUS.** MY DAD. HE WAS SKINNY. HE HAD A **DUMB** MOUSTACHE, AND A PONY TAIL, SO HE'D LOOK YOUNGER, I SUPPOSE. HE WAS A LAWYER.
I MEAN, MY FATHER WAS THE MOST **BORING** MAN I EVER MET.
I **LIKED** HIM OKAY. HE WAS MY DAD. YOU KNOW. BUT I THOUGHT I KNEW HIM.
AND **LOOK** AT THIS SHIT. **LOOK** AT IT. JESUS. I MEAN, **MY FATHER**. DAD. GOOD OL' BERNIE CAPAX.
YOU KNOW WHAT **THESE ARE?** KRUGERRANDS. **GOLD** KRUGERRANDS. TWO HUNDRED OF THEM. LOOK.
ONE BAG OF **BROWN** POWDER. MY GUESS IS **SMACK**. ONE BAG OF **WHITE** POWDER. I TASTED IT AND IT MADE MY TONGUE GO ALL NUMB, SO I FIGURE IT'S **PROB**ABLY COCAINE.
I NEVER **DID** DRUGS. DAD USED TO COME DOWN REALLY HEAVY ON US. HE DIDN'T EVEN LIKE MOM **DRINKING**. YOU **KNOW?**
GUNS AND KNIVES ARE IN THE **TOP** DRAWER.

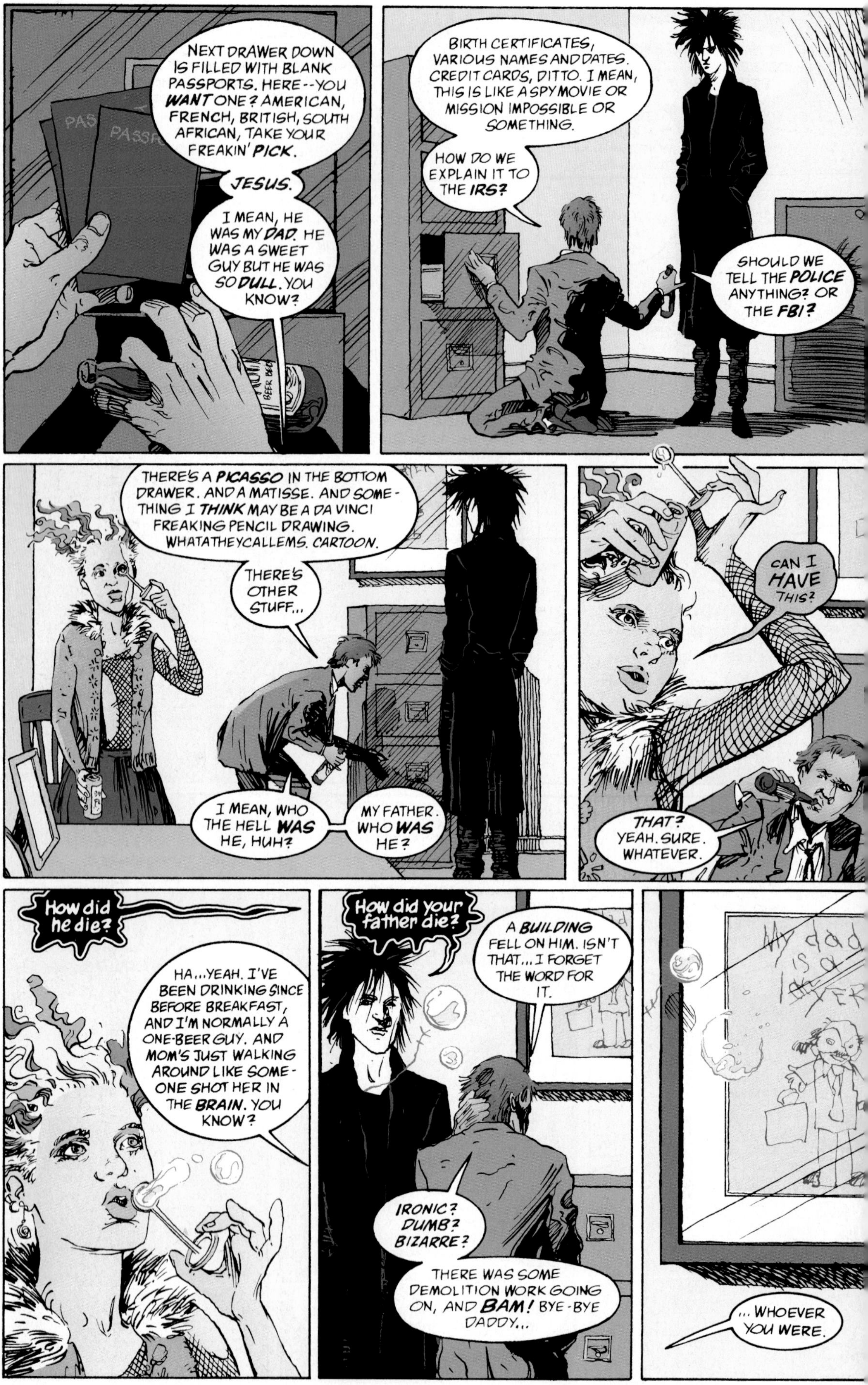
NEXT DRAWER DOWN IS FILLED WITH BLANK PASSPORTS. HERE--YOU WANT ONE? AMERICAN, FRENCH, BRITISH, SOUTH AFRICAN, TAKE YOUR FREAKIN' PICK.
JESUS.
I MEAN, HE WAS MY DAD. HE WAS A SWEET GUY BUT HE WAS SO DULL. YOU KNOW?
BIRTH CERTIFICATES, VARIOUS NAMES AND DATES. CREDIT CARDS, DITTO. I MEAN, THIS IS LIKE A SPY MOVIE OR MISSION IMPOSSIBLE OR SOMETHING.
HOW DO WE EXPLAIN IT TO THE IRS?
SHOULD WE TELL THE POLICE ANYTHING? OR THE FBI?
THERE'S A PICASSO IN THE BOTTOM DRAWER. AND A MATISSE. AND SOMETHING I THINK MAY BE A DA VINCI FREAKING PENCIL DRAWING. WHATATHEYCALLEMS. CARTOON.
THERE'S OTHER STUFF...
I MEAN, WHO THE HELL WAS HE, HUH?
MY FATHER. WHO WAS HE?
CAN I HAVE THIS?
THAT? YEAH. SURE. WHATEVER.
How did he die?
HA...YEAH. I'VE BEEN DRINKING SINCE BEFORE BREAKFAST, AND I'M NORMALLY A ONE-BEER GUY. AND MOM'S JUST WALKING AROUND LIKE SOMEONE SHOT HER IN THE BRAIN. YOU KNOW?
How did your father die?
A BUILDING FELL ON HIM. ISN'T THAT... I FORGET THE WORD FOR IT.
IRONIC? DUMB? BIZARRE?
THERE WAS SOME DEMOLITION WORK GOING ON, AND BAM! BYE-BYE DADDY...
...WHOEVER YOU WERE.

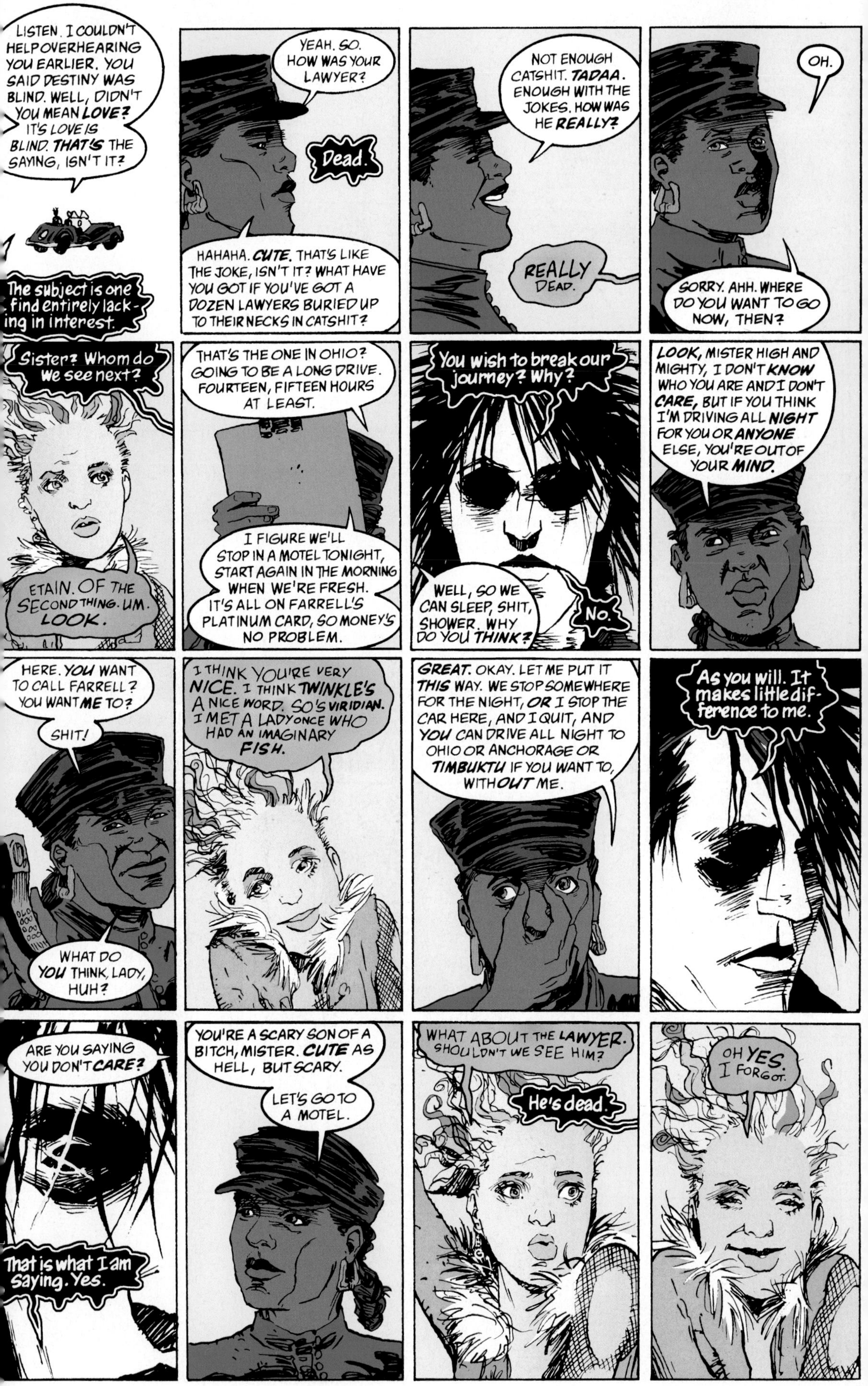

LISTEN. I COULDN'T HELP OVERHEARING YOU EARLIER. YOU SAID DESTINY WAS BLIND. WELL, DIDN'T YOU MEAN LOVE? IT'S LOVE IS BLIND. THAT'S THE SAYING, ISN'T IT?
The subject is one I find entirely lacking in interest.
YEAH. SO. HOW WAS YOUR LAWYER?
Dead.
HAHAHA. CUTE. THAT'S LIKE THE JOKE, ISN'T IT? WHAT HAVE YOU GOT IF YOU'VE GOT A DOZEN LAWYERS BURIED UP TO THEIR NECKS IN CATSHIT?
NOT ENOUGH CATSHIT. TADAA. ENOUGH WITH THE JOKES. HOW WAS HE REALLY?
REALLY DEAD.
OH.
SORRY. AHH. WHERE DO YOU WANT TO GO NOW, THEN?
Sister? Whom do we see next?
ETAIN. OF THE SECOND THING. UM. LOOK.
THAT'S THE ONE IN OHIO? GOING TO BE A LONG DRIVE. FOURTEEN, FIFTEEN HOURS AT LEAST.
I FIGURE WE'LL STOP IN A MOTEL TONIGHT, START AGAIN IN THE MORNING WHEN WE'RE FRESH. IT'S ALL ON FARRELL'S PLATINUM CARD, SO MONEY'S NO PROBLEM.
You wish to break our journey? Why?
WELL, SO WE CAN SLEEP, SHIT, SHOWER. WHY DO YOU THINK?
No.
LOOK, MISTER HIGH AND MIGHTY, I DON'T KNOW WHO YOU ARE AND I DON'T CARE, BUT IF YOU THINK I'M DRIVING ALL NIGHT FOR YOU OR ANYONE ELSE, YOU'RE OUT OF YOUR MIND.
HERE. YOU WANT TO CALL FARRELL? YOU WANT ME TO?
SHIT!
WHAT DO YOU THINK, LADY, HUH?
I THINK YOU'RE VERY NICE. I THINK TWINKLE'S A NICE WORD. SO'S VIRIDIAN. I MET A LADY ONCE WHO HAD AN IMAGINARY FISH.
GREAT. OKAY. LET ME PUT IT THIS WAY. WE STOP SOMEWHERE FOR THE NIGHT, OR I STOP THE CAR HERE, AND I QUIT, AND YOU CAN DRIVE ALL NIGHT TO OHIO OR ANCHORAGE OR TIMBUKTU IF YOU WANT TO, WITHOUT ME.
As you will. It makes little difference to me.
ARE YOU SAYING YOU DON'T CARE?
That is what I am saying. Yes.
YOU'RE A SCARY SON OF A BITCH, MISTER. CUTE AS HELL, BUT SCARY.
LET'S GO TO A MOTEL.
WHAT ABOUT THE LAWYER. SHOULDN'T WE SEE HIM?
He's dead.
OH YES. I FORGOT.

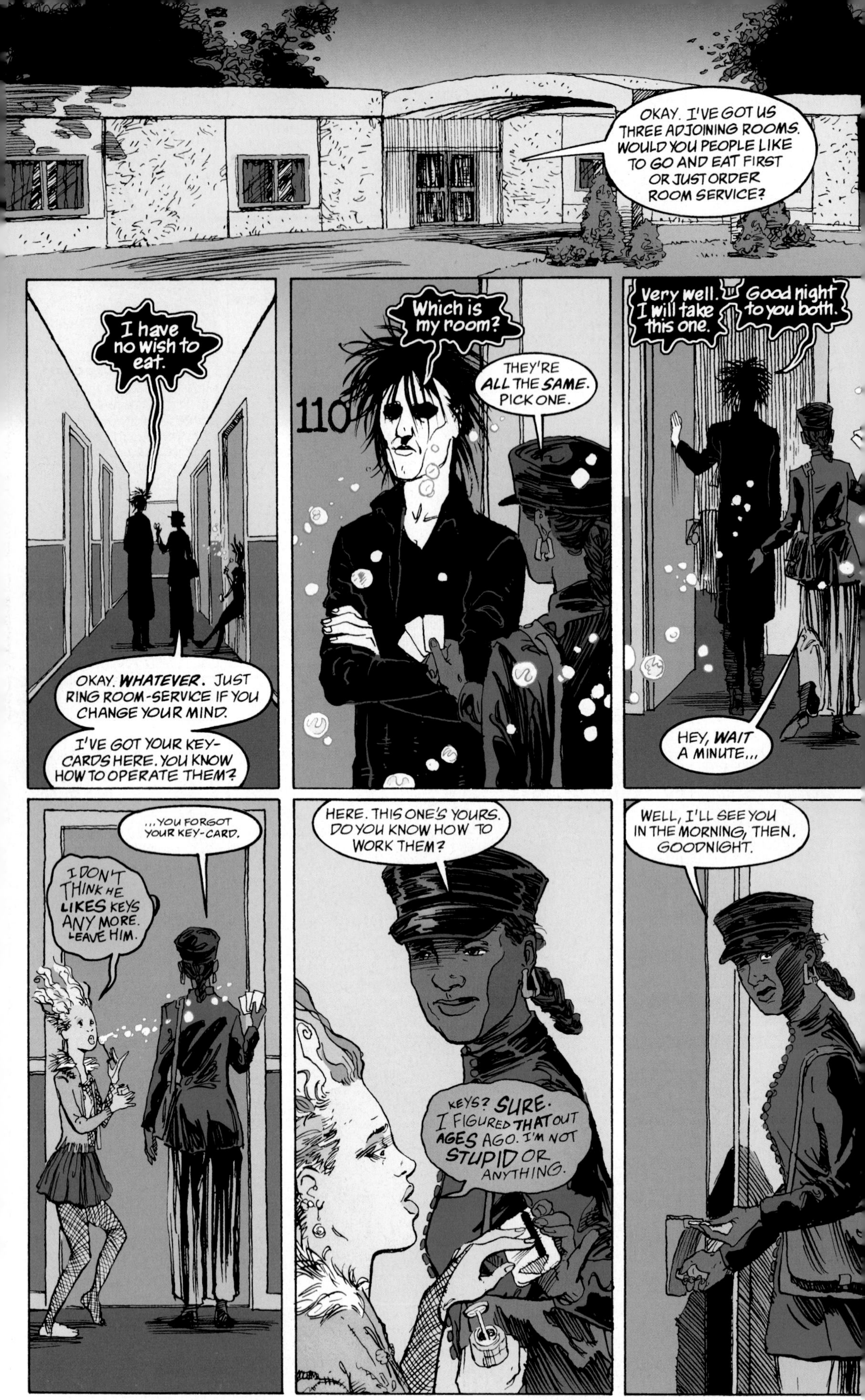
OKAY. I'VE GOT US THREE ADJOINING ROOMS. WOULD YOU PEOPLE LIKE TO GO AND EAT FIRST OR JUST ORDER ROOM SERVICE?
I have no wish to eat.
OKAY. WHATEVER. JUST RING ROOM-SERVICE IF YOU CHANGE YOUR MIND.
I'VE GOT YOUR KEY-CARDS HERE. YOU KNOW HOW TO OPERATE THEM?
Which is my room?
110
THEY'RE ALL THE SAME. PICK ONE.
Very well. I will take this one.
Good night to you both.
HEY, WAIT A MINUTE...
...YOU FORGOT YOUR KEY-CARD.
I DON'T THINK HE LIKES KEYS ANY MORE. LEAVE HIM.
HERE. THIS ONE'S YOURS. DO YOU KNOW HOW TO WORK THEM?
KEYS? SURE. I FIGURED THAT OUT AGES AGO. I'M NOT STUPID OR ANYTHING.
WELL, I'LL SEE YOU IN THE MORNING, THEN. GOODNIGHT.

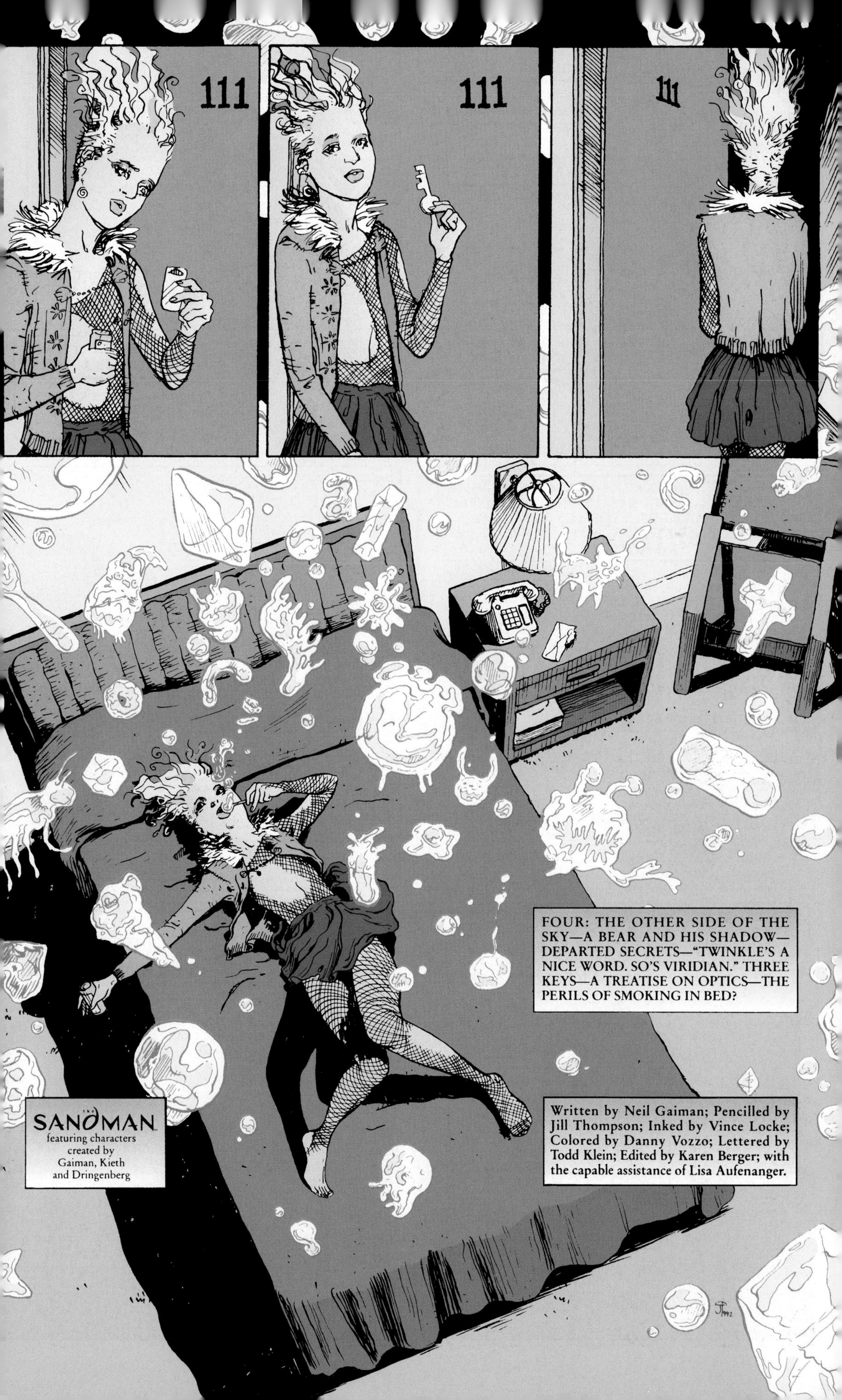

111
111
111
FOUR: THE OTHER SIDE OF THE SKY—A BEAR AND HIS SHADOW—DEPARTED SECRETS—"TWINKLE'S A NICE WORD. SO'S VIRIDIAN." THREE KEYS—A TREATISE ON OPTICS—THE PERILS OF SMOKING IN BED?
THE SANDMAN featuring characters created by Gaiman, Kieth and Dringenberg
Written by Neil Gaiman; Pencilled by Jill Thompson; Inked by Vince Locke; Colored by Danny Vozzo; Lettered by Todd Klein; Edited by Karen Berger; with the capable assistance of Lisa Aufenanger.

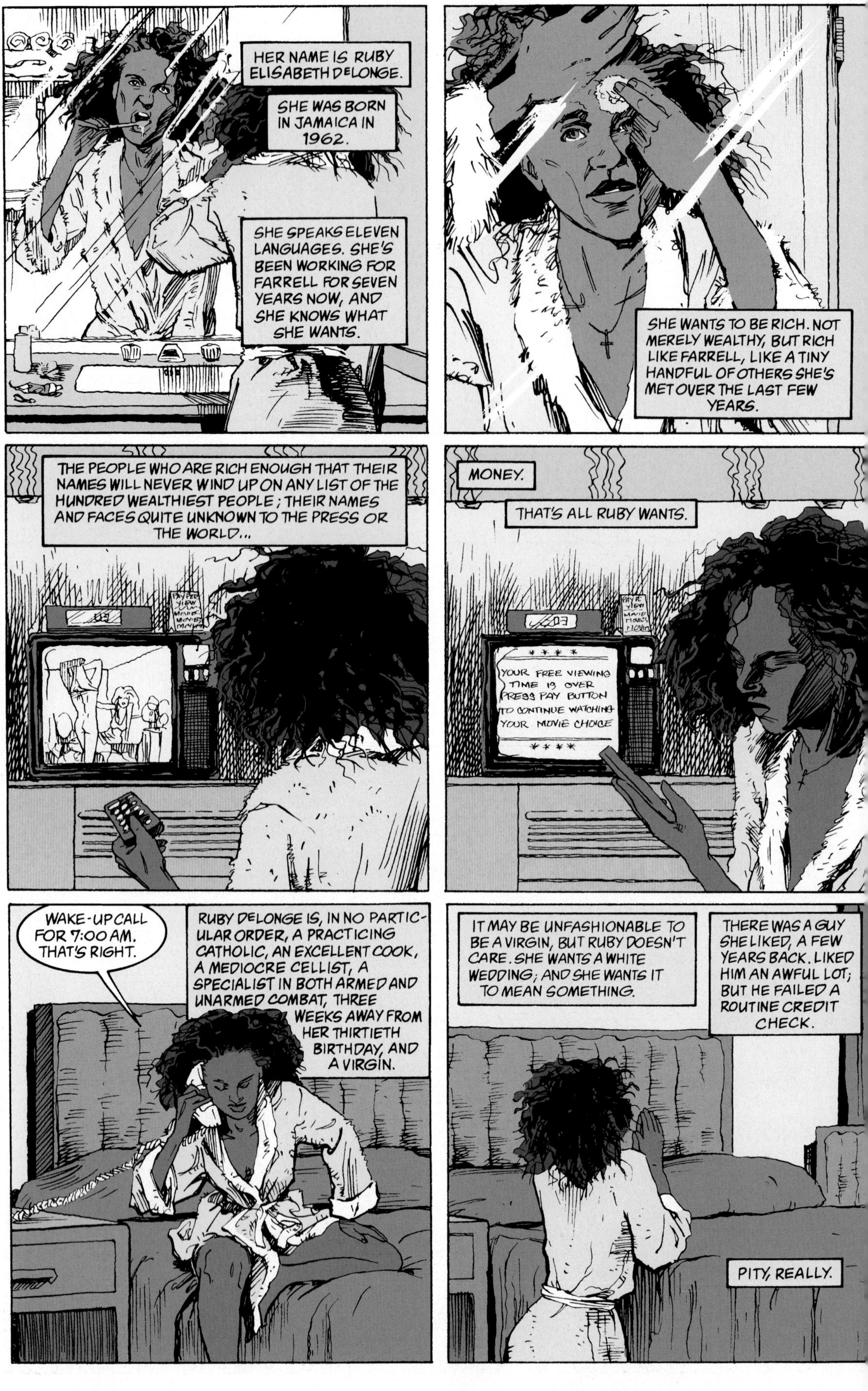
HER NAME IS RUBY ELISABETH DeLONGE.
SHE WAS BORN IN JAMAICA IN 1962.
SHE SPEAKS ELEVEN LANGUAGES. SHE'S BEEN WORKING FOR FARRELL FOR SEVEN YEARS NOW, AND SHE KNOWS WHAT SHE WANTS.
SHE WANTS TO BE RICH. NOT MERELY WEALTHY, BUT RICH LIKE FARRELL, LIKE A TINY HANDFUL OF OTHERS SHE'S MET OVER THE LAST FEW YEARS.
THE PEOPLE WHO ARE RICH ENOUGH THAT THEIR NAMES WILL NEVER WIND UP ON ANY LIST OF THE HUNDRED WEALTHIEST PEOPLE; THEIR NAMES AND FACES QUITE UNKNOWN TO THE PRESS OR THE WORLD...
MONEY.
THAT'S ALL RUBY WANTS.
YOUR FREE VIEWING TIME IS OVER PRESS PAY BUTTON TO CONTINUE WATCHING YOUR MOVIE CHOICE
WAKE-UP CALL FOR 7:00 AM. THAT'S RIGHT.
RUBY DeLONGE IS, IN NO PARTICULAR ORDER, A PRACTICING CATHOLIC, AN EXCELLENT COOK, A MEDIOCRE CELLIST, A SPECIALIST IN BOTH ARMED AND UNARMED COMBAT, THREE WEEKS AWAY FROM HER THIRTIETH BIRTHDAY, AND A VIRGIN.
IT MAY BE UNFASHIONABLE TO BE A VIRGIN, BUT RUBY DOESN'T CARE. SHE WANTS A WHITE WEDDING; AND SHE WANTS IT TO MEAN SOMETHING.
THERE WAS A GUY SHE LIKED, A FEW YEARS BACK. LIKED HIM AN AWFUL LOT; BUT HE FAILED A ROUTINE CREDIT CHECK.
PITY, REALLY.

SOMETIMES SHE STILL MISSES HIM.

AND SHE WANTS TO BE *SO* GODDAMNED RICH...

AND SHE WANTS SOMEONE TO LOVE...

AND SHE WANTS TO BE HAPPY...

TOMORROW SHE'LL BE BACK ON THE ROAD, DRIVING FARRELL'S PALE CRAZIES OFF TO THEIR NEXT LUNATIC DESTINATION.

TIRED. SHE'S TIRED.

DESTINY IS BLIND?

ONE CIGARETTE. A GIRL NEEDS HER NICOTINE FIX, AND SHE'S ALREADY CUT DOWN TO FIVE A DAY.

SHE DRAWS THE BLUE SMOKE DEEP INTO HER LUNGS, FEELS HER HEAD GO SWIMMY AND HER INSIDES RELAX.

SHE'S GOT TO GIVE IT UP. SHE REALLY MUST. THESE THINGS ARE GOING TO KILL HER.

IT'S NOT DESTINY. IT'S LOVE.

112

SHE WAS RIGHT. HE WAS WRONG.

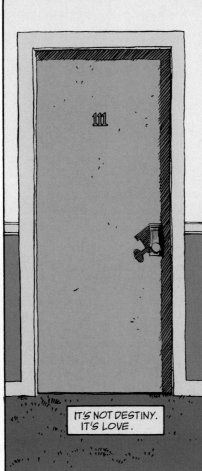

111

IT'S NOT DESTINY. IT'S LOVE.

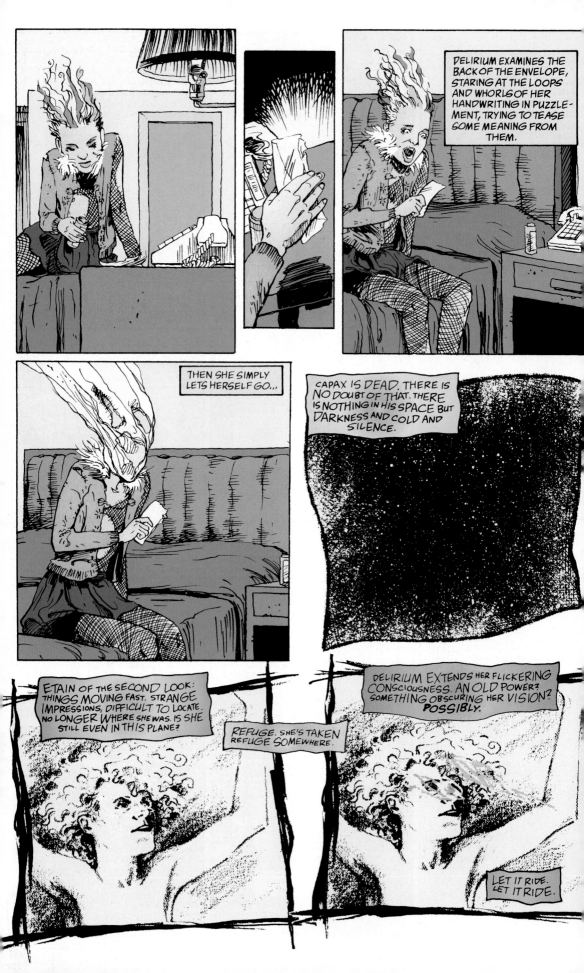

DELIRIUM EXAMINES THE BACK OF THE ENVELOPE, STARING AT THE LOOPS AND WHORLS OF HER HANDWRITING IN PUZZLEMENT, TRYING TO TEASE SOME MEANING FROM THEM.

THEN SHE SIMPLY LETS HERSELF GO...

CAPAX IS DEAD. THERE IS NO DOUBT OF THAT. THERE IS NOTHING IN HIS SPACE BUT DARKNESS AND COLD AND SILENCE.

ETAIN OF THE SECOND LOOK: THINGS MOVING FAST. STRANGE IMPRESSIONS, DIFFICULT TO LOCATE. NO LONGER WHERE SHE WAS. IS SHE STILL EVEN IN THIS PLANE?

REFUGE. SHE'S TAKEN REFUGE SOMEWHERE.

DELIRIUM EXTENDS HER FLICKERING CONSCIOUSNESS. AN OLD POWER? SOMETHING OBSCURING HER VISION? POSSIBLY.

LET IT RIDE. LET IT RIDE.

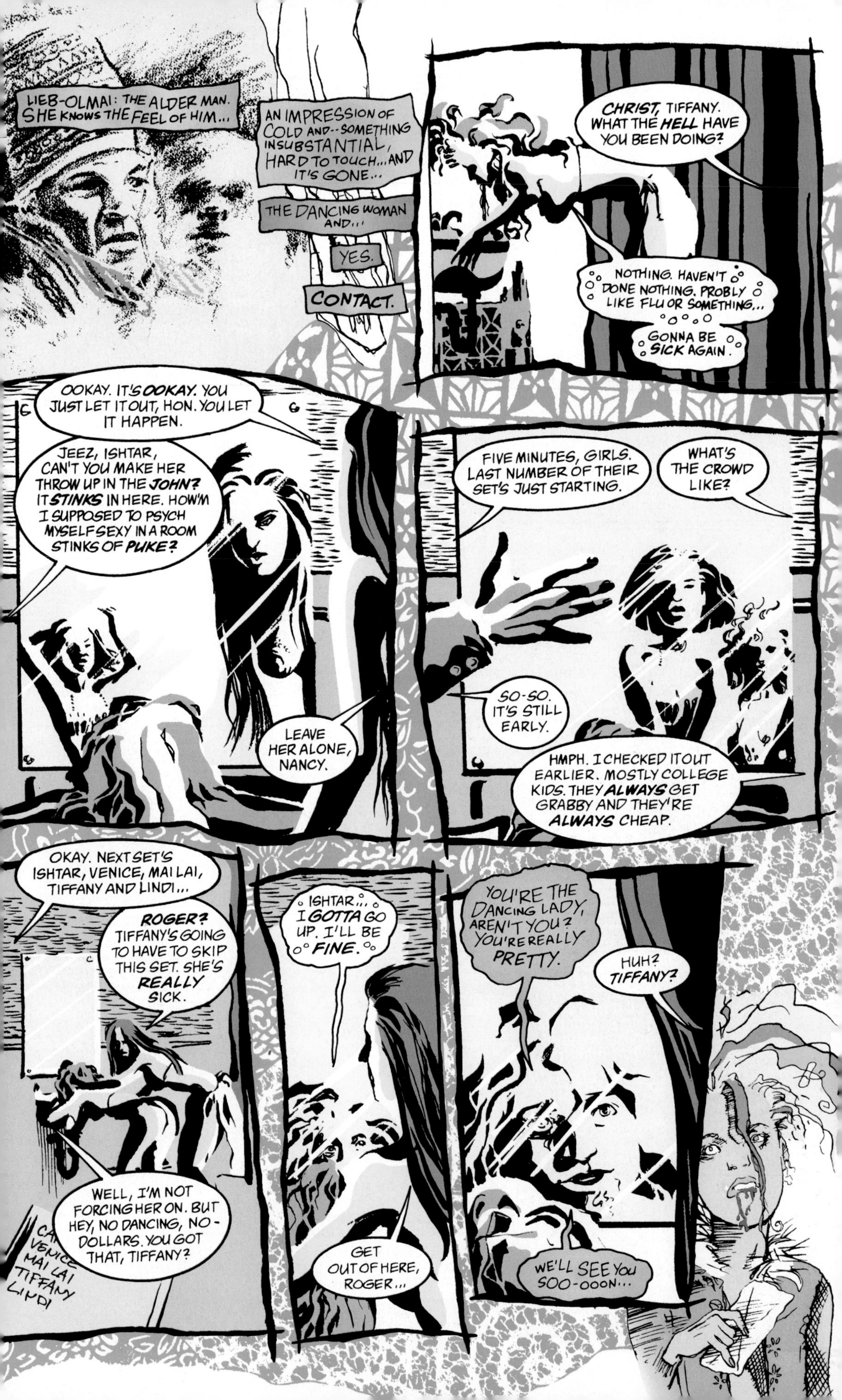

LIEB-OLMAI: THE ALDER MAN. SHE KNOWS THE FEEL OF HIM...
AN IMPRESSION OF COLD AND--SOMETHING INSUBSTANTIAL, HARD TO TOUCH... AND IT'S GONE...
THE DANCING WOMAN AND...
YES.
CONTACT.
CHRIST, TIFFANY. WHAT THE HELL HAVE YOU BEEN DOING?
NOTHING. HAVEN'T DONE NOTHING. PROBLY LIKE FLU OR SOMETHING...
GONNA BE SICK AGAIN.
OOKAY. IT'S OOKAY. YOU JUST LET IT OUT, HON. YOU LET IT HAPPEN.
JEEZ, ISHTAR, CAN'T YOU MAKE HER THROW UP IN THE JOHN? IT STINKS IN HERE. HOW'M I SUPPOSED TO PSYCH MYSELF SEXY IN A ROOM STINKS OF PUKE?
LEAVE HER ALONE, NANCY.
FIVE MINUTES, GIRLS. LAST NUMBER OF THEIR SET'S JUST STARTING.
WHAT'S THE CROWD LIKE?
SO-SO. IT'S STILL EARLY.
HMPH. I CHECKED IT OUT EARLIER. MOSTLY COLLEGE KIDS. THEY ALWAYS GET GRABBY AND THEY'RE ALWAYS CHEAP.
OKAY. NEXT SET'S ISHTAR, VENICE, MAI LAI, TIFFANY AND LINDI...
ROGER? TIFFANY'S GOING TO HAVE TO SKIP THIS SET. SHE'S REALLY SICK.
WELL, I'M NOT FORCING HER ON. BUT HEY, NO DANCING, NO-DOLLARS. YOU GOT THAT, TIFFANY?
MAI LAI
TIFFANY
LINDI
ISHTAR... I GOTTA GO UP. I'LL BE FINE.
GET OUT OF HERE, ROGER...
YOU'RE THE DANCING LADY, AREN'T YOU? YOU'RE REALLY PRETTY.
HUH? TIFFANY?
WE'LL SEE YOU SOO-OOON...

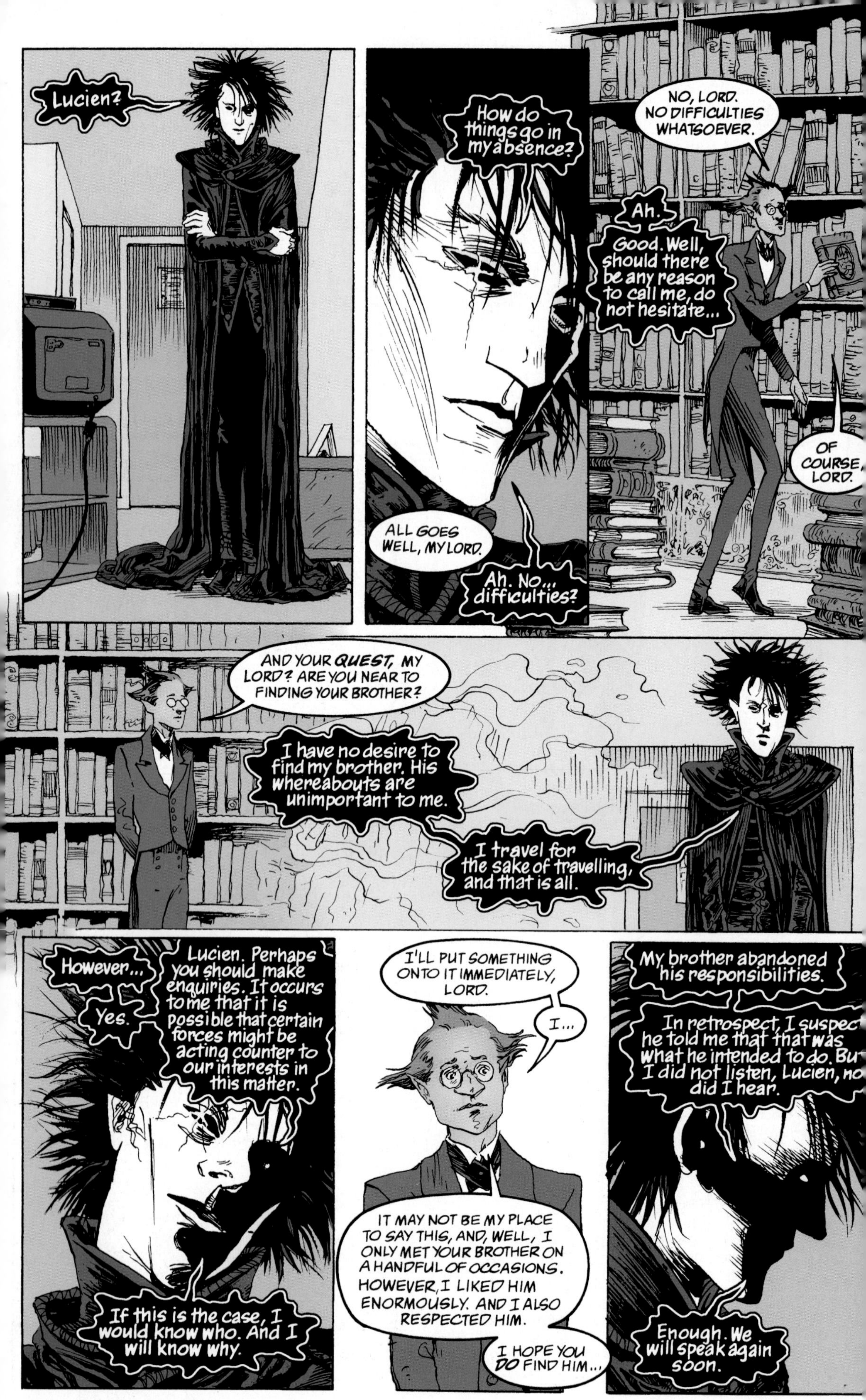

Lucien?
How do things go in my absence?
ALL GOES WELL, MY LORD.
Ah. No... difficulties?
NO, LORD. NO DIFFICULTIES WHATSOEVER.
Ah.
Good. Well, should there be any reason to call me, do not hesitate...
OF COURSE, LORD.
AND YOUR QUEST, MY LORD? ARE YOU NEAR TO FINDING YOUR BROTHER?
I have no desire to find my brother. His whereabouts are unimportant to me.
I travel for the sake of travelling, and that is all.
However...
Yes.
Lucien. Perhaps you should make enquiries. It occurs to me that it is possible that certain forces might be acting counter to our interests in this matter.
If this is the case, I would know who. And I will know why.
I'LL PUT SOMETHING ONTO IT IMMEDIATELY, LORD.
I...
IT MAY NOT BE MY PLACE TO SAY THIS, AND, WELL, I ONLY MET YOUR BROTHER ON A HANDFUL OF OCCASIONS. HOWEVER, I LIKED HIM ENORMOUSLY. AND I ALSO RESPECTED HIM.
I HOPE YOU DO FIND HIM...
My brother abandoned his responsibilities.
In retrospect, I suspec he told me that that was what he intended to do. Bu I did not listen, Lucien, no did I hear.
Enough. We will speak again soon.

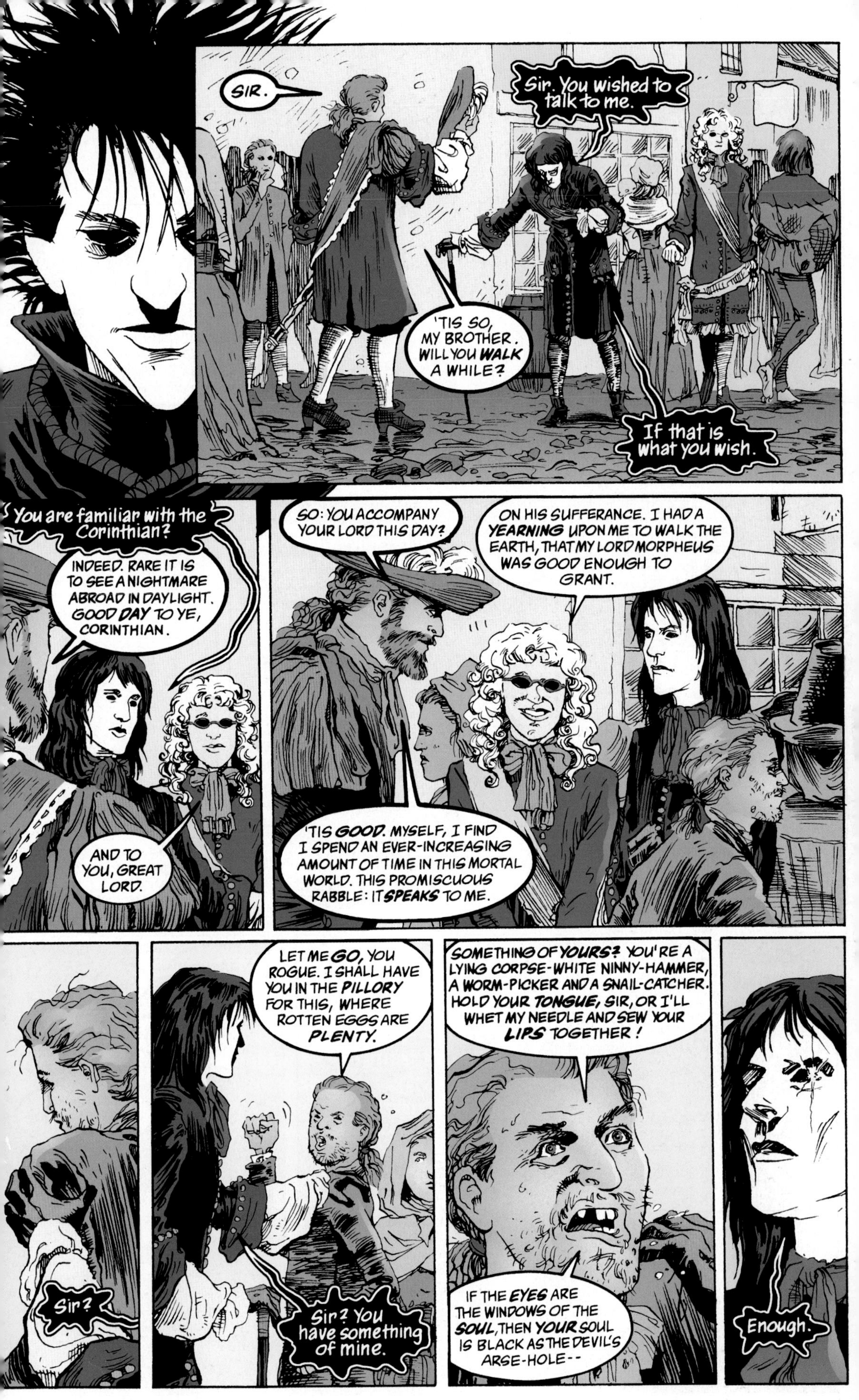

SIR.
Sir. You wished to talk to me.
'TIS SO, MY BROTHER. WILL YOU WALK A WHILE?
If that is what you wish.
You are familiar with the Corinthian?
INDEED. RARE IT IS TO SEE A NIGHTMARE ABROAD IN DAYLIGHT. GOOD DAY TO YE, CORINTHIAN.
AND TO YOU, GREAT LORD.
SO: YOU ACCOMPANY YOUR LORD THIS DAY?
ON HIS SUFFERANCE. I HAD A YEARNING UPON ME TO WALK THE EARTH, THAT MY LORD MORPHEUS WAS GOOD ENOUGH TO GRANT.
'TIS GOOD. MYSELF, I FIND I SPEND AN EVER-INCREASING AMOUNT OF TIME IN THIS MORTAL WORLD. THIS PROMISCUOUS RABBLE: IT SPEAKS TO ME.
Sir?
LET ME GO, YOU ROGUE. I SHALL HAVE YOU IN THE PILLORY FOR THIS, WHERE ROTTEN EGGS ARE PLENTY.
Sir? You have something of mine.
SOMETHING OF YOURS? YOU'RE A LYING CORPSE-WHITE NINNY-HAMMER, A WORM-PICKER AND A SNAIL-CATCHER. HOLD YOUR TONGUE, SIR, OR I'LL WHET MY NEEDLE AND SEW YOUR LIPS TOGETHER!
IF THE EYES ARE THE WINDOWS OF THE SOUL, THEN YOUR SOUL IS BLACK AS THE DEVIL'S ARSE-HOLE--
Enough.

You are Dickon Hawksthorne.

YOU *KNOW* ME?

Aye. After my fashion.

Tell me, Master Hawksthorne, was it wise to return from transportation? When they find you out, you'll swing for it.

THAT'S *A LIE!*

It is rare that I tell fortunes. But Tyburn tree haunts your dreams, Master Hawksthorne, and it will continue so to do, until you are hung there in chains, *without* benefit of clergy.

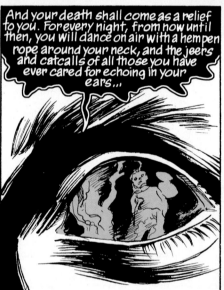

And your death shall come as a relief to you. For every night, from now until then, you will dance on air with a hempen rope around your neck, and the jeers and catcalls of all those you have ever cared for echoing in your ears...

HERE -- *TAKE* YOUR *DAMNED* STONE, YOU *WIGHT!* I WILL HAVE *NONE* OF IT!

YOU COULD SIMPLY HAVE TAKEN IT BACK FROM HIM. YOU DID NOT *NEED* TO DO THAT.

I do not tell you how to conduct your affairs, brother.

I must confess I see no reason for you to tell me how to conduct mine.

MY AFFAIRS.

YES.

I HAVE GIVEN MUCH *THOUGHT* TO MY AFFAIRS IN RECENT YEARS.

TIMES ARE *CHANGING,* MY BROTHER.

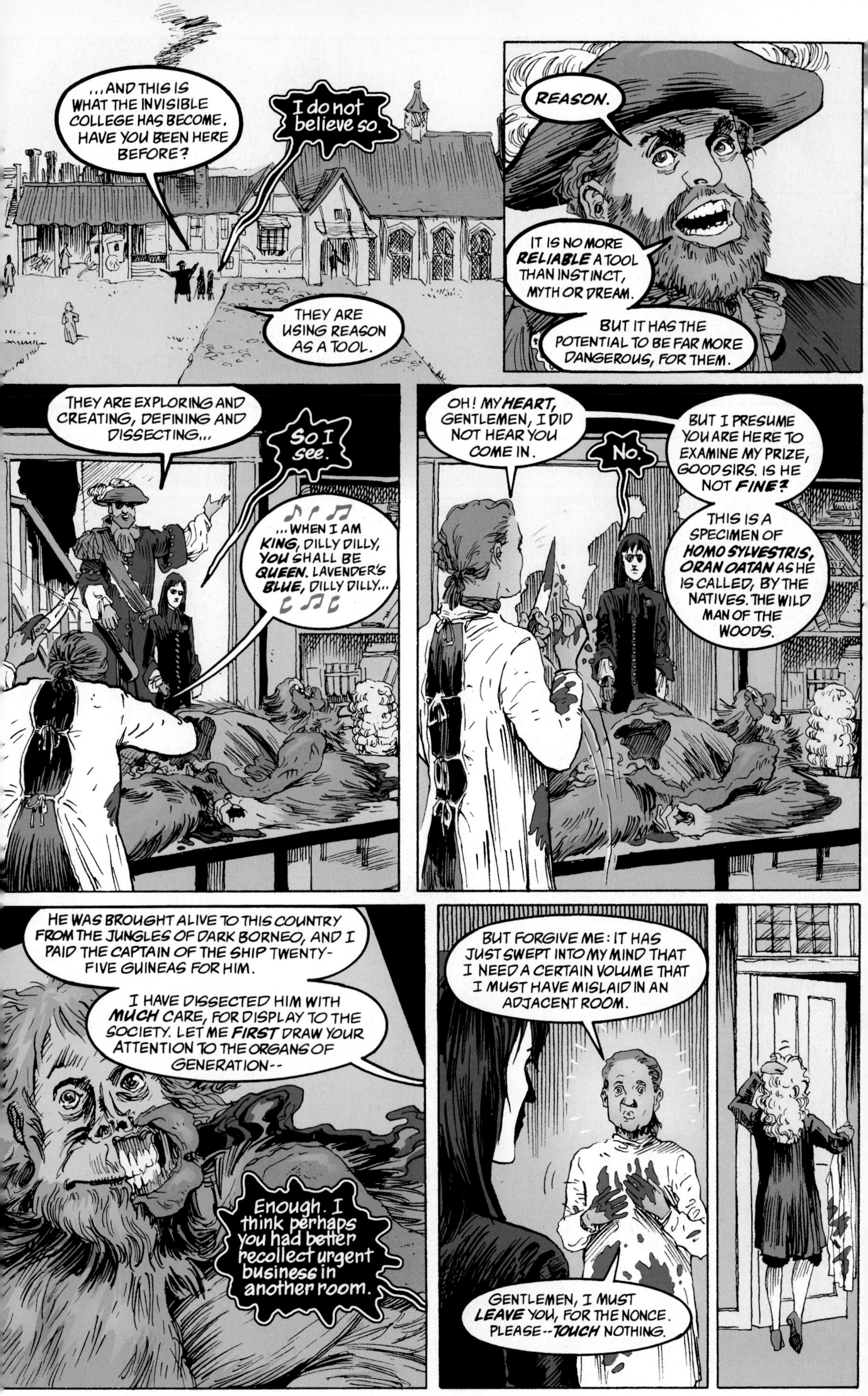

...AND THIS IS WHAT THE INVISIBLE COLLEGE HAS BECOME. HAVE YOU BEEN HERE BEFORE?
I do not believe so.
THEY ARE USING REASON AS A TOOL.
REASON.
IT IS NO MORE RELIABLE A TOOL THAN INSTINCT, MYTH OR DREAM.
BUT IT HAS THE POTENTIAL TO BE FAR MORE DANGEROUS, FOR THEM.
THEY ARE EXPLORING AND CREATING, DEFINING AND DISSECTING...
So I see.
...WHEN I AM KING, DILLY DILLY, YOU SHALL BE QUEEN. LAVENDER'S BLUE, DILLY DILLY...
OH! MY HEART, GENTLEMEN, I DID NOT HEAR YOU COME IN.
No.
BUT I PRESUME YOU ARE HERE TO EXAMINE MY PRIZE, GOOD SIRS. IS HE NOT FINE?
THIS IS A SPECIMEN OF HOMO SYLVESTRIS, ORAN OATAN AS HE IS CALLED, BY THE NATIVES. THE WILD MAN OF THE WOODS.
HE WAS BROUGHT ALIVE TO THIS COUNTRY FROM THE JUNGLES OF DARK BORNEO, AND I PAID THE CAPTAIN OF THE SHIP TWENTY-FIVE GUINEAS FOR HIM.
I HAVE DISSECTED HIM WITH MUCH CARE, FOR DISPLAY TO THE SOCIETY. LET ME FIRST DRAW YOUR ATTENTION TO THE ORGANS OF GENERATION--
Enough. I think perhaps you had better recollect urgent business in another room.
BUT FORGIVE ME: IT HAS JUST SWEPT INTO MY MIND THAT I NEED A CERTAIN VOLUME THAT I MUST HAVE MISLAID IN AN ADJACENT ROOM.
GENTLEMEN, I MUST LEAVE YOU, FOR THE NONCE. PLEASE--TOUCH NOTHING.

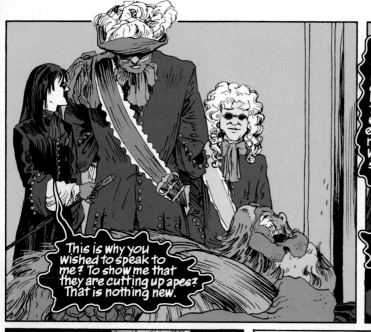

This is why you wished to speak to me? To show me that they are cutting up apes? That is nothing new.

Do they think that they can impale the soul of it on their knives? That if they cut deep enough they can extract its dreams, naked and writhing and screaming, from its head?

Reason is a flawed tool at best, my brother.

ONE of them has prismed the sun's rays into beams of discrete color.

A pretty phenomenon, indeed.

MISTER NEWTON--THE YOUNG GENTLEMAN WHO ORDERED THE RAINBOW--HAS MUCH ELSE TO SAY ON THE SUBJECT OF OPTICKS.

"ARE NOT LIGHT AND GROSS BODIES INTRACONVERTIBLE?"

HE HAS ALREADY POSED THAT QUESTION; ALTHOUGH AT PRESENT IT IS BUT AN IDLE NOTION, AND I DOUBT HE WILL RETURN TO IT. HE HAS TOO MANY OTHER THINGS TO OCCUPY HIS MIND.

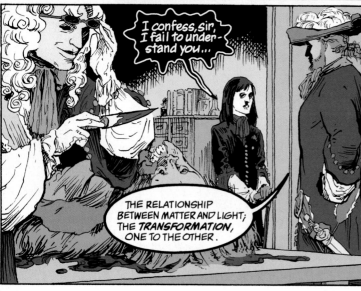

I confess, sir, I fail to understand you...

THE RELATIONSHIP BETWEEN MATTER AND LIGHT; THE TRANSFORMATION, ONE TO THE OTHER.

I HAVE BEEN HERE BEFORE. AFTER A WHILE CERTAIN IDEAS BECOME INEVITABLE.

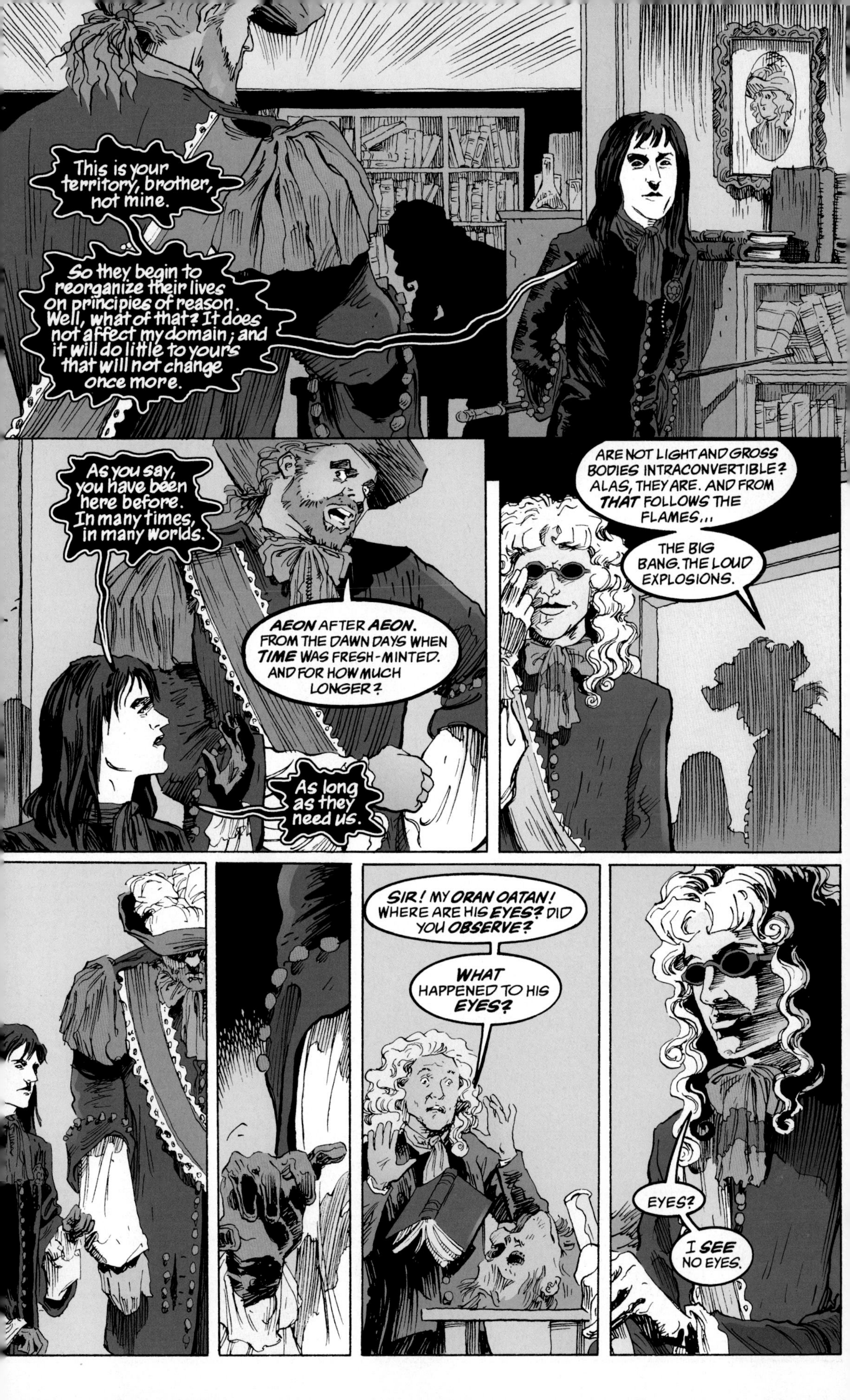
This is your territory, brother, not mine.
So they begin to reorganize their lives on principles of reason. Well, what of that? It does not affect my domain; and it will do little to yours that will not change once more.
As you say, you have been here before. In many times, in many worlds.
AEON AFTER AEON. FROM THE DAWN DAYS WHEN TIME WAS FRESH-MINTED. AND FOR HOW MUCH LONGER?
As long as they need us.
ARE NOT LIGHT AND GROSS BODIES INTRACONVERTIBLE? ALAS, THEY ARE. AND FROM THAT FOLLOWS THE FLAMES...
THE BIG BANG. THE LOUD EXPLOSIONS.
SIR! MY ORAN OATAN! WHERE ARE HIS EYES? DID YOU OBSERVE?
WHAT HAPPENED TO HIS EYES?
EYES?
I SEE NO EYES.

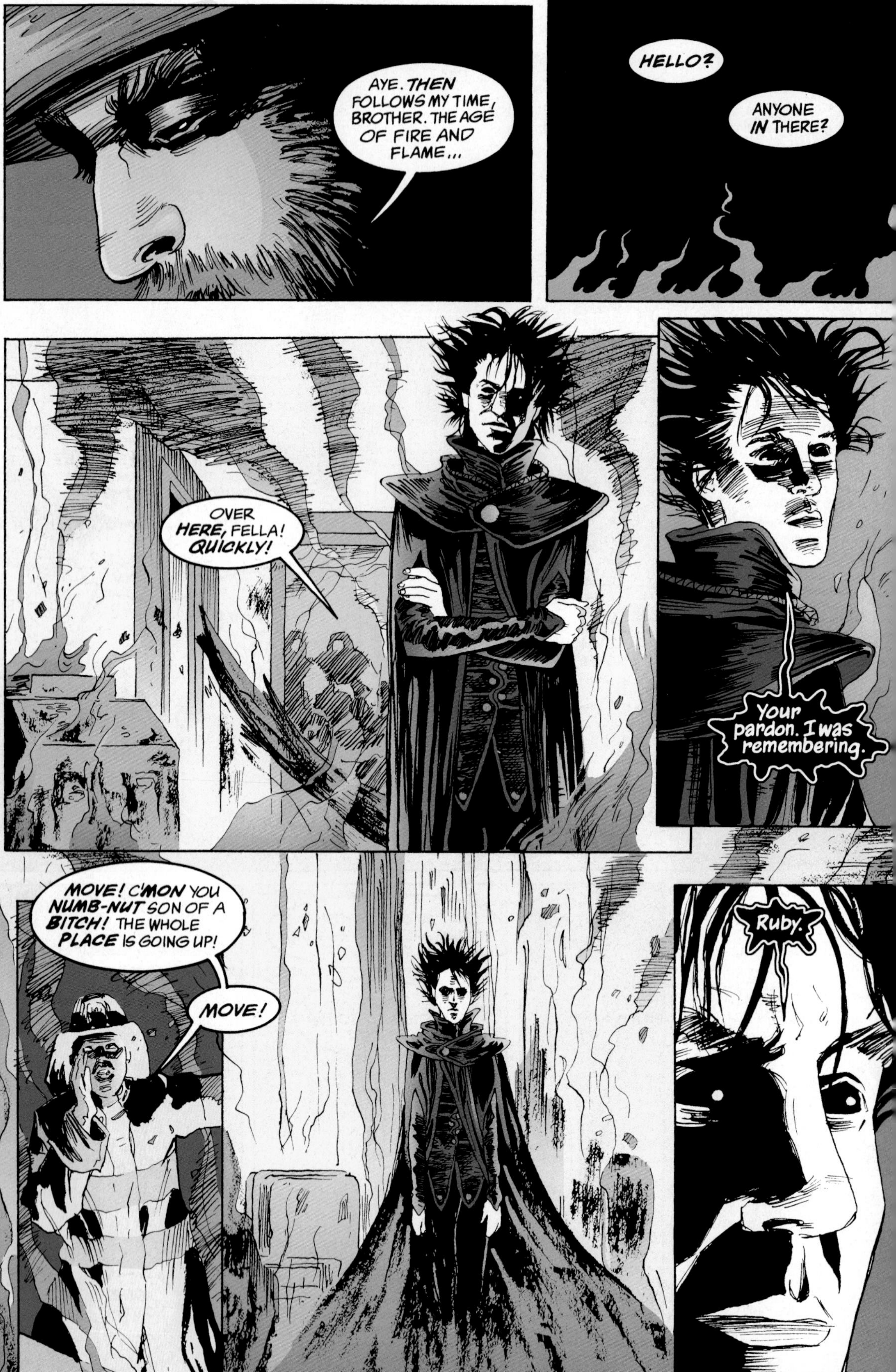

AYE. THEN FOLLOWS MY TIME, BROTHER. THE AGE OF FIRE AND FLAME...
HELLO?
ANYONE IN THERE?
OVER HERE, FELLA! QUICKLY!
Your pardon. I was remembering.
MOVE! C'MON YOU NUMB-NUT SON OF A BITCH! THE WHOLE PLACE IS GOING UP!
MOVE!
Ruby.

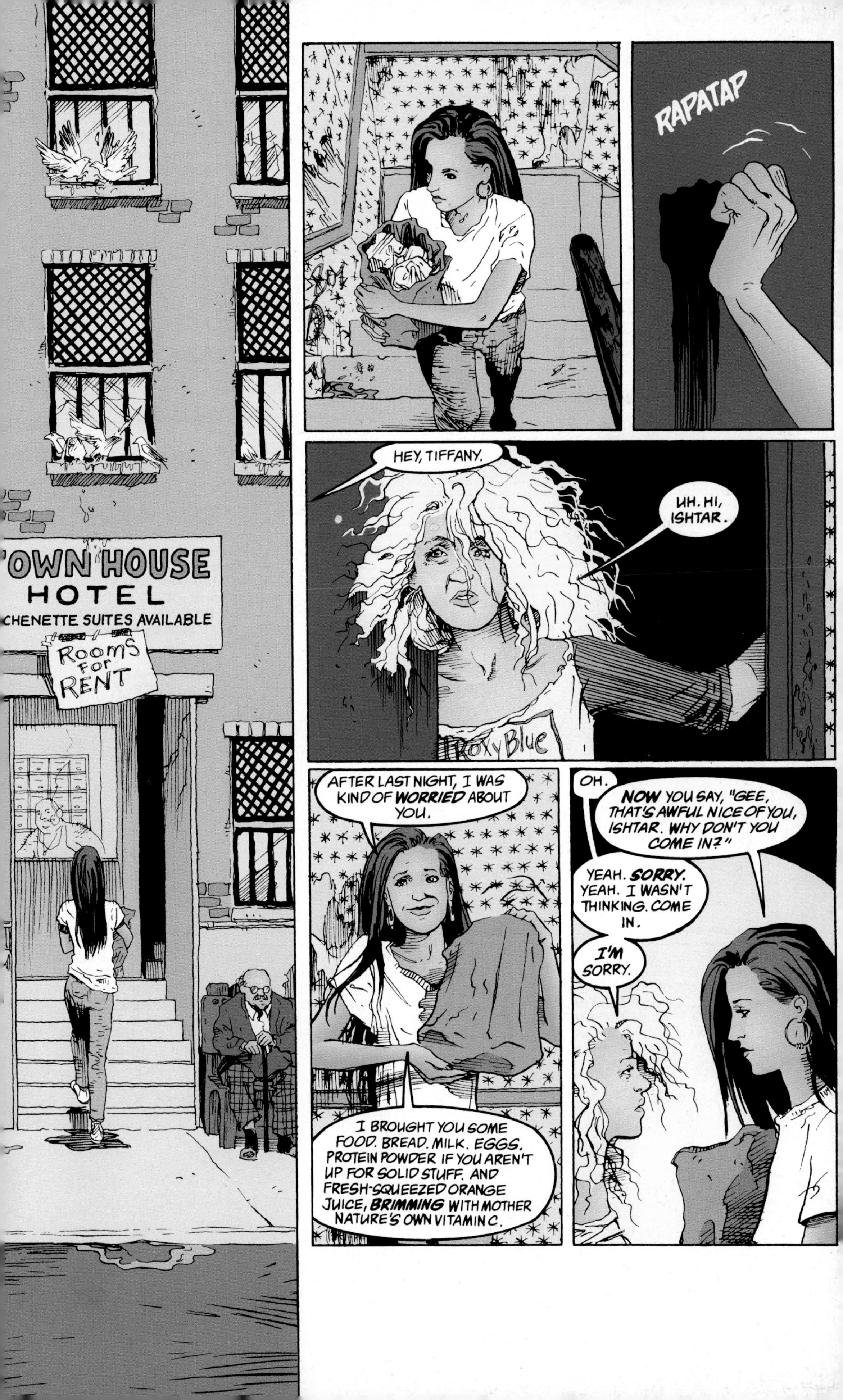

OWN HOUSE
HOTEL
CHENETTE SUITES AVAILABLE
Rooms For RENT
RAPATAP
HEY, TIFFANY.
UH. HI, ISHTAR.
Roxy Blue
AFTER LAST NIGHT, I WAS KIND OF WORRIED ABOUT YOU.
I BROUGHT YOU SOME FOOD. BREAD. MILK. EGGS. PROTEIN POWDER IF YOU AREN'T UP FOR SOLID STUFF. AND FRESH-SQUEEZED ORANGE JUICE, BRIMMING WITH MOTHER NATURE'S OWN VITAMIN C.
OH.
NOW YOU SAY, "GEE, THAT'S AWFUL NICE OF YOU, ISHTAR. WHY DON'T YOU COME IN?"
YEAH. SORRY. YEAH. I WASN'T THINKING. COME IN.
I'M SORRY.

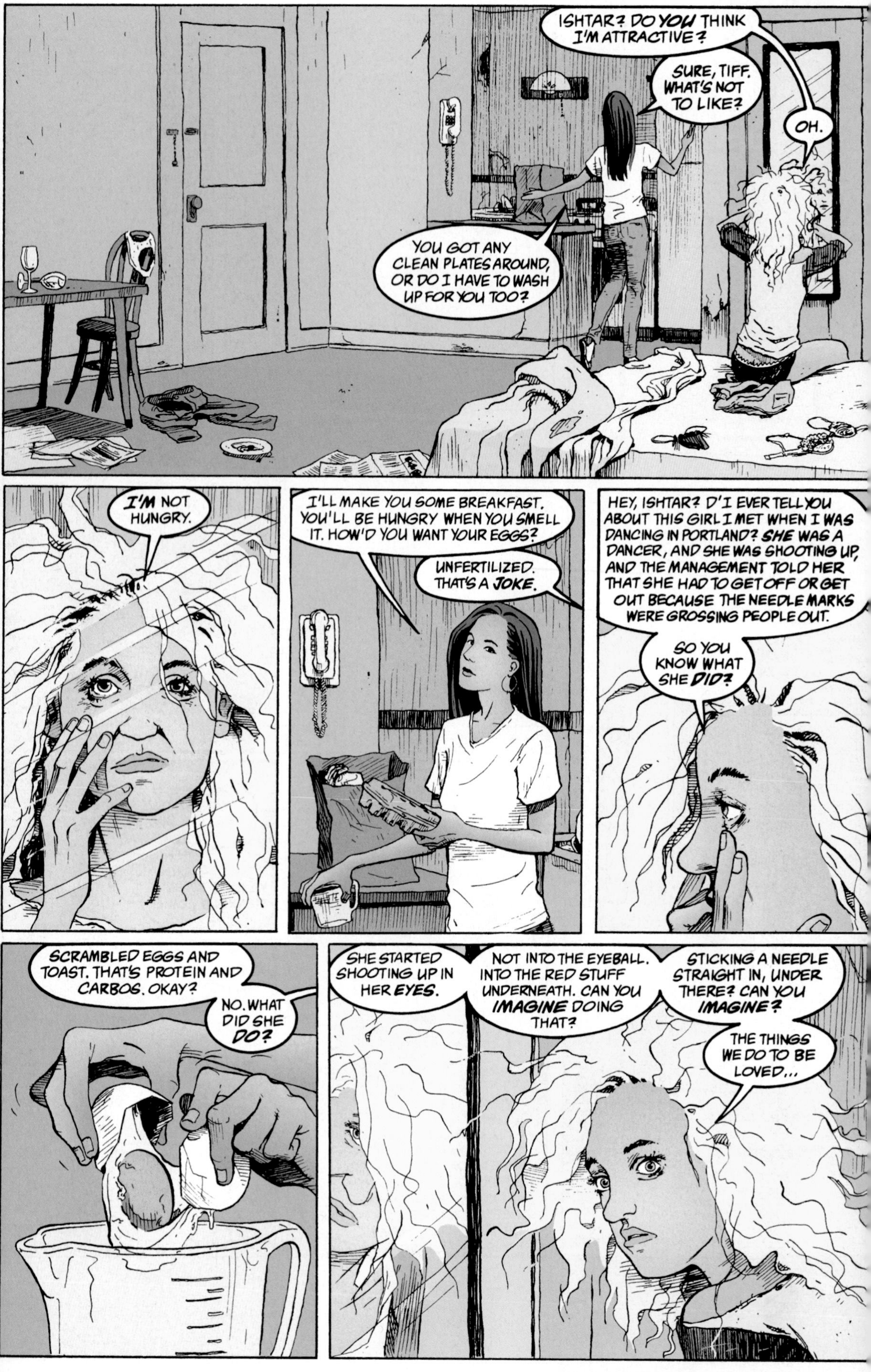
ISHTAR? DO YOU THINK I'M ATTRACTIVE?
SURE, TIFF. WHAT'S NOT TO LIKE?
OH.
YOU GOT ANY CLEAN PLATES AROUND, OR DO I HAVE TO WASH UP FOR YOU TOO?
I'M NOT HUNGRY.
I'LL MAKE YOU SOME BREAKFAST. YOU'LL BE HUNGRY WHEN YOU SMELL IT. HOW'D YOU WANT YOUR EGGS?
UNFERTILIZED. THAT'S A JOKE.
HEY, ISHTAR? D'I EVER TELL YOU ABOUT THIS GIRL I MET WHEN I WAS DANCING IN PORTLAND? SHE WAS A DANCER, AND SHE WAS SHOOTING UP, AND THE MANAGEMENT TOLD HER THAT SHE HAD TO GET OFF OR GET OUT BECAUSE THE NEEDLE MARKS WERE GROSSING PEOPLE OUT.
SO YOU KNOW WHAT SHE DID?
SCRAMBLED EGGS AND TOAST. THAT'S PROTEIN AND CARBOS. OKAY?
NO. WHAT DID SHE DO?
SHE STARTED SHOOTING UP IN HER EYES.
NOT INTO THE EYEBALL. INTO THE RED STUFF UNDERNEATH. CAN YOU IMAGINE DOING THAT?
STICKING A NEEDLE STRAIGHT IN, UNDER THERE? CAN YOU IMAGINE?
THE THINGS WE DO TO BE LOVED...

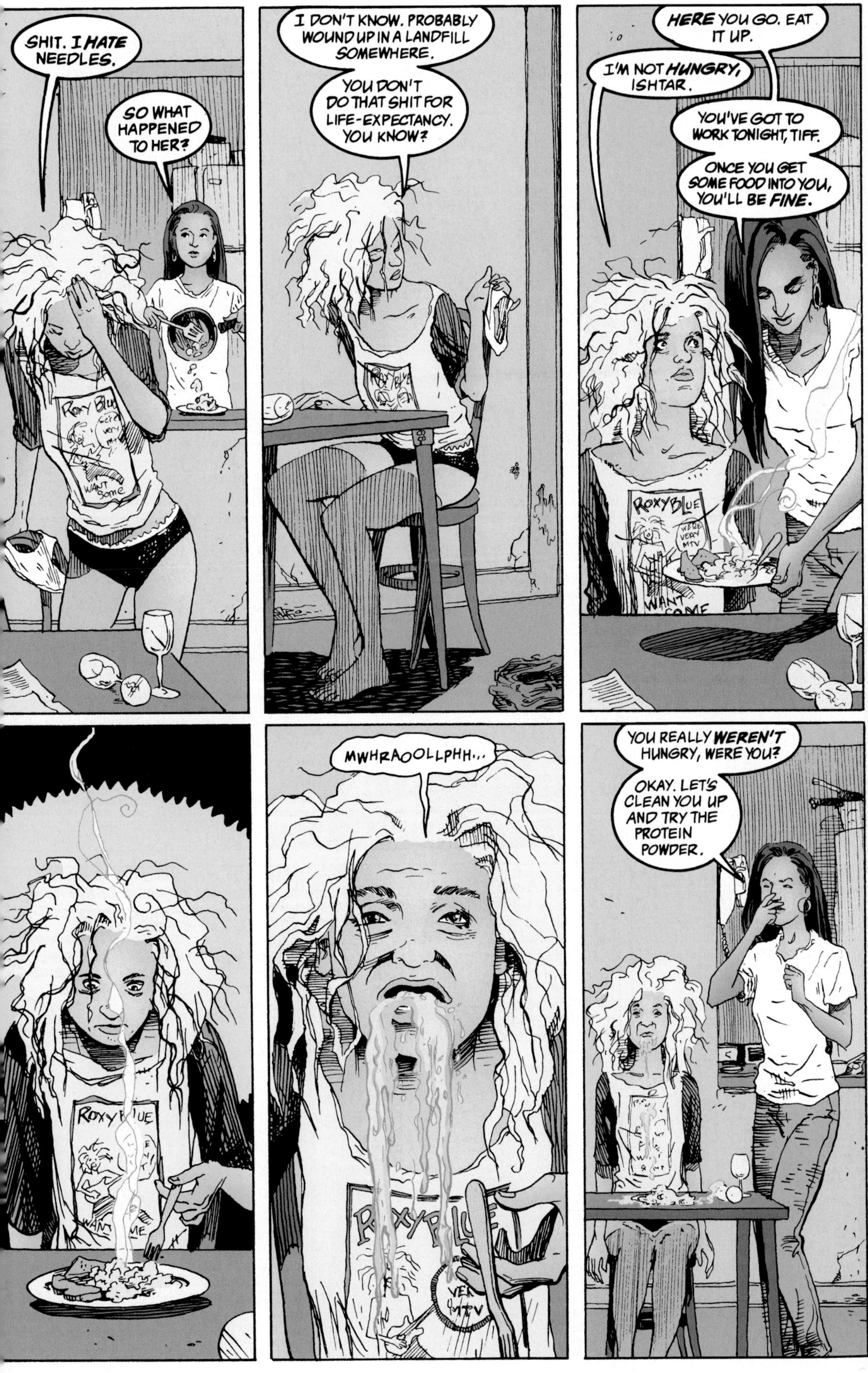
SHIT. I HATE NEEDLES.
SO WHAT HAPPENED TO HER?
I DON'T KNOW. PROBABLY WOUND UP IN A LANDFILL SOMEWHERE.
YOU DON'T DO THAT SHIT FOR LIFE-EXPECTANCY. YOU KNOW?
HERE YOU GO. EAT IT UP.
I'M NOT HUNGRY, ISHTAR.
YOU'VE GOT TO WORK TONIGHT, TIFF.
ONCE YOU GET SOME FOOD INTO YOU, YOU'LL BE FINE.
MWHRAOOLLPHH...
YOU REALLY WEREN'T HUNGRY, WERE YOU?
OKAY. LET'S CLEAN YOU UP AND TRY THE PROTEIN POWDER.

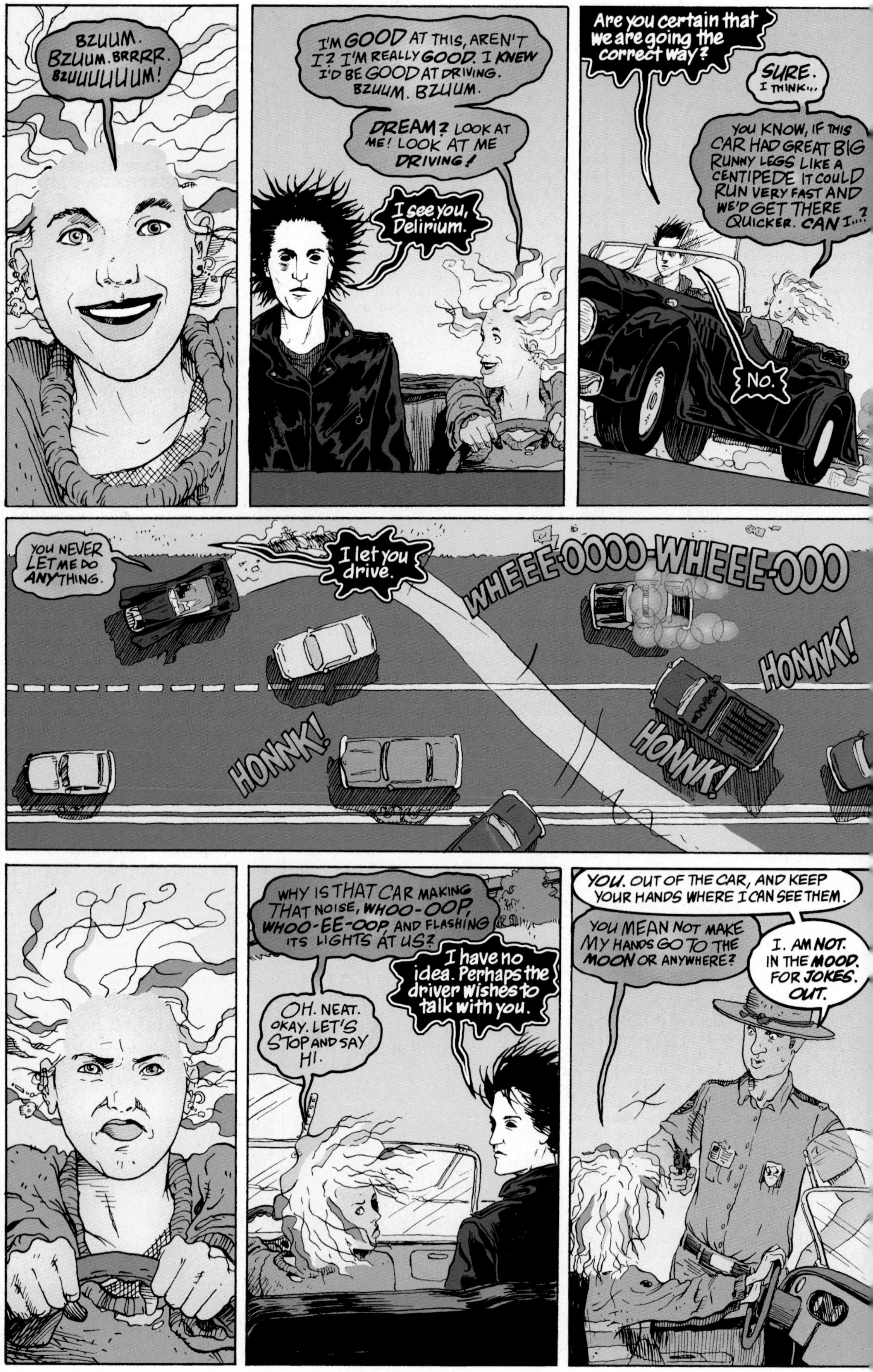
BZUUM. BZUUM. BRRRR. BZUUUUUUM!
I'M GOOD AT THIS, AREN'T I? I'M REALLY GOOD. I KNEW I'D BE GOOD AT DRIVING. BZUUM. BZUUM.
DREAM? LOOK AT ME! LOOK AT ME DRIVING!
I see you, Delirium.
Are you certain that we are going the correct way?
SURE. I THINK...
YOU KNOW, IF THIS CAR HAD GREAT BIG RUNNY LEGS LIKE A CENTIPEDE IT COULD RUN VERY FAST AND WE'D GET THERE QUICKER. CAN I...?
No.
YOU NEVER LET ME DO ANYTHING.
I let you drive.
WHEEE-OOOO-WHEEE-OOO
HONNK!
HONNK!
HONNK!
WHY IS THAT CAR MAKING THAT NOISE, WHOO-OOP, WHOO-EE-OOP AND FLASHING ITS LIGHTS AT US?
I have no idea. Perhaps the driver wishes to talk with you.
OH. NEAT. OKAY. LET'S STOP AND SAY HI.
YOU. OUT OF THE CAR, AND KEEP YOUR HANDS WHERE I CAN SEE THEM.
YOU MEAN NOT MAKE MY HANDS GO TO THE MOON OR ANYWHERE?
I. AM NOT. IN THE MOOD. FOR JOKES. OUT.

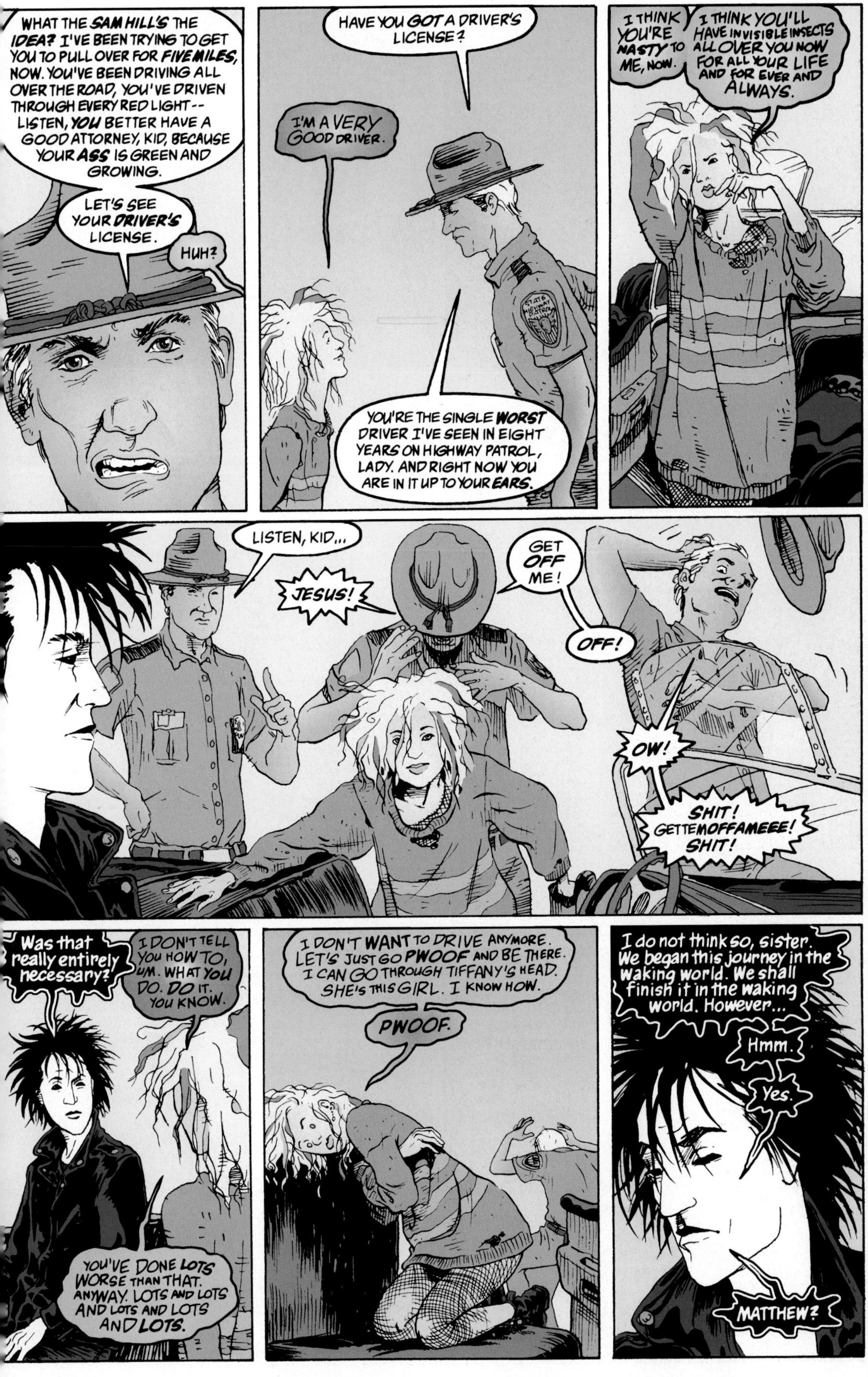
WHAT THE SAM HILL'S THE IDEA? I'VE BEEN TRYING TO GET YOU TO PULL OVER FOR FIVE MILES, NOW. YOU'VE BEEN DRIVING ALL OVER THE ROAD, YOU'VE DRIVEN THROUGH EVERY RED LIGHT-- LISTEN, YOU BETTER HAVE A GOOD ATTORNEY, KID, BECAUSE YOUR ASS IS GREEN AND GROWING.
LET'S SEE YOUR DRIVER'S LICENSE.
HUH?
HAVE YOU GOT A DRIVER'S LICENSE?
I'M A VERY GOOD DRIVER.
YOU'RE THE SINGLE WORST DRIVER I'VE SEEN IN EIGHT YEARS ON HIGHWAY PATROL, LADY. AND RIGHT NOW YOU ARE IN IT UP TO YOUR EARS.
I THINK YOU'RE NASTY TO ME, NOW.
I THINK YOU'LL HAVE INVISIBLE INSECTS ALL OVER YOU NOW FOR ALL YOUR LIFE AND FOR EVER AND ALWAYS.
LISTEN, KID...
JESUS!
GET OFF ME!
OFF!
OW!
SHIT! GETTEMOFFAMEEE! SHIT!
Was that really entirely necessary?
I DON'T TELL YOU HOW TO, UM. WHAT YOU DO. DO IT. YOU KNOW.
YOU'VE DONE LOTS WORSE THAN THAT. ANYWAY. LOTS AND LOTS AND LOTS AND LOTS AND LOTS.
I DON'T WANT TO DRIVE ANYMORE. LET'S JUST GO PWOOF AND BE THERE. I CAN GO THROUGH TIFFANY'S HEAD. SHE'S THIS GIRL. I KNOW HOW.
PWOOF.
I do not think so, sister. We began this journey in the waking world. We shall finish it in the waking world. However...
Hmm.
Yes.
MATTHEW?

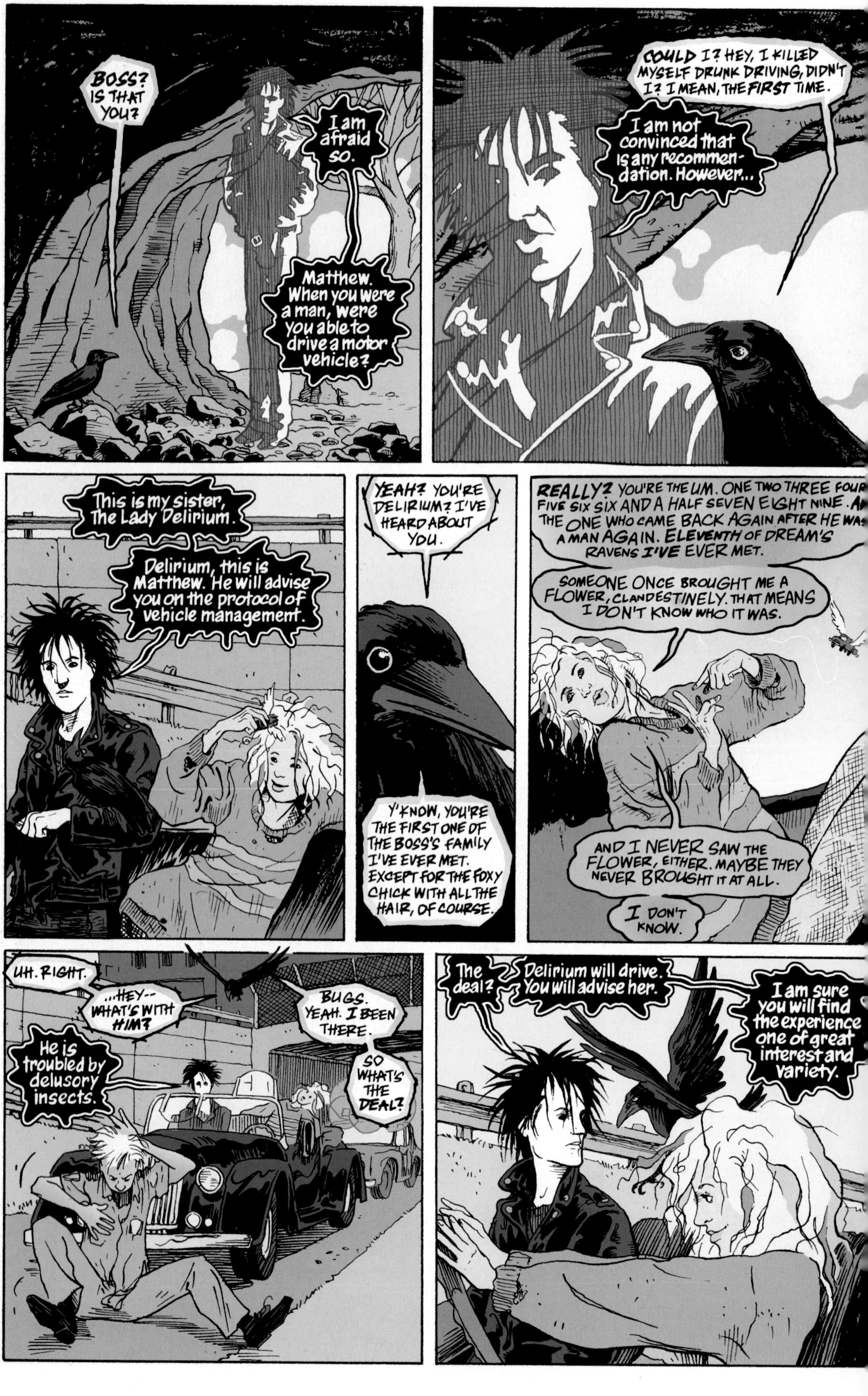
BOSS? IS THAT YOU?
I am afraid so.
Matthew. When you were a man, were you able to drive a motor vehicle?
COULD I? HEY, I KILLED MYSELF DRUNK DRIVING, DIDN'T I? I MEAN, THE FIRST TIME.
I am not convinced that is any recommendation. However...
This is my sister, the Lady Delirium.
Delirium, this is Matthew. He will advise you on the protocol of vehicle management.
YEAH? YOU'RE DELIRIUM? I'VE HEARD ABOUT YOU.
Y'KNOW, YOU'RE THE FIRST ONE OF THE BOSS'S FAMILY I'VE EVER MET. EXCEPT FOR THE FOXY CHICK WITH ALL THE HAIR, OF COURSE.
REALLY? YOU'RE THE UM. ONE TWO THREE FOUR FIVE SIX SIX AND A HALF SEVEN EIGHT NINE. A THE ONE WHO CAME BACK AGAIN AFTER HE WAS A MAN AGAIN. ELEVENTH OF DREAM'S RAVENS I'VE EVER MET.
SOMEONE ONCE BROUGHT ME A FLOWER, CLANDESTINELY. THAT MEANS I DON'T KNOW WHO IT WAS.
AND I NEVER SAW THE FLOWER, EITHER. MAYBE THEY NEVER BROUGHT IT AT ALL.
I DON'T KNOW.
UH. RIGHT.
...HEY-- WHAT'S WITH HIM?
He is troubled by delusory insects.
BUGS. YEAH. I BEEN THERE.
SO WHAT'S THE DEAL?
The deal?
Delirium will drive. You will advise her.
I am sure you will find the experience one of great interest and variety.

HOW'D I LOOK?

MUCH BETTER.

HEY, WHEN YOU'RE *UP*, YOU'RE *UP*, Y'KNOW? WATCH OUT, WORLD, HERE COMES TIFFANY CALHOUN.

≤SNF≥

MADONNA BLONDE AMBITION

WHY'D YOU PICK *ISHTAR*?

WHAT?

AS A NAME? I MEAN, IT WAS A *LOUSY* MOVIE.

IT GOES WAY BACK. WHY'D *YOU* PICK TIFFANY?

YOU *REALLY* WANT TO KNOW? OKAY.

MY MOM HAD A TIFFANY WATCH. IT WAS THE *ONLY* PRETTY THING SHE HAD. SHE KEPT IT IN THIS BOX BY HER BED. IF I WAS *REALLY GOOD* SHE'D LET ME TRY IT ON.

I'D WEAR IT IN FRONT OF A MIRROR. WHEN I WAS LITTLE.

WHEN I LEFT HOME IT WAS THE ONLY THING I TOOK AWAY WITH ME.

SHE GAVE IT TO YOU?

SHIT, NO. ARE YOU *KIDDING*? MY MOM *LOVED* THAT WATCH.

MADONNA BLONDE ITION

WHAT WAS YOUR NAME BEFORE IT WAS TIFFANY CALHOUN?

IT'S A *REALLY* SHITTY NAME. YOU DON'T WANT TO KNOW.

SURE I DO.

ALVA. ALVA ELLEN RASMUSSEN. *YICKY*, HUH?

I WAS FIFTEEN WHEN I LEFT HOME, AND MY MOM SAID, YOU DON'T KNOW SHIT, ALVA. YOU'LL STARVE.

SOMETHING *ELSE* SHE WAS WRONG ABOUT. I MAY NOT KNOW SHIT, BUT I CAN DANCE.

MADONNA BLONDE AMBITION

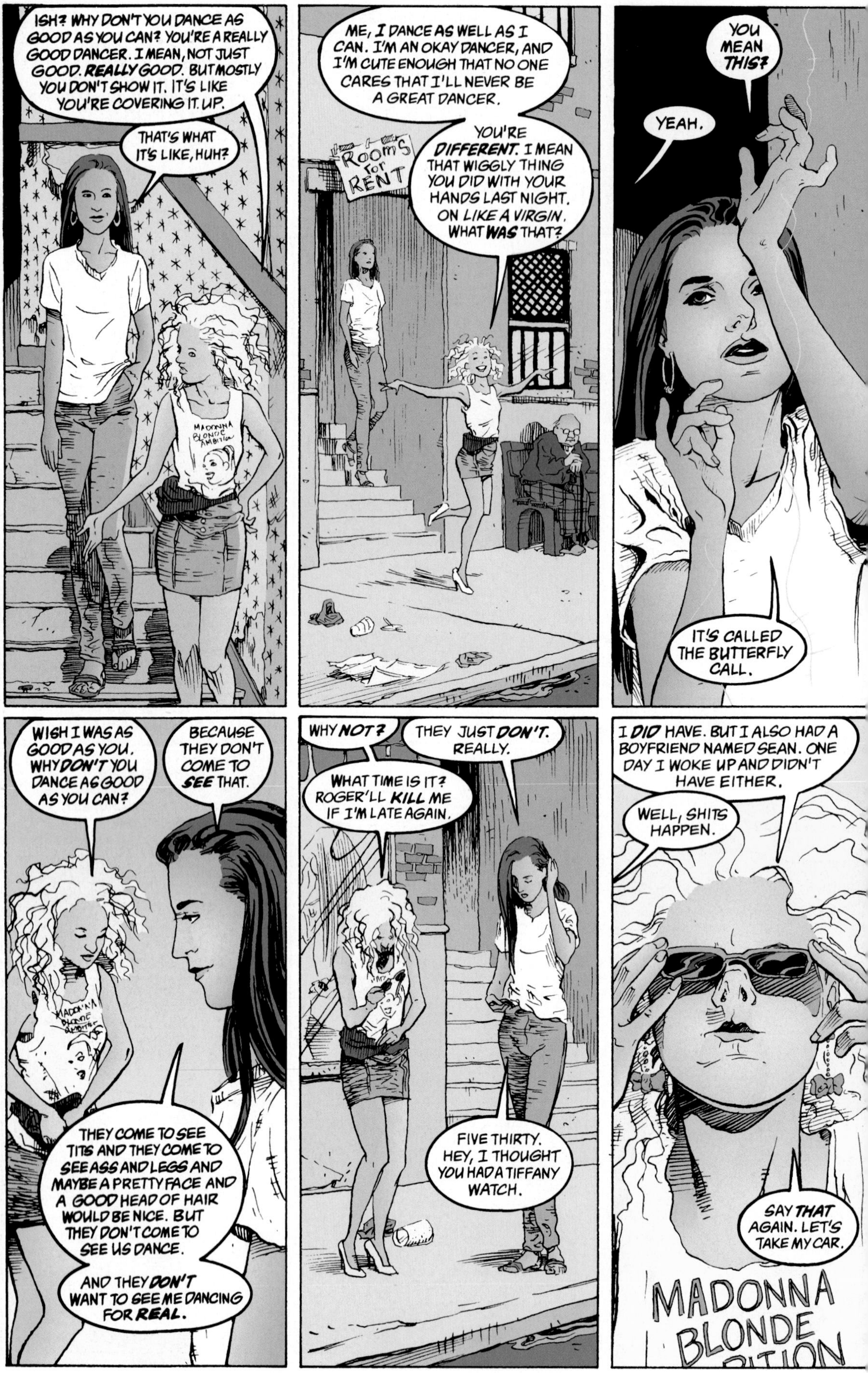
ISH? WHY DON'T YOU DANCE AS GOOD AS YOU CAN? YOU'RE A REALLY GOOD DANCER. I MEAN, NOT JUST GOOD. REALLY GOOD. BUT MOSTLY YOU DON'T SHOW IT. IT'S LIKE YOU'RE COVERING IT UP.
THAT'S WHAT IT'S LIKE, HUH?
MADONNA BLONDE AMBITION
ME, I DANCE AS WELL AS I CAN. I'M AN OKAY DANCER, AND I'M CUTE ENOUGH THAT NO ONE CARES THAT I'LL NEVER BE A GREAT DANCER.
ROOMS for RENT
YOU'RE DIFFERENT. I MEAN THAT WIGGLY THING YOU DID WITH YOUR HANDS LAST NIGHT. ON LIKE A VIRGIN. WHAT WAS THAT?
YOU MEAN THIS?
YEAH.
IT'S CALLED THE BUTTERFLY CALL.
WISH I WAS AS GOOD AS YOU. WHY DON'T YOU DANCE AS GOOD AS YOU CAN?
BECAUSE THEY DON'T COME TO SEE THAT.
THEY COME TO SEE TITS AND THEY COME TO SEE ASS AND LEGS AND MAYBE A PRETTY FACE AND A GOOD HEAD OF HAIR WOULD BE NICE. BUT THEY DON'T COME TO SEE US DANCE.
AND THEY DON'T WANT TO SEE ME DANCING FOR REAL.
WHY NOT?
THEY JUST DON'T. REALLY.
WHAT TIME IS IT? ROGER'LL KILL ME IF I'M LATE AGAIN.
FIVE THIRTY. HEY, I THOUGHT YOU HAD A TIFFANY WATCH.
I DID HAVE. BUT I ALSO HAD A BOYFRIEND NAMED SEAN. ONE DAY I WOKE UP AND DIDN'T HAVE EITHER.
WELL, SHITS HAPPEN.
SAY THAT AGAIN. LET'S TAKE MY CAR.
MADONNA BLONDE

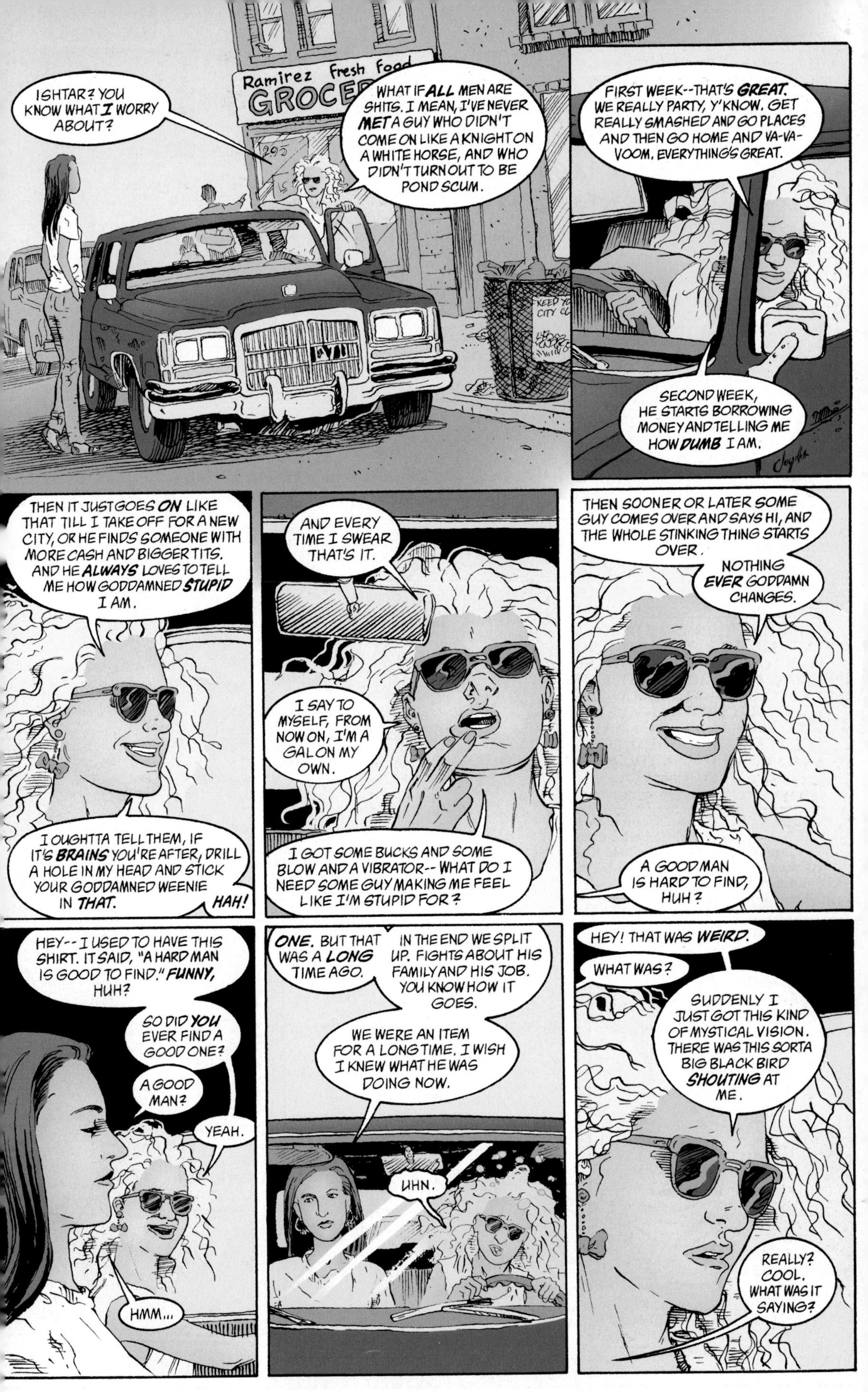
ISHTAR? YOU KNOW WHAT I WORRY ABOUT?
Ramirez Fresh Food GROCER
WHAT IF ALL MEN ARE SHITS. I MEAN, I'VE NEVER MET A GUY WHO DIDN'T COME ON LIKE A KNIGHT ON A WHITE HORSE, AND WHO DIDN'T TURN OUT TO BE POND SCUM.
FIRST WEEK--THAT'S GREAT. WE REALLY PARTY, Y'KNOW. GET REALLY SMASHED AND GO PLACES AND THEN GO HOME AND VA-VA-VOOM. EVERYTHING'S GREAT.
SECOND WEEK, HE STARTS BORROWING MONEY AND TELLING ME HOW DUMB I AM.
THEN IT JUST GOES ON LIKE THAT TILL I TAKE OFF FOR A NEW CITY, OR HE FINDS SOMEONE WITH MORE CASH AND BIGGER TITS. AND HE ALWAYS LOVES TO TELL ME HOW GODDAMNED STUPID I AM.
I OUGHTTA TELL THEM, IF IT'S BRAINS YOU'RE AFTER, DRILL A HOLE IN MY HEAD AND STICK YOUR GODDAMNED WEENIE IN THAT.
HAH!
AND EVERY TIME I SWEAR THAT'S IT.
I SAY TO MYSELF, FROM NOW ON, I'M A GAL ON MY OWN.
I GOT SOME BUCKS AND SOME BLOW AND A VIBRATOR-- WHAT DO I NEED SOME GUY MAKING ME FEEL LIKE I'M STUPID FOR?
THEN SOONER OR LATER SOME GUY COMES OVER AND SAYS HI, AND THE WHOLE STINKING THING STARTS OVER.
NOTHING EVER GODDAMN CHANGES.
A GOOD MAN IS HARD TO FIND, HUH?
HEY-- I USED TO HAVE THIS SHIRT. IT SAID, "A HARD MAN IS GOOD TO FIND." FUNNY, HUH?
SO DID YOU EVER FIND A GOOD ONE?
A GOOD MAN?
YEAH.
HMM...
ONE. BUT THAT WAS A LONG TIME AGO.
IN THE END WE SPLIT UP. FIGHTS ABOUT HIS FAMILY AND HIS JOB. YOU KNOW HOW IT GOES.
WE WERE AN ITEM FOR A LONG TIME. I WISH I KNEW WHAT HE WAS DOING NOW.
UHN.
HEY! THAT WAS WEIRD.
WHAT WAS?
SUDDENLY I JUST GOT THIS KIND OF MYSTICAL VISION. THERE WAS THIS SORTA BIG BLACK BIRD SHOUTING AT ME.
REALLY? COOL. WHAT WAS IT SAYING?

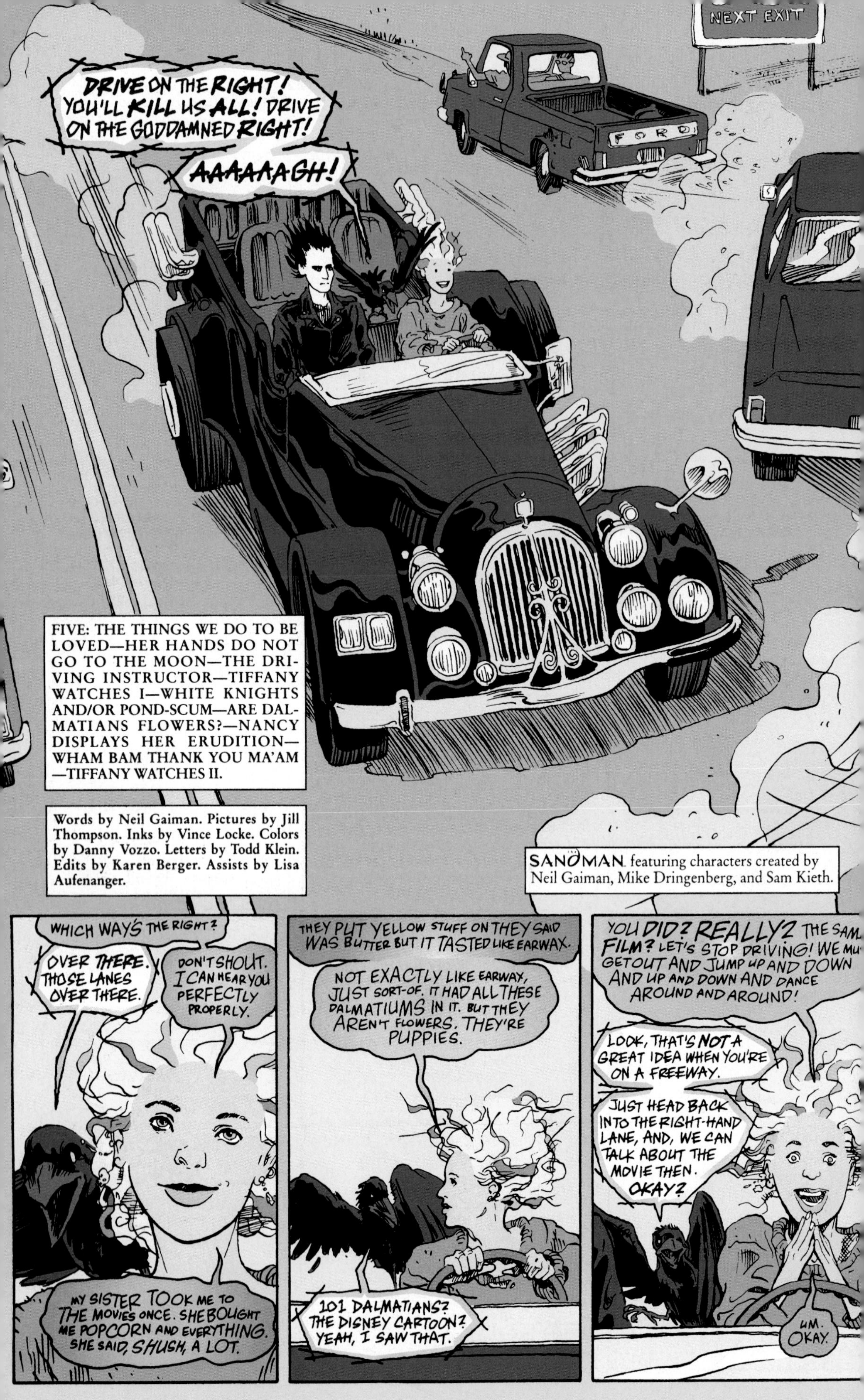

NEXT EXIT
DRIVE ON THE RIGHT! YOU'LL KILL US ALL! DRIVE ON THE GODDAMNED RIGHT!
AAAAAAGH!
FORD
FIVE: THE THINGS WE DO TO BE LOVED—HER HANDS DO NOT GO TO THE MOON—THE DRIVING INSTRUCTOR—TIFFANY WATCHES I—WHITE KNIGHTS AND/OR POND-SCUM—ARE DALMATIANS FLOWERS?—NANCY DISPLAYS HER ERUDITION—WHAM BAM THANK YOU MA'AM—TIFFANY WATCHES II.
Words by Neil Gaiman. Pictures by Jill Thompson. Inks by Vince Locke. Colors by Danny Vozzo. Letters by Todd Klein. Edits by Karen Berger. Assists by Lisa Aufenanger.
SANDMAN featuring characters created by Neil Gaiman, Mike Dringenberg, and Sam Kieth.
WHICH WAY'S THE RIGHT?
OVER THERE. THOSE LANES OVER THERE.
DON'T SHOUT. I CAN HEAR YOU PERFECTLY PROPERLY.
MY SISTER TOOK ME TO THE MOVIES ONCE. SHE BOUGHT ME POPCORN AND EVERYTHING. SHE SAID, SHUSH, A LOT.
THEY PUT YELLOW STUFF ON THEY SAID WAS BUTTER BUT IT TASTED LIKE EARWAX.
NOT EXACTLY LIKE EARWAX, JUST SORT-OF. IT HAD ALL THESE DALMATIUMS IN IT. BUT THEY AREN'T FLOWERS. THEY'RE PUPPIES.
101 DALMATIANS? THE DISNEY CARTOON? YEAH, I SAW THAT.
YOU DID? REALLY? THE SAM FILM? LET'S STOP DRIVING! WE MU GET OUT AND JUMP UP AND DOWN AND UP AND DOWN AND DANCE AROUND AND AROUND!
LOOK, THAT'S NOT A GREAT IDEA WHEN YOU'RE ON A FREEWAY.
JUST HEAD BACK INTO THE RIGHT-HAND LANE, AND, WE CAN TALK ABOUT THE MOVIE THEN. OKAY?
UM. OKAY.

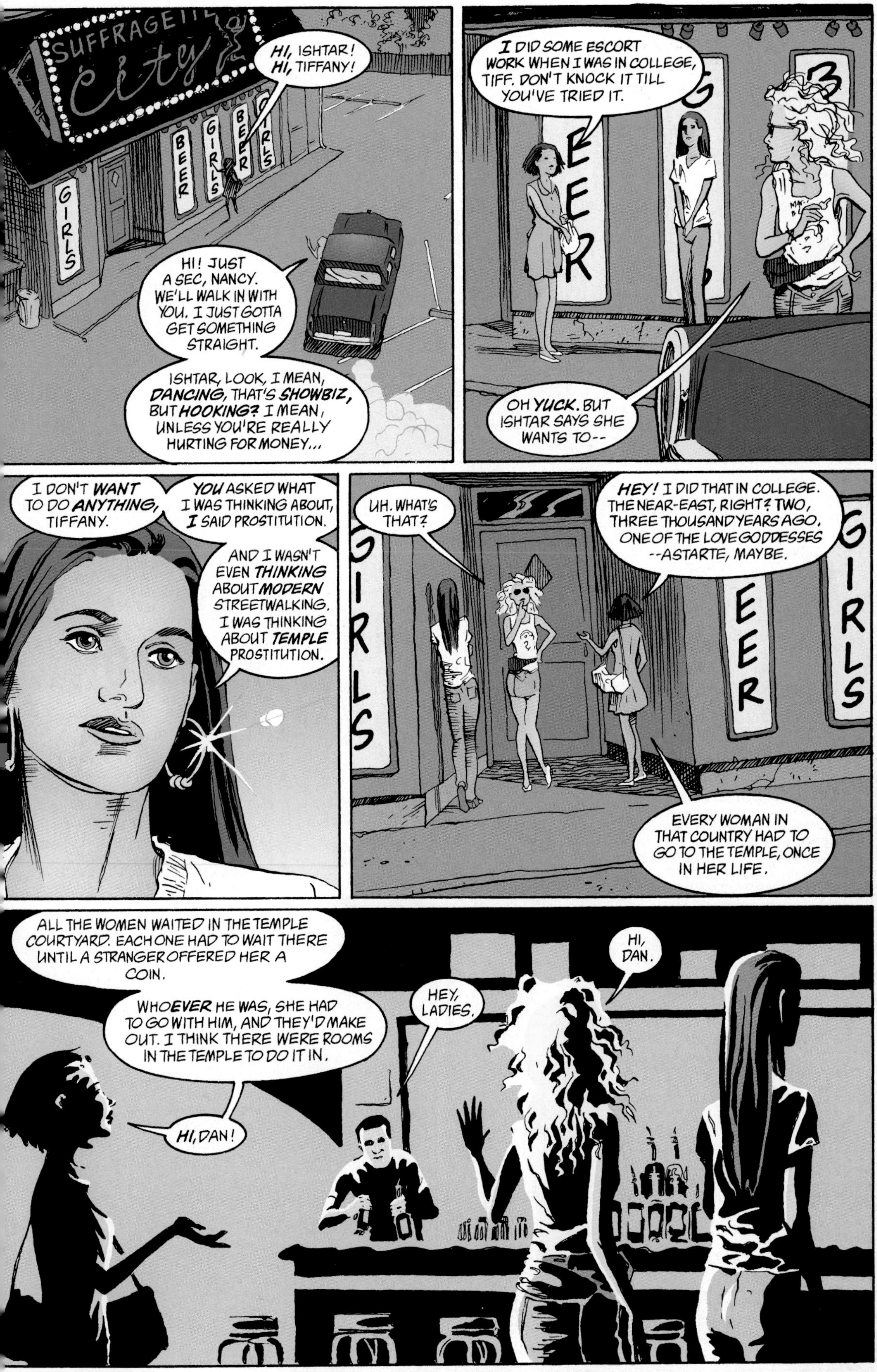
SUFFRAGETTE
city
GIRLS
BEER
GIRLS
BEER
GIRLS
HI, ISHTAR! HI, TIFFANY!
HI! JUST A SEC, NANCY. WE'LL WALK IN WITH YOU. I JUST GOTTA GET SOMETHING STRAIGHT.
ISHTAR, LOOK, I MEAN, DANCING, THAT'S SHOWBIZ, BUT HOOKING? I MEAN, UNLESS YOU'RE REALLY HURTING FOR MONEY...
I DID SOME ESCORT WORK WHEN I WAS IN COLLEGE, TIFF. DON'T KNOCK IT TILL YOU'VE TRIED IT.
OH YUCK. BUT ISHTAR SAYS SHE WANTS TO--
I DON'T WANT TO DO ANYTHING, TIFFANY.
YOU ASKED WHAT I WAS THINKING ABOUT, I SAID PROSTITUTION.
AND I WASN'T EVEN THINKING ABOUT MODERN STREETWALKING. I WAS THINKING ABOUT TEMPLE PROSTITUTION.
UH. WHAT'S THAT?
HEY! I DID THAT IN COLLEGE. THE NEAR-EAST, RIGHT? TWO, THREE THOUSAND YEARS AGO, ONE OF THE LOVE GODDESSES --ASTARTE, MAYBE.
EVERY WOMAN IN THAT COUNTRY HAD TO GO TO THE TEMPLE, ONCE IN HER LIFE.
ALL THE WOMEN WAITED IN THE TEMPLE COURTYARD. EACH ONE HAD TO WAIT THERE UNTIL A STRANGER OFFERED HER A COIN.
WHOEVER HE WAS, SHE HAD TO GO WITH HIM, AND THEY'D MAKE OUT. I THINK THERE WERE ROOMS IN THE TEMPLE TO DO IT IN.
HI, DAN!
HEY, LADIES.
HI, DAN.

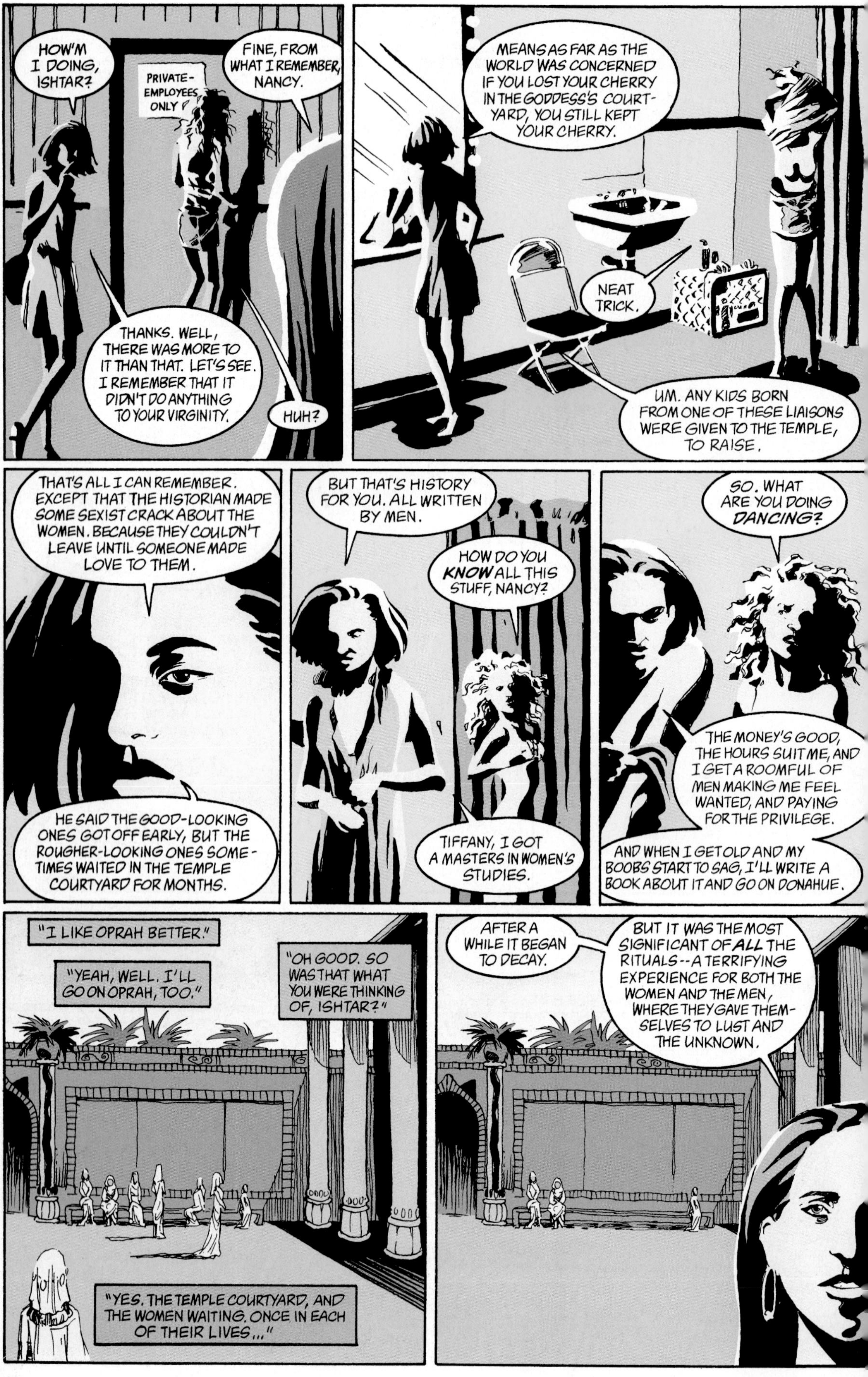
HOW'M I DOING, ISHTAR?
PRIVATE-EMPLOYEES ONLY
FINE, FROM WHAT I REMEMBER, NANCY.
THANKS. WELL, THERE WAS MORE TO IT THAN THAT. LET'S SEE. I REMEMBER THAT IT DIDN'T DO ANYTHING TO YOUR VIRGINITY.
HUH?
MEANS AS FAR AS THE WORLD WAS CONCERNED IF YOU LOST YOUR CHERRY IN THE GODDESS'S COURTYARD, YOU STILL KEPT YOUR CHERRY.
NEAT TRICK.
UM. ANY KIDS BORN FROM ONE OF THESE LIAISONS WERE GIVEN TO THE TEMPLE, TO RAISE.
THAT'S ALL I CAN REMEMBER. EXCEPT THAT THE HISTORIAN MADE SOME SEXIST CRACK ABOUT THE WOMEN. BECAUSE THEY COULDN'T LEAVE UNTIL SOMEONE MADE LOVE TO THEM.
HE SAID THE GOOD-LOOKING ONES GOT OFF EARLY, BUT THE ROUGHER-LOOKING ONES SOMETIMES WAITED IN THE TEMPLE COURTYARD FOR MONTHS.
BUT THAT'S HISTORY FOR YOU. ALL WRITTEN BY MEN.
HOW DO YOU KNOW ALL THIS STUFF, NANCY?
TIFFANY, I GOT A MASTERS IN WOMEN'S STUDIES.
SO. WHAT ARE YOU DOING DANCING?
THE MONEY'S GOOD, THE HOURS SUIT ME, AND I GET A ROOMFUL OF MEN MAKING ME FEEL WANTED, AND PAYING FOR THE PRIVILEGE.
AND WHEN I GET OLD AND MY BOOBS START TO SAG, I'LL WRITE A BOOK ABOUT IT AND GO ON DONAHUE.
"I LIKE OPRAH BETTER."
"YEAH, WELL. I'LL GO ON OPRAH, TOO."
"OH GOOD. SO WAS THAT WHAT YOU WERE THINKING OF, ISHTAR?"
"YES. THE TEMPLE COURTYARD, AND THE WOMEN WAITING. ONCE IN EACH OF THEIR LIVES..."
AFTER A WHILE IT BEGAN TO DECAY.
BUT IT WAS THE MOST SIGNIFICANT OF ALL THE RITUALS--A TERRIFYING EXPERIENCE FOR BOTH THE WOMEN AND THE MEN, WHERE THEY GAVE THEMSELVES TO LUST AND THE UNKNOWN.

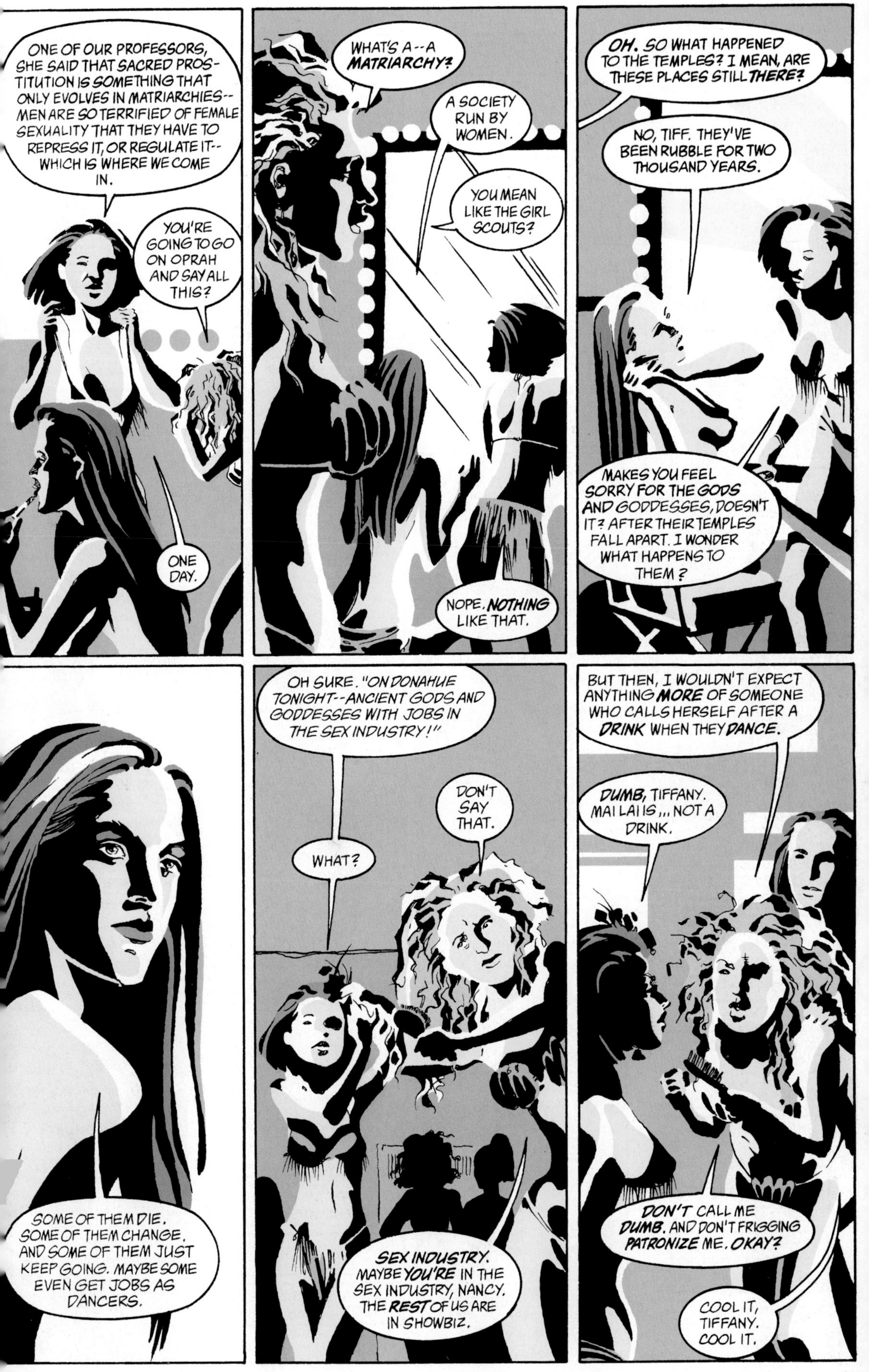
ONE OF OUR PROFESSORS, SHE SAID THAT SACRED PROSTITUTION IS SOMETHING THAT ONLY EVOLVES IN MATRIARCHIES-- MEN ARE SO TERRIFIED OF FEMALE SEXUALITY THAT THEY HAVE TO REPRESS IT, OR REGULATE IT-- WHICH IS WHERE WE COME IN.
YOU'RE GOING TO GO ON OPRAH AND SAY ALL THIS?
ONE DAY.
WHAT'S A--A MATRIARCHY?
A SOCIETY RUN BY WOMEN.
YOU MEAN LIKE THE GIRL SCOUTS?
NOPE, NOTHING LIKE THAT.
OH. SO WHAT HAPPENED TO THE TEMPLES? I MEAN, ARE THESE PLACES STILL THERE?
NO, TIFF. THEY'VE BEEN RUBBLE FOR TWO THOUSAND YEARS.
MAKES YOU FEEL SORRY FOR THE GODS AND GODDESSES, DOESN'T IT? AFTER THEIR TEMPLES FALL APART. I WONDER WHAT HAPPENS TO THEM?
SOME OF THEM DIE. SOME OF THEM CHANGE. AND SOME OF THEM JUST KEEP GOING. MAYBE SOME EVEN GET JOBS AS DANCERS.
OH SURE. "ON DONAHUE TONIGHT--ANCIENT GODS AND GODDESSES WITH JOBS IN THE SEX INDUSTRY!"
DON'T SAY THAT.
WHAT?
SEX INDUSTRY. MAYBE YOU'RE IN THE SEX INDUSTRY, NANCY. THE REST OF US ARE IN SHOWBIZ.
BUT THEN, I WOULDN'T EXPECT ANYTHING MORE OF SOMEONE WHO CALLS HERSELF AFTER A DRINK WHEN THEY DANCE.
DUMB, TIFFANY. MAI LAI IS,,, NOT A DRINK.
DON'T CALL ME DUMB. AND DON'T FRIGGING PATRONIZE ME. OKAY?
COOL IT, TIFFANY. COOL IT.

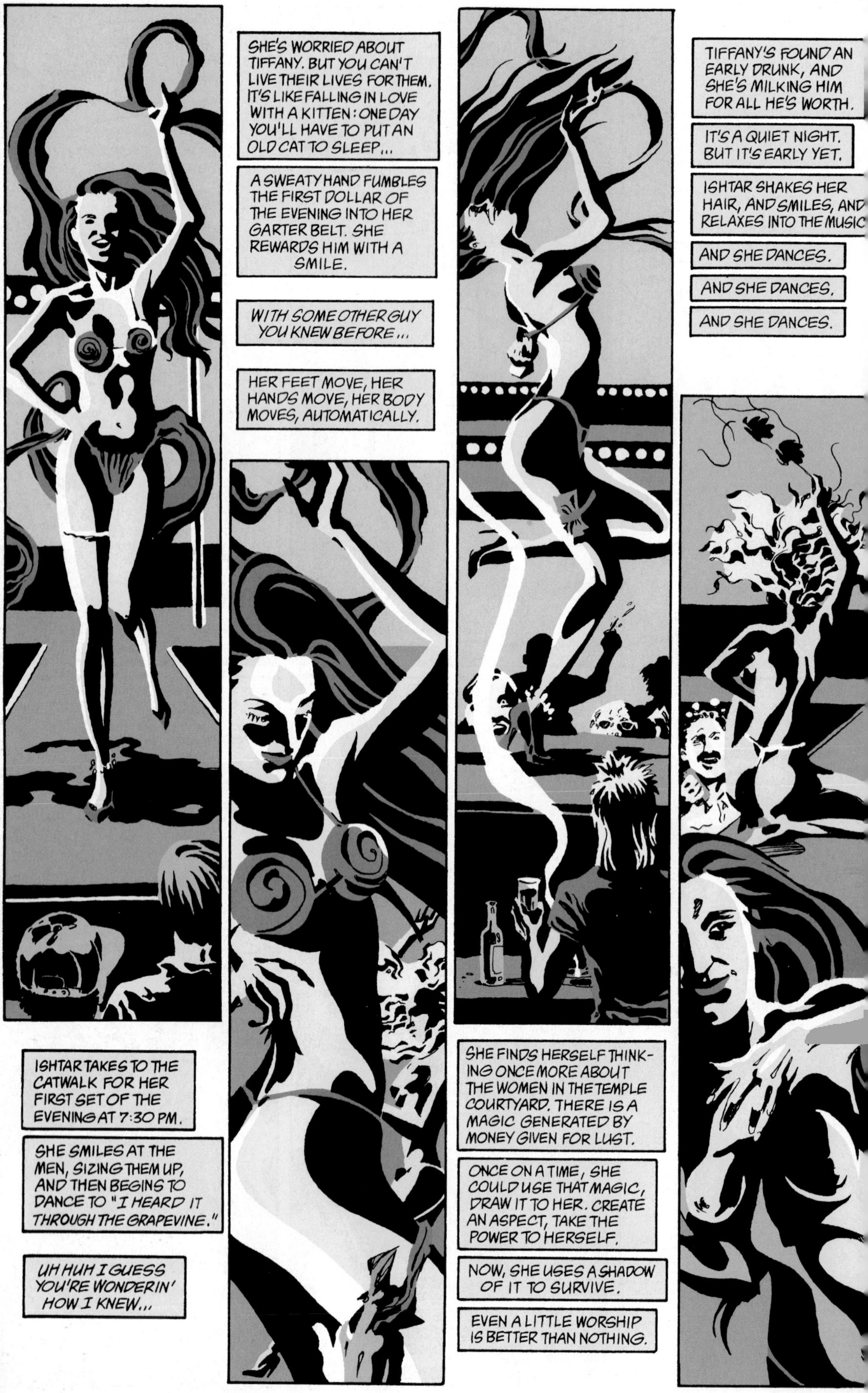

SHE'S WORRIED ABOUT TIFFANY. BUT YOU CAN'T LIVE THEIR LIVES FOR THEM. IT'S LIKE FALLING IN LOVE WITH A KITTEN: ONE DAY YOU'LL HAVE TO PUT AN OLD CAT TO SLEEP...
A SWEATY HAND FUMBLES THE FIRST DOLLAR OF THE EVENING INTO HER GARTER BELT. SHE REWARDS HIM WITH A SMILE.
WITH SOME OTHER GUY YOU KNEW BEFORE...
HER FEET MOVE, HER HANDS MOVE, HER BODY MOVES, AUTOMATICALLY.
ISHTAR TAKES TO THE CATWALK FOR HER FIRST SET OF THE EVENING AT 7:30 PM.
SHE SMILES AT THE MEN, SIZING THEM UP, AND THEN BEGINS TO DANCE TO "I HEARD IT THROUGH THE GRAPEVINE."
UH HUH I GUESS YOU'RE WONDERIN' HOW I KNEW...
SHE FINDS HERSELF THINKING ONCE MORE ABOUT THE WOMEN IN THE TEMPLE COURTYARD. THERE IS A MAGIC GENERATED BY MONEY GIVEN FOR LUST.
ONCE ON A TIME, SHE COULD USE THAT MAGIC, DRAW IT TO HER. CREATE AN ASPECT, TAKE THE POWER TO HERSELF.
NOW, SHE USES A SHADOW OF IT TO SURVIVE.
EVEN A LITTLE WORSHIP IS BETTER THAN NOTHING.
TIFFANY'S FOUND AN EARLY DRUNK, AND SHE'S MILKING HIM FOR ALL HE'S WORTH.
IT'S A QUIET NIGHT. BUT IT'S EARLY YET.
ISHTAR SHAKES HER HAIR, AND SMILES, AND RELAXES INTO THE MUSIC
AND SHE DANCES.
AND SHE DANCES.
AND SHE DANCES.

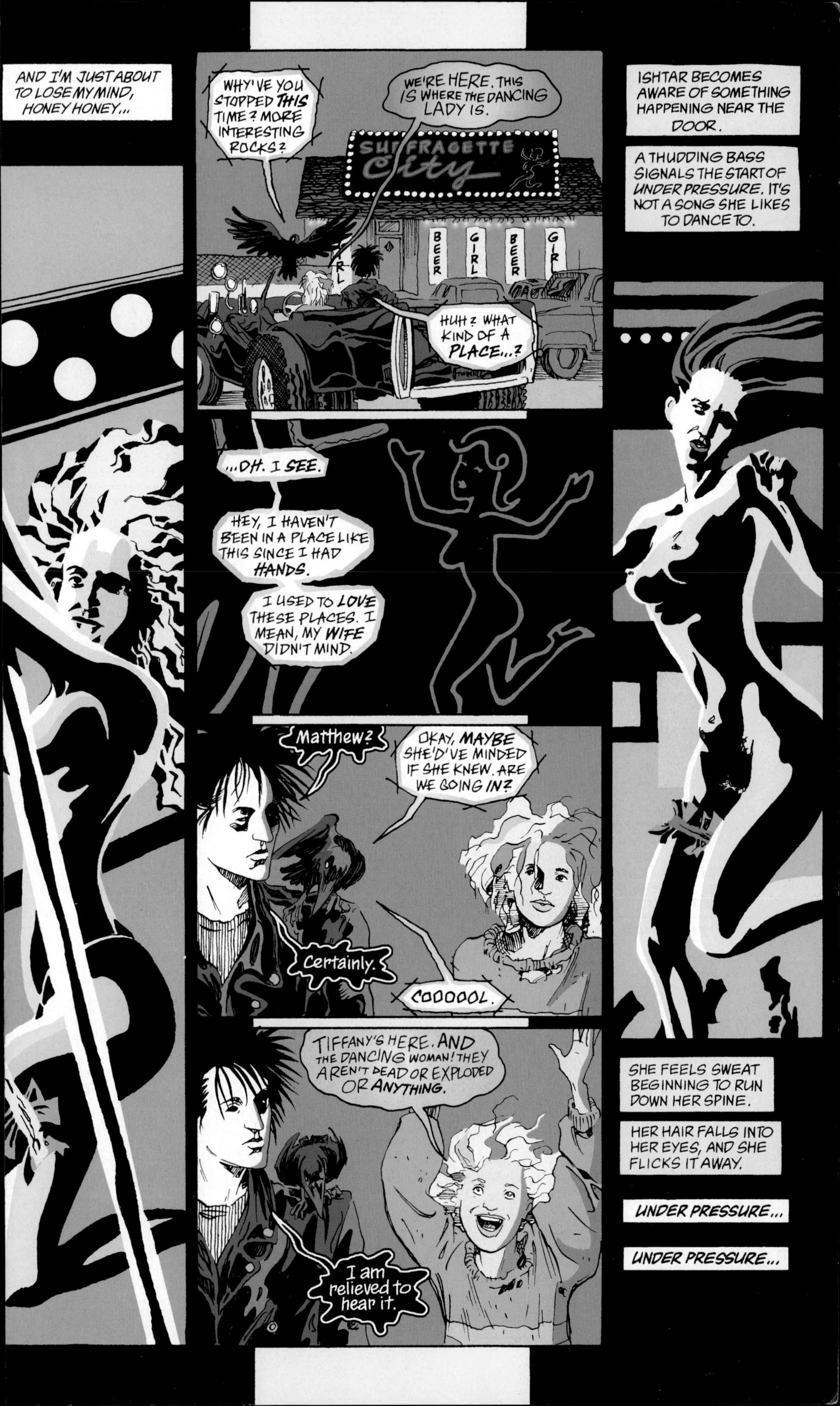

AND I'M JUST ABOUT TO LOSE MY MIND, HONEY HONEY...
WHY'VE YOU STOPPED THIS TIME? MORE INTERESTING ROCKS?
WE'RE HERE. THIS IS WHERE THE DANCING LADY IS.
SUFFRAGETTE City
BEER
GIRL
BEER
HUH? WHAT KIND OF A PLACE...?
ISHTAR BECOMES AWARE OF SOMETHING HAPPENING NEAR THE DOOR.
A THUDDING BASS SIGNALS THE START OF UNDER PRESSURE. IT'S NOT A SONG SHE LIKES TO DANCE TO.
...OH. I SEE.
HEY, I HAVEN'T BEEN IN A PLACE LIKE THIS SINCE I HAD HANDS.
I USED TO LOVE THESE PLACES. I MEAN, MY WIFE DIDN'T MIND.
Matthew?
OKAY, MAYBE SHE'D'VE MINDED IF SHE KNEW. ARE WE GOING IN?
Certainly.
COOOOOL.
TIFFANY'S HERE. AND THE DANCING WOMAN! THEY AREN'T DEAD OR EXPLODED OR ANYTHING.
I am relieved to hear it.
SHE FEELS SWEAT BEGINNING TO RUN DOWN HER SPINE.
HER HAIR FALLS INTO HER EYES, AND SHE FLICKS IT AWAY.
UNDER PRESSURE...
UNDER PRESSURE...

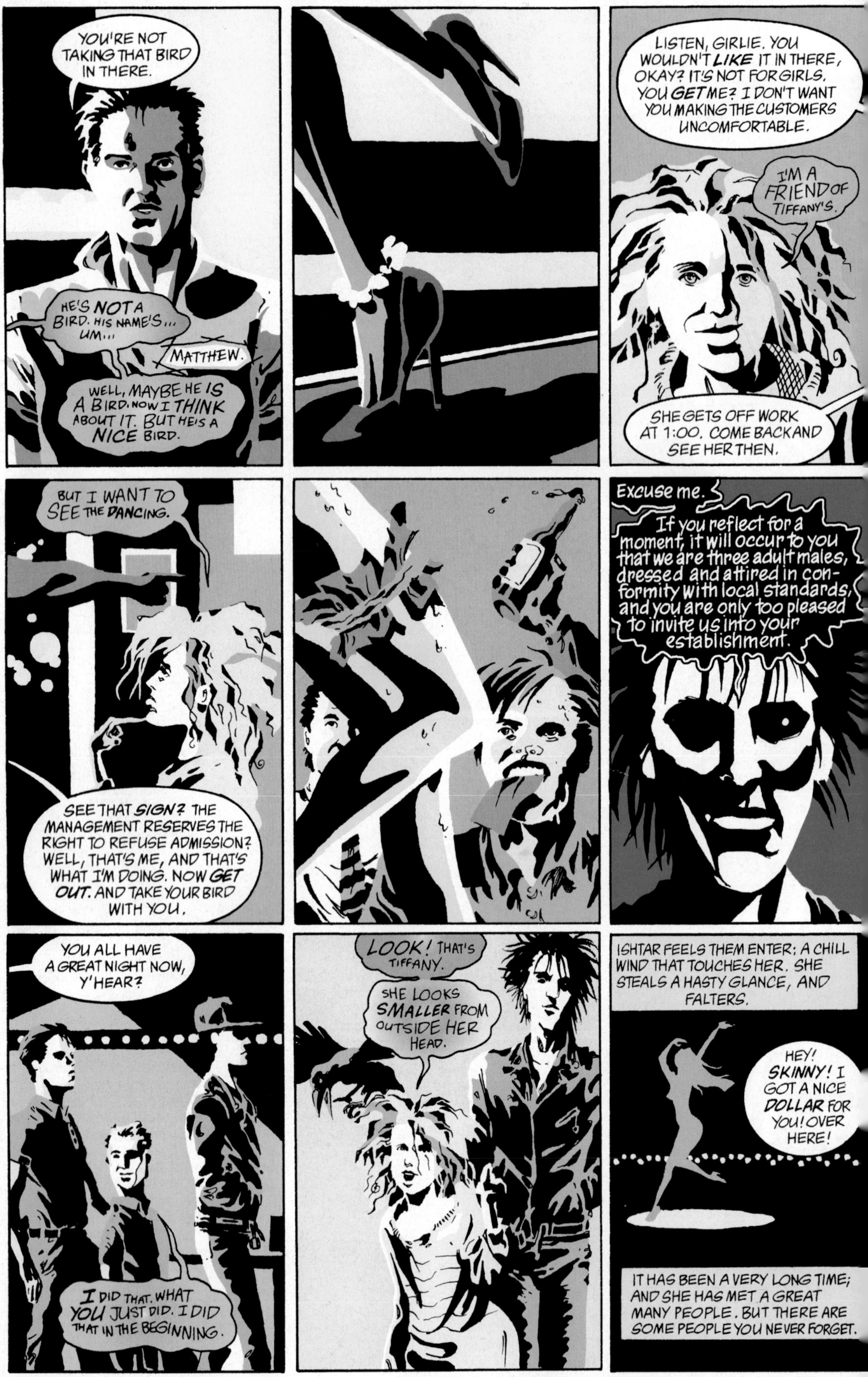

YOU'RE NOT TAKING THAT BIRD IN THERE.
HE'S NOT A BIRD. HIS NAME'S... UM...
MATTHEW.
WELL, MAYBE HE IS A BIRD. NOW I THINK ABOUT IT. BUT HE'S A NICE BIRD.
LISTEN, GIRLIE. YOU WOULDN'T LIKE IT IN THERE, OKAY? IT'S NOT FOR GIRLS. YOU GET ME? I DON'T WANT YOU MAKING THE CUSTOMERS UNCOMFORTABLE.
I'M A FRIEND OF TIFFANY'S.
SHE GETS OFF WORK AT 1:00. COME BACK AND SEE HER THEN.
BUT I WANT TO SEE THE DANCING.
SEE THAT SIGN? THE MANAGEMENT RESERVES THE RIGHT TO REFUSE ADMISSION? WELL, THAT'S ME, AND THAT'S WHAT I'M DOING. NOW GET OUT. AND TAKE YOUR BIRD WITH YOU.
Excuse me.
If you reflect for a moment, it will occur to you that we are three adult males, dressed and attired in conformity with local standards, and you are only too pleased to invite us into your establishment.
YOU ALL HAVE A GREAT NIGHT NOW, Y'HEAR?
I DID THAT. WHAT YOU JUST DID. I DID THAT IN THE BEGINNING.
LOOK! THAT'S TIFFANY.
SHE LOOKS SMALLER FROM OUTSIDE HER HEAD.
ISHTAR FEELS THEM ENTER: A CHILL WIND THAT TOUCHES HER. SHE STEALS A HASTY GLANCE, AND FALTERS.
HEY! SKINNY! I GOT A NICE DOLLAR FOR YOU! OVER HERE!
IT HAS BEEN A VERY LONG TIME; AND SHE HAS MET A GREAT MANY PEOPLE. BUT THERE ARE SOME PEOPLE YOU NEVER FORGET.

HEY!

WHEREYAGOIN'?

OW!

ISHTAR? WHAT THE BLAZES DO YOU THINK YOU'RE DOING? YOU CAN'T JUST RUN OFF...

OUT OF MY WAY, ROGER.

PRIVATE— EMPLOYEES ONLY

ISHTAR? HEY, AREN'T YOU MEANT TO BE ON NOW?

YOU LOOK LIKE YOU'VE SEEN A GHOST.

YOU OKAY?

HEY, BUD. YOU CAN'T GO IN THERE.

PRIVATE— EMPLOYEES ONLY

HEY, WAS IT YOU THAT UPSET ISHTAR LIKE THAT? 'CUZ I'M TELLING YOU...

NO. You are not telling me anything. You will, however, remove your hand from my arm.

I will talk to the lady Ishtar, and I will talk to her in private. Now. Do you understand me?

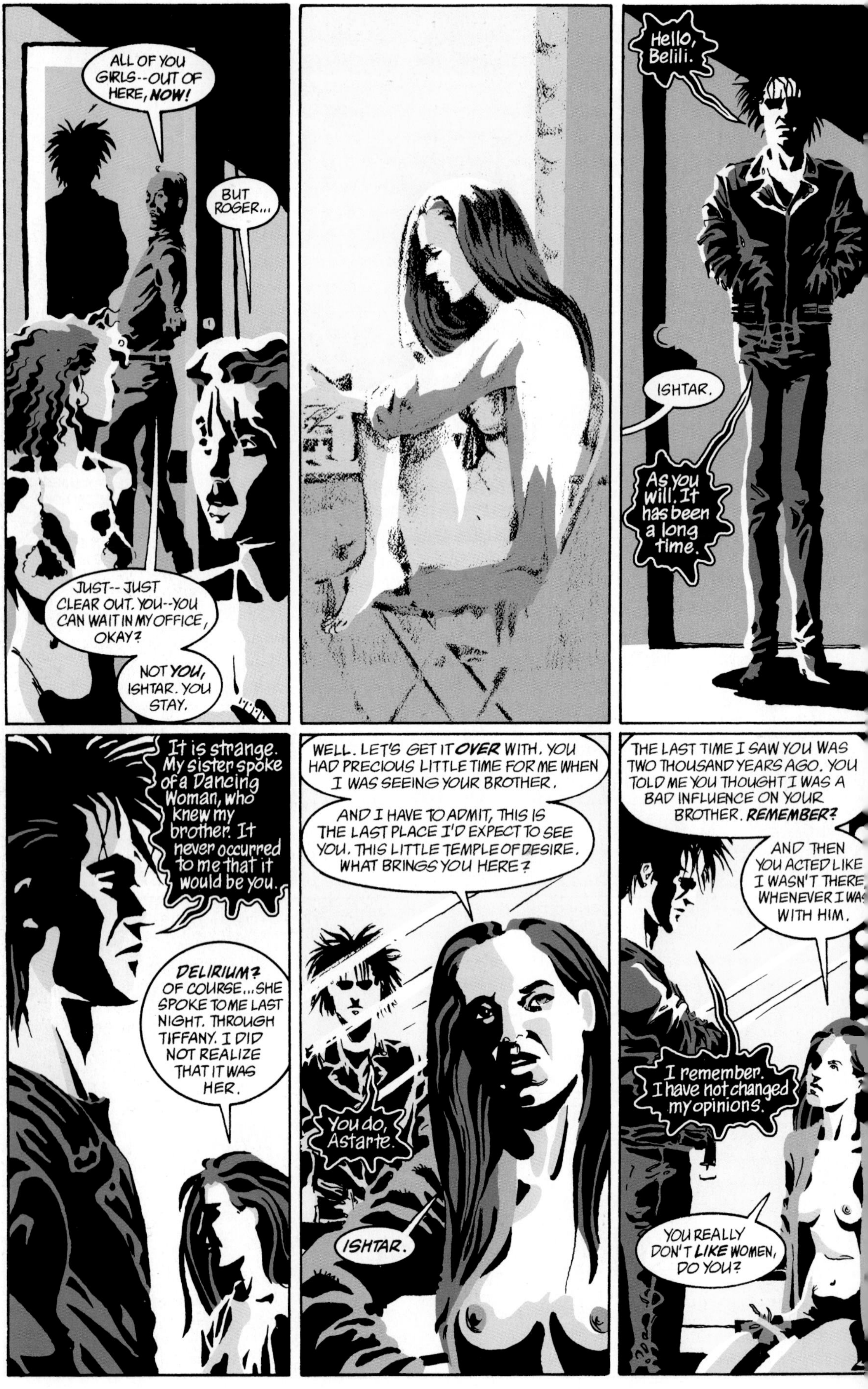
ALL OF YOU GIRLS--OUT OF HERE, **NOW!**
BUT ROGER...
JUST-- JUST CLEAR OUT. YOU--YOU CAN WAIT IN MY OFFICE, OKAY?
NOT **YOU**, ISHTAR. YOU STAY.
Hello, Belili.
ISHTAR.
As you will. It has been a long time.
It is strange. My sister spoke of a Dancing Woman, who knew my brother. It never occurred to me that it would be you.
DELIRIUM? OF COURSE...SHE SPOKE TO ME LAST NIGHT. THROUGH TIFFANY. I DID NOT REALIZE THAT IT WAS HER.
WELL. LET'S GET IT **OVER** WITH. YOU HAD PRECIOUS LITTLE TIME FOR ME WHEN I WAS SEEING YOUR BROTHER.
AND I HAVE TO ADMIT, THIS IS THE LAST PLACE I'D EXPECT TO SEE YOU. THIS LITTLE TEMPLE OF DESIRE. WHAT BRINGS YOU HERE?
You do, Astarte.
ISHTAR.
THE LAST TIME I SAW YOU WAS TWO THOUSAND YEARS AGO. YOU TOLD ME YOU THOUGHT I WAS A BAD INFLUENCE ON YOUR BROTHER. **REMEMBER?**
AND THEN YOU ACTED LIKE I WASN'T THERE WHENEVER I WAS WITH HIM.
I remember. I have not changed my opinions.
YOU REALLY DON'T **LIKE** WOMEN, DO YOU?

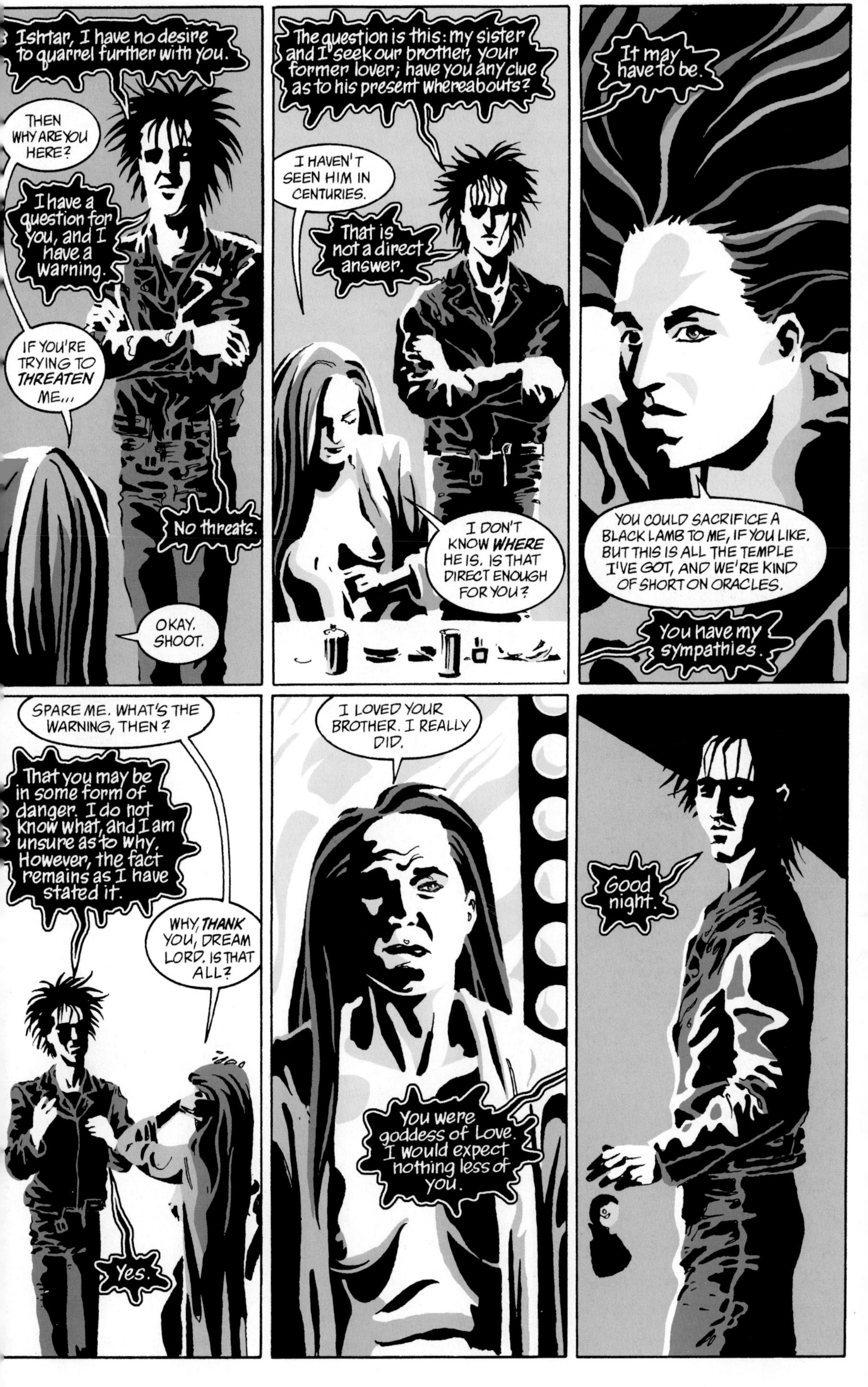

Ishtar, I have no desire to quarrel further with you.
THEN WHY ARE YOU HERE?
I have a question for you, and I have a warning.
IF YOU'RE TRYING TO THREATEN ME...
No threats.
OKAY. SHOOT.
The question is this: my sister and I seek our brother, your former lover; have you any clue as to his present whereabouts?
I HAVEN'T SEEN HIM IN CENTURIES.
That is not a direct answer.
I DON'T KNOW WHERE HE IS. IS THAT DIRECT ENOUGH FOR YOU?
It may have to be.
YOU COULD SACRIFICE A BLACK LAMB TO ME, IF YOU LIKE. BUT THIS IS ALL THE TEMPLE I'VE GOT, AND WE'RE KIND OF SHORT ON ORACLES.
You have my sympathies.
SPARE ME. WHAT'S THE WARNING, THEN?
That you may be in some form of danger. I do not know what, and I am unsure as to why. However, the fact remains as I have stated it.
WHY, THANK YOU, DREAM LORD. IS THAT ALL?
Yes.
I LOVED YOUR BROTHER. I REALLY DID.
You were goddess of Love. I would expect nothing less of you.
Good night.

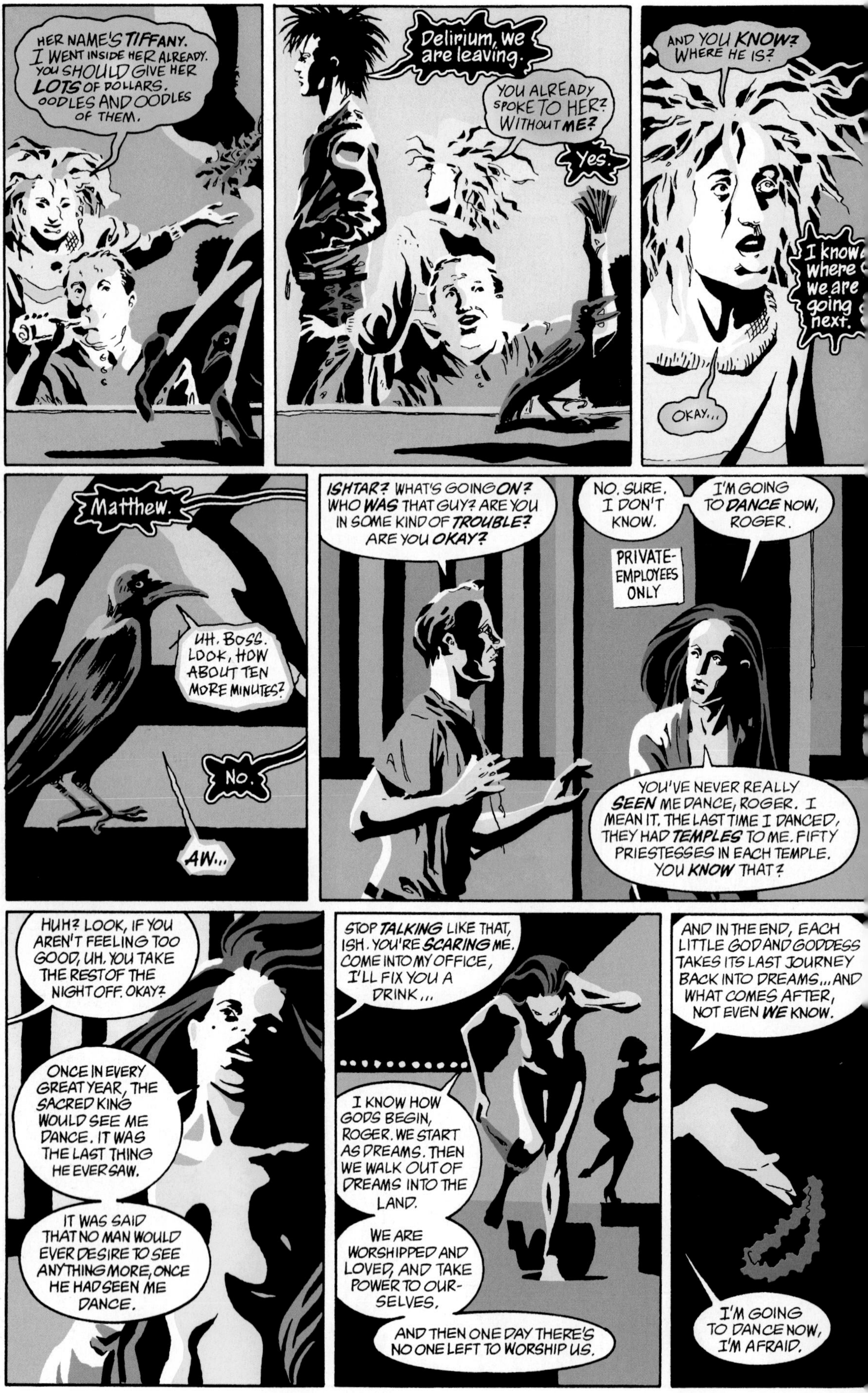
HER NAME'S TIFFANY. I WENT INSIDE HER ALREADY. YOU SHOULD GIVE HER LOTS OF DOLLARS. OODLES AND OODLES OF THEM.
Delirium, we are leaving.
YOU ALREADY SPOKE TO HER? WITHOUT ME?
Yes.
AND YOU KNOW? WHERE HE IS?
I know where we are going next.
OKAY...
Matthew.
UH. BOSS. LOOK, HOW ABOUT TEN MORE MINUTES?
No.
AW...
ISHTAR? WHAT'S GOING ON? WHO WAS THAT GUY? ARE YOU IN SOME KIND OF TROUBLE? ARE YOU OKAY?
NO. SURE. I DON'T KNOW.
I'M GOING TO DANCE NOW, ROGER.
PRIVATE-EMPLOYEES ONLY
YOU'VE NEVER REALLY SEEN ME DANCE, ROGER. I MEAN IT. THE LAST TIME I DANCED, THEY HAD TEMPLES TO ME. FIFTY PRIESTESSES IN EACH TEMPLE. YOU KNOW THAT?
HUH? LOOK, IF YOU AREN'T FEELING TOO GOOD, UH. YOU TAKE THE REST OF THE NIGHT OFF. OKAY?
ONCE IN EVERY GREAT YEAR, THE SACRED KING WOULD SEE ME DANCE. IT WAS THE LAST THING HE EVER SAW.
IT WAS SAID THAT NO MAN WOULD EVER DESIRE TO SEE ANYTHING MORE, ONCE HE HAD SEEN ME DANCE.
STOP TALKING LIKE THAT, ISH. YOU'RE SCARING ME. COME INTO MY OFFICE, I'LL FIX YOU A DRINK...
I KNOW HOW GODS BEGIN, ROGER. WE START AS DREAMS. THEN WE WALK OUT OF DREAMS INTO THE LAND.
WE ARE WORSHIPPED AND LOVED, AND TAKE POWER TO OUR-SELVES.
AND THEN ONE DAY THERE'S NO ONE LEFT TO WORSHIP US.
AND IN THE END, EACH LITTLE GOD AND GODDESS TAKES ITS LAST JOURNEY BACK INTO DREAMS... AND WHAT COMES AFTER, NOT EVEN WE KNOW.
I'M GOING TO DANCE NOW, I'M AFRAID.

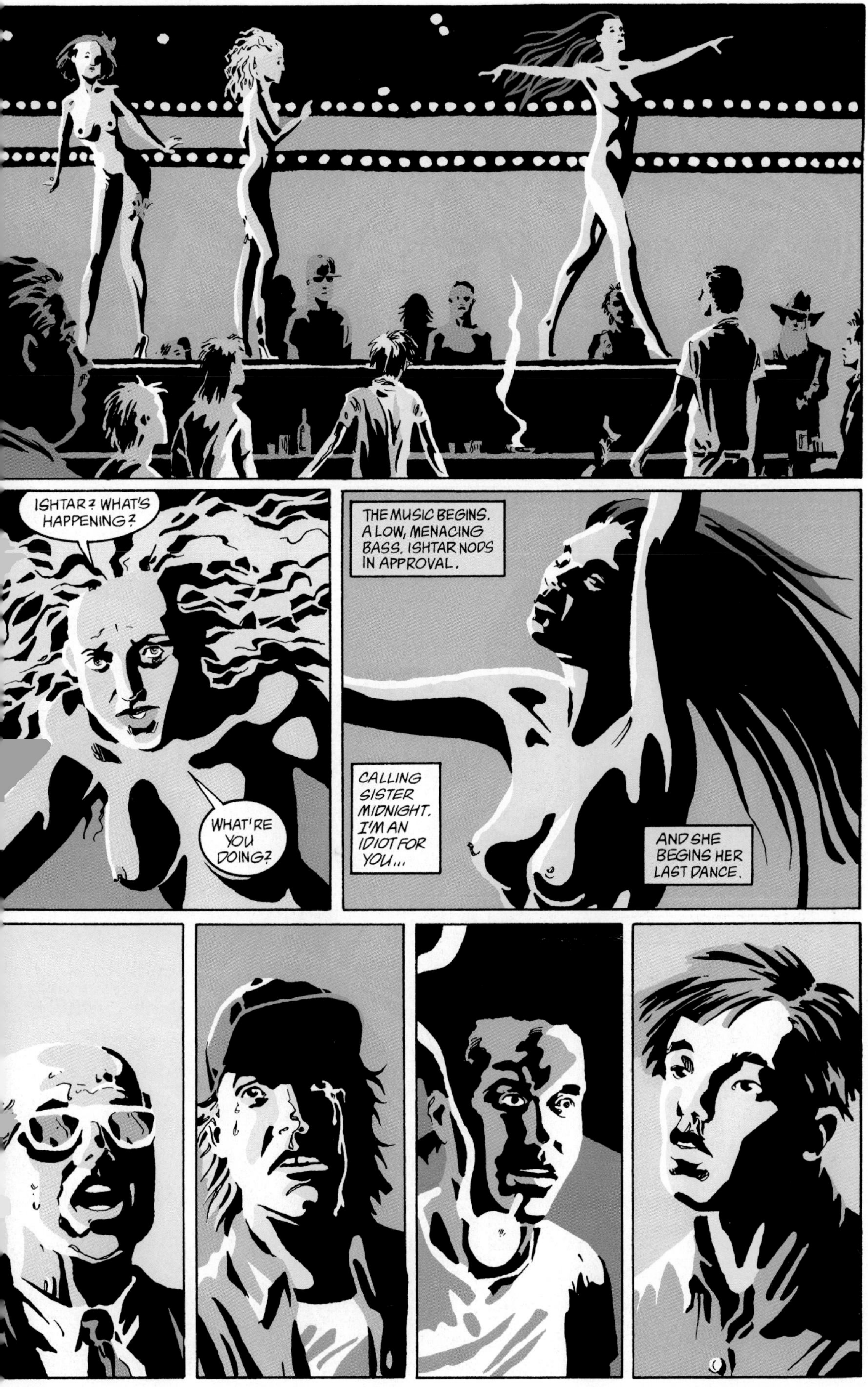
ISHTAR? WHAT'S HAPPENING?
WHAT'RE YOU DOING?
THE MUSIC BEGINS. A LOW, MENACING BASS. ISHTAR NODS IN APPROVAL.
CALLING SISTER MIDNIGHT. I'M AN IDIOT FOR YOU...
AND SHE BEGINS HER LAST DANCE.

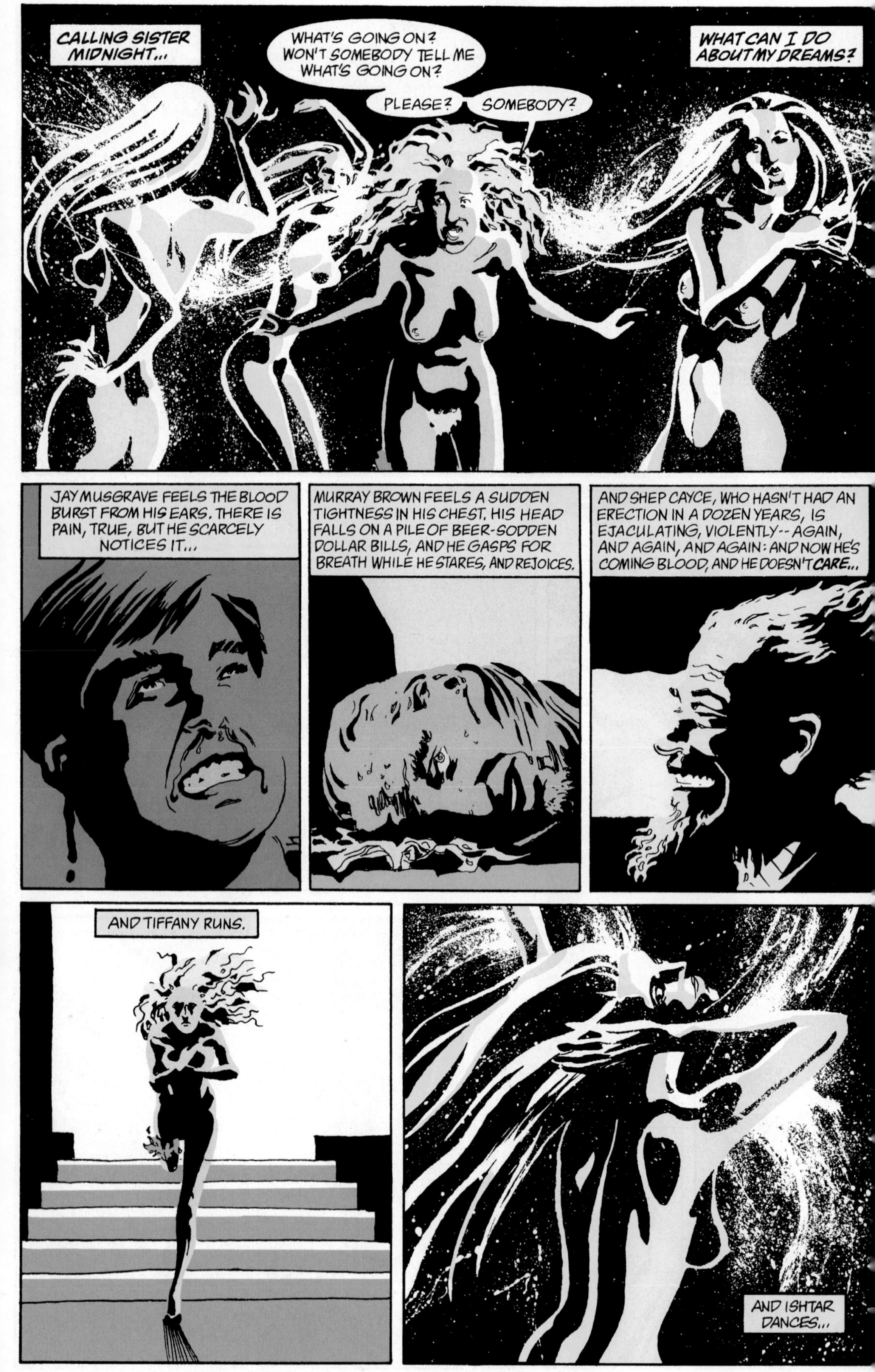
CALLING SISTER MIDNIGHT...
WHAT'S GOING ON? WON'T SOMEBODY TELL ME WHAT'S GOING ON?
PLEASE?
SOMEBODY?
WHAT CAN I DO ABOUT MY DREAMS?
JAY MUSGRAVE FEELS THE BLOOD BURST FROM HIS EARS. THERE IS PAIN, TRUE, BUT HE SCARCELY NOTICES IT...
MURRAY BROWN FEELS A SUDDEN TIGHTNESS IN HIS CHEST. HIS HEAD FALLS ON A PILE OF BEER-SODDEN DOLLAR BILLS, AND HE GASPS FOR BREATH WHILE HE STARES, AND REJOICES.
AND SHEP CAYCE, WHO HASN'T HAD AN ERECTION IN A DOZEN YEARS, IS EJACULATING, VIOLENTLY-- AGAIN, AND AGAIN, AND AGAIN: AND NOW HE'S COMING BLOOD, AND HE DOESN'T CARE...
AND TIFFANY RUNS.
AND ISHTAR DANCES...

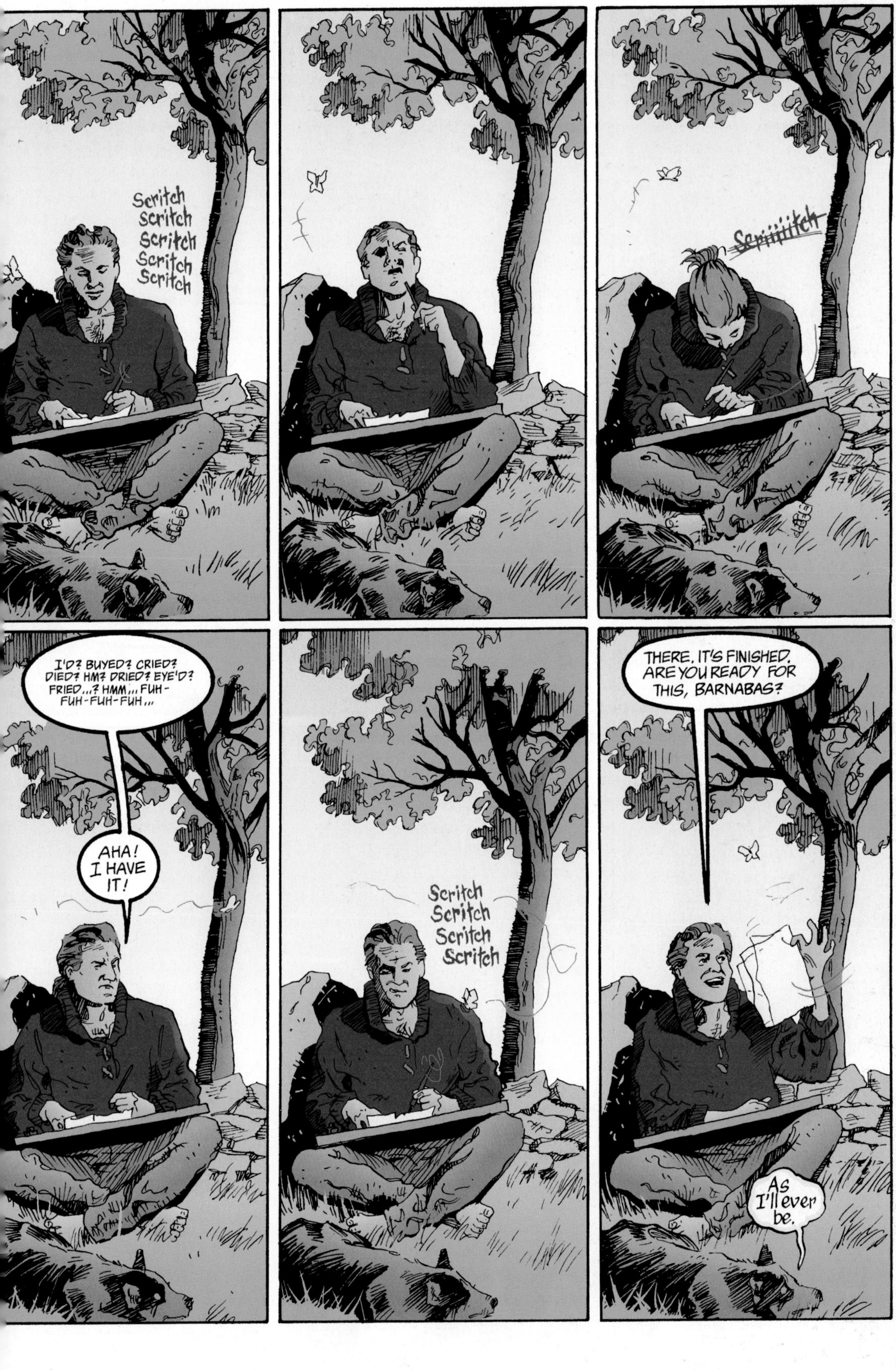
Scritch scritch Scritch Scritch Scritch
Scriiiiitch
I'D? BUYED? CRIED? DIED? HM? DRIED? EYE'D? FRIED...? HMM... FUH-FUH-FUH-FUH...
AHA! I HAVE IT!
Scritch Scritch Scritch Scritch
THERE. IT'S FINISHED. ARE YOU READY FOR THIS, BARNABAS?
As I'll ever be.

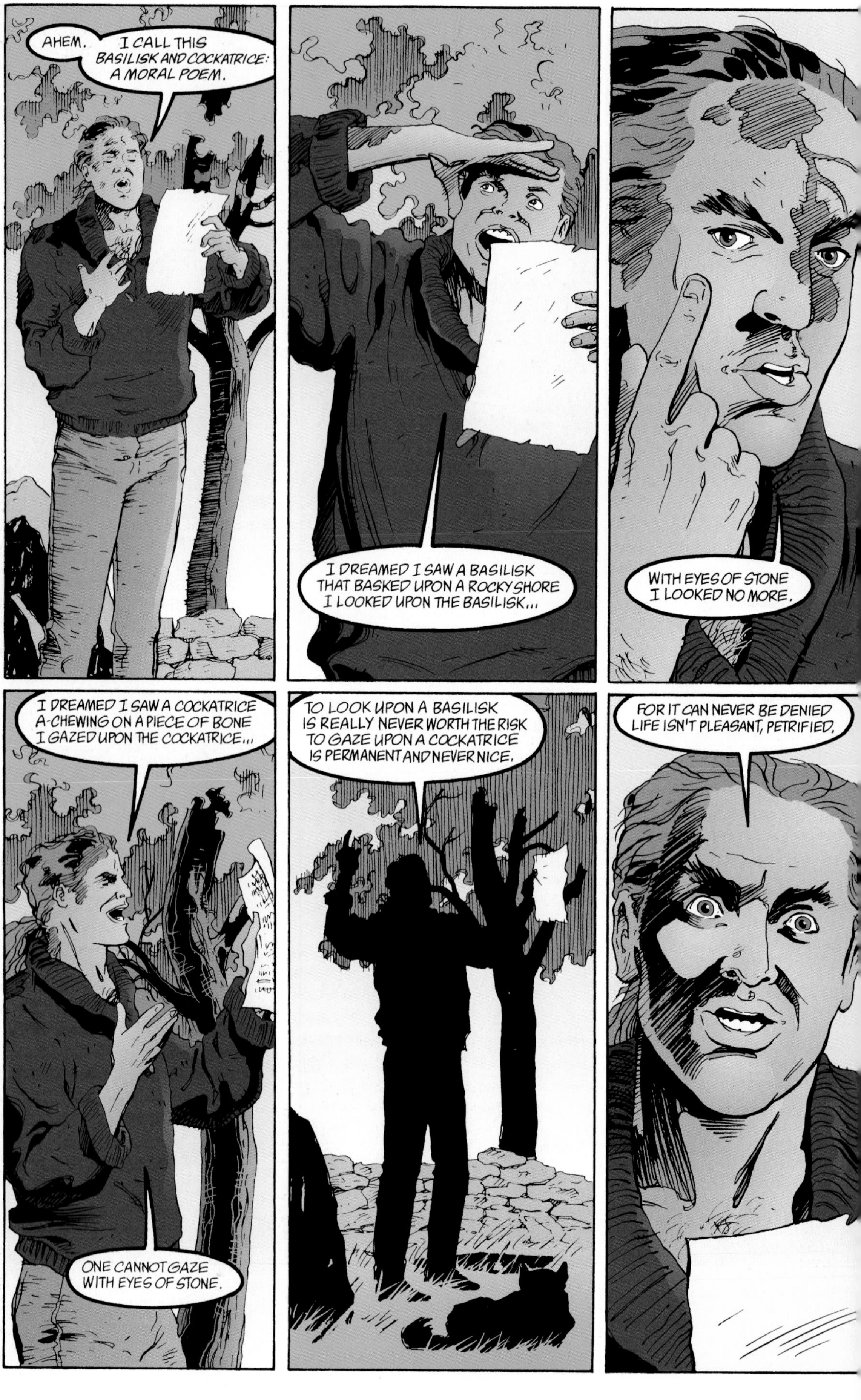
AHEM. I CALL THIS BASILISK AND COCKATRICE: A MORAL POEM.
I DREAMED I SAW A BASILISK THAT BASKED UPON A ROCKY SHORE I LOOKED UPON THE BASILISK...
WITH EYES OF STONE I LOOKED NO MORE.
I DREAMED I SAW A COCKATRICE A-CHEWING ON A PIECE OF BONE I GAZED UPON THE COCKATRICE...
ONE CANNOT GAZE WITH EYES OF STONE.
TO LOOK UPON A BASILISK IS REALLY NEVER WORTH THE RISK TO GAZE UPON A COCKATRICE IS PERMANENT AND NEVER NICE.
FOR IT CAN NEVER BE DENIED LIFE ISN'T PLEASANT, PETRIFIED.

Is that it?

IT IS INDEED.

Ah. Well, at least it wasn't long.

I TAKE IT YOU WEREN'T OVERLY IMPRESSED, THEN.

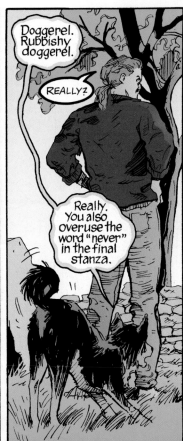

Doggerel. Rubbishy doggerel.

REALLY?

Really. You also overuse the word "never" in the final stanza.

WELL, YOU'D KNOW. EH? **DOG**GEREL? EH?

Spare me. So, what remarkable feats are we going to accomplish today?

THE USUAL. *I'M* GOING TO WORK ON A PAINTING. *YOU'RE* GOING TO SIT IN THE SUN, SCRATCH FOR FLEAS, ROMP ABOUT, EAT AND SLEEP.

MAYBE YOU'LL GAZE UP AT ME ADORINGLY FROM TIME TO TIME, MY FAITHFUL HOUND.

Hmph. In your dreams.

I DON'T DREAM. WOULDN'T DO TO GIVE TOO MUCH AWAY. ESPECIALLY NOT NOW.

I don't see what you're so worried about.

NO? AH, BARNABAS, THAT'S BECAUSE YOU NEVER MET MY FAMILY.

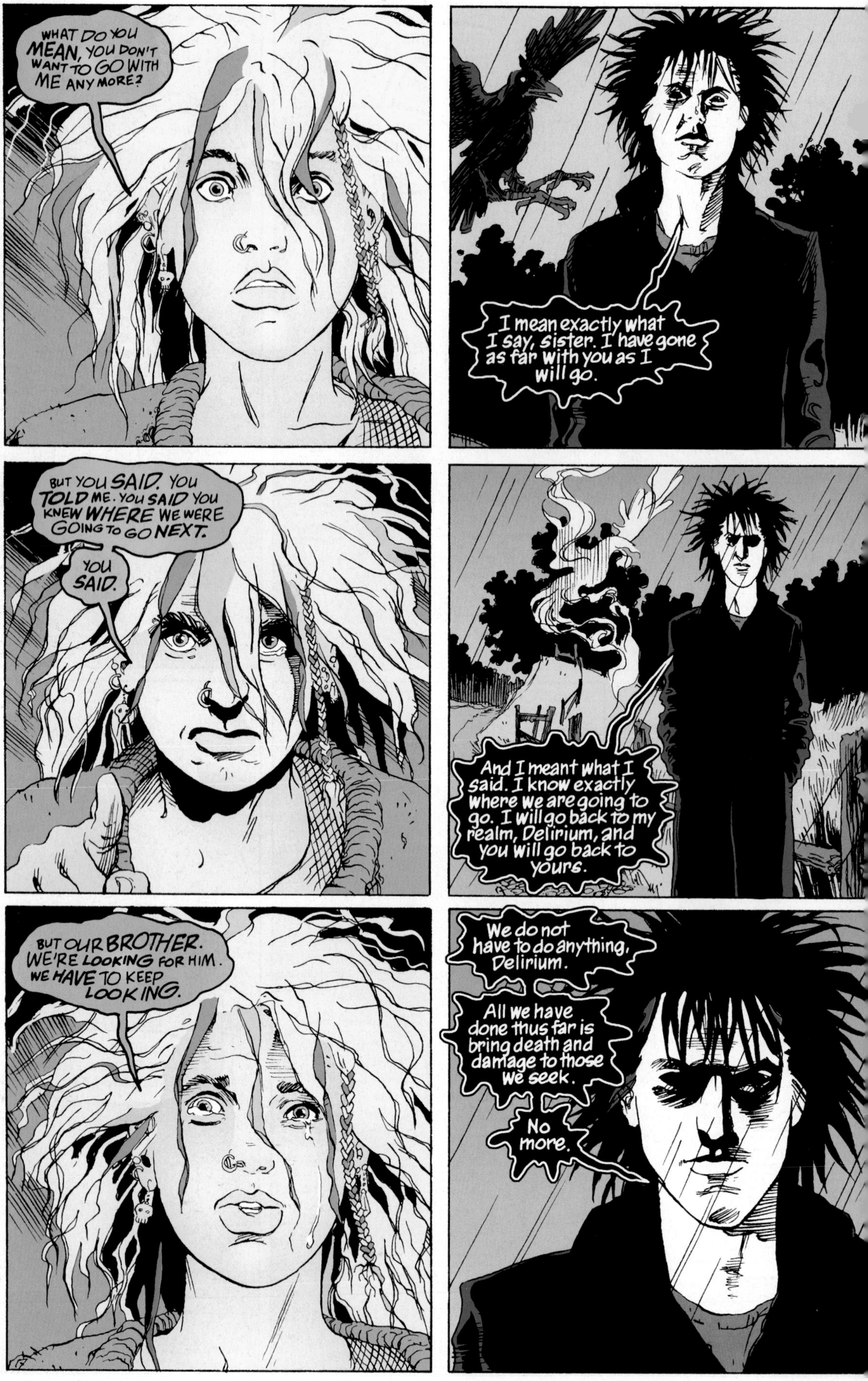
WHAT DO YOU MEAN, YOU DON'T WANT TO GO WITH ME ANY MORE?
I mean exactly what I say, sister. I have gone as far with you as I will go.
BUT YOU SAID. YOU TOLD ME. YOU SAID YOU KNEW WHERE WE WERE GOING TO GO NEXT.
YOU SAID.
And I meant what I said. I know exactly where we are going to go. I will go back to my realm, Delirium, and you will go back to yours.
BUT OUR BROTHER. WE'RE LOOKING FOR HIM. WE HAVE TO KEEP LOOKING.
We do not have to do anything, Delirium.
All we have done thus far is bring death and damage to those we seek.
No more.

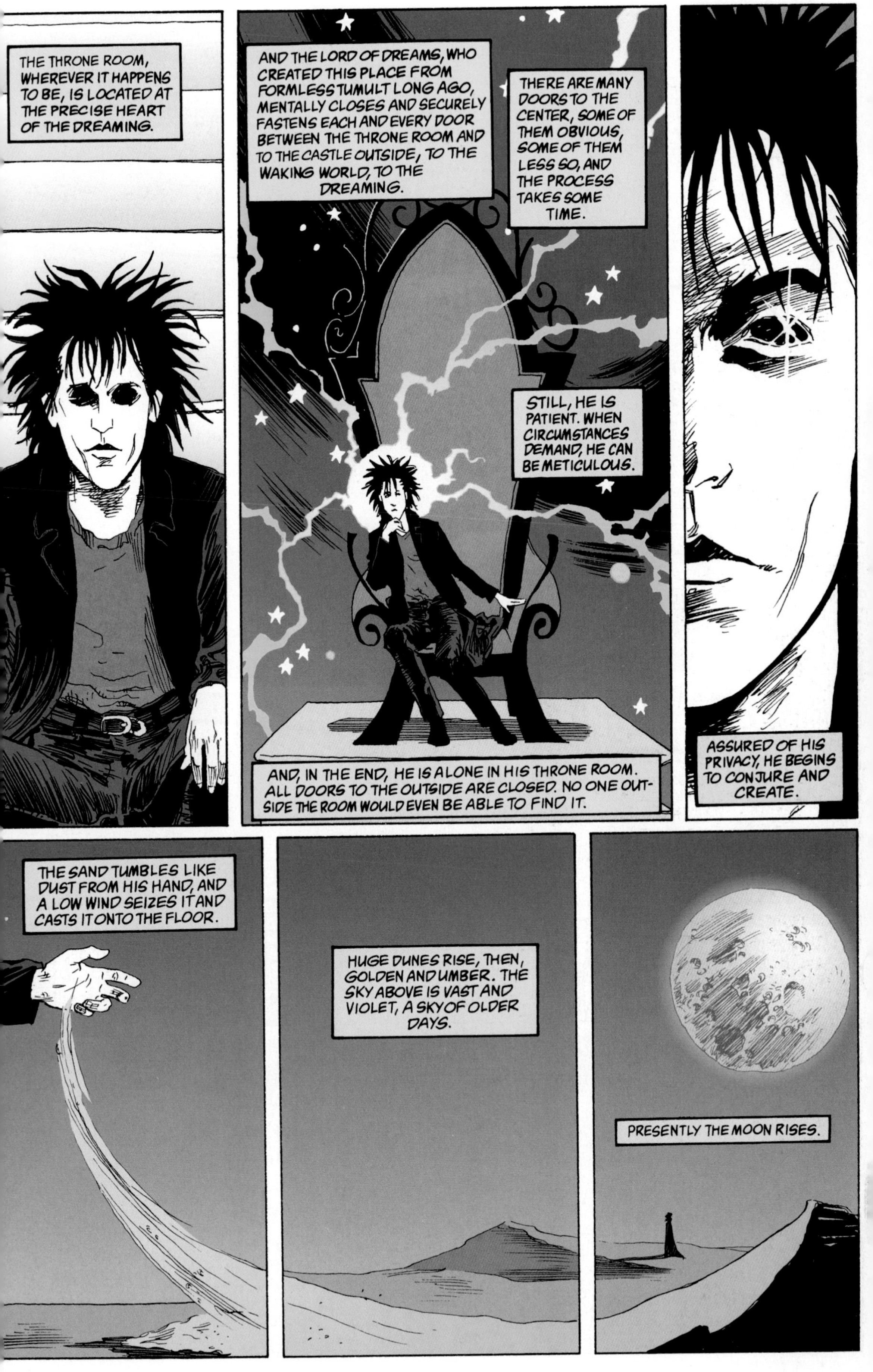
THE THRONE ROOM, WHEREVER IT HAPPENS TO BE, IS LOCATED AT THE PRECISE HEART OF THE DREAMING.
AND THE LORD OF DREAMS, WHO CREATED THIS PLACE FROM FORMLESS TUMULT LONG AGO, MENTALLY CLOSES AND SECURELY FASTENS EACH AND EVERY DOOR BETWEEN THE THRONE ROOM AND TO THE CASTLE OUTSIDE, TO THE WAKING WORLD, TO THE DREAMING.
THERE ARE MANY DOORS TO THE CENTER, SOME OF THEM OBVIOUS, SOME OF THEM LESS SO, AND THE PROCESS TAKES SOME TIME.
STILL, HE IS PATIENT. WHEN CIRCUMSTANCES DEMAND, HE CAN BE METICULOUS.
AND, IN THE END, HE IS ALONE IN HIS THRONE ROOM. ALL DOORS TO THE OUTSIDE ARE CLOSED. NO ONE OUTSIDE THE ROOM WOULD EVEN BE ABLE TO FIND IT.
ASSURED OF HIS PRIVACY, HE BEGINS TO CONJURE AND CREATE.
THE SAND TUMBLES LIKE DUST FROM HIS HAND, AND A LOW WIND SEIZES IT AND CASTS IT ONTO THE FLOOR.
HUGE DUNES RISE, THEN, GOLDEN AND UMBER. THE SKY ABOVE IS VAST AND VIOLET, A SKY OF OLDER DAYS.
PRESENTLY THE MOON RISES.

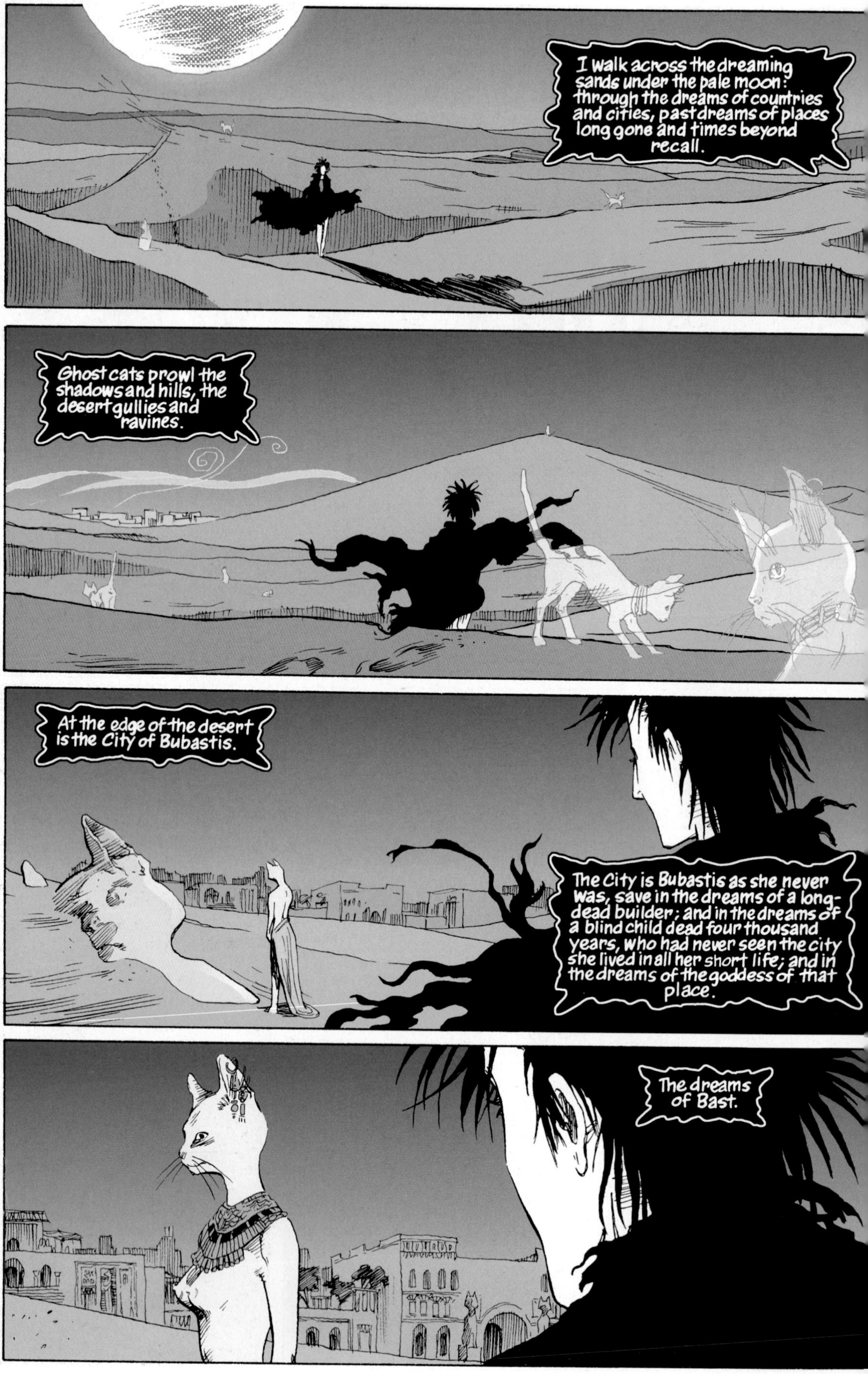
I walk across the dreaming sands under the pale moon: through the dreams of countries and cities, past dreams of places long gone and times beyond recall.
Ghost cats prowl the shadows and hills, the desert gullies and ravines.
At the edge of the desert is the City of Bubastis.
The City is Bubastis as she never was, save in the dreams of a long-dead builder; and in the dreams of a blind child dead four thousand years, who had never seen the city she lived in all her short life; and in the dreams of the goddess of that place.
The dreams of Bast.

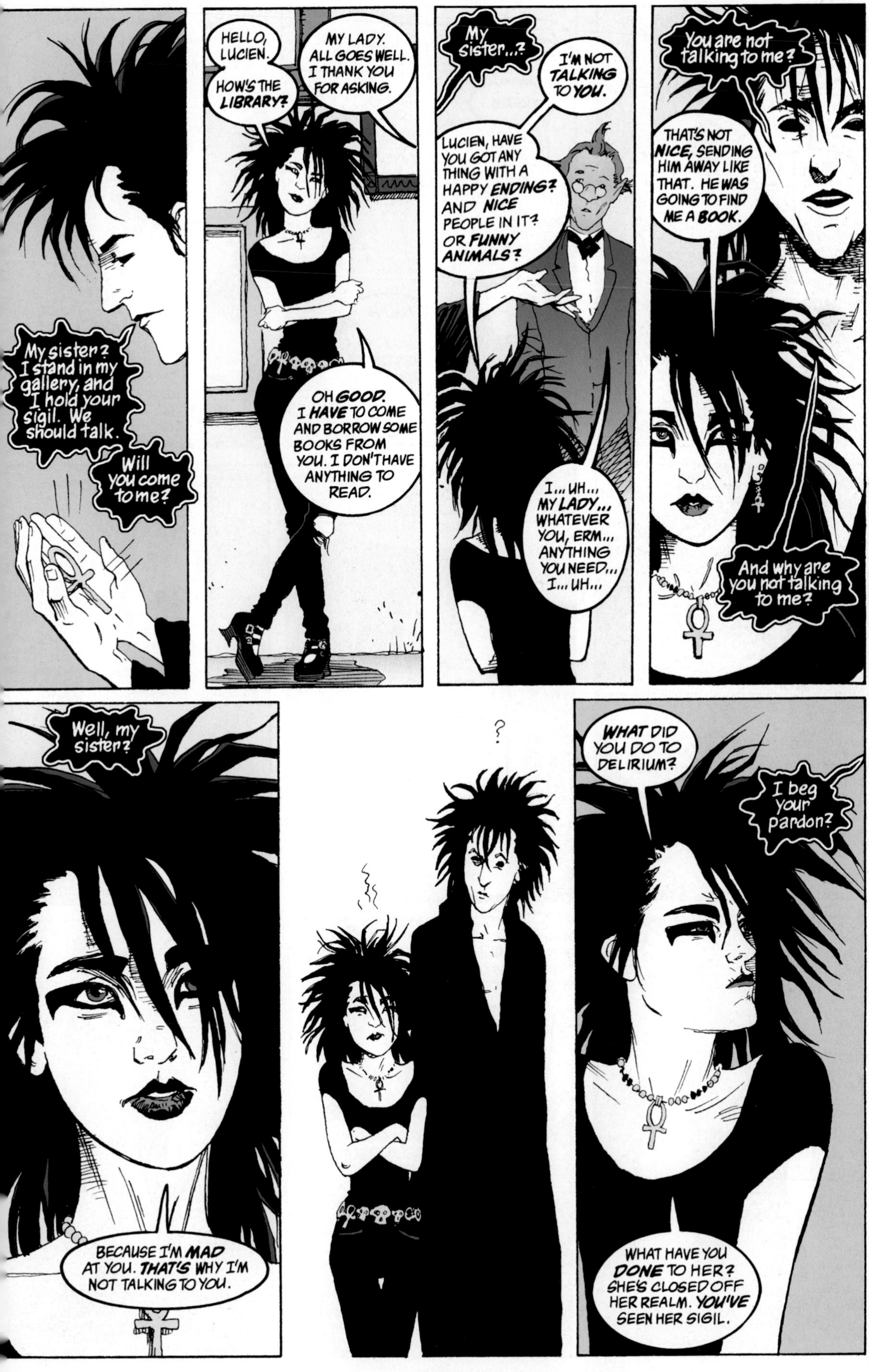
My sister? I stand in my gallery, and I hold your sigil. We should talk.
Will you come to me?
HELLO, LUCIEN.
HOW'S THE LIBRARY?
MY LADY. ALL GOES WELL. I THANK YOU FOR ASKING.
OH GOOD. I HAVE TO COME AND BORROW SOME BOOKS FROM YOU. I DON'T HAVE ANYTHING TO READ.
My sister...?
I'M NOT TALKING TO YOU.
LUCIEN, HAVE YOU GOT ANY THING WITH A HAPPY ENDING? AND NICE PEOPLE IN IT? OR FUNNY ANIMALS?
I... UH... MY LADY... WHATEVER YOU, ERM... ANYTHING YOU NEED... I... UH...
You are not talking to me?
THAT'S NOT NICE, SENDING HIM AWAY LIKE THAT. HE WAS GOING TO FIND ME A BOOK.
And why are you not talking to me?
Well, my sister?
BECAUSE I'M MAD AT YOU. THAT'S WHY I'M NOT TALKING TO YOU.
?
WHAT DID YOU DO TO DELIRIUM?
I beg your pardon?
WHAT HAVE YOU DONE TO HER? SHE'S CLOSED OFF HER REALM. YOU'VE SEEN HER SIGIL.

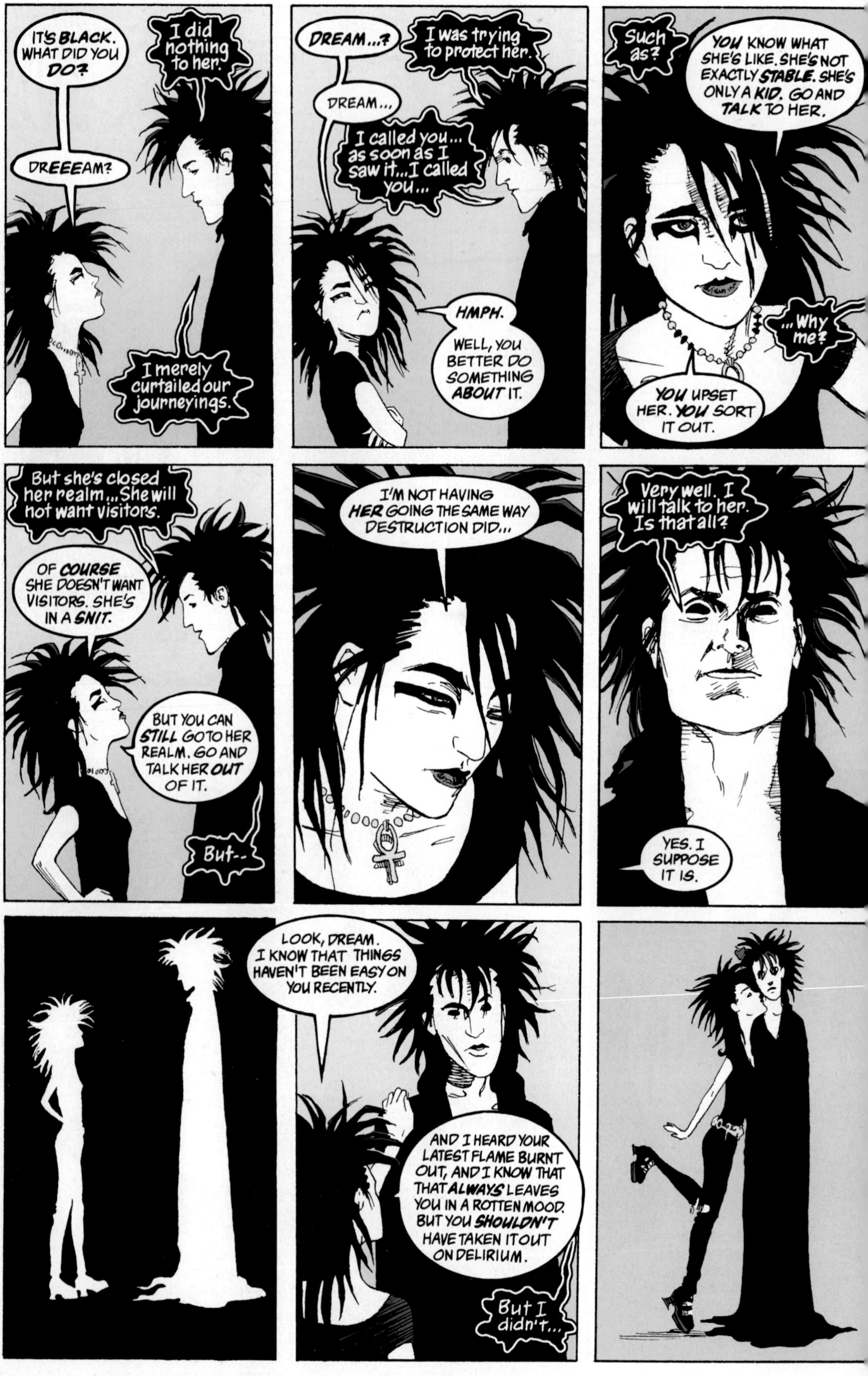
IT'S BLACK. WHAT DID YOU DO?
I did nothing to her.
DREEEAM?
I merely curtailed our journeyings.
DREAM...?
I was trying to protect her.
DREAM...
I called you... as soon as I saw it... I called you...
HMPH.
WELL, YOU BETTER DO SOMETHING ABOUT IT.
Such as?
YOU KNOW WHAT SHE'S LIKE. SHE'S NOT EXACTLY STABLE. SHE'S ONLY A KID. GO AND TALK TO HER.
...Why me?
YOU UPSET HER. YOU SORT IT OUT.
But she's closed her realm... She will not want visitors.
OF COURSE SHE DOESN'T WANT VISITORS. SHE'S IN A SNIT.
BUT YOU CAN STILL GO TO HER REALM. GO AND TALK HER OUT OF IT.
But--
I'M NOT HAVING HER GOING THE SAME WAY DESTRUCTION DID...
Very well. I will talk to her. Is that all?
YES. I SUPPOSE IT IS.
LOOK, DREAM. I KNOW THAT THINGS HAVEN'T BEEN EASY ON YOU RECENTLY.
AND I HEARD YOUR LATEST FLAME BURNT OUT, AND I KNOW THAT THAT ALWAYS LEAVES YOU IN A ROTTEN MOOD. BUT YOU SHOULDN'T HAVE TAKEN IT OUT ON DELIRIUM.
But I didn't...

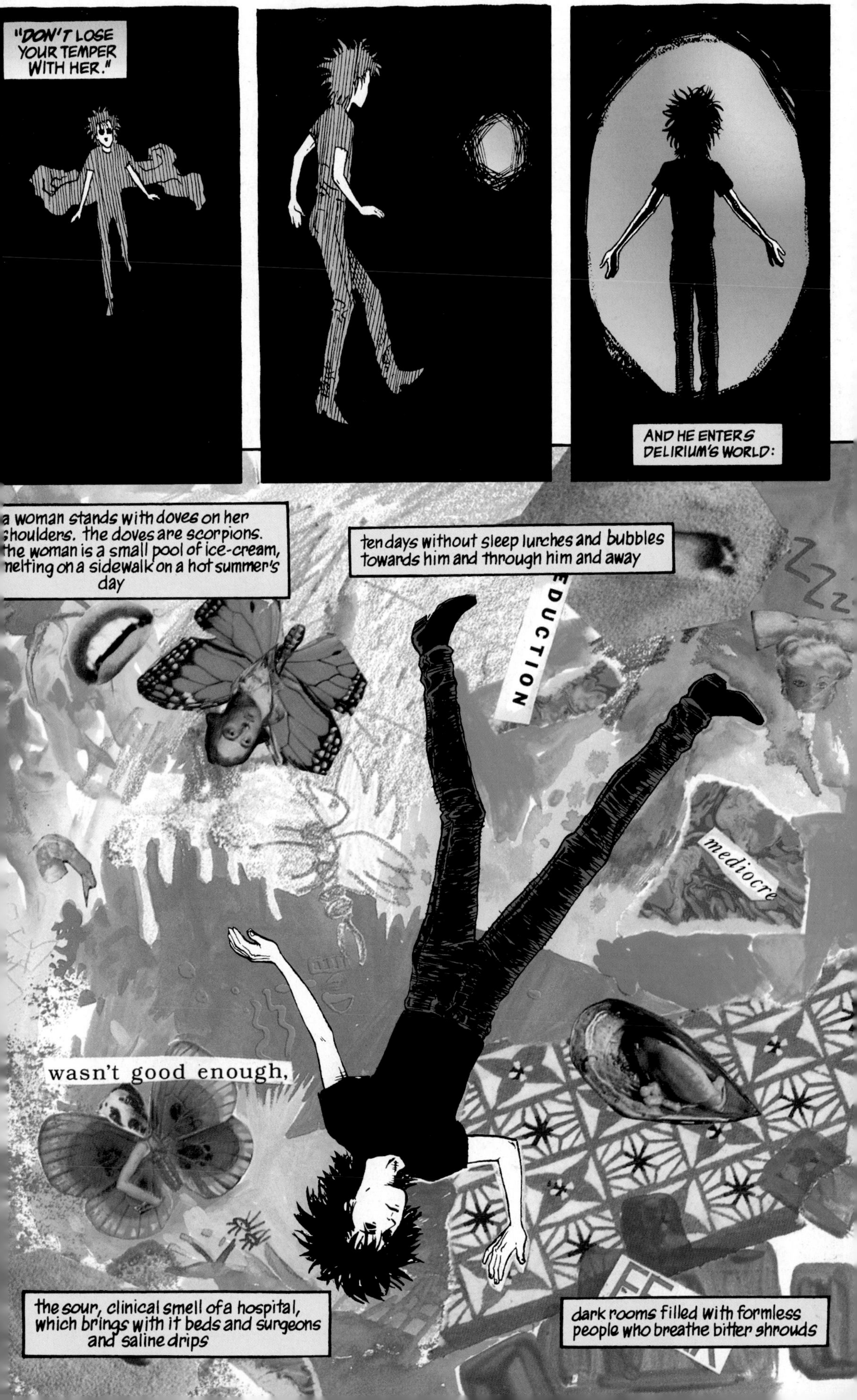

"DON'T LOSE YOUR TEMPER WITH HER."
AND HE ENTERS DELIRIUM'S WORLD:
a woman stands with doves on her shoulders. the doves are scorpions. the woman is a small pool of ice-cream, melting on a sidewalk on a hot summer's day
ten days without sleep lurches and bubbles towards him and through him and away
EDUCTION
Zzz
mediocre
wasn't good enough,
the sour, clinical smell of a hospital, which brings with it beds and surgeons and saline drips
dark rooms filled with formless people who breathe bitter shrouds

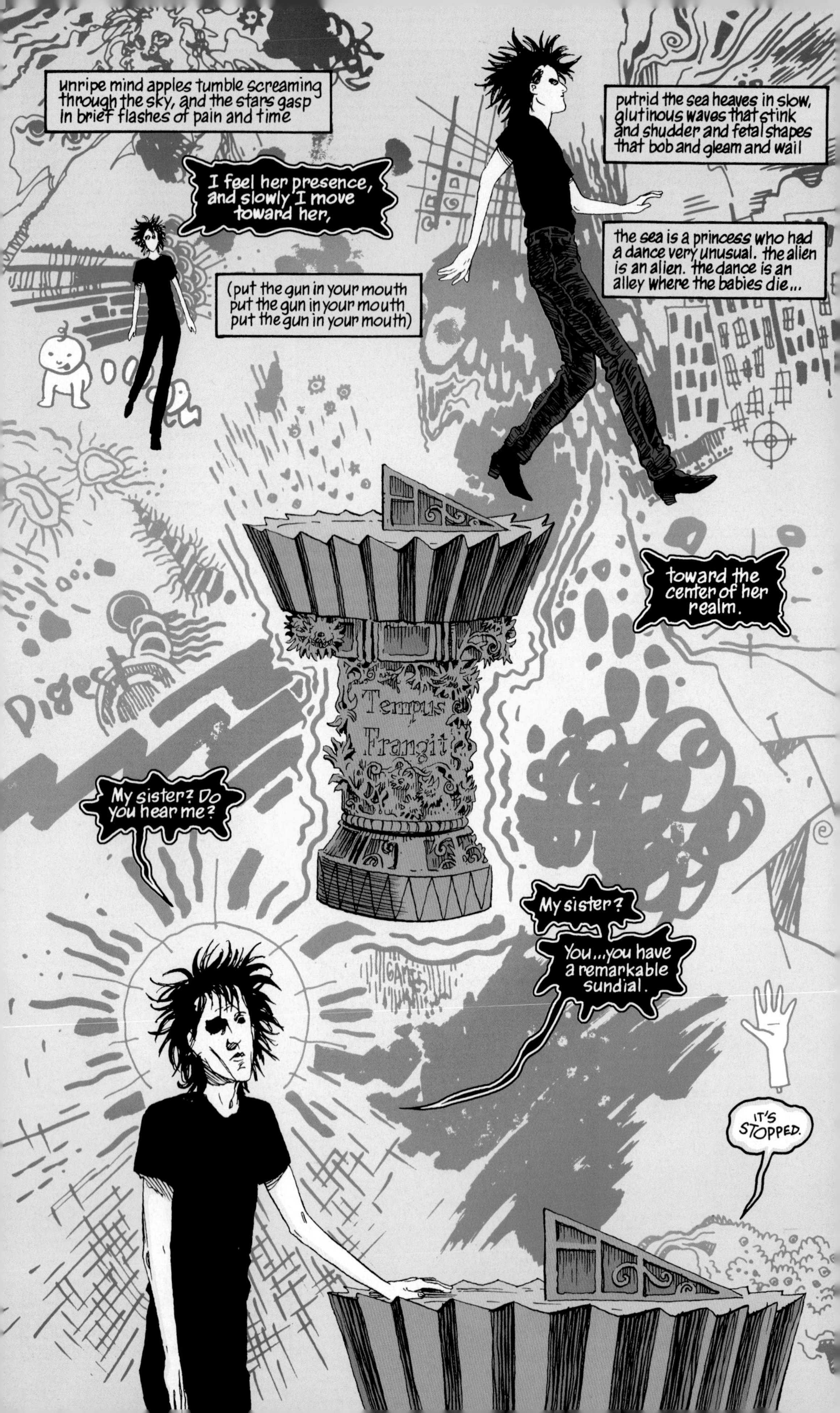

unripe mind apples tumble screaming through the sky, and the stars gasp in brief flashes of pain and time
putrid the sea heaves in slow, glutinous waves that stink and shudder and fetal shapes that bob and gleam and wail
I feel her presence, and slowly I move toward her,
the sea is a princess who had a dance very unusual. the alien is an alien. the dance is an alley where the babies die...
(put the gun in your mouth put the gun in your mouth put the gun in your mouth)
toward the center of her realm.
Tempus Frangit
My sister? Do you hear me?
My sister?
You...you have a remarkable sundial.
IT'S STOPPED.

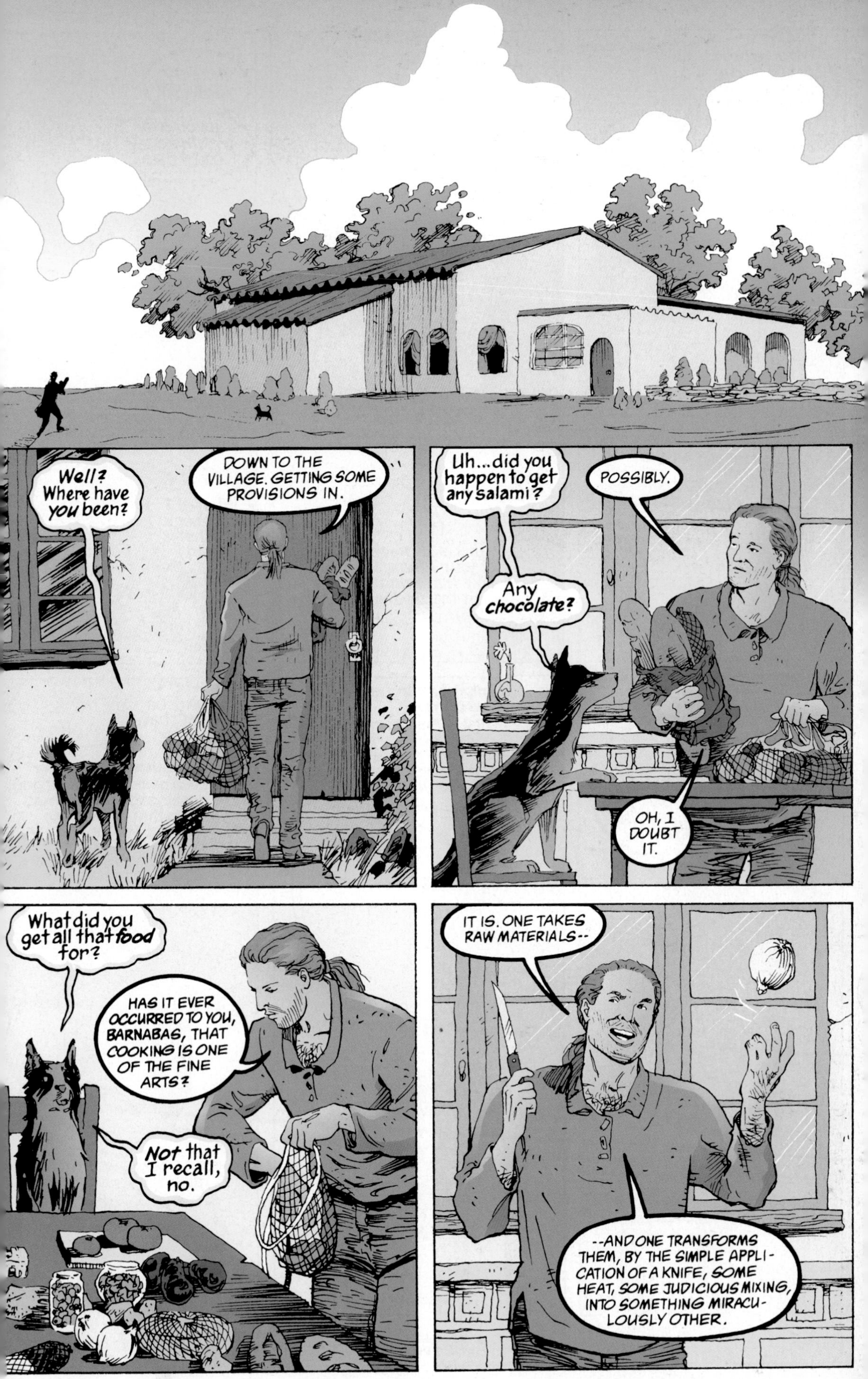
Well? Where have you been?
DOWN TO THE VILLAGE. GETTING SOME PROVISIONS IN.
Uh...did you happen to get any salami?
POSSIBLY.
Any chocolate?
OH, I DOUBT IT.
What did you get all that food for?
HAS IT EVER OCCURRED TO YOU, BARNABAS, THAT COOKING IS ONE OF THE FINE ARTS?
Not that I recall, no.
IT IS. ONE TAKES RAW MATERIALS--
--AND ONE TRANSFORMS THEM, BY THE SIMPLE APPLICATION OF A KNIFE, SOME HEAT, SOME JUDICIOUS MIXING, INTO SOMETHING MIRACULOUSLY OTHER.

You've never cooked anything as long as I've known you.

HAVEN'T I?

No.

Am I going to get any of this heavenly repast, once it's complete?

THAT DEPENDS ON HOW IT TURNS OUT.

This is another one of your *ideas*, isn't it? Like that *thing* you left in the garden.

THING? THING?

BARNABAS, THAT *THING* IS A SCULPTURE.

What *of*? A big rock with holes in it?

HAAA! HAHAHAHA HAHAHA!

I'LL TELL YOU WHAT, BARNABAS.

THE HAMMER AND CHISEL ARE OUTSIDE IN THE HALL. THERE'S ANOTHER MARBLE BLOCK UPSTAIRS. WHY DON'T *YOU* DO YOUR *OWN* SCULPTURE, AND *I'LL* LAUGH AT WHAT *YOU* MAKE?

Hmph. Leaving aside the issue of hands, I have *no* desire to ruin a perfectly good piece of marble. Dogs have more *sense*. We don't make fools of ourselves like you do.

OF *COURSE* YOU DON'T.

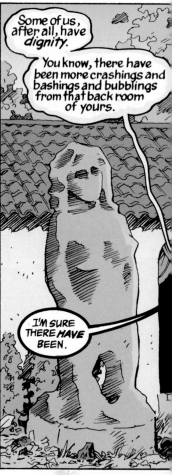

Some of us, after all, have *dignity*.

You know, there have been more crashings and bashings and bubblings from that back room of yours.

I'M SURE THERE *HAVE* BEEN.

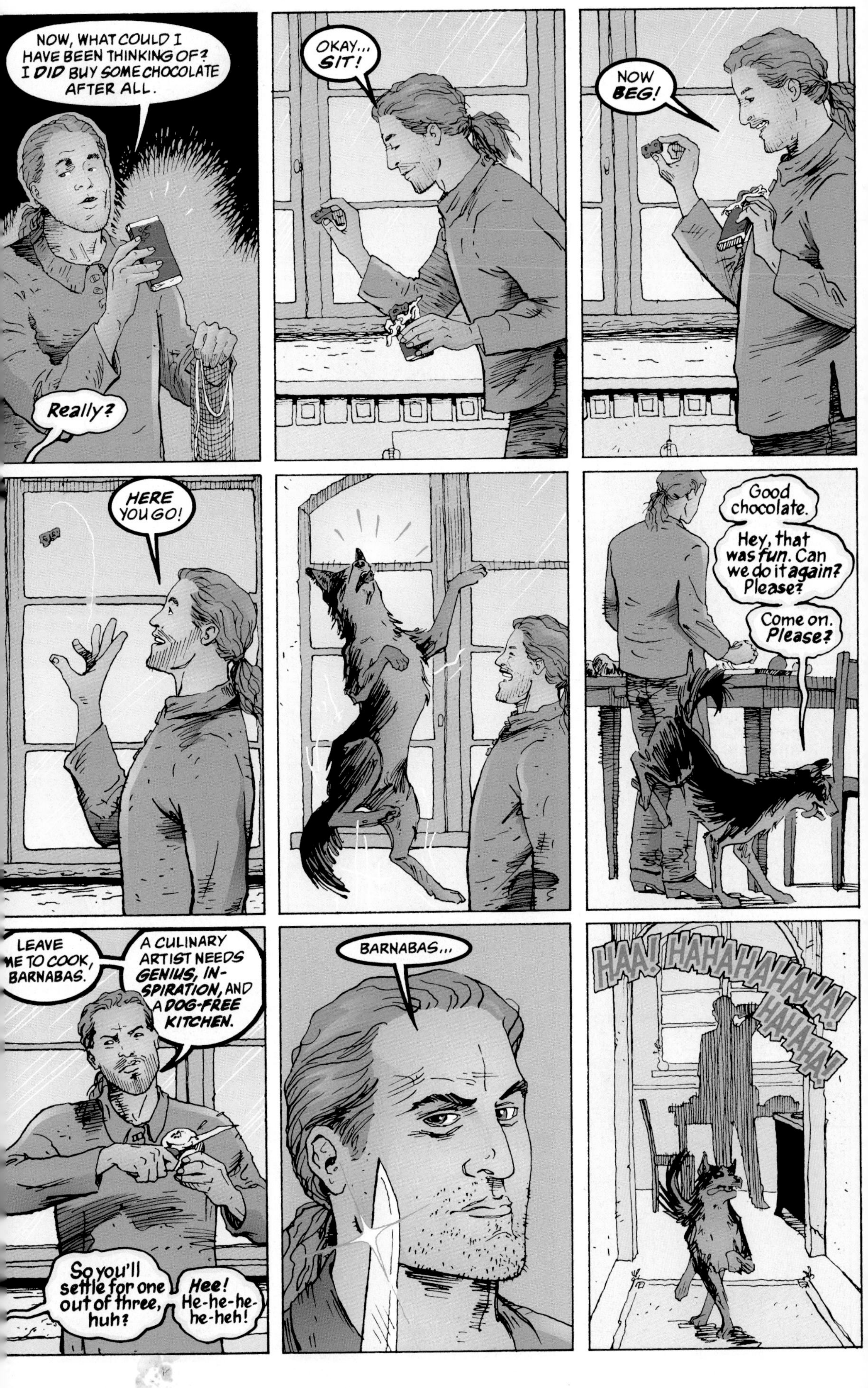

NOW, WHAT COULD I HAVE BEEN THINKING OF? I DID BUY SOME CHOCOLATE AFTER ALL.
Really?
OKAY... SIT!
NOW BEG!
HERE YOU GO!
Good chocolate.
Hey, that was fun. Can we do it again? Please?
Come on. Please?
LEAVE ME TO COOK, BARNABAS.
A CULINARY ARTIST NEEDS GENIUS, INSPIRATION, AND A DOG-FREE KITCHEN.
So you'll settle for one out of three, huh?
Hee! He-he-he-he-heh!
BARNABAS...
HAA! HAHAHAHAHAHA! HAHAHA!

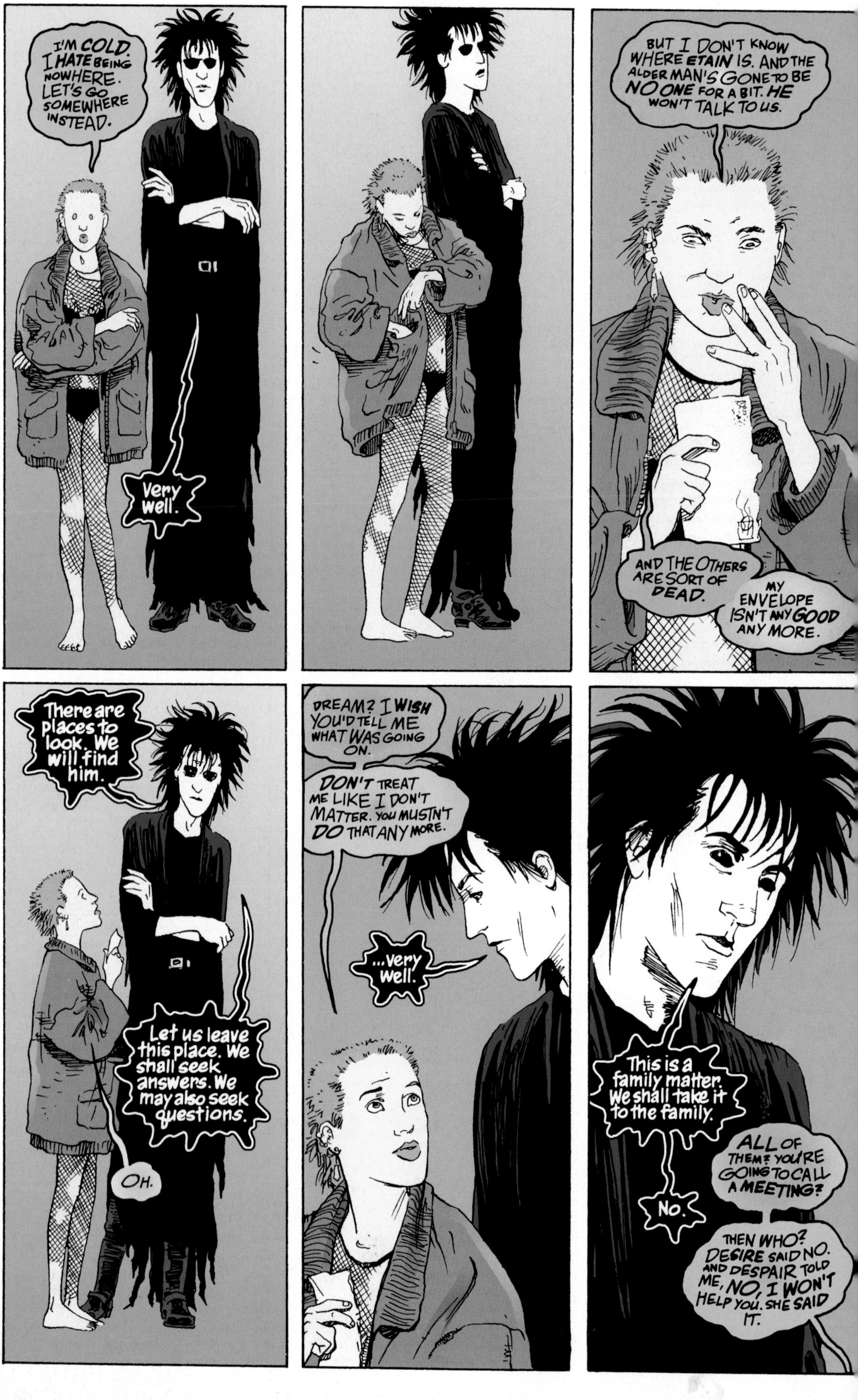

I'M COLD. I HATE BEING NOWHERE. LET'S GO SOMEWHERE INSTEAD.
Very well.
BUT I DON'T KNOW WHERE ETAIN IS. AND THE ALDER MAN'S GONE TO BE NO ONE FOR A BIT. HE WON'T TALK TO US.
AND THE OTHERS ARE SORT OF DEAD.
MY ENVELOPE ISN'T ANY GOOD ANY MORE.
There are places to look. We will find him.
Let us leave this place. We shall seek answers. We may also seek questions.
OH.
DREAM? I WISH YOU'D TELL ME WHAT WAS GOING ON.
DON'T TREAT ME LIKE I DON'T MATTER. YOU MUSTN'T DO THAT ANY MORE.
...very well.
This is a family matter. We shall take it to the family.
No.
ALL OF THEM? YOU'RE GOING TO CALL A MEETING?
THEN WHO? DESIRE SAID NO. AND DESPAIR TOLD ME, NO, I WON'T HELP YOU. SHE SAID IT.

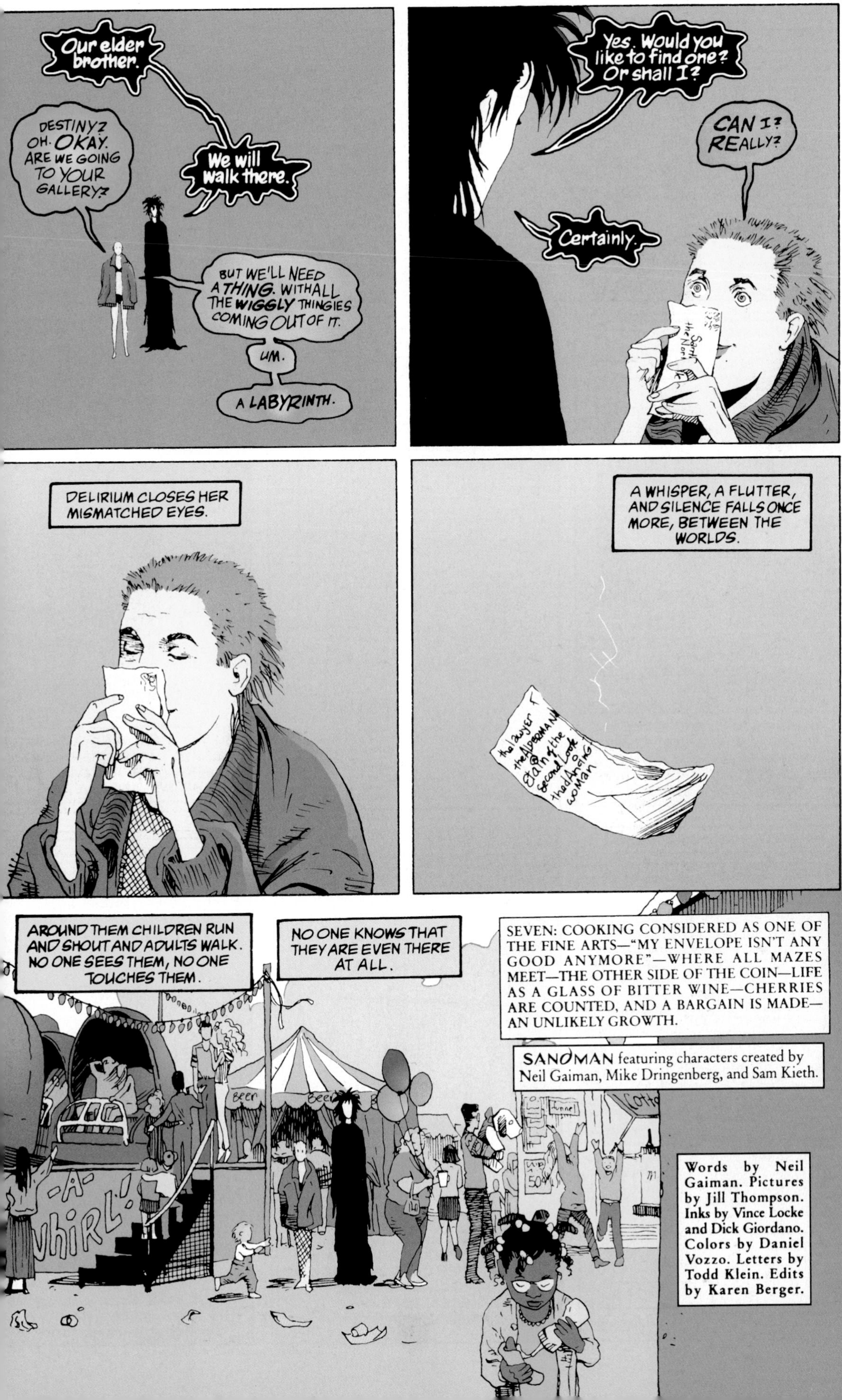
Our elder brother.
DESTINY? OH. OKAY. ARE WE GOING TO YOUR GALLERY?
We will walk there.
BUT WE'LL NEED A THING. WITH ALL THE WIGGLY THINGIES COMING OUT OF IT.
UM.
A LABYRINTH.
Yes. Would you like to find one? Or shall I?
CAN I? REALLY?
Certainly.
DELIRIUM CLOSES HER MISMATCHED EYES.
A WHISPER, A FLUTTER, AND SILENCE FALLS ONCE MORE, BETWEEN THE WORLDS.
AROUND THEM CHILDREN RUN AND SHOUT AND ADULTS WALK. NO ONE SEES THEM, NO ONE TOUCHES THEM.
NO ONE KNOWS THAT THEY ARE EVEN THERE AT ALL.
SEVEN: COOKING CONSIDERED AS ONE OF THE FINE ARTS—"MY ENVELOPE ISN'T ANY GOOD ANYMORE"—WHERE ALL MAZES MEET—THE OTHER SIDE OF THE COIN—LIFE AS A GLASS OF BITTER WINE—CHERRIES ARE COUNTED, AND A BARGAIN IS MADE—AN UNLIKELY GROWTH.
SANDMAN featuring characters created by Neil Gaiman, Mike Dringenberg, and Sam Kieth.
Beer
Beer
Funnel
-A-WHIRL!
Words by Neil Gaiman. Pictures by Jill Thompson. Inks by Vince Locke and Dick Giordano. Colors by Daniel Vozzo. Letters by Todd Klein. Edits by Karen Berger.

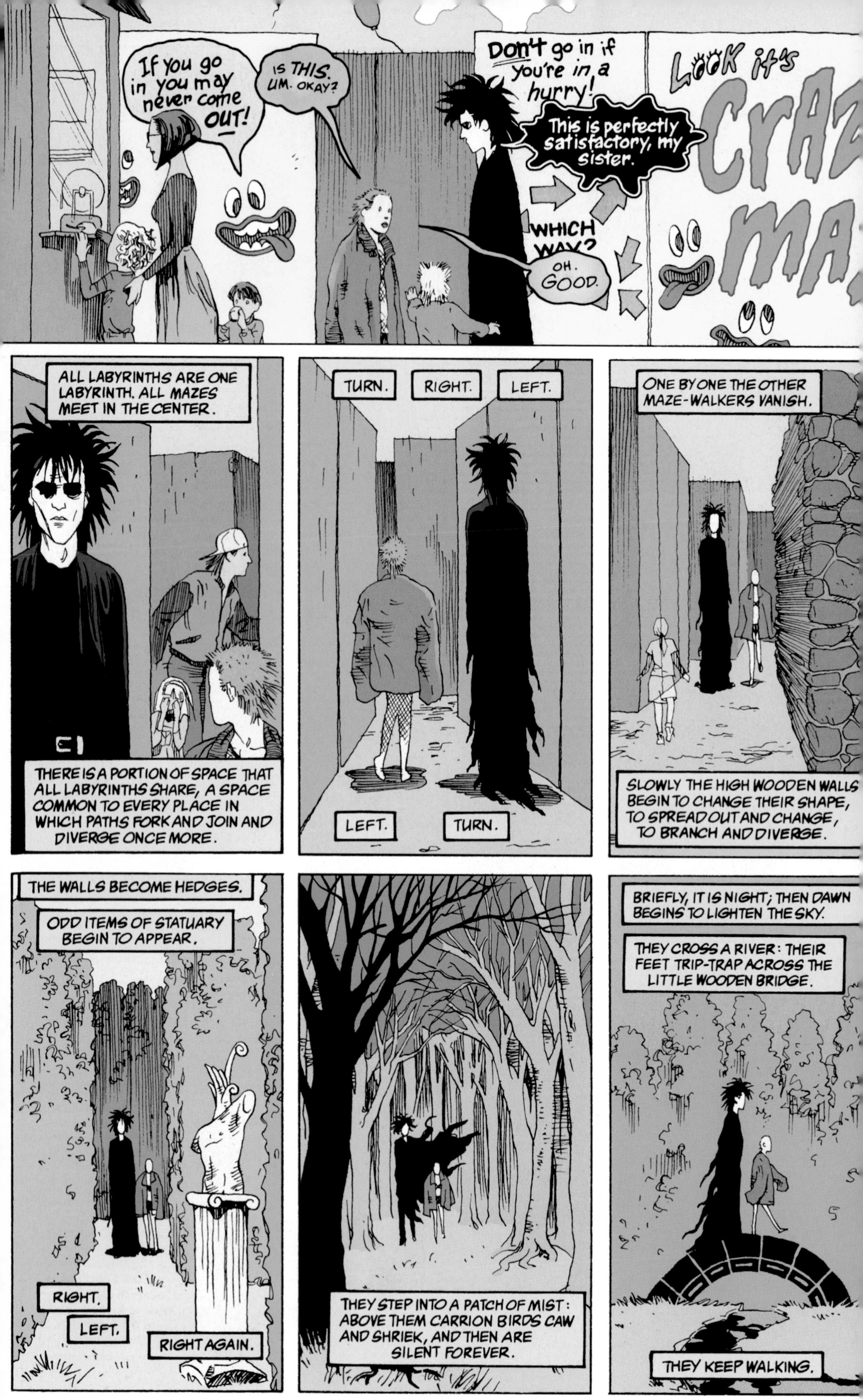

If you go in you may never come OUT!
IS THIS. UM. OKAY?
Don't go in if you're in a hurry!
This is perfectly satisfactory, my sister.
WHICH WAY?
OH. GOOD.
LOOK it's CRAZ MAZ
ALL LABYRINTHS ARE ONE LABYRINTH. ALL MAZES MEET IN THE CENTER.
THERE IS A PORTION OF SPACE THAT ALL LABYRINTHS SHARE, A SPACE COMMON TO EVERY PLACE IN WHICH PATHS FORK AND JOIN AND DIVERGE ONCE MORE.
TURN.
RIGHT.
LEFT.
LEFT.
TURN.
ONE BY ONE THE OTHER MAZE-WALKERS VANISH.
SLOWLY THE HIGH WOODEN WALLS BEGIN TO CHANGE THEIR SHAPE, TO SPREAD OUT AND CHANGE, TO BRANCH AND DIVERGE.
THE WALLS BECOME HEDGES.
ODD ITEMS OF STATUARY BEGIN TO APPEAR.
RIGHT.
LEFT.
RIGHT AGAIN.
THEY STEP INTO A PATCH OF MIST: ABOVE THEM CARRION BIRDS CAW AND SHRIEK, AND THEN ARE SILENT FOREVER.
BRIEFLY, IT IS NIGHT; THEN DAWN BEGINS TO LIGHTEN THE SKY.
THEY CROSS A RIVER: THEIR FEET TRIP-TRAP ACROSS THE LITTLE WOODEN BRIDGE.
THEY KEEP WALKING.

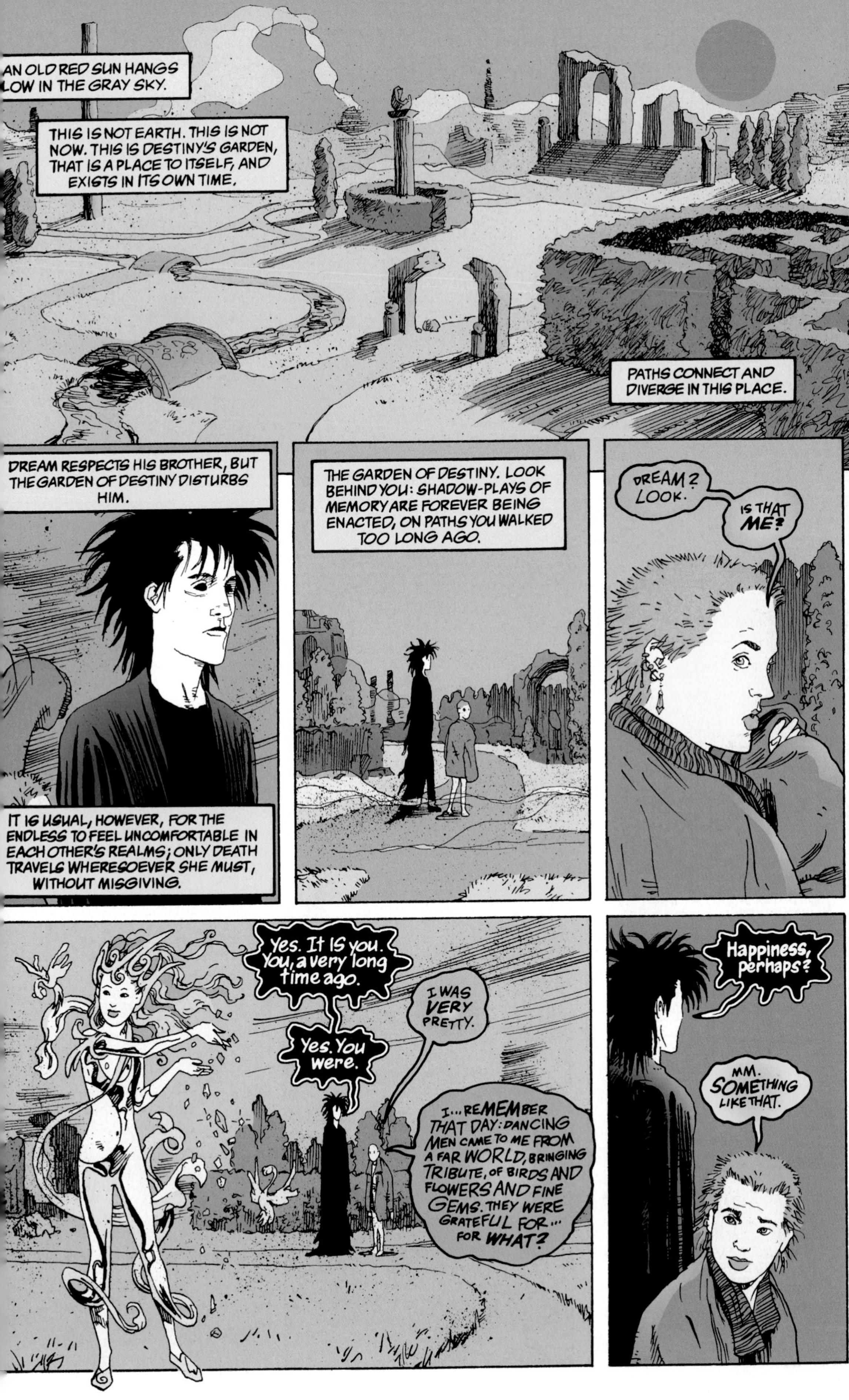
AN OLD RED SUN HANGS LOW IN THE GRAY SKY.
THIS IS NOT EARTH. THIS IS NOT NOW. THIS IS DESTINY'S GARDEN, THAT IS A PLACE TO ITSELF, AND EXISTS IN ITS OWN TIME.
PATHS CONNECT AND DIVERGE IN THIS PLACE.
DREAM RESPECTS HIS BROTHER, BUT THE GARDEN OF DESTINY DISTURBS HIM.
IT IS USUAL, HOWEVER, FOR THE ENDLESS TO FEEL UNCOMFORTABLE IN EACH OTHER'S REALMS; ONLY DEATH TRAVELS WHERESOEVER SHE MUST, WITHOUT MISGIVING.
THE GARDEN OF DESTINY. LOOK BEHIND YOU: SHADOW-PLAYS OF MEMORY ARE FOREVER BEING ENACTED, ON PATHS YOU WALKED TOO LONG AGO.
DREAM? LOOK.
IS THAT ME?
Yes. It IS you. You, a very long time ago.
I WAS VERY PRETTY.
Yes. You were.
I... REMEMBER THAT DAY: DANCING MEN CAME TO ME FROM A FAR WORLD, BRINGING TRIBUTE, OF BIRDS AND FLOWERS AND FINE GEMS. THEY WERE GRATEFUL FOR... FOR WHAT?
Happiness, perhaps?
MM. SOMETHING LIKE THAT.

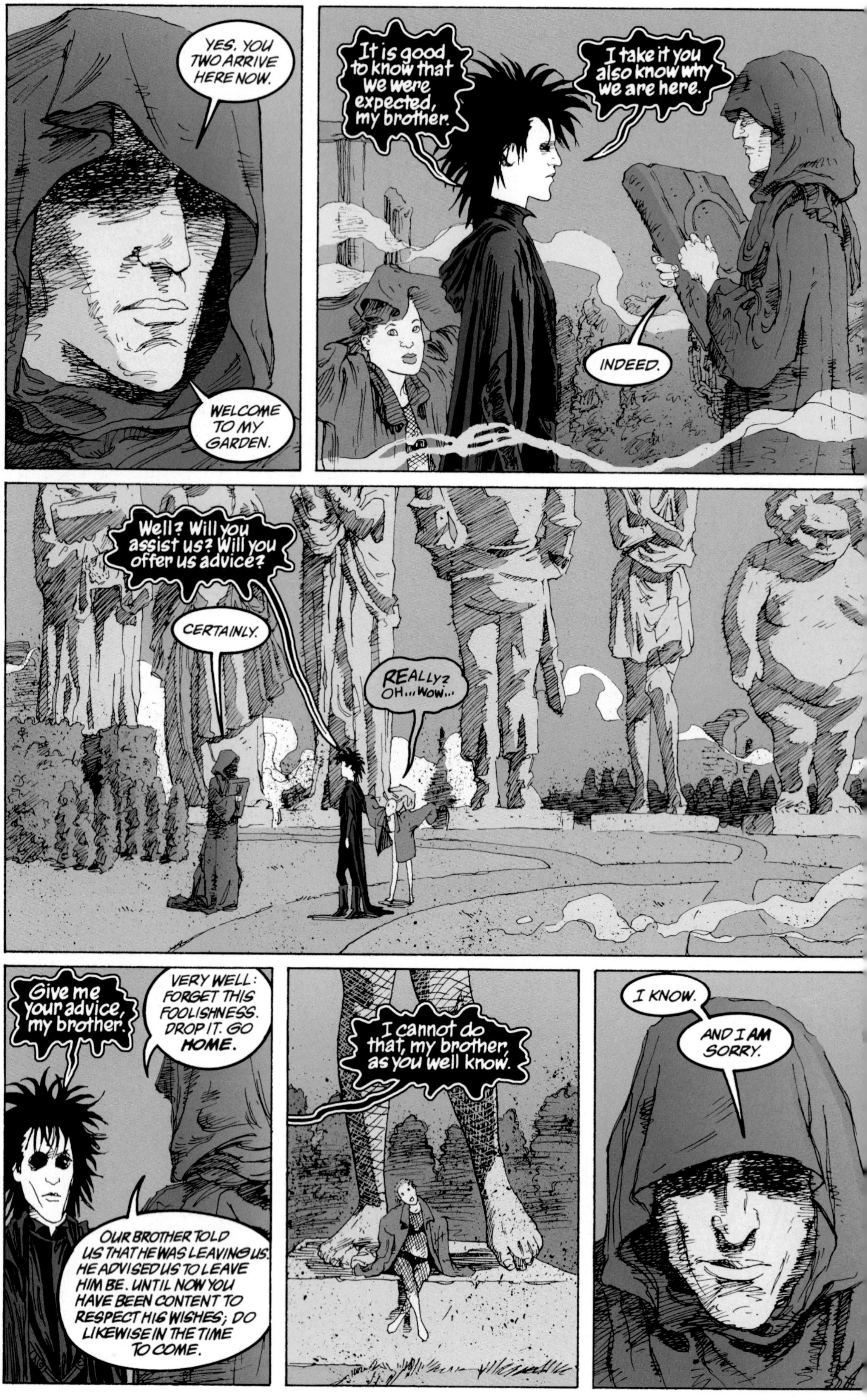
YES. YOU TWO ARRIVE HERE NOW.
WELCOME TO MY GARDEN.
It is good to know that we were expected, my brother.
I take it you also know why we are here.
INDEED.
Well? Will you assist us? Will you offer us advice?
CERTAINLY.
REAllY? OH...WOW...
Give me your advice, my brother.
VERY WELL: FORGET THIS FOOLISHNESS. DROP IT. GO HOME.
OUR BROTHER TOLD US THAT HE WAS LEAVING US. HE ADVISED US TO LEAVE HIM BE. UNTIL NOW YOU HAVE BEEN CONTENT TO RESPECT HIS WISHES; DO LIKEWISE IN THE TIME TO COME.
I cannot do that, my brother, as you well know.
I KNOW.
AND I AM SORRY.

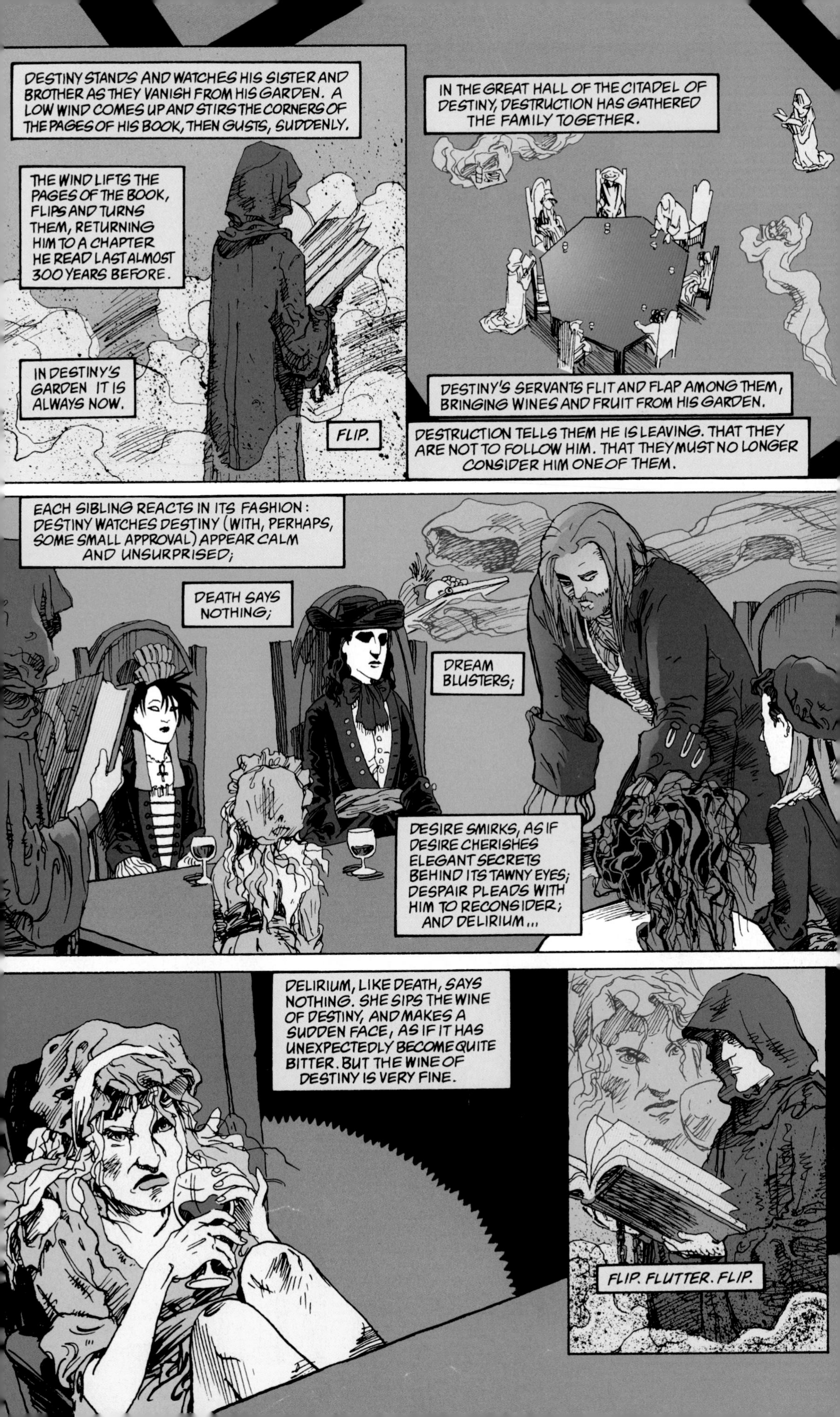
DESTINY STANDS AND WATCHES HIS SISTER AND BROTHER AS THEY VANISH FROM HIS GARDEN. A LOW WIND COMES UP AND STIRS THE CORNERS OF THE PAGES OF HIS BOOK, THEN GUSTS, SUDDENLY.
THE WIND LIFTS THE PAGES OF THE BOOK, FLIPS AND TURNS THEM, RETURNING HIM TO A CHAPTER HE READ LAST ALMOST 300 YEARS BEFORE.
IN DESTINY'S GARDEN IT IS ALWAYS NOW.
FLIP.
IN THE GREAT HALL OF THE CITADEL OF DESTINY, DESTRUCTION HAS GATHERED THE FAMILY TOGETHER.
DESTINY'S SERVANTS FLIT AND FLAP AMONG THEM, BRINGING WINES AND FRUIT FROM HIS GARDEN.
DESTRUCTION TELLS THEM HE IS LEAVING. THAT THEY ARE NOT TO FOLLOW HIM. THAT THEY MUST NO LONGER CONSIDER HIM ONE OF THEM.
EACH SIBLING REACTS IN ITS FASHION: DESTINY WATCHES DESTINY (WITH, PERHAPS, SOME SMALL APPROVAL) APPEAR CALM AND UNSURPRISED;
DEATH SAYS NOTHING;
DREAM BLUSTERS;
DESIRE SMIRKS, AS IF DESIRE CHERISHES ELEGANT SECRETS BEHIND ITS TAWNY EYES; DESPAIR PLEADS WITH HIM TO RECONSIDER; AND DELIRIUM...
DELIRIUM, LIKE DEATH, SAYS NOTHING. SHE SIPS THE WINE OF DESTINY, AND MAKES A SUDDEN FACE, AS IF IT HAS UNEXPECTEDLY BECOME QUITE BITTER. BUT THE WINE OF DESTINY IS VERY FINE.
FLIP. FLUTTER. FLIP.

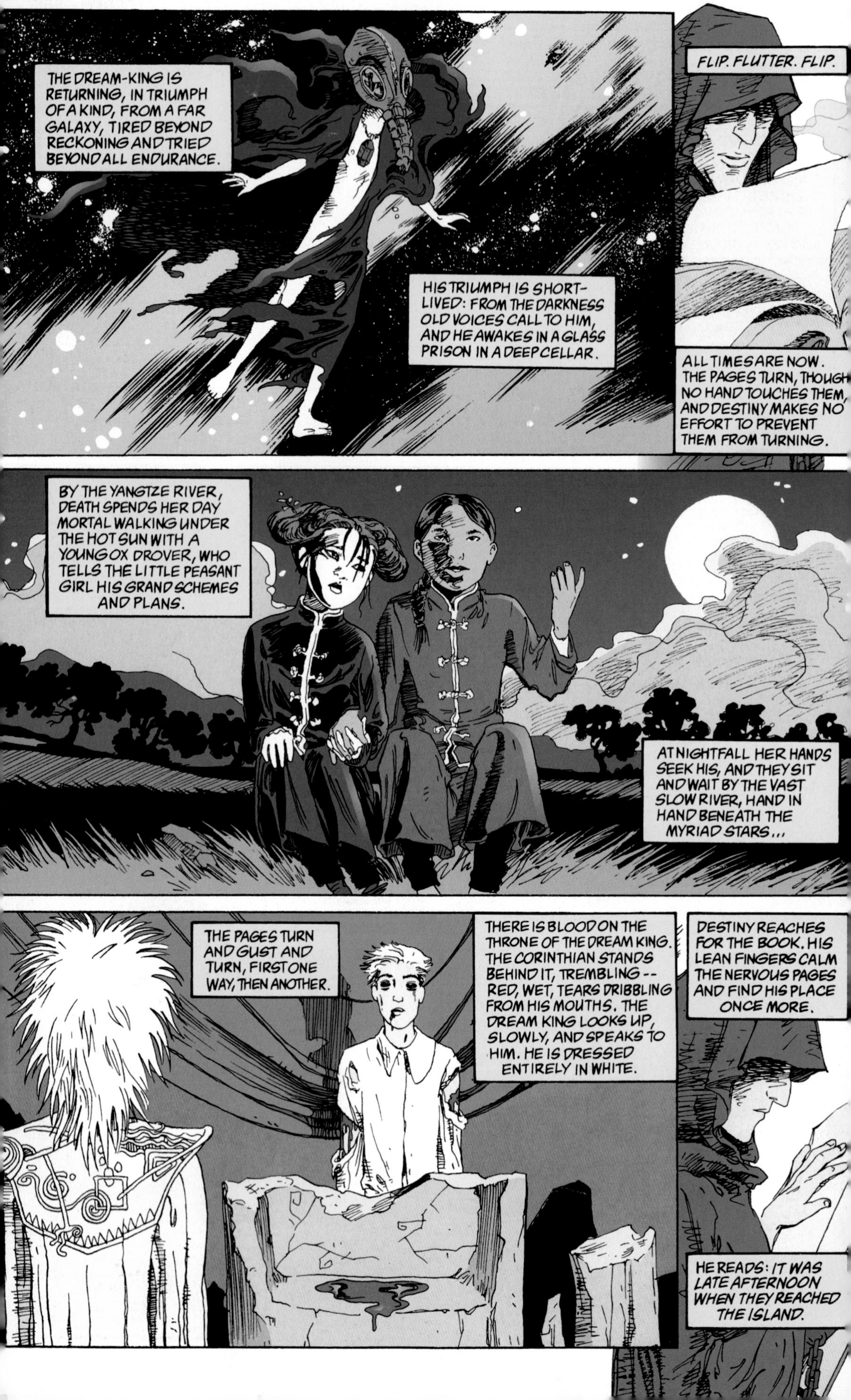

THE DREAM-KING IS RETURNING, IN TRIUMPH OF A KIND, FROM A FAR GALAXY, TIRED BEYOND RECKONING AND TRIED BEYOND ALL ENDURANCE.
HIS TRIUMPH IS SHORT-LIVED: FROM THE DARKNESS OLD VOICES CALL TO HIM, AND HE AWAKES IN A GLASS PRISON IN A DEEP CELLAR.
FLIP. FLUTTER. FLIP.
ALL TIMES ARE NOW. THE PAGES TURN, THOUGH NO HAND TOUCHES THEM, AND DESTINY MAKES NO EFFORT TO PREVENT THEM FROM TURNING.
BY THE YANGTZE RIVER, DEATH SPENDS HER DAY MORTAL WALKING UNDER THE HOT SUN WITH A YOUNG OX DROVER, WHO TELLS THE LITTLE PEASANT GIRL HIS GRAND SCHEMES AND PLANS.
AT NIGHTFALL HER HANDS SEEK HIS, AND THEY SIT AND WAIT BY THE VAST SLOW RIVER, HAND IN HAND BENEATH THE MYRIAD STARS...
THE PAGES TURN AND GUST AND TURN, FIRST ONE WAY, THEN ANOTHER.
THERE IS BLOOD ON THE THRONE OF THE DREAM KING. THE CORINTHIAN STANDS BEHIND IT, TREMBLING -- RED, WET, TEARS DRIBBLING FROM HIS MOUTHS. THE DREAM KING LOOKS UP, SLOWLY, AND SPEAKS TO HIM. HE IS DRESSED ENTIRELY IN WHITE.
DESTINY REACHES FOR THE BOOK. HIS LEAN FINGERS CALM THE NERVOUS PAGES AND FIND HIS PLACE ONCE MORE.
HE READS: IT WAS LATE AFTERNOON WHEN THEY REACHED THE ISLAND.

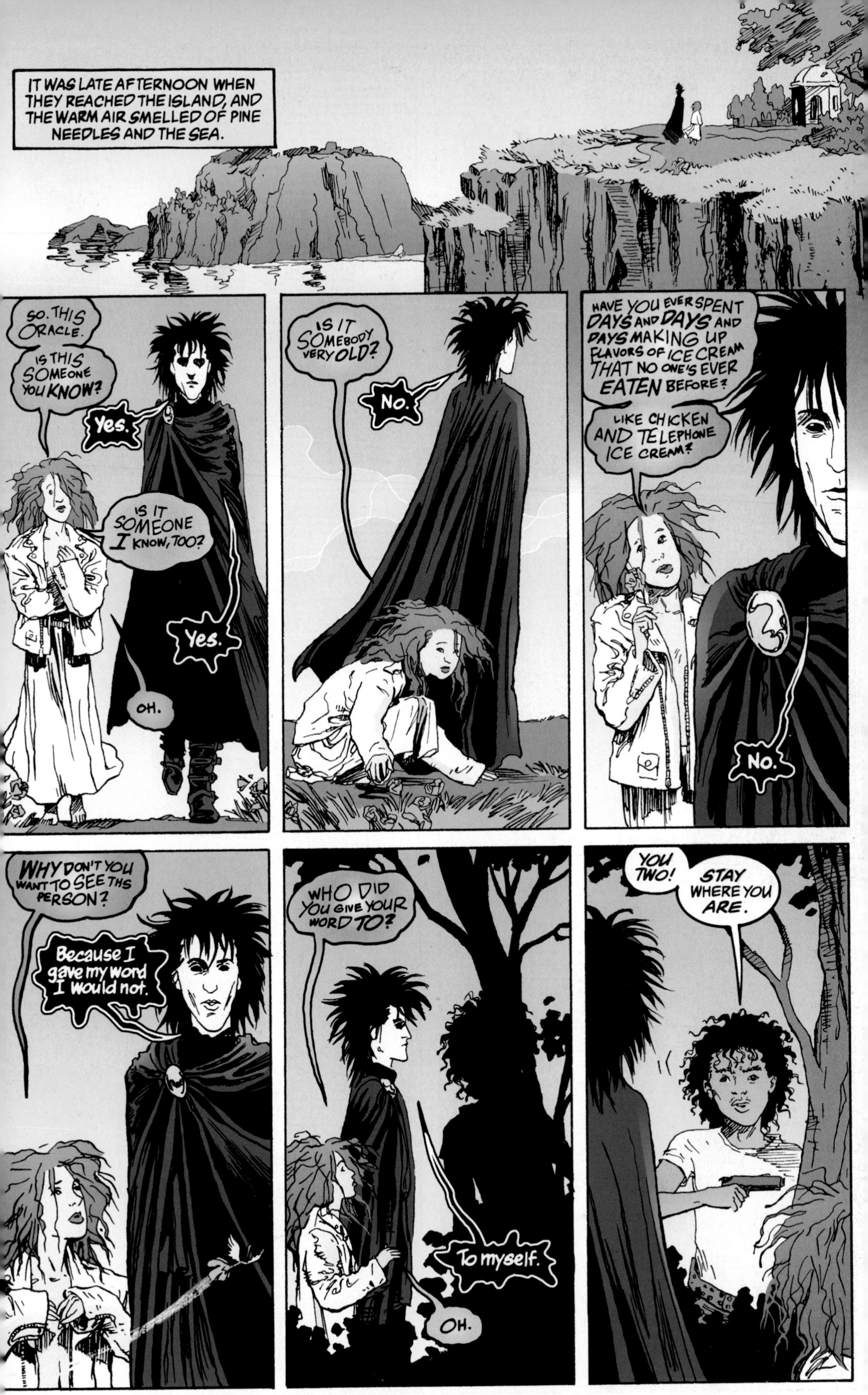
IT WAS LATE AFTERNOON WHEN THEY REACHED THE ISLAND, AND THE WARM AIR SMELLED OF PINE NEEDLES AND THE SEA.
SO. THIS ORACLE.
IS THIS SOMEONE YOU KNOW?
Yes.
IS IT SOMEONE I KNOW, TOO?
Yes.
OH.
IS IT SOMEBODY VERY OLD?
No.
HAVE YOU EVER SPENT DAYS AND DAYS AND DAYS MAKING UP FLAVORS OF ICE CREAM THAT NO ONE'S EVER EATEN BEFORE?
LIKE CHICKEN AND TELEPHONE ICE CREAM?
No.
WHY DON'T YOU WANT TO SEE THIS PERSON?
Because I gave my word I would not.
WHO DID YOU GIVE YOUR WORD TO?
To myself.
OH.
YOU TWO!
STAY WHERE YOU ARE.

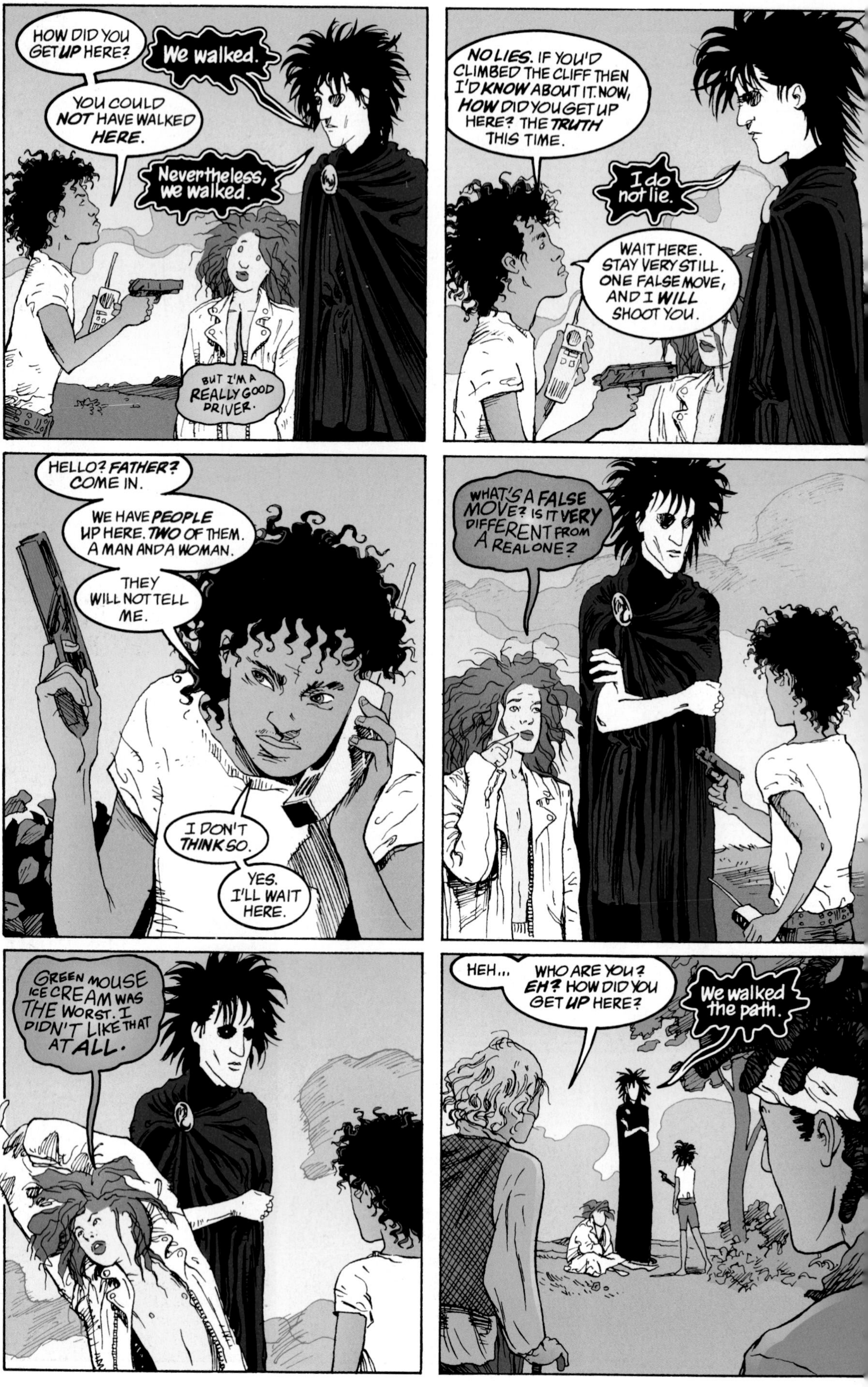
HOW DID YOU GET UP HERE?
We walked.
YOU COULD NOT HAVE WALKED HERE.
Nevertheless, we walked.
BUT I'M A REALLY GOOD DRIVER.
NO LIES. IF YOU'D CLIMBED THE CLIFF THEN I'D KNOW ABOUT IT. NOW, HOW DID YOU GET UP HERE? THE TRUTH THIS TIME.
I do not lie.
WAIT HERE. STAY VERY STILL. ONE FALSE MOVE, AND I WILL SHOOT YOU.
HELLO? FATHER? COME IN.
WE HAVE PEOPLE UP HERE. TWO OF THEM. A MAN AND A WOMAN.
THEY WILL NOT TELL ME.
I DON'T THINK SO.
YES. I'LL WAIT HERE.
WHAT'S A FALSE MOVE? IS IT VERY DIFFERENT FROM A REAL ONE?
GREEN MOUSE ICE CREAM WAS THE WORST. I DIDN'T LIKE THAT AT ALL.
HEH...
WHO ARE YOU? EH? HOW DID YOU GET UP HERE?
We walked the path.

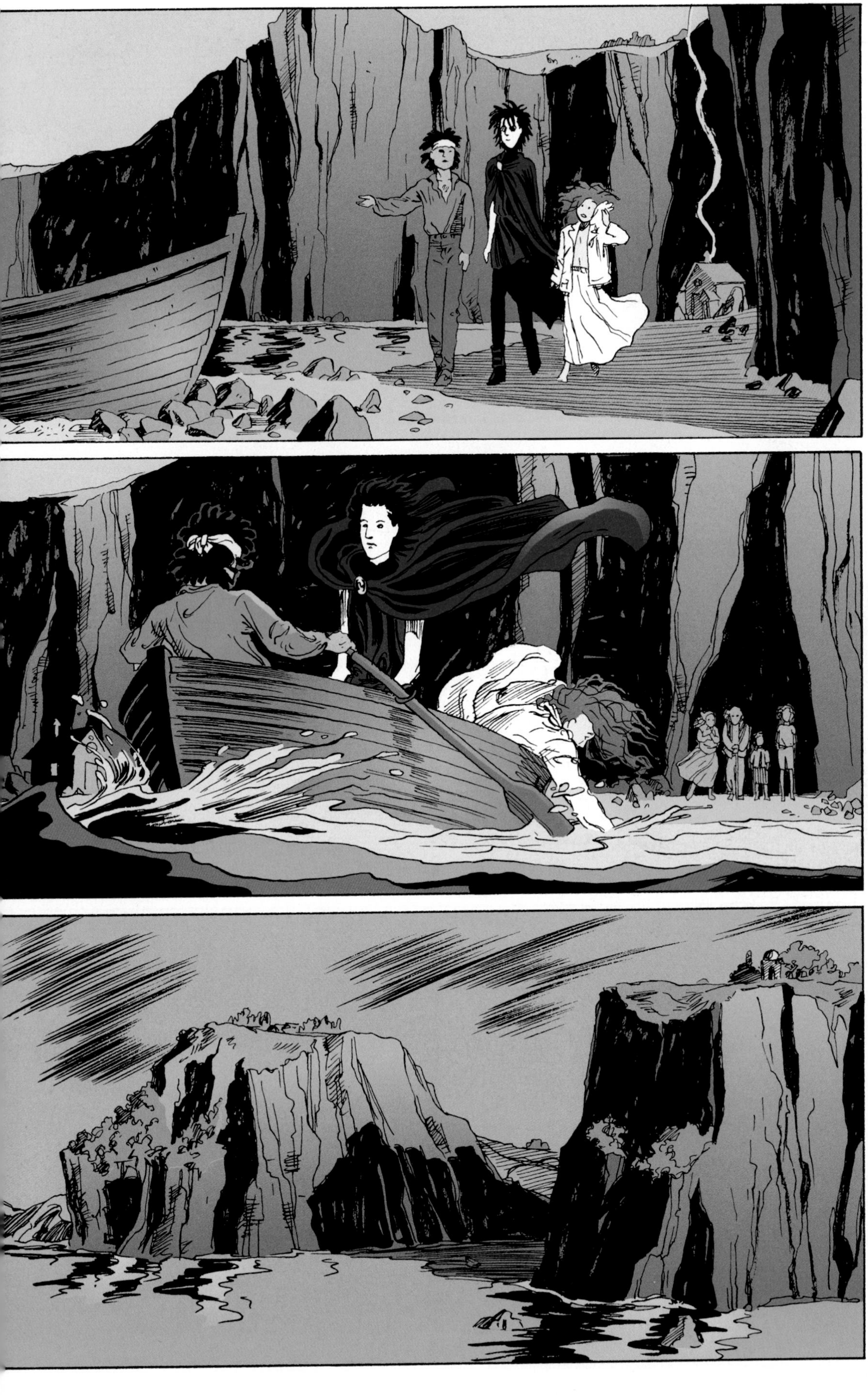

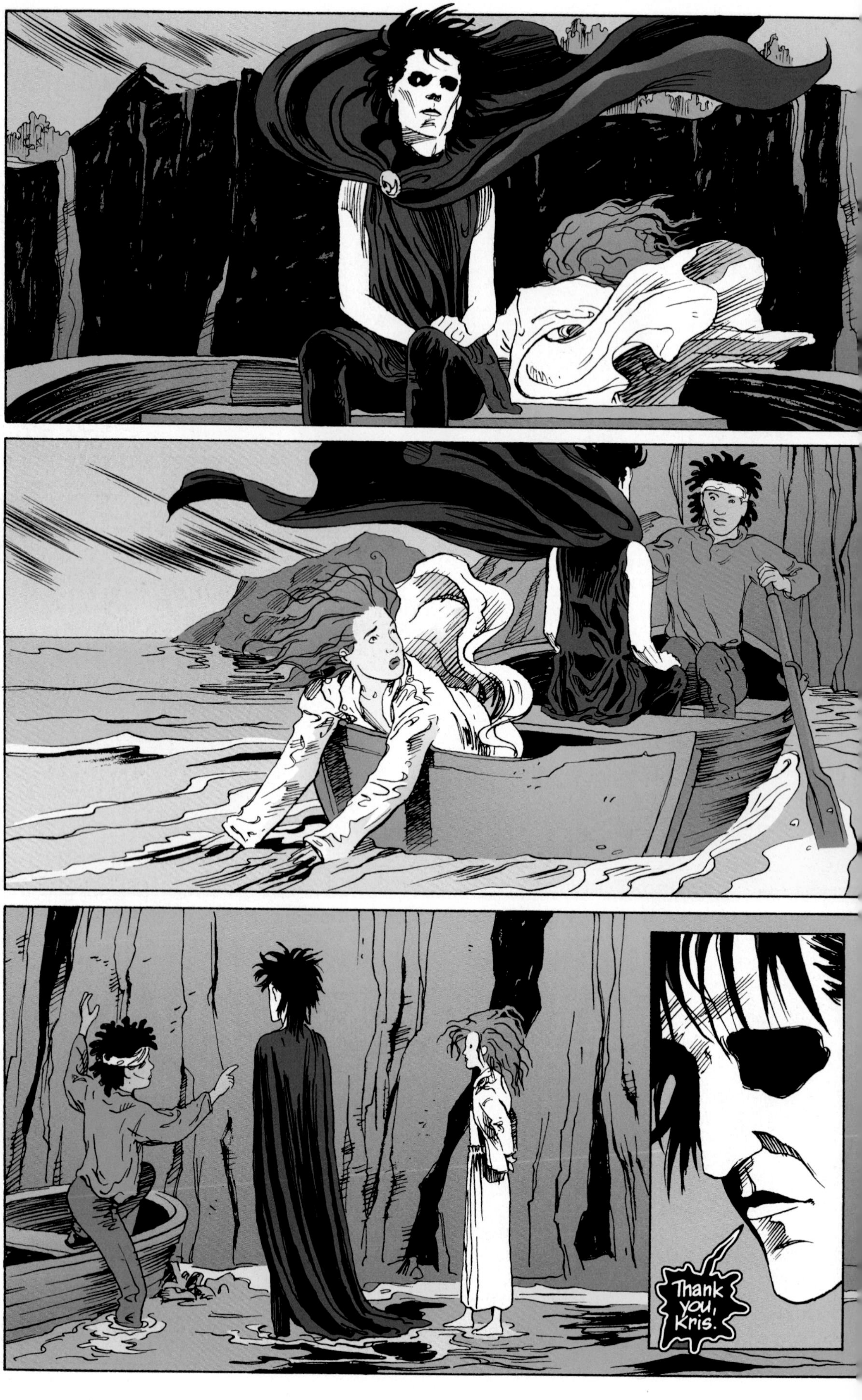
Thank you, Kris.

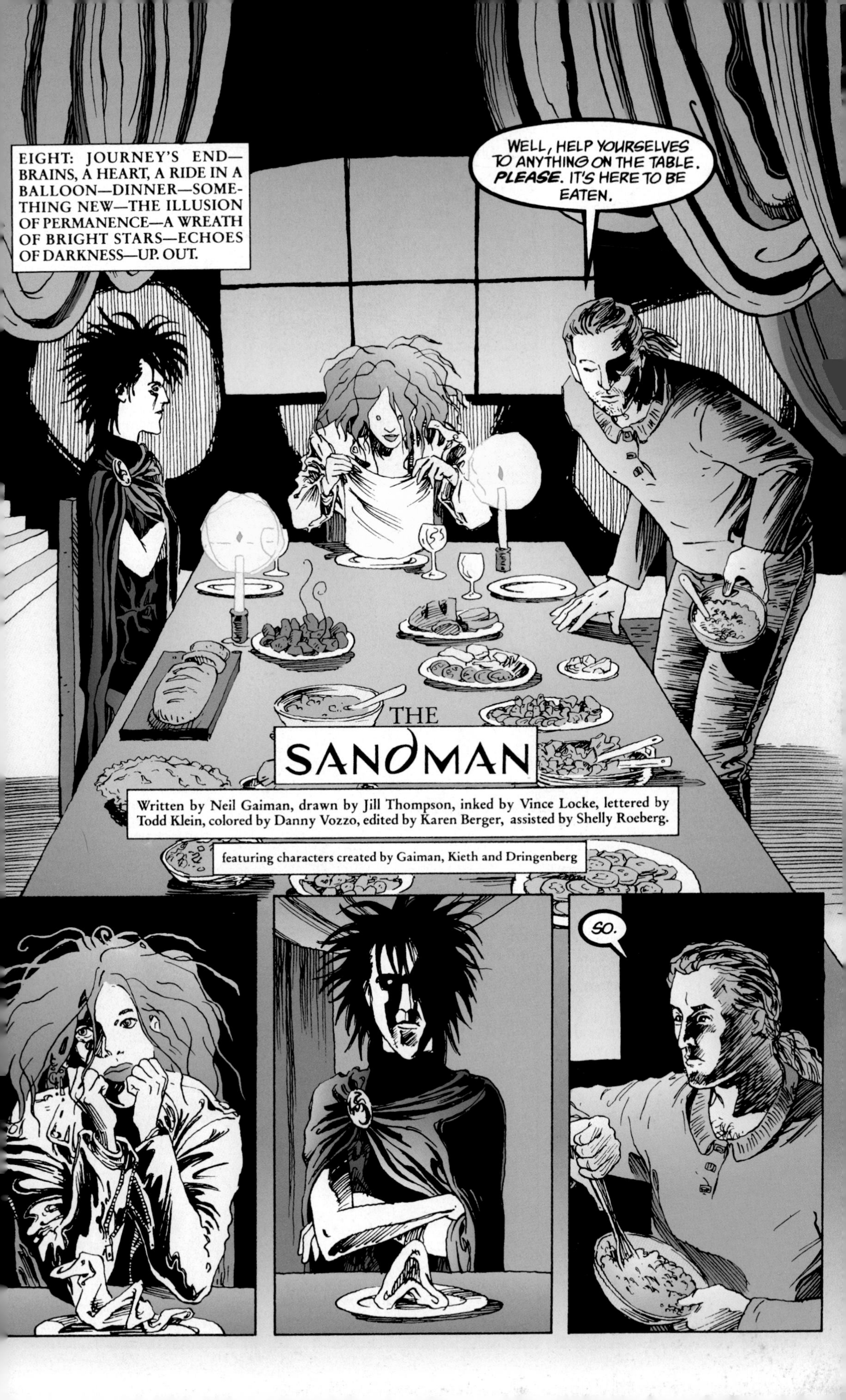
EIGHT: JOURNEY'S END—BRAINS, A HEART, A RIDE IN A BALLOON—DINNER—SOMETHING NEW—THE ILLUSION OF PERMANENCE—A WREATH OF BRIGHT STARS—ECHOES OF DARKNESS—UP. OUT.
WELL, HELP YOURSELVES TO ANYTHING ON THE TABLE. PLEASE. IT'S HERE TO BE EATEN.
THE SANDMAN
Written by Neil Gaiman, drawn by Jill Thompson, inked by Vince Locke, lettered by Todd Klein, colored by Danny Vozzo, edited by Karen Berger, assisted by Shelly Roeberg.
featuring characters created by Gaiman, Kieth and Dringenberg
SO.

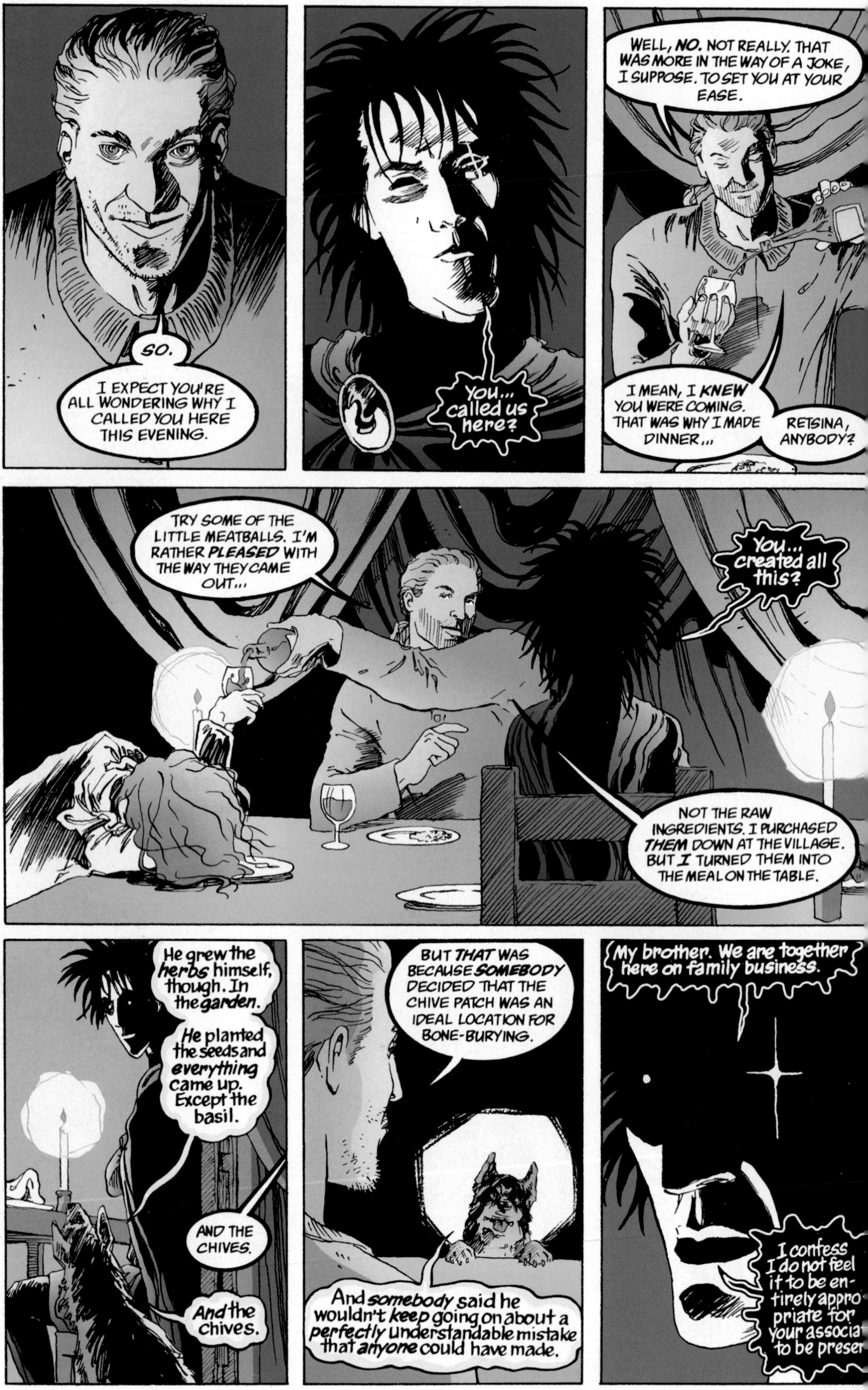
SO.
I EXPECT YOU'RE ALL WONDERING WHY I CALLED YOU HERE THIS EVENING.
You... called us here?
WELL, NO. NOT REALLY. THAT WAS MORE IN THE WAY OF A JOKE, I SUPPOSE. TO SET YOU AT YOUR EASE.
I MEAN, I KNEW YOU WERE COMING. THAT WAS WHY I MADE DINNER...
RETSINA, ANYBODY?
TRY SOME OF THE LITTLE MEATBALLS. I'M RATHER PLEASED WITH THE WAY THEY CAME OUT...
You... created all this?
NOT THE RAW INGREDIENTS. I PURCHASED THEM DOWN AT THE VILLAGE. BUT I TURNED THEM INTO THE MEAL ON THE TABLE.
He grew the herbs himself, though. In the garden.
He planted the seeds and everything came up. Except the basil.
AND THE CHIVES.
And the chives.
BUT THAT WAS BECAUSE SOMEBODY DECIDED THAT THE CHIVE PATCH WAS AN IDEAL LOCATION FOR BONE-BURYING.
And somebody said he wouldn't keep going on about a perfectly understandable mistake that anyone could have made.
My brother. We are together here on family business.
I confess I do not feel it to be entirely appropriate for your associa to be preser

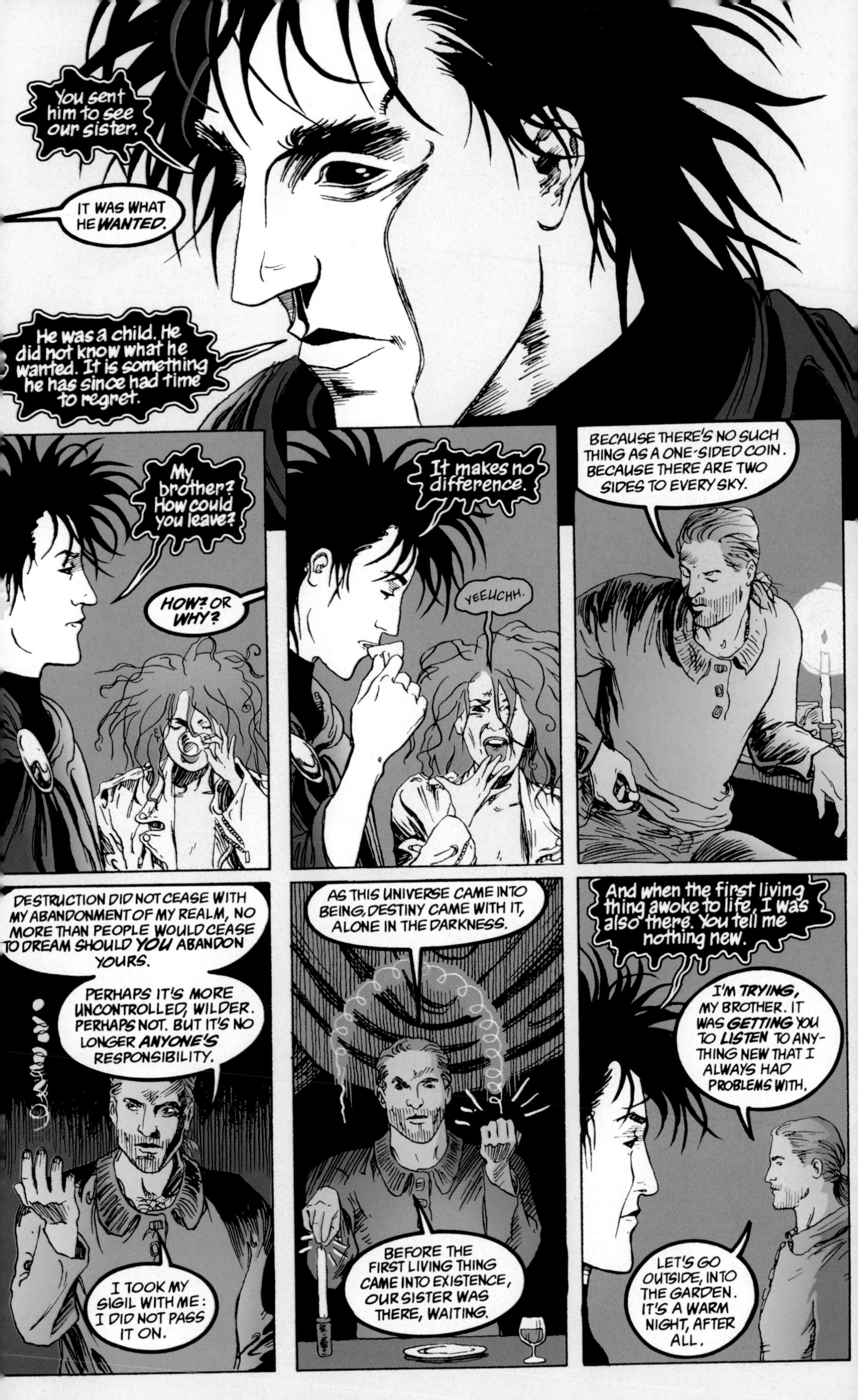
You sent him to see our sister.
IT WAS WHAT HE WANTED.
He was a child. He did not know what he wanted. It is something he has since had time to regret.
My brother? How could you leave?
HOW? OR WHY?
It makes no difference.
YEEUCHH.
BECAUSE THERE'S NO SUCH THING AS A ONE-SIDED COIN. BECAUSE THERE ARE TWO SIDES TO EVERY SKY.
DESTRUCTION DID NOT CEASE WITH MY ABANDONMENT OF MY REALM, NO MORE THAN PEOPLE WOULD CEASE TO DREAM SHOULD YOU ABANDON YOURS.
PERHAPS IT'S MORE UNCONTROLLED, WILDER. PERHAPS NOT. BUT IT'S NO LONGER ANYONE'S RESPONSIBILITY.
I TOOK MY SIGIL WITH ME: I DID NOT PASS IT ON.
AS THIS UNIVERSE CAME INTO BEING, DESTINY CAME WITH IT, ALONE IN THE DARKNESS.
BEFORE THE FIRST LIVING THING CAME INTO EXISTENCE, OUR SISTER WAS THERE, WAITING.
And when the first living thing awoke to life, I was also there. You tell me nothing new.
I'M TRYING, MY BROTHER. IT WAS GETTING YOU TO LISTEN TO ANYTHING NEW THAT I ALWAYS HAD PROBLEMS WITH.
LET'S GO OUTSIDE, INTO THE GARDEN. IT'S A WARM NIGHT, AFTER ALL.

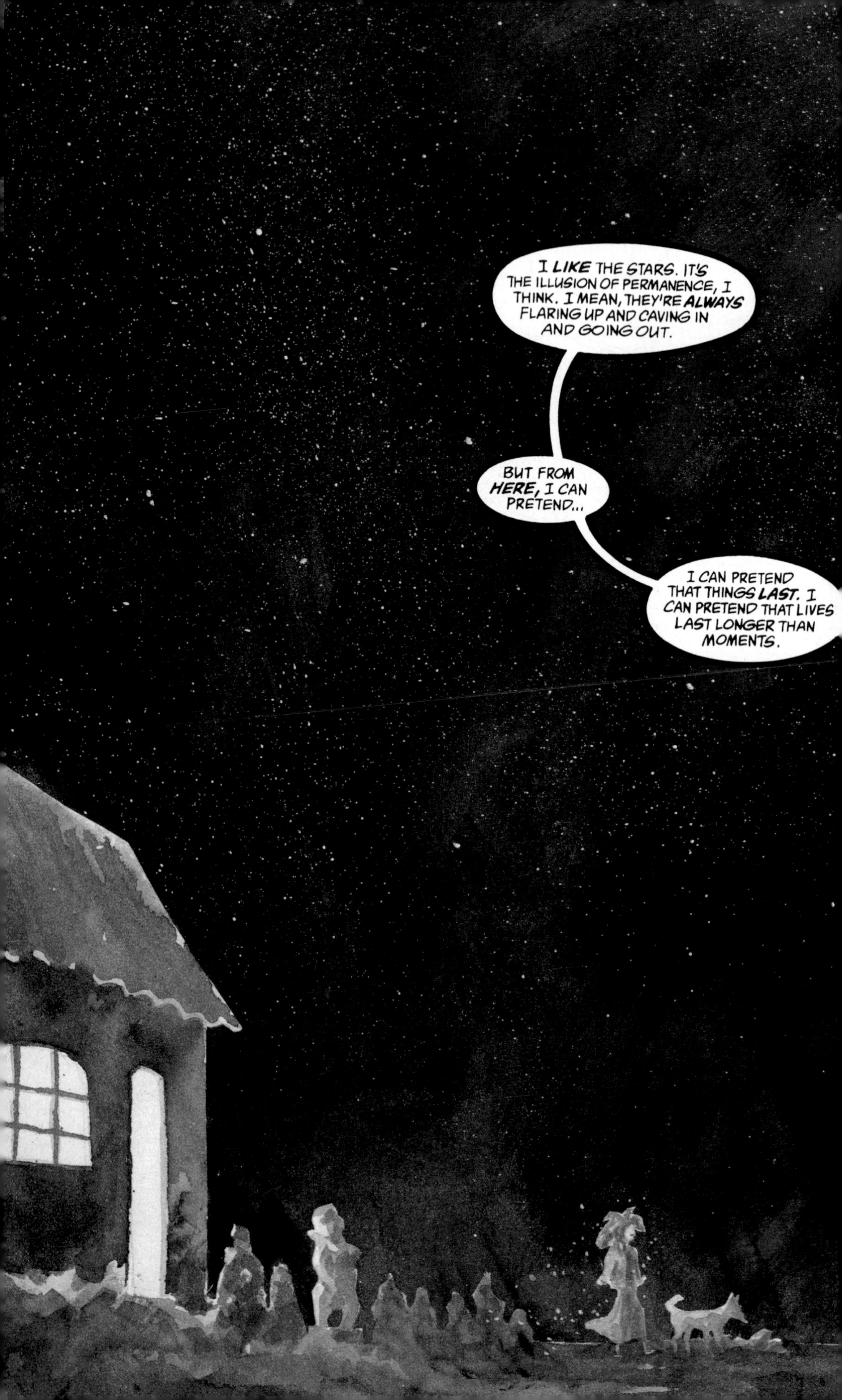
I LIKE THE STARS. IT'S THE ILLUSION OF PERMANENCE, I THINK. I MEAN, THEY'RE ALWAYS FLARING UP AND CAVING IN AND GOING OUT.
BUT FROM HERE, I CAN PRETEND...
I CAN PRETEND THAT THINGS LAST. I CAN PRETEND THAT LIVES LAST LONGER THAN MOMENTS.

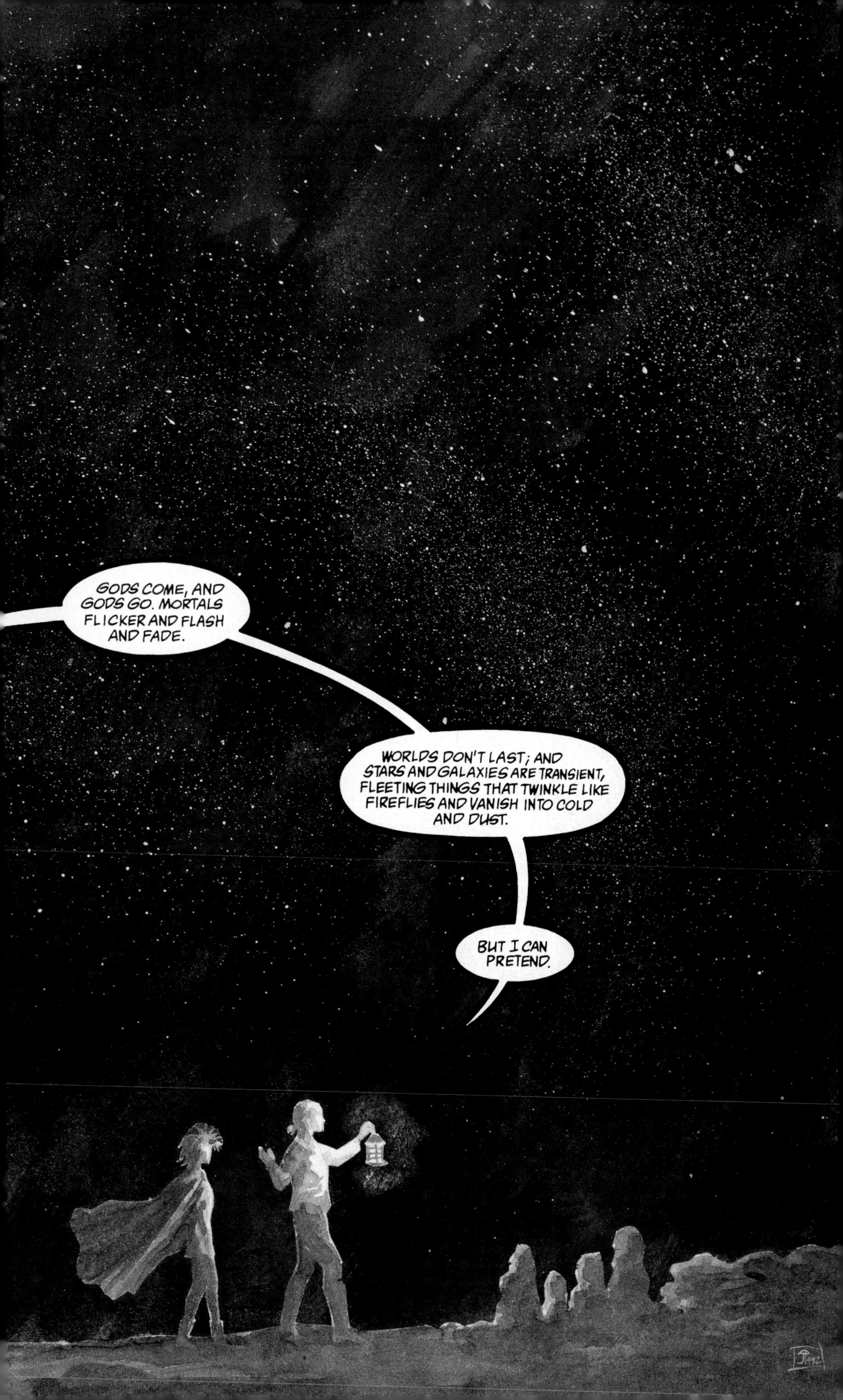
GODS COME, AND GODS GO. MORTALS FLICKER AND FLASH AND FADE.
WORLDS DON'T LAST; AND STARS AND GALAXIES ARE TRANSIENT, FLEETING THINGS THAT TWINKLE LIKE FIREFLIES AND VANISH INTO COLD AND DUST.
BUT I CAN PRETEND.

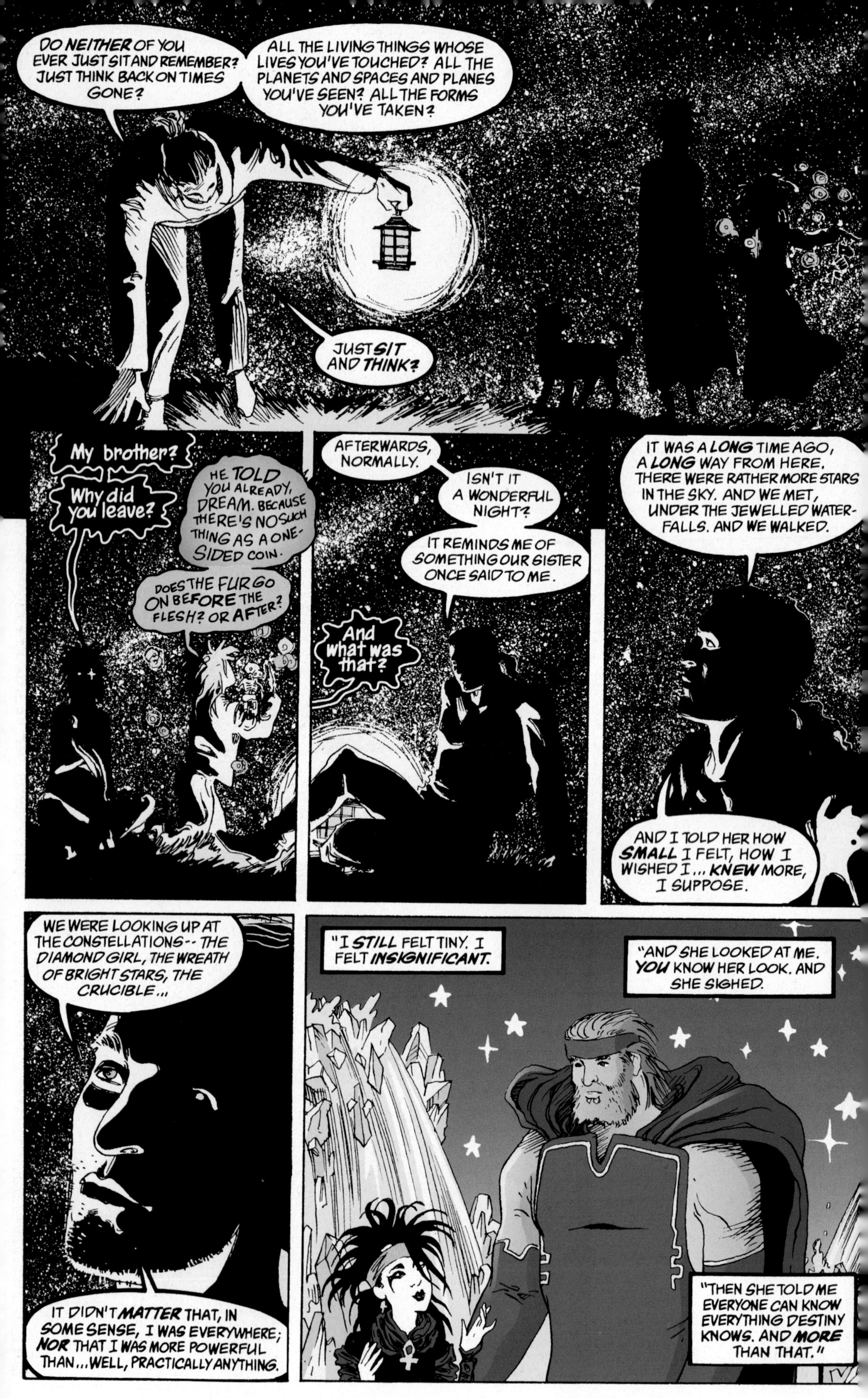
DO NEITHER OF YOU EVER JUST SIT AND REMEMBER? JUST THINK BACK ON TIMES GONE?
ALL THE LIVING THINGS WHOSE LIVES YOU'VE TOUCHED? ALL THE PLANETS AND SPACES AND PLANES YOU'VE SEEN? ALL THE FORMS YOU'VE TAKEN?
JUST SIT AND THINK?
My brother?
Why did you leave?
HE TOLD YOU ALREADY, DREAM. BECAUSE THERE'S NO SUCH THING AS A ONE-SIDED COIN.
DOES THE FUR GO ON BEFORE THE FLESH? OR AFTER?
AFTERWARDS, NORMALLY.
ISN'T IT A WONDERFUL NIGHT?
IT REMINDS ME OF SOMETHING OUR SISTER ONCE SAID TO ME.
And what was that?
IT WAS A LONG TIME AGO, A LONG WAY FROM HERE. THERE WERE RATHER MORE STARS IN THE SKY. AND WE MET, UNDER THE JEWELLED WATER-FALLS. AND WE WALKED.
AND I TOLD HER HOW SMALL I FELT, HOW I WISHED I... KNEW MORE, I SUPPOSE.
WE WERE LOOKING UP AT THE CONSTELLATIONS-- THE DIAMOND GIRL, THE WREATH OF BRIGHT STARS, THE CRUCIBLE...
IT DIDN'T MATTER THAT, IN SOME SENSE, I WAS EVERYWHERE; NOR THAT I WAS MORE POWERFUL THAN... WELL, PRACTICALLY ANYTHING.
"I STILL FELT TINY. I FELT INSIGNIFICANT.
"AND SHE LOOKED AT ME. YOU KNOW HER LOOK. AND SHE SIGHED.
"THEN SHE TOLD ME EVERYONE CAN KNOW EVERYTHING DESTINY KNOWS. AND MORE THAN THAT."

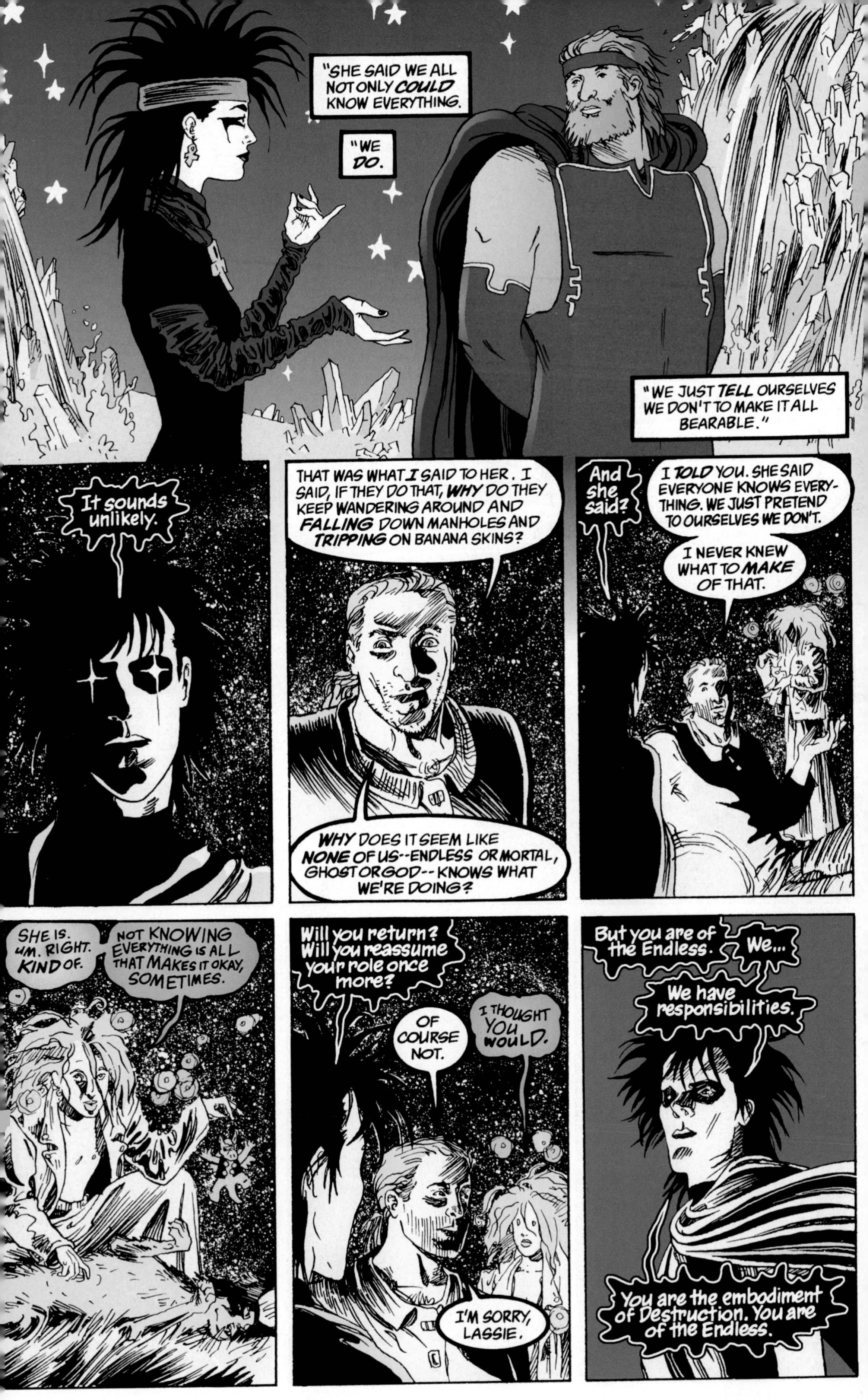

"SHE SAID WE ALL NOT ONLY COULD KNOW EVERYTHING.
"WE DO.
"WE JUST TELL OURSELVES WE DON'T TO MAKE IT ALL BEARABLE."
It sounds unlikely.
THAT WAS WHAT I SAID TO HER. I SAID, IF THEY DO THAT, WHY DO THEY KEEP WANDERING AROUND AND FALLING DOWN MANHOLES AND TRIPPING ON BANANA SKINS?
WHY DOES IT SEEM LIKE NONE OF US--ENDLESS OR MORTAL, GHOST OR GOD--KNOWS WHAT WE'RE DOING?
And she said?
I TOLD YOU. SHE SAID EVERYONE KNOWS EVERY-THING. WE JUST PRETEND TO OURSELVES WE DON'T.
I NEVER KNEW WHAT TO MAKE OF THAT.
SHE IS. UM. RIGHT. KIND OF.
NOT KNOWING EVERYTHING IS ALL THAT MAKES IT OKAY, SOMETIMES.
Will you return? Will you reassume your role once more?
OF COURSE NOT.
I THOUGHT YOU WOULD.
I'M SORRY, LASSIE.
But you are of the Endless.
We...
We have responsibilities.
You are the embodiment of Destruction. You are of the Endless.

THE *ENDLESS?* THE ENDLESS ARE MERELY *PATTERNS.* THE ENDLESS ARE *IDEAS.* THE ENDLESS ARE *WAVE FUNCTIONS.* THE ENDLESS ARE *REPEATING MOTIFS.*

THE ENDLESS ARE *ECHOES* OF *DARKNESS,* AND NOTHING MORE. WE HAVE NO *RIGHT* TO PLAY WITH THEIR LIVES, TO ORDER THEIR DREAMS AND THEIR DESIRES.

AND EVEN *OUR* EXISTENCES ARE BRIEF AND BOUNDED. *NONE* OF US WILL LAST LONGER THAN THIS VERSION OF THE UNIVERSE.

EXCEPT OUR *SISTER.*

So we suppose.

I FILLED MY ROLE *MORE* THAN ADEQUATELY FOR OVER TEN BILLION YEARS.

A TWO-SIDED COIN: DESTRUCTION IS NEEDED. NOTHING NEW CAN EXIST WITHOUT DESTROYING THE OLD.

THINGS ARE CREATED. THEY LAST FOR SOME LITTLE WHILE, AND THEN THEY ARE GONE. EMPIRES, CITIES, POEMS AND PEOPLE. ATOMS AND WORLDS.

ONE CANNOT BEGIN A NEW DREAM WITHOUT ABANDONING THE LAST, *EH,* BROTHER?

WHOOMPF

OUR SISTER DEFINES LIFE, JUST AS DESPAIR DEFINES HOPE, OR DESIRE DEFINES HATRED, OR AS DESTINY DEFINES FREEDOM.

And what do *I* define, by this theory of yours.

REALITY, PERHAPS?

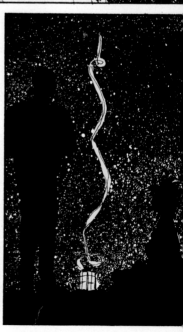

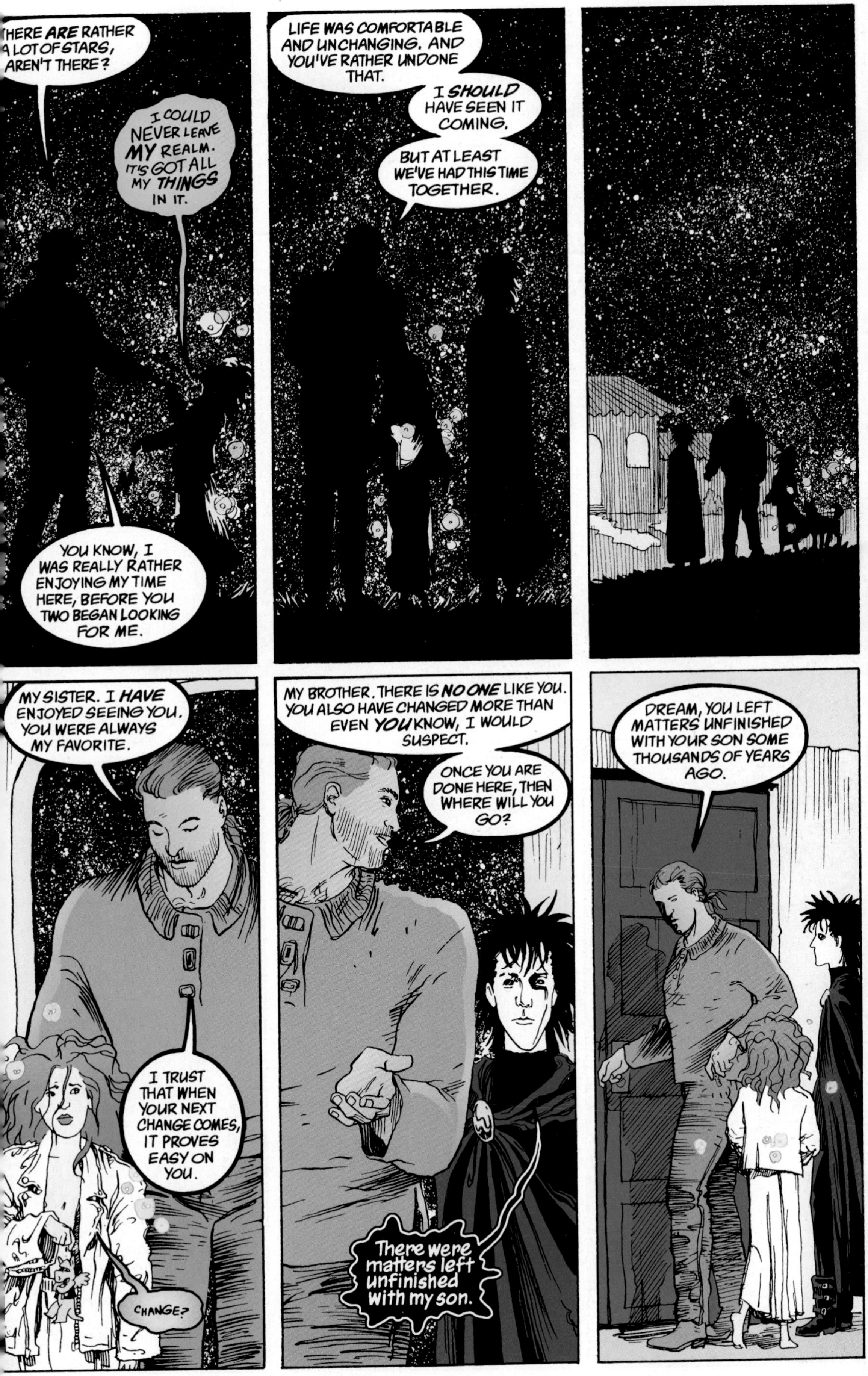

THERE ARE RATHER A LOT OF STARS, AREN'T THERE?
I COULD NEVER LEAVE MY REALM. IT'S GOT ALL MY THINGS IN IT.
YOU KNOW, I WAS REALLY RATHER ENJOYING MY TIME HERE, BEFORE YOU TWO BEGAN LOOKING FOR ME.
LIFE WAS COMFORTABLE AND UNCHANGING. AND YOU'VE RATHER UNDONE THAT.
I SHOULD HAVE SEEN IT COMING.
BUT AT LEAST WE'VE HAD THIS TIME TOGETHER.
MY SISTER. I HAVE ENJOYED SEEING YOU. YOU WERE ALWAYS MY FAVORITE.
I TRUST THAT WHEN YOUR NEXT CHANGE COMES, IT PROVES EASY ON YOU.
CHANGE?
MY BROTHER. THERE IS NO ONE LIKE YOU. YOU ALSO HAVE CHANGED MORE THAN EVEN YOU KNOW, I WOULD SUSPECT.
ONCE YOU ARE DONE HERE, THEN WHERE WILL YOU GO?
There were matters left unfinished with my son.
DREAM, YOU LEFT MATTERS UNFINISHED WITH YOUR SON SOME THOUSANDS OF YEARS AGO.

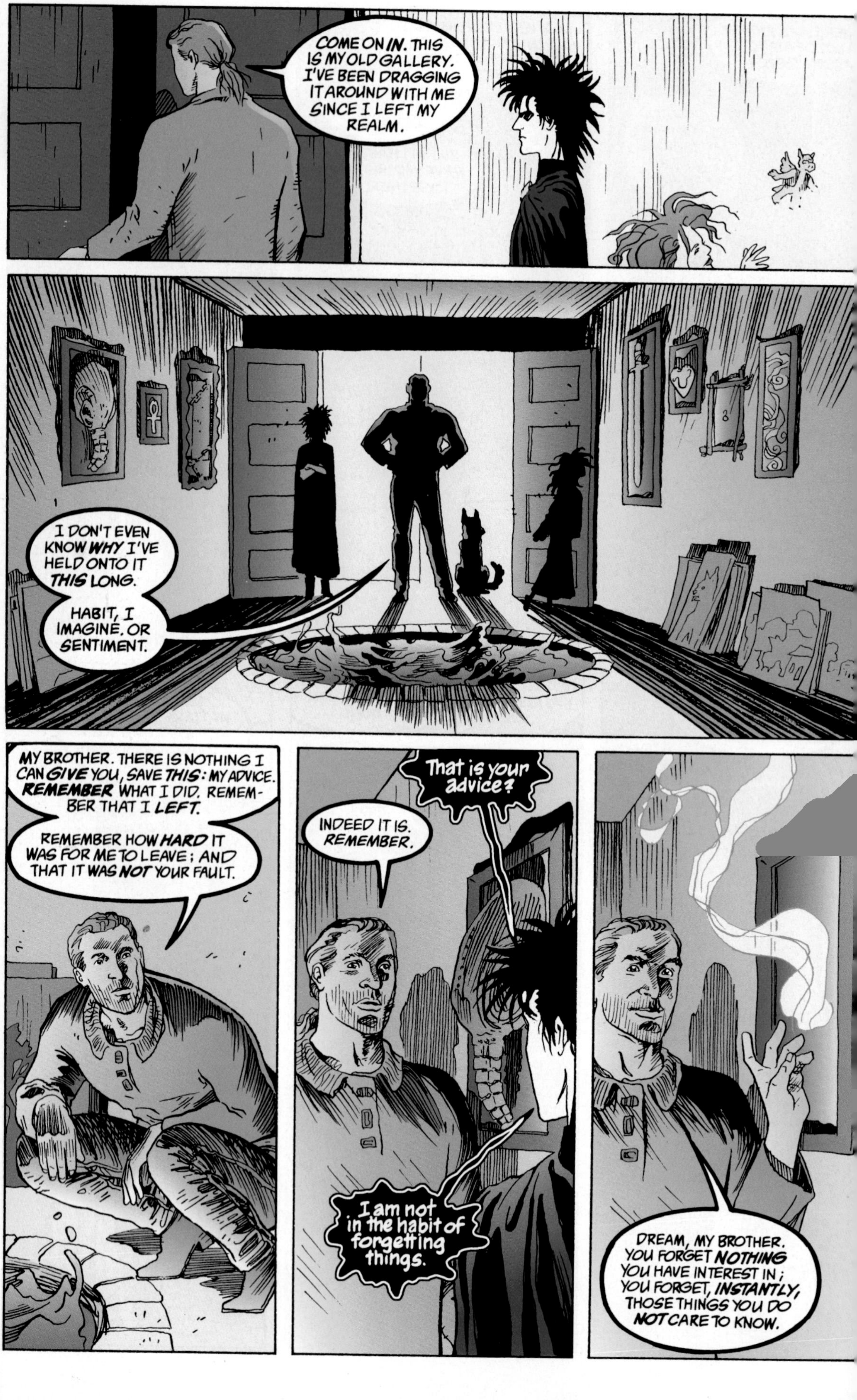
COME ON IN. THIS IS MY OLD GALLERY. I'VE BEEN DRAGGING IT AROUND WITH ME SINCE I LEFT MY REALM.
I DON'T EVEN KNOW WHY I'VE HELD ONTO IT THIS LONG.
HABIT, I IMAGINE. OR SENTIMENT.
MY BROTHER. THERE IS NOTHING I CAN GIVE YOU, SAVE THIS: MY ADVICE. REMEMBER WHAT I DID. REMEMBER THAT I LEFT.
REMEMBER HOW HARD IT WAS FOR ME TO LEAVE; AND THAT IT WAS NOT YOUR FAULT.
That is your advice?
INDEED IT IS. REMEMBER.
I am not in the habit of forgetting things.
DREAM, MY BROTHER. YOU FORGET NOTHING YOU HAVE INTEREST IN; YOU FORGET, INSTANTLY, THOSE THINGS YOU DO NOT CARE TO KNOW.

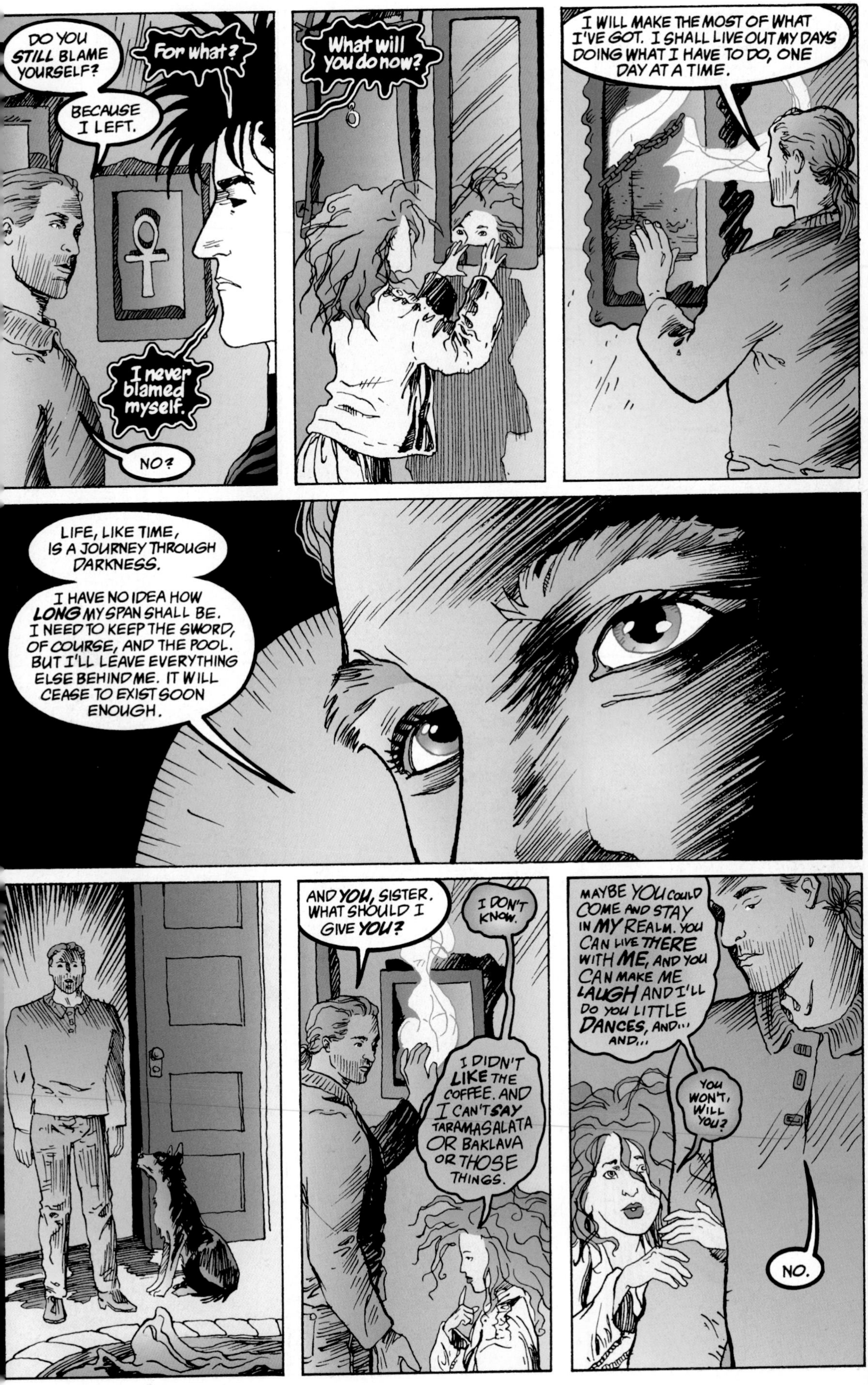

DO YOU STILL BLAME YOURSELF?
For what?
BECAUSE I LEFT.
I never blamed myself.
NO?
What will you do now?
I WILL MAKE THE MOST OF WHAT I'VE GOT. I SHALL LIVE OUT MY DAYS DOING WHAT I HAVE TO DO, ONE DAY AT A TIME.
LIFE, LIKE TIME, IS A JOURNEY THROUGH DARKNESS.
I HAVE NO IDEA HOW LONG MY SPAN SHALL BE. I NEED TO KEEP THE SWORD, OF COURSE, AND THE POOL. BUT I'LL LEAVE EVERYTHING ELSE BEHIND ME. IT WILL CEASE TO EXIST SOON ENOUGH.
AND YOU, SISTER. WHAT SHOULD I GIVE YOU?
I DON'T KNOW.
I DIDN'T LIKE THE COFFEE. AND I CAN'T SAY TARAMASALATA OR BAKLAVA OR THOSE THINGS.
MAYBE YOU COULD COME AND STAY IN MY REALM. YOU CAN LIVE THERE WITH ME, AND YOU CAN MAKE ME LAUGH AND I'LL DO YOU LITTLE DANCES, AND... AND...
YOU WON'T, WILL YOU?
NO.

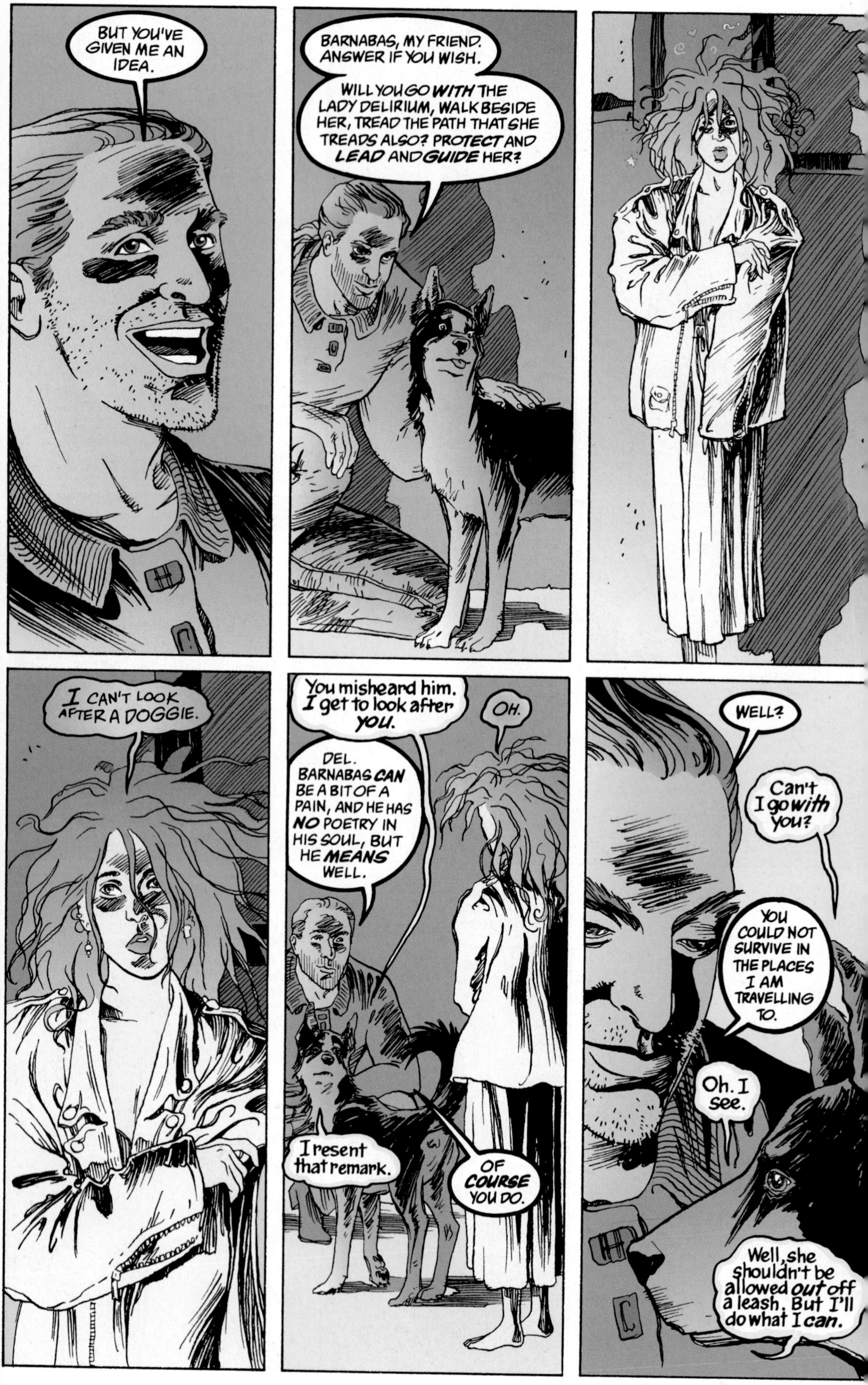
BUT YOU'VE GIVEN ME AN IDEA.
BARNABAS, MY FRIEND. ANSWER IF YOU WISH.
WILL YOU GO WITH THE LADY DELIRIUM, WALK BESIDE HER, TREAD THE PATH THAT SHE TREADS ALSO? PROTECT AND LEAD AND GUIDE HER?
I CAN'T LOOK AFTER A DOGGIE.
You misheard him. I get to look after YOU.
OH.
DEL. BARNABAS CAN BE A BIT OF A PAIN, AND HE HAS NO POETRY IN HIS SOUL, BUT HE MEANS WELL.
I resent that remark.
OF COURSE YOU DO.
WELL?
Can't I go with you?
YOU COULD NOT SURVIVE IN THE PLACES I AM TRAVELLING TO.
Oh. I see.
Well, she shouldn't be allowed out off a leash. But I'll do what I can.

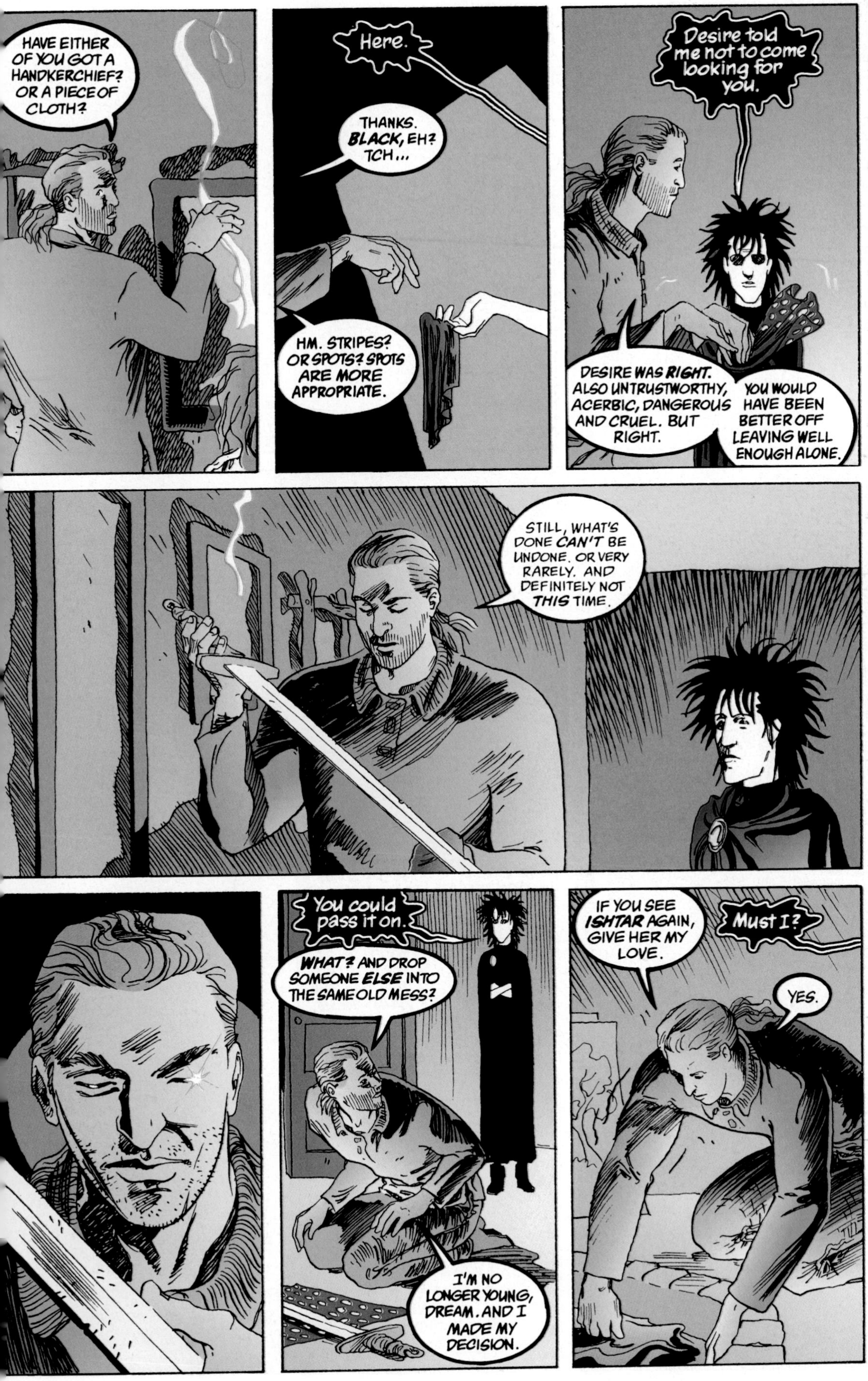
HAVE EITHER OF YOU GOT A HANDKERCHIEF? OR A PIECE OF CLOTH?
Here.
THANKS. BLACK, EH? TCH...
HM. STRIPES? OR SPOTS? SPOTS ARE MORE APPROPRIATE.
Desire told me not to come looking for you.
DESIRE WAS RIGHT. ALSO UNTRUSTWORTHY, ACERBIC, DANGEROUS AND CRUEL. BUT RIGHT.
YOU WOULD HAVE BEEN BETTER OFF LEAVING WELL ENOUGH ALONE.
STILL, WHAT'S DONE CAN'T BE UNDONE. OR VERY RARELY. AND DEFINITELY NOT THIS TIME.
You could pass it on.
WHAT? AND DROP SOMEONE ELSE INTO THE SAME OLD MESS?
I'M NO LONGER YOUNG, DREAM. AND I MADE MY DECISION.
IF YOU SEE ISHTAR AGAIN, GIVE HER MY LOVE.
Must I?
YES.

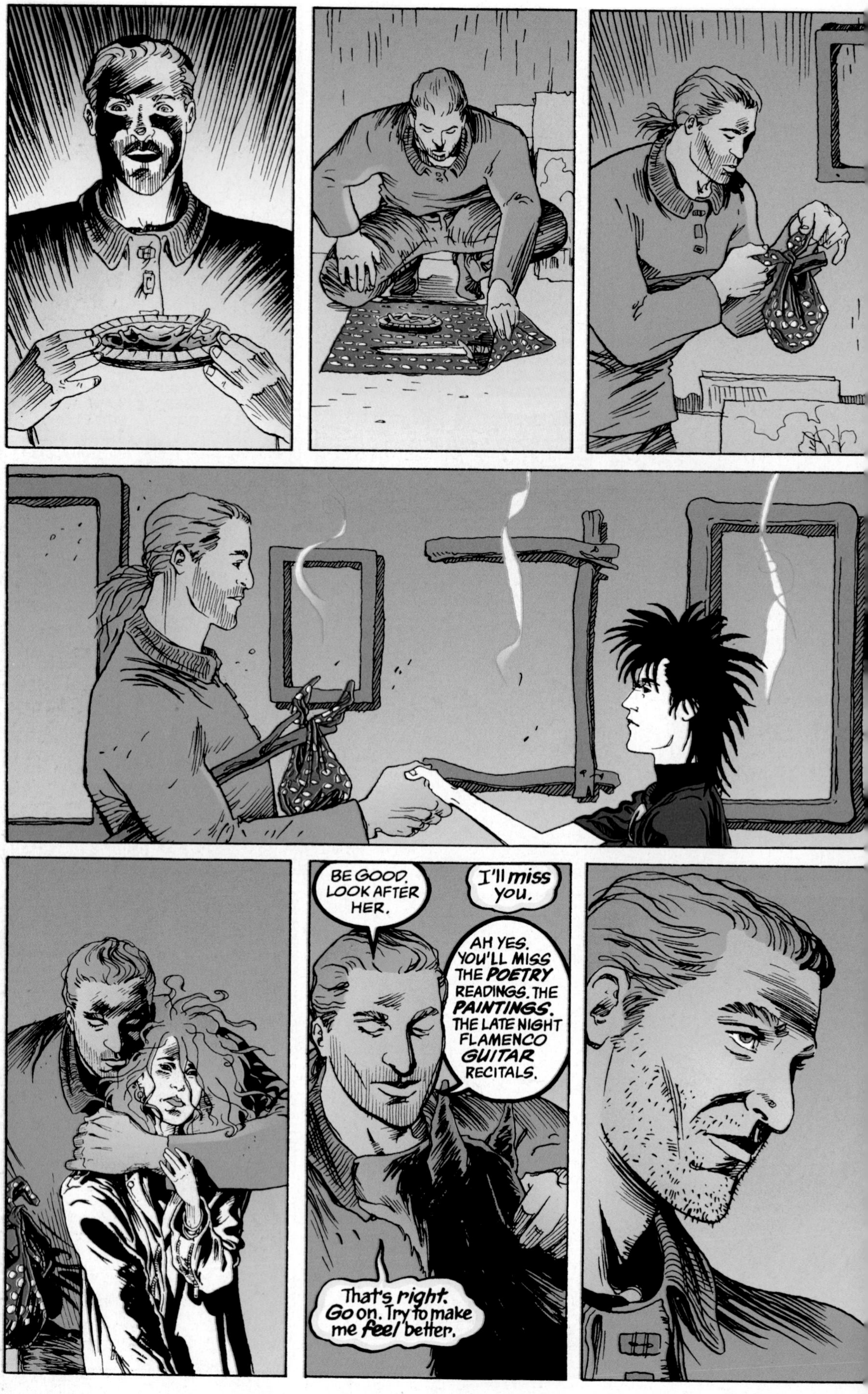
BE GOOD. LOOK AFTER HER.
I'll miss you.
AH YES. YOU'LL MISS THE POETRY READINGS. THE PAINTINGS. THE LATE NIGHT FLAMENCO GUITAR RECITALS.
That's right. Go on. Try to make me feel better.

NINE: FAREWELLS—ANSWERED PRAYERS—THE FLOWERS OF ROMANCE—JOURNEY'S END—THE GATES OF HORN—THINGS UNLOOKED FOR—BRIEF LIVES.

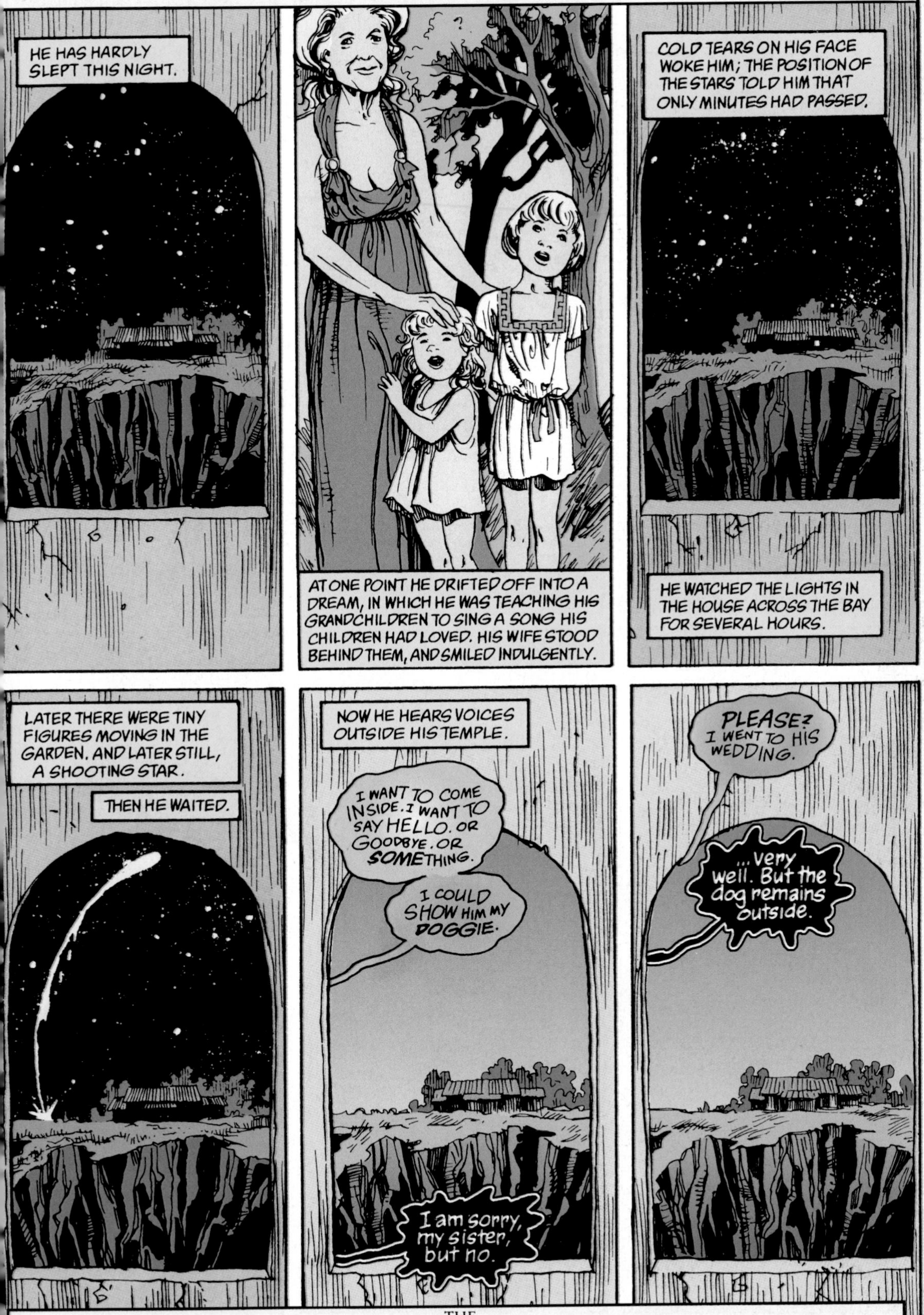

HE HAS HARDLY SLEPT THIS NIGHT.
AT ONE POINT HE DRIFTED OFF INTO A DREAM, IN WHICH HE WAS TEACHING HIS GRANDCHILDREN TO SING A SONG HIS CHILDREN HAD LOVED. HIS WIFE STOOD BEHIND THEM, AND SMILED INDULGENTLY.
COLD TEARS ON HIS FACE WOKE HIM; THE POSITION OF THE STARS TOLD HIM THAT ONLY MINUTES HAD PASSED.
HE WATCHED THE LIGHTS IN THE HOUSE ACROSS THE BAY FOR SEVERAL HOURS.
LATER THERE WERE TINY FIGURES MOVING IN THE GARDEN. AND LATER STILL, A SHOOTING STAR.
THEN HE WAITED.
NOW HE HEARS VOICES OUTSIDE HIS TEMPLE.
I WANT TO COME INSIDE. I WANT TO SAY HELLO. OR GOODBYE. OR SOMETHING.
I COULD SHOW HIM MY DOGGIE.
I am sorry, my sister, but no.
PLEASE? I WENT TO HIS WEDDING.
...very well. But the dog remains outside.

THE

SANDMAN™

Written by Neil Gaiman, drawn by Jill Thompson, inked by Vince Locke, lettered by Todd Klein, colored by Danny Vozzo, edited by Karen Berger, assisted by Shelly Roeberg.

featuring characters created by Gaiman, Kieth and Dringenberg

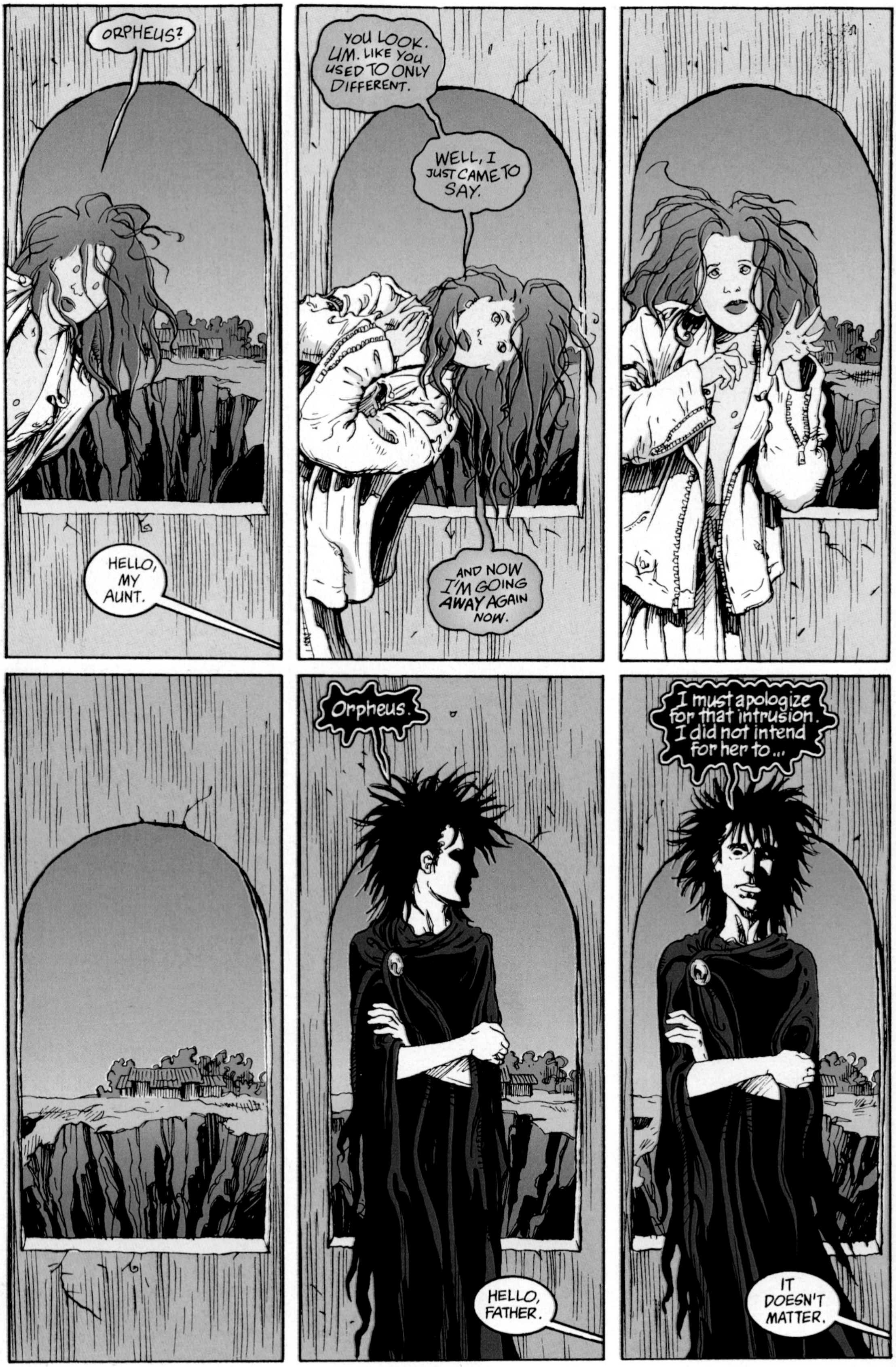

ORPHEUS?
HELLO, MY AUNT.
YOU LOOK. UM. LIKE YOU USED TO ONLY DIFFERENT.
WELL, I JUST CAME TO SAY.
AND NOW I'M GOING AWAY AGAIN NOW.
Orpheus.
HELLO, FATHER.
I must apologize for that intrusion. I did not intend for her to...
IT DOESN'T MATTER.

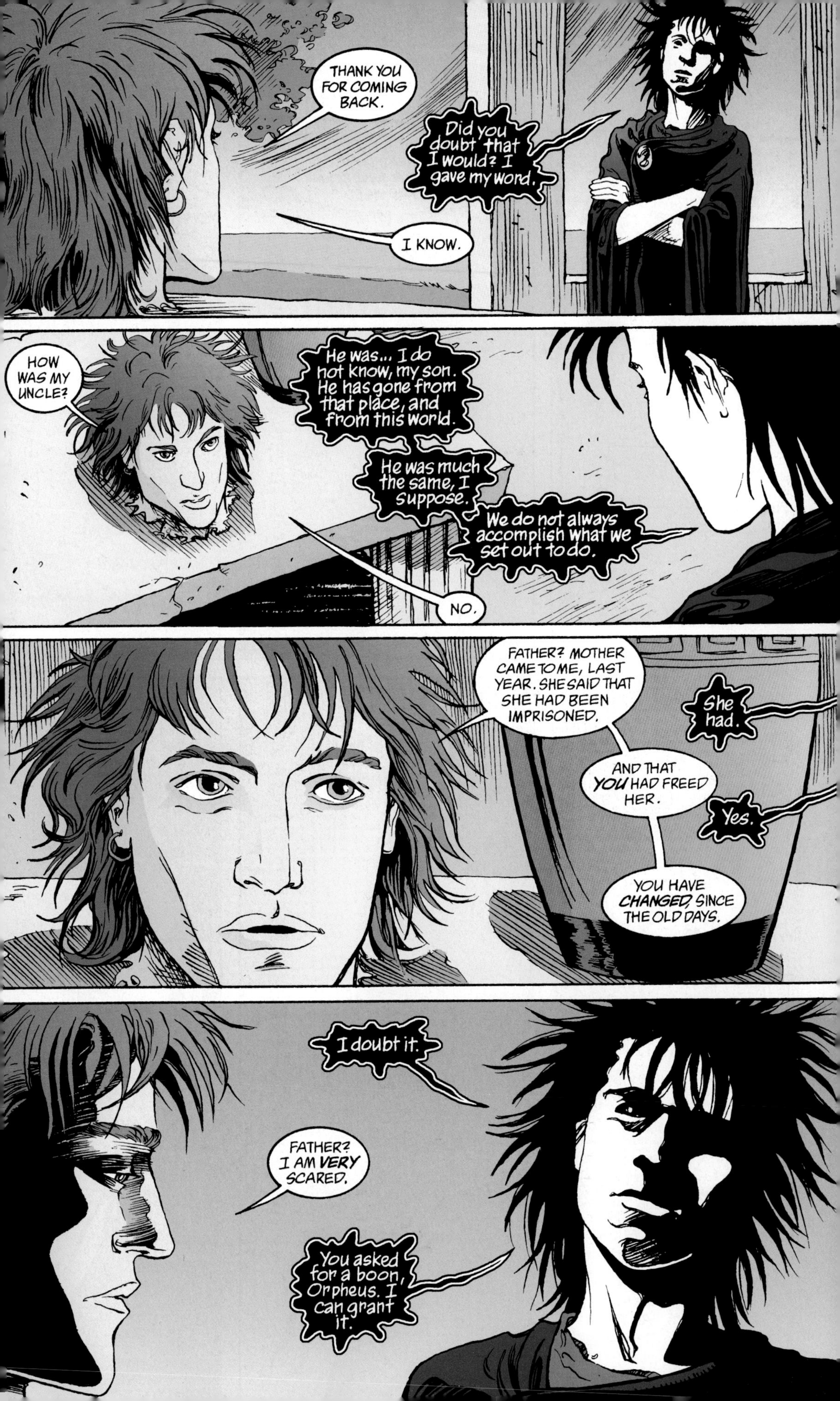
THANK YOU FOR COMING BACK.
Did you doubt that I would? I gave my word.
I KNOW.
HOW WAS MY UNCLE?
He was... I do not know, my son. He has gone from that place, and from this world.
He was much the same, I suppose.
We do not always accomplish what we set out to do.
NO.
FATHER? MOTHER CAME TO ME, LAST YEAR. SHE SAID THAT SHE HAD BEEN IMPRISONED.
She had.
AND THAT YOU HAD FREED HER.
Yes.
YOU HAVE CHANGED, SINCE THE OLD DAYS.
I doubt it.
FATHER? I AM VERY SCARED.
You asked for a boon, Orpheus. I can grant it.

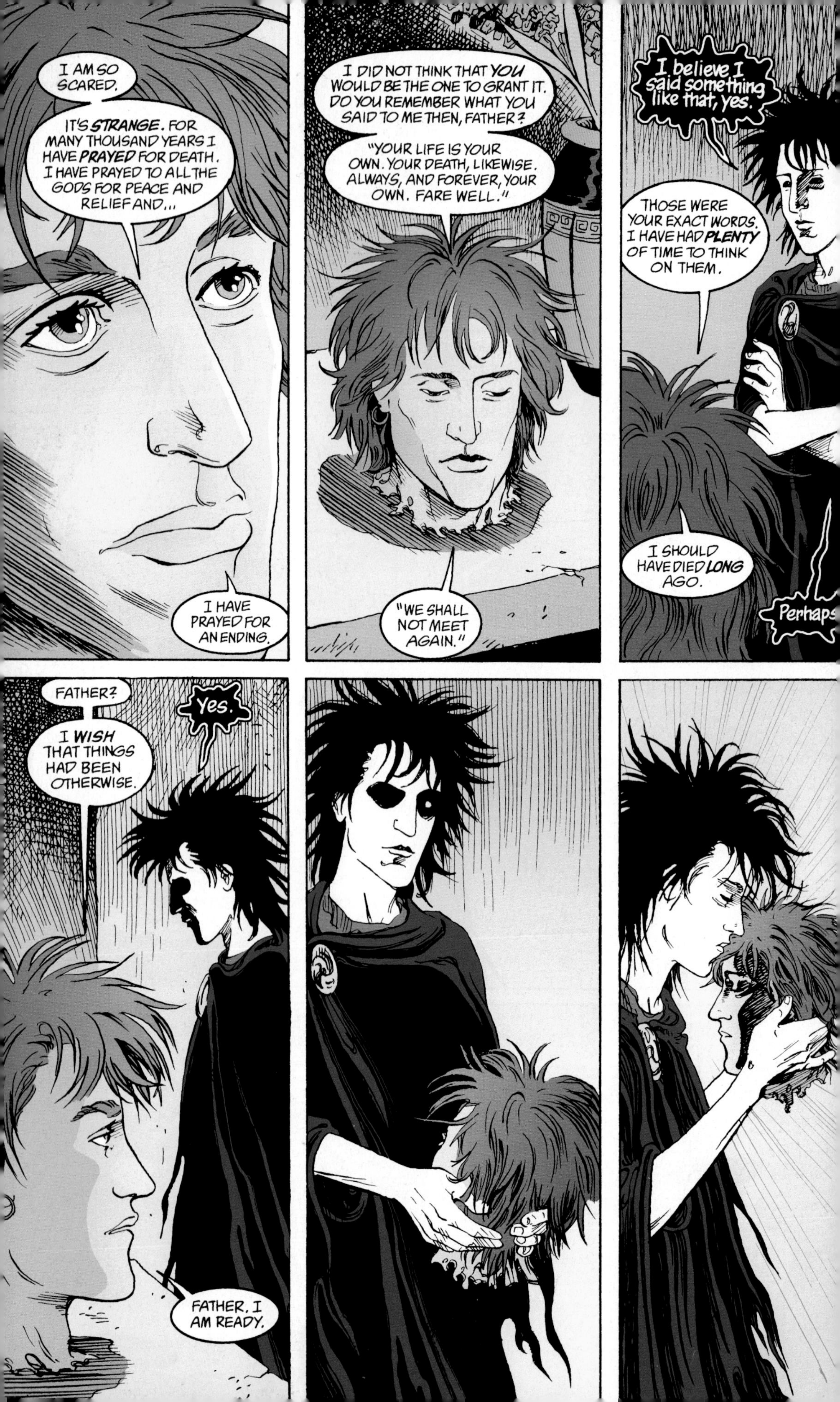
I AM SO SCARED.
IT'S STRANGE. FOR MANY THOUSAND YEARS I HAVE PRAYED FOR DEATH. I HAVE PRAYED TO ALL THE GODS FOR PEACE AND RELIEF AND...
I HAVE PRAYED FOR AN ENDING.
I DID NOT THINK THAT YOU WOULD BE THE ONE TO GRANT IT. DO YOU REMEMBER WHAT YOU SAID TO ME THEN, FATHER?
"YOUR LIFE IS YOUR OWN. YOUR DEATH, LIKEWISE. ALWAYS, AND FOREVER, YOUR OWN. FARE WELL."
"WE SHALL NOT MEET AGAIN."
I believe I said something like that, yes.
THOSE WERE YOUR EXACT WORDS. I HAVE HAD PLENTY OF TIME TO THINK ON THEM.
I SHOULD HAVE DIED LONG AGO.
Perhaps
FATHER?
I WISH THAT THINGS HAD BEEN OTHERWISE.
Yes.
FATHER. I AM READY.

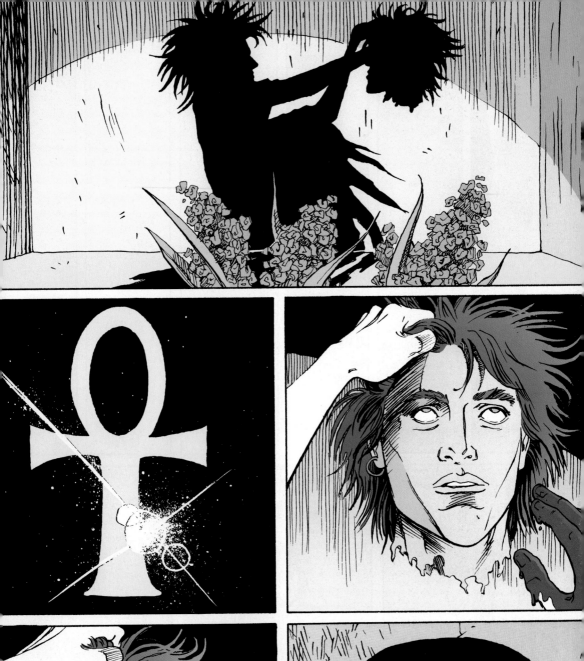

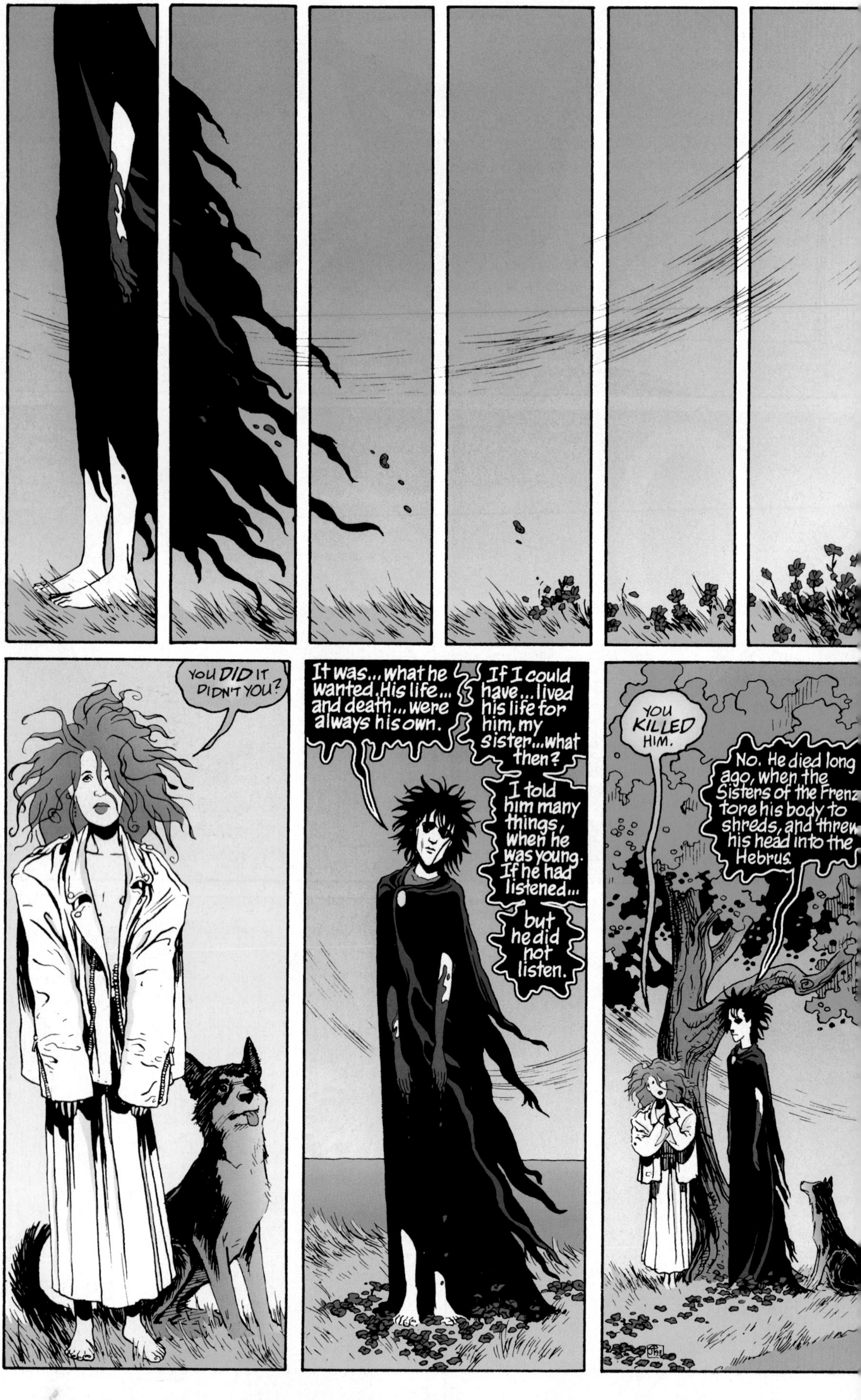

YOU DID IT DIDN'T YOU?
It was... what he wanted. His life... and death... were always his own.
If I could have... lived his life for him, my sister... what then?
I told him many things, when he was young. If he had listened...
but he did not listen.
YOU KILLED HIM.
No. He died long ago, when the Sisters of the Frenz tore his body to shreds, and threw his head into the Hebrus.

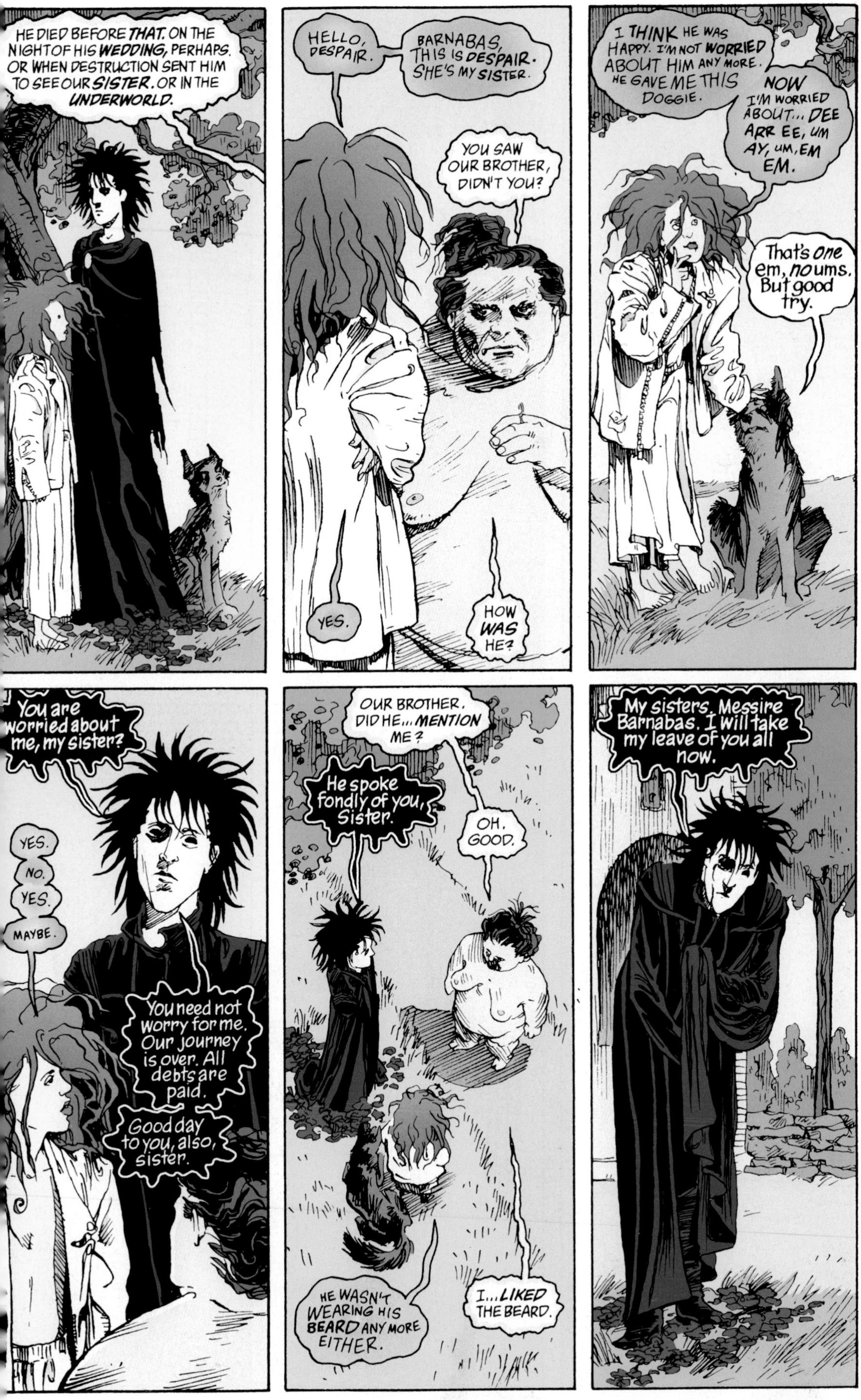
HE DIED BEFORE THAT. ON THE NIGHT OF HIS WEDDING, PERHAPS. OR WHEN DESTRUCTION SENT HIM TO SEE OUR SISTER. OR IN THE UNDERWORLD.
HELLO, DESPAIR.
BARNABAS, THIS IS DESPAIR. SHE'S MY SISTER.
YOU SAW OUR BROTHER, DIDN'T YOU?
YES.
HOW WAS HE?
I THINK HE WAS HAPPY. I'M NOT WORRIED ABOUT HIM ANY MORE. HE GAVE ME THIS DOGGIE.
NOW I'M WORRIED ABOUT... DEE ARR EE, UM AY, UM, EM EM.
That's one em, no ums. But good try.
You are worried about me, my sister?
YES.
NO.
YES.
MAYBE.
You need not worry for me. Our journey is over. All debts are paid.
Good day to you, also, sister.
OUR BROTHER. DID HE... MENTION ME?
He spoke fondly of you, Sister.
OH. GOOD.
HE WASN'T WEARING HIS BEARD ANY MORE EITHER.
I... LIKED THE BEARD.
My sisters. Messire Barnabas. I will take my leave of you all now.

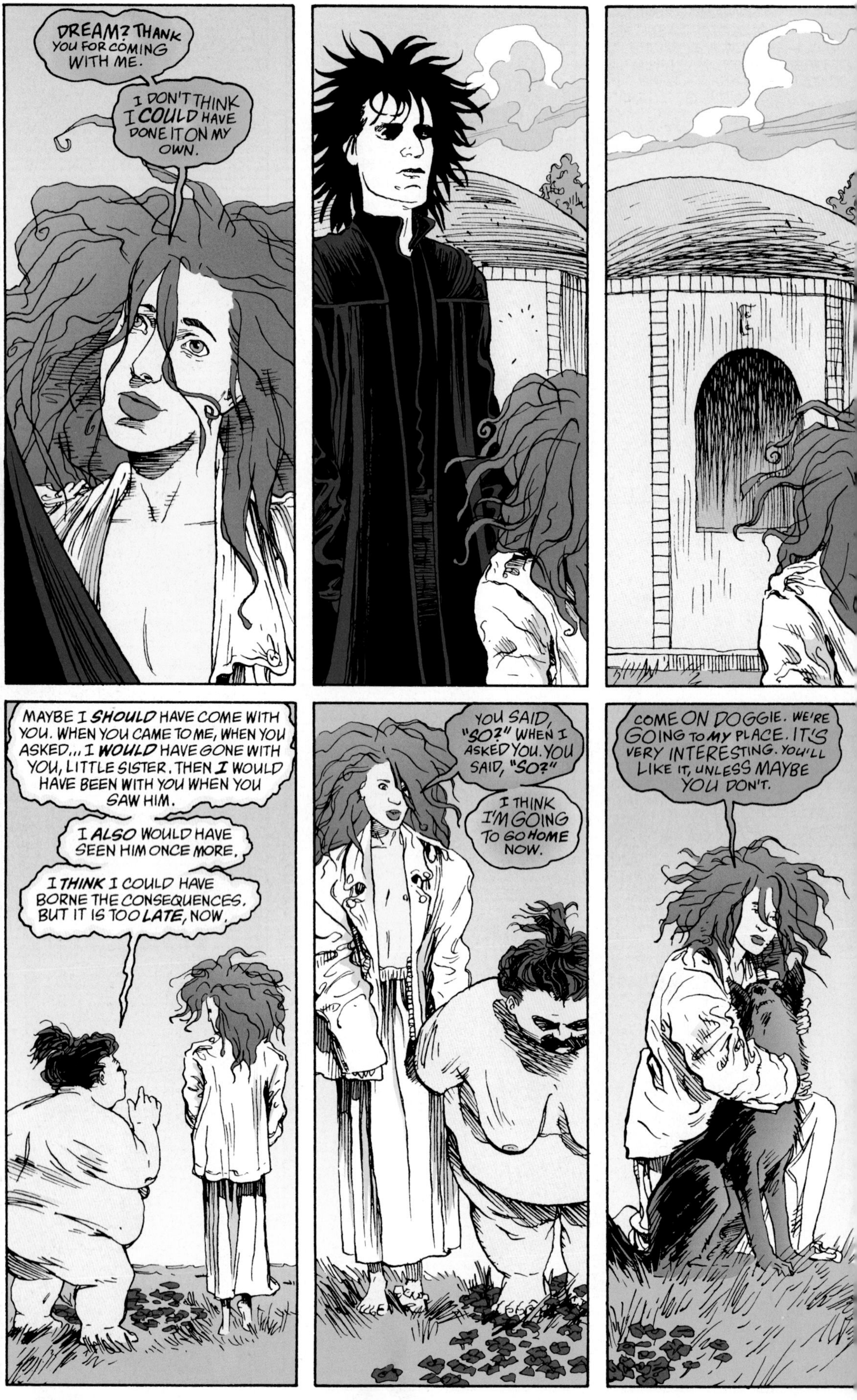
DREAM? THANK YOU FOR COMING WITH ME.
I DON'T THINK I COULD HAVE DONE IT ON MY OWN.
MAYBE I SHOULD HAVE COME WITH YOU. WHEN YOU CAME TO ME, WHEN YOU ASKED... I WOULD HAVE GONE WITH YOU, LITTLE SISTER. THEN I WOULD HAVE BEEN WITH YOU WHEN YOU SAW HIM.
I ALSO WOULD HAVE SEEN HIM ONCE MORE.
I THINK I COULD HAVE BORNE THE CONSEQUENCES. BUT IT IS TOO LATE, NOW.
YOU SAID, "SO?" WHEN I ASKED YOU. YOU SAID, "SO?"
I THINK I'M GOING TO GO HOME NOW.
COME ON DOGGIE. WE'RE GOING TO MY PLACE. IT'S VERY INTERESTING. YOU'LL LIKE IT, UNLESS MAYBE YOU DON'T.

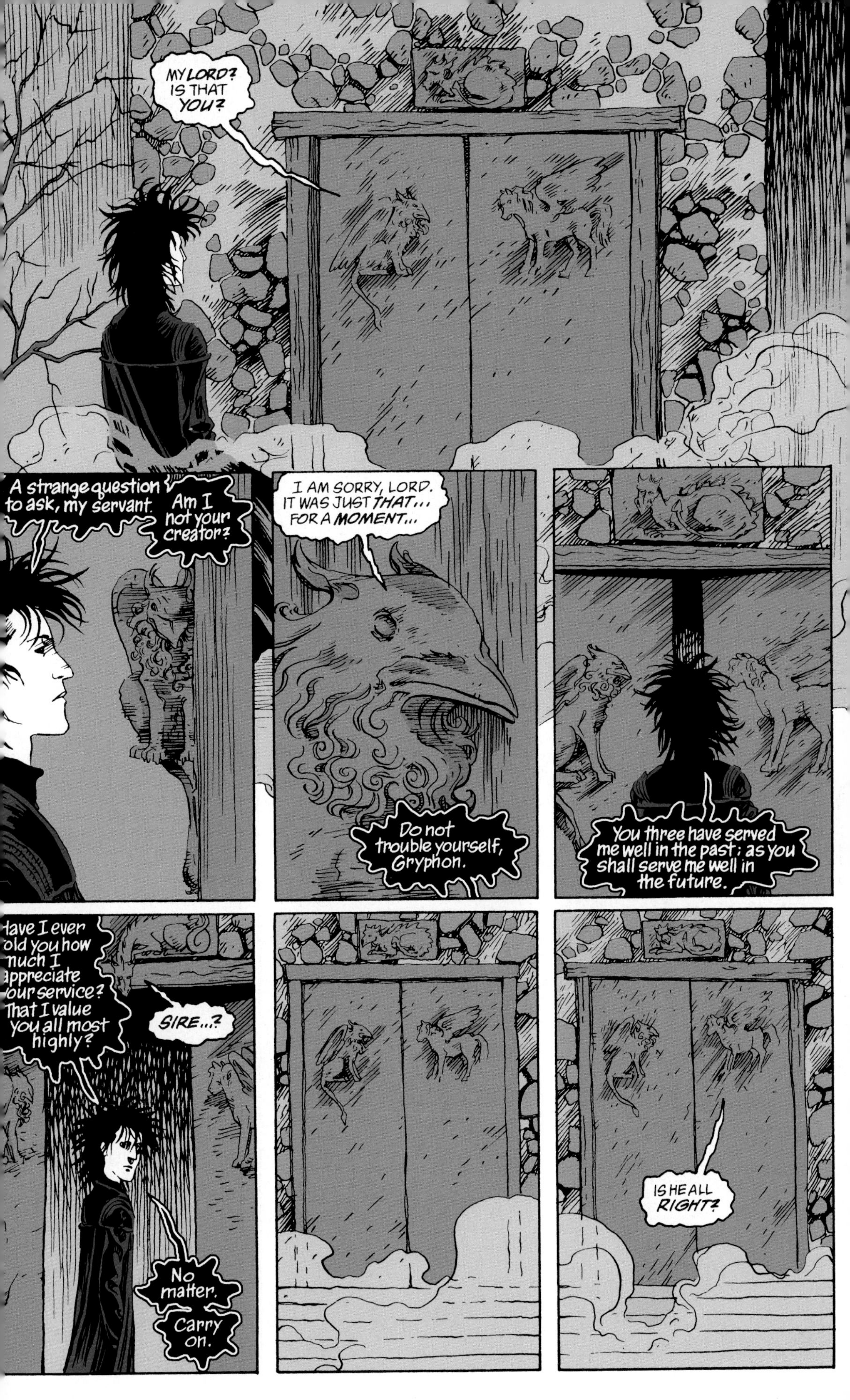

MY LORD? IS THAT YOU?
A strange question to ask, my servant.
Am I not your creator?
I AM SORRY, LORD. IT WAS JUST THAT... FOR A MOMENT...
Do not trouble yourself, Gryphon.
You three have served me well in the past; as you shall serve me well in the future.
ave I ever old you how nuch I appreciate our service? That I value you all most highly?
SIRE...?
No matter.
Carry on.
IS HE ALL RIGHT?

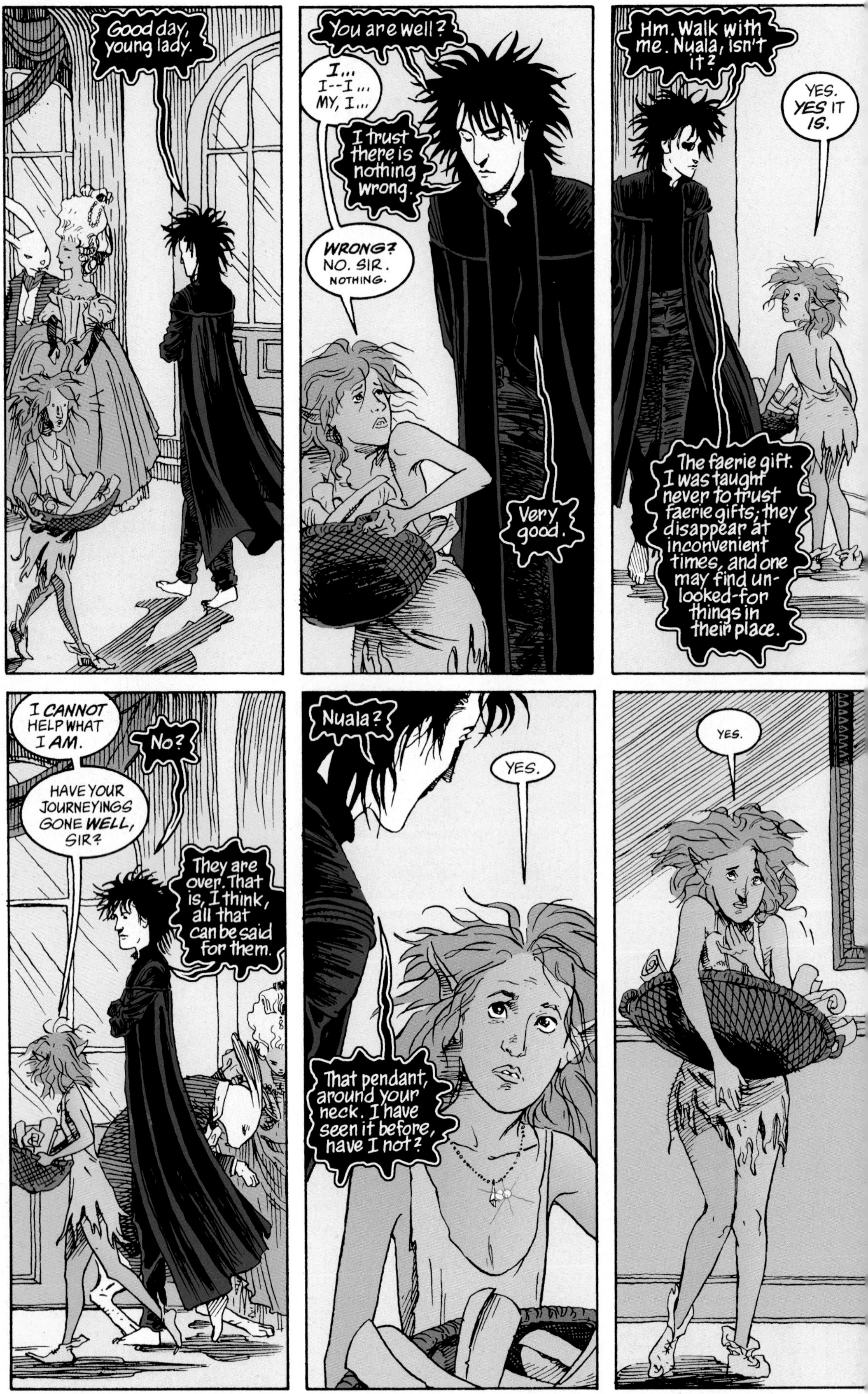
Good day, young lady.
You are well?
I... I--I... MY, I...
I trust there is nothing wrong.
WRONG? NO. SIR. NOTHING.
Very good.
Hm. Walk with me. Nuala, isn't it?
YES. YES IT IS.
The faerie gift. I was taught never to trust faerie gifts; they disappear at inconvenient times, and one may find unlooked-for things in their place.
I CANNOT HELP WHAT I AM.
No?
HAVE YOUR JOURNEYINGS GONE WELL, SIR?
They are over. That is, I think, all that can be said for them.
Nuala?
YES.
That pendant, around your neck. I have seen it before, have I not?
YES.

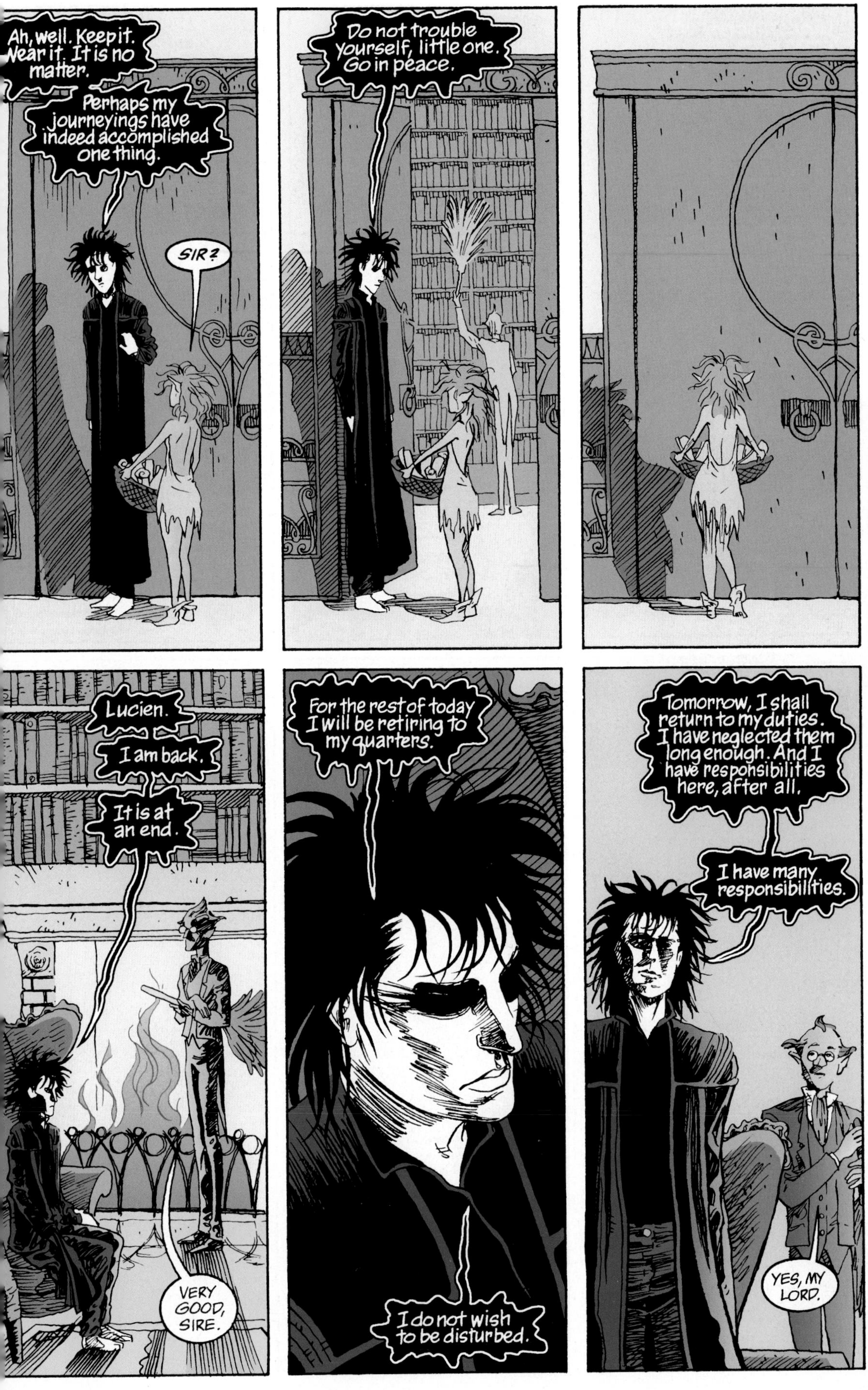

Ah, well. Keep it. Wear it. It is no matter.
Perhaps my journeyings have indeed accomplished one thing.
SIR?
Do not trouble yourself, little one. Go in peace.
Lucien.
I am back.
It is at an end.
VERY GOOD, SIRE.
For the rest of today I will be retiring to my quarters.
I do not wish to be disturbed.
Tomorrow, I shall return to my duties. I have neglected them long enough. And I have responsibilities here, after all.
I have many responsibilities.
YES, MY LORD.

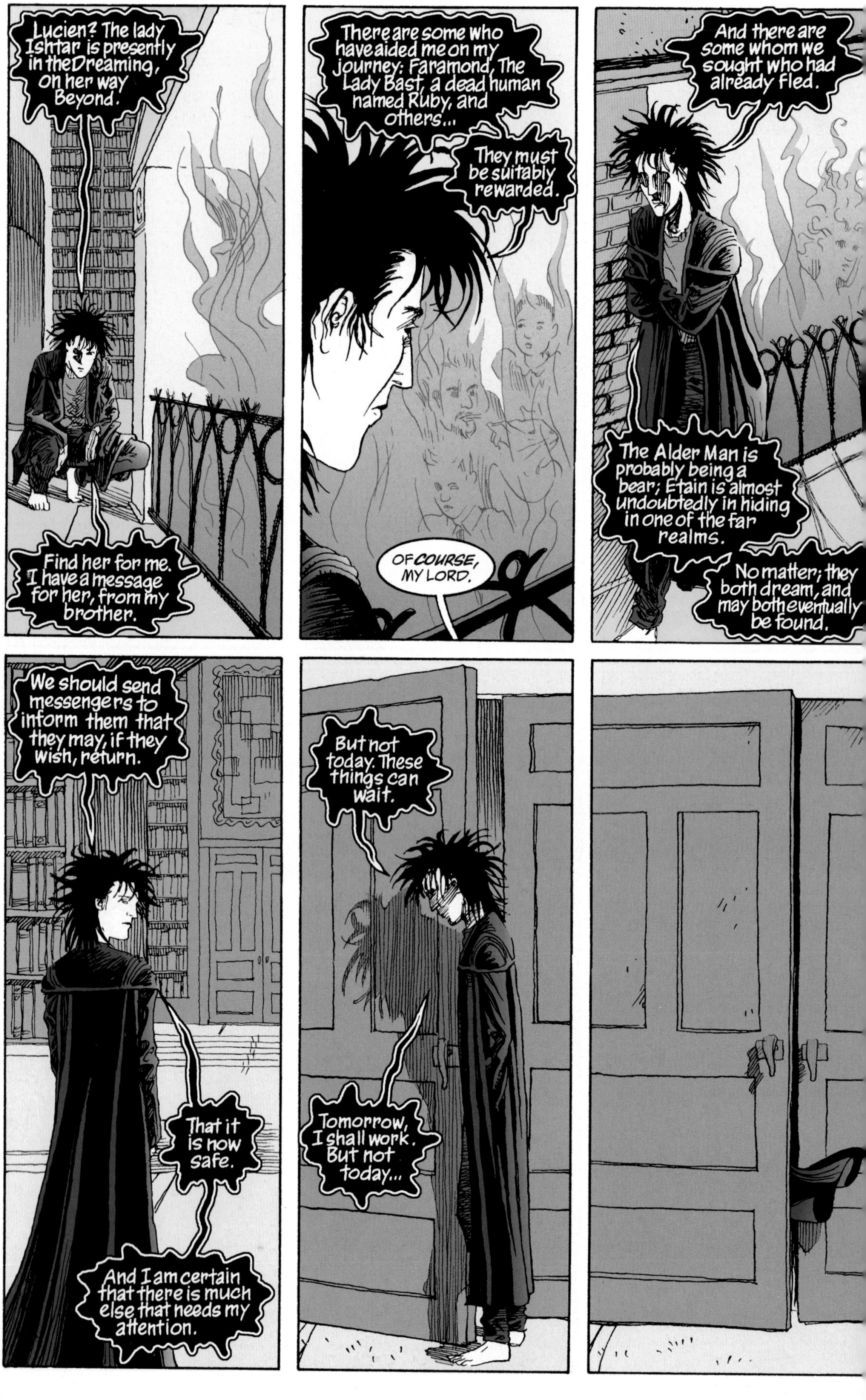
Lucien? The lady Ishtar is presently in the Dreaming, on her way Beyond.
Find her for me. I have a message for her, from my brother.
There are some who have aided me on my journey: Faramond, The Lady Bast, a dead human named Ruby, and others...
They must be suitably rewarded.
OF COURSE, MY LORD.
And there are some whom we sought who had already fled.
The Alder Man is probably being a bear; Etain is almost undoubtedly in hiding in one of the far realms.
No matter; they both dream, and may both eventually be found.
We should send messengers to inform them that they may, if they wish, return.
That it is now safe.
And I am certain that there is much else that needs my attention.
But not today. These things can wait.
Tomorrow, I shall work. But not today...

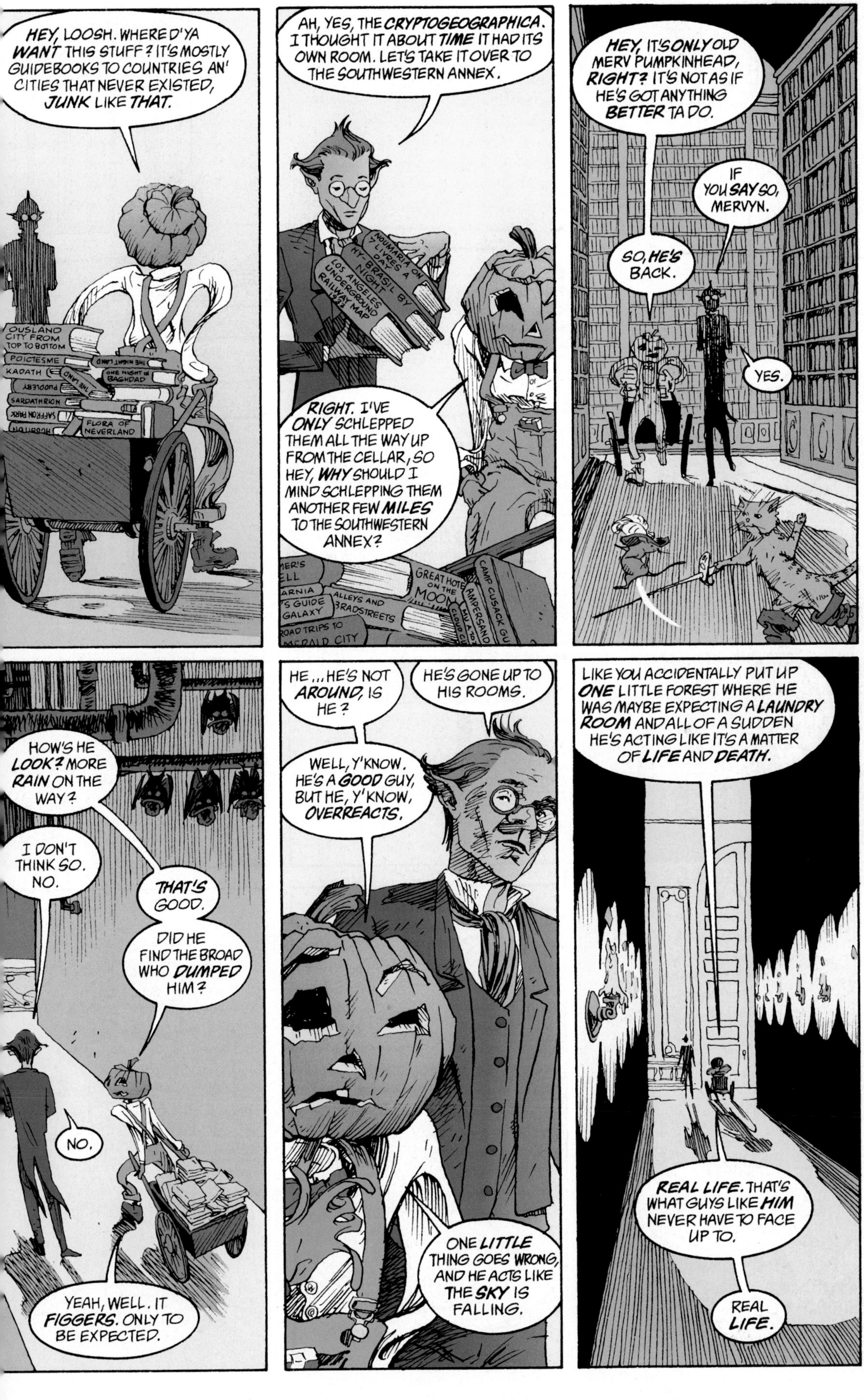

HEY, LOOSH. WHERE D'YA WANT THIS STUFF? IT'S MOSTLY GUIDEBOOKS TO COUNTRIES AN' CITIES THAT NEVER EXISTED, JUNK LIKE THAT.
OUSLAND CITY FROM TOP TO BOTTOM
POICTESME
KADATH
SARDATHRION
SAFFRON PARK
FLORA OF NEVERLAND
ONE NIGHT IN BAGHDAD
AH, YES, THE CRYPTOGEOGRAPHICA. I THOUGHT IT ABOUT TIME IT HAD ITS OWN ROOM. LET'S TAKE IT OVER TO THE SOUTHWESTERN ANNEX.
HY-BRASIL BY NIGHT
LOS ANGELES UNDERGROUND RAILWAY MAP
RIGHT. I'VE ONLY SCHLEPPED THEM ALL THE WAY UP FROM THE CELLAR, SO HEY, WHY SHOULD I MIND SCHLEPPING THEM ANOTHER FEW MILES TO THE SOUTHWESTERN ANNEX?
GREAT HOTEL ON THE MOON
ALLEYS AND BRADSTREETS
AMPERSAND
HEY, IT'S ONLY OLD MERV PUMPKINHEAD, RIGHT? IT'S NOT AS IF HE'S GOT ANYTHING BETTER TA DO.
IF YOU SAY SO, MERVYN.
SO, HE'S BACK.
YES.
HOW'S HE LOOK? MORE RAIN ON THE WAY?
I DON'T THINK SO. NO.
THAT'S GOOD.
DID HE FIND THE BROAD WHO DUMPED HIM?
NO.
YEAH, WELL. IT FIGGERS. ONLY TO BE EXPECTED.
HE... HE'S NOT AROUND, IS HE?
HE'S GONE UP TO HIS ROOMS.
WELL, Y'KNOW. HE'S A GOOD GUY, BUT HE, Y'KNOW, OVERREACTS.
ONE LITTLE THING GOES WRONG, AND HE ACTS LIKE THE SKY IS FALLING.
LIKE YOU ACCIDENTALLY PUT UP ONE LITTLE FOREST WHERE HE WAS MAYBE EXPECTING A LAUNDRY ROOM AND ALL OF A SUDDEN HE'S ACTING LIKE IT'S A MATTER OF LIFE AND DEATH.
REAL LIFE. THAT'S WHAT GUYS LIKE HIM NEVER HAVE TO FACE UP TO.
REAL LIFE.

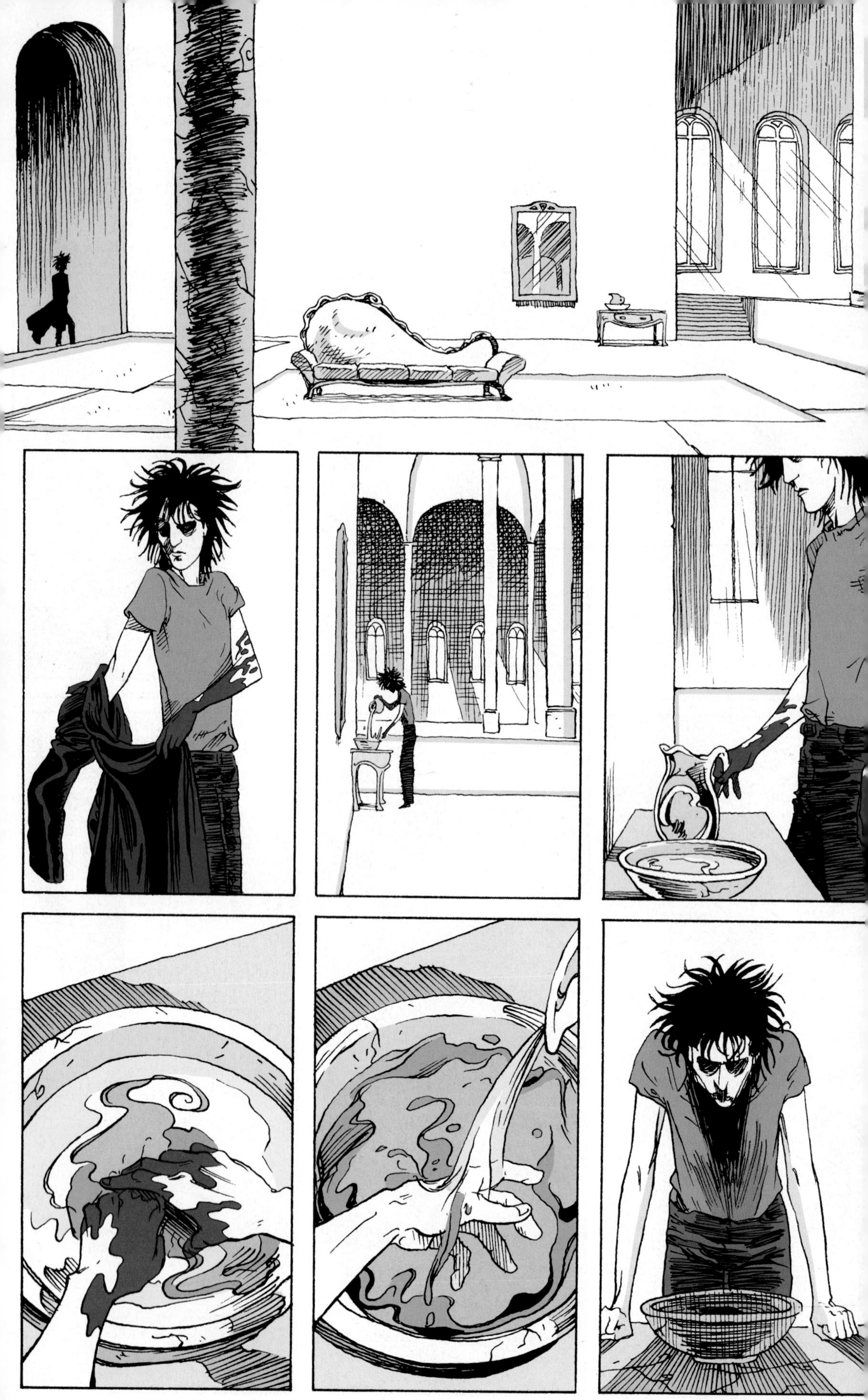

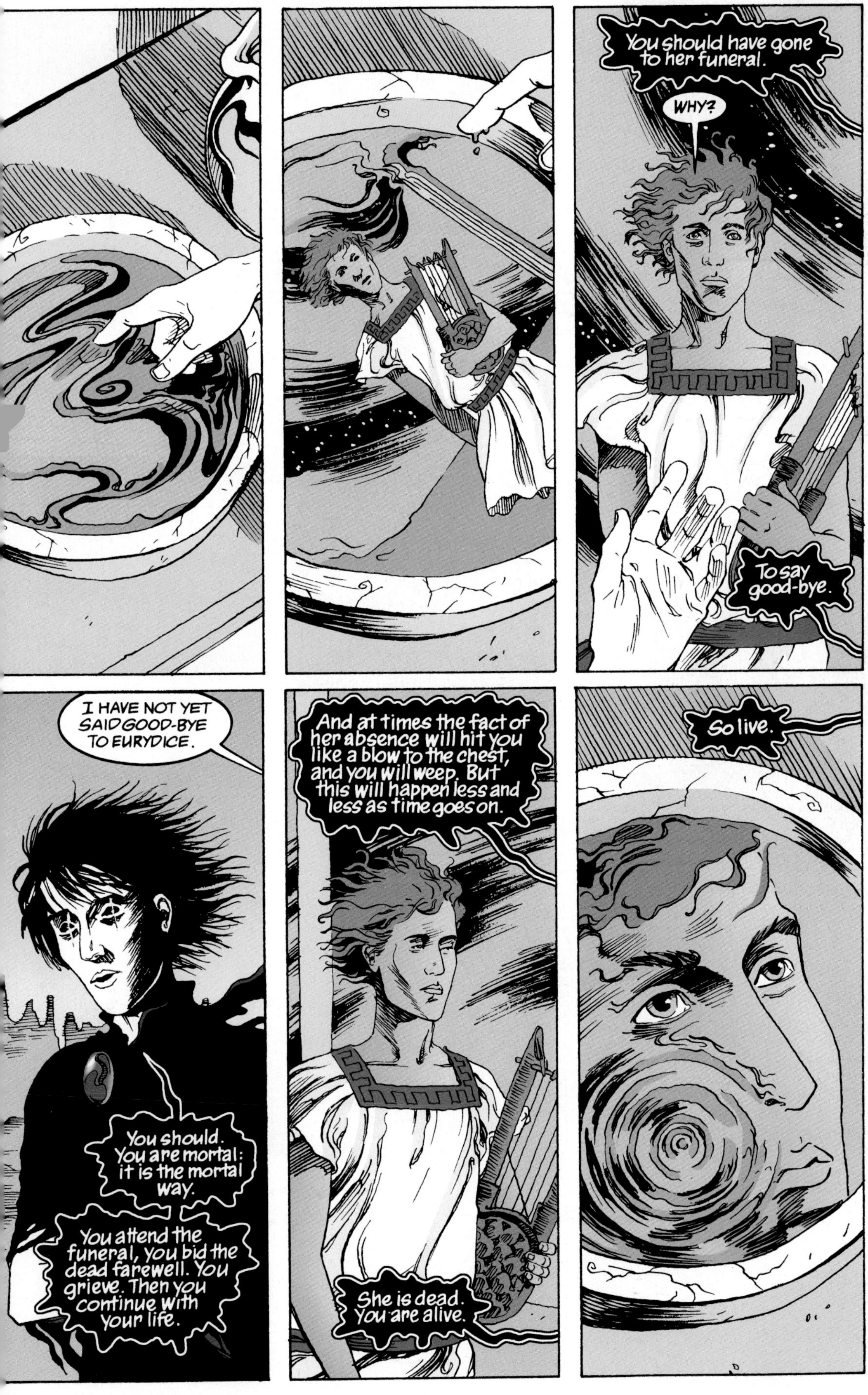
You should have gone to her funeral.
WHY?
To say good-bye.
I HAVE NOT YET SAID GOOD-BYE TO EURYDICE.
You should. You are mortal: it is the mortal way.
You attend the funeral, you bid the dead farewell. You grieve. Then you continue with your life.
And at times the fact of her absence will hit you like a blow to the chest, and you will weep. But this will happen less and less as time goes on.
She is dead. You are alive.
So live.

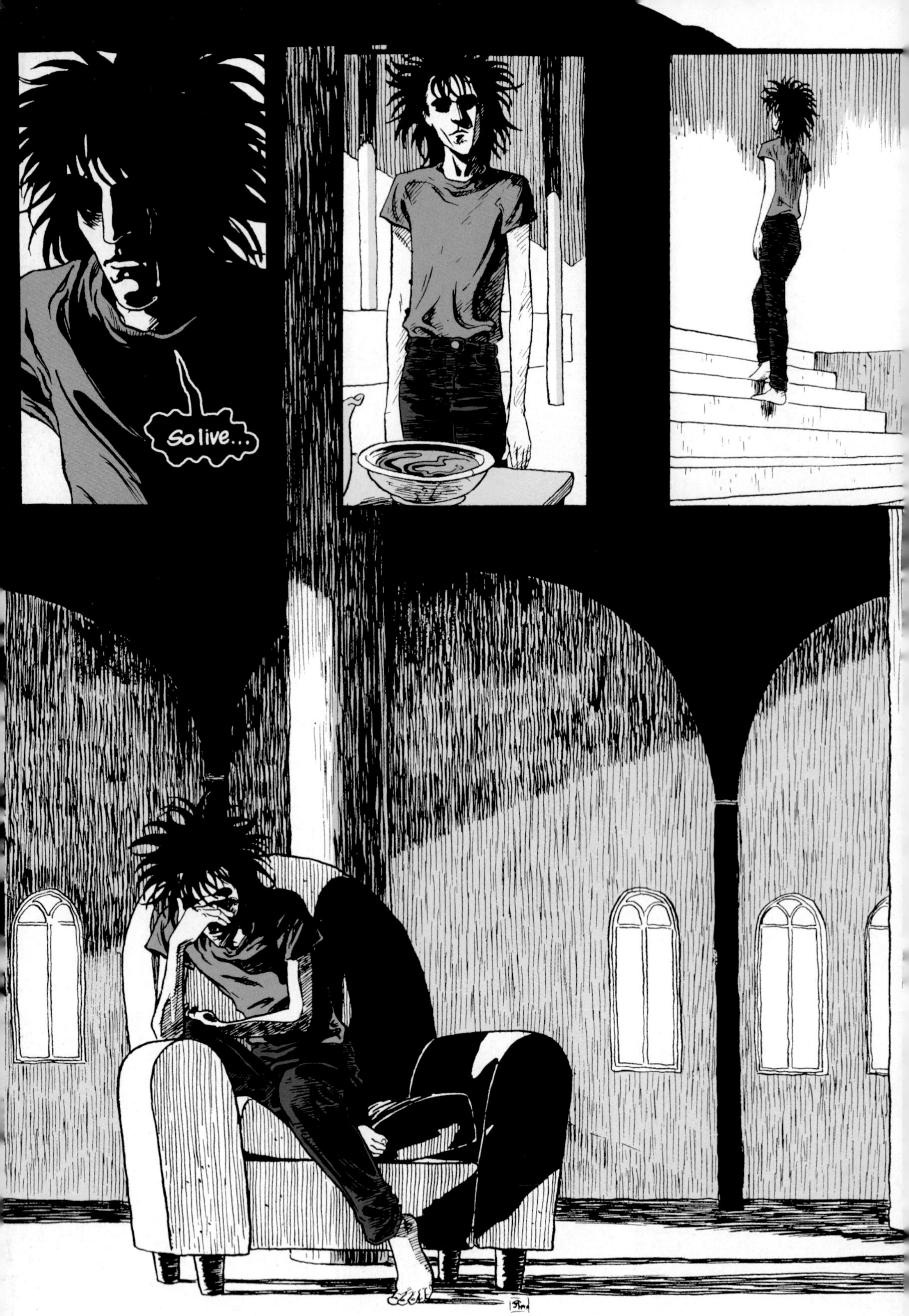
So live...

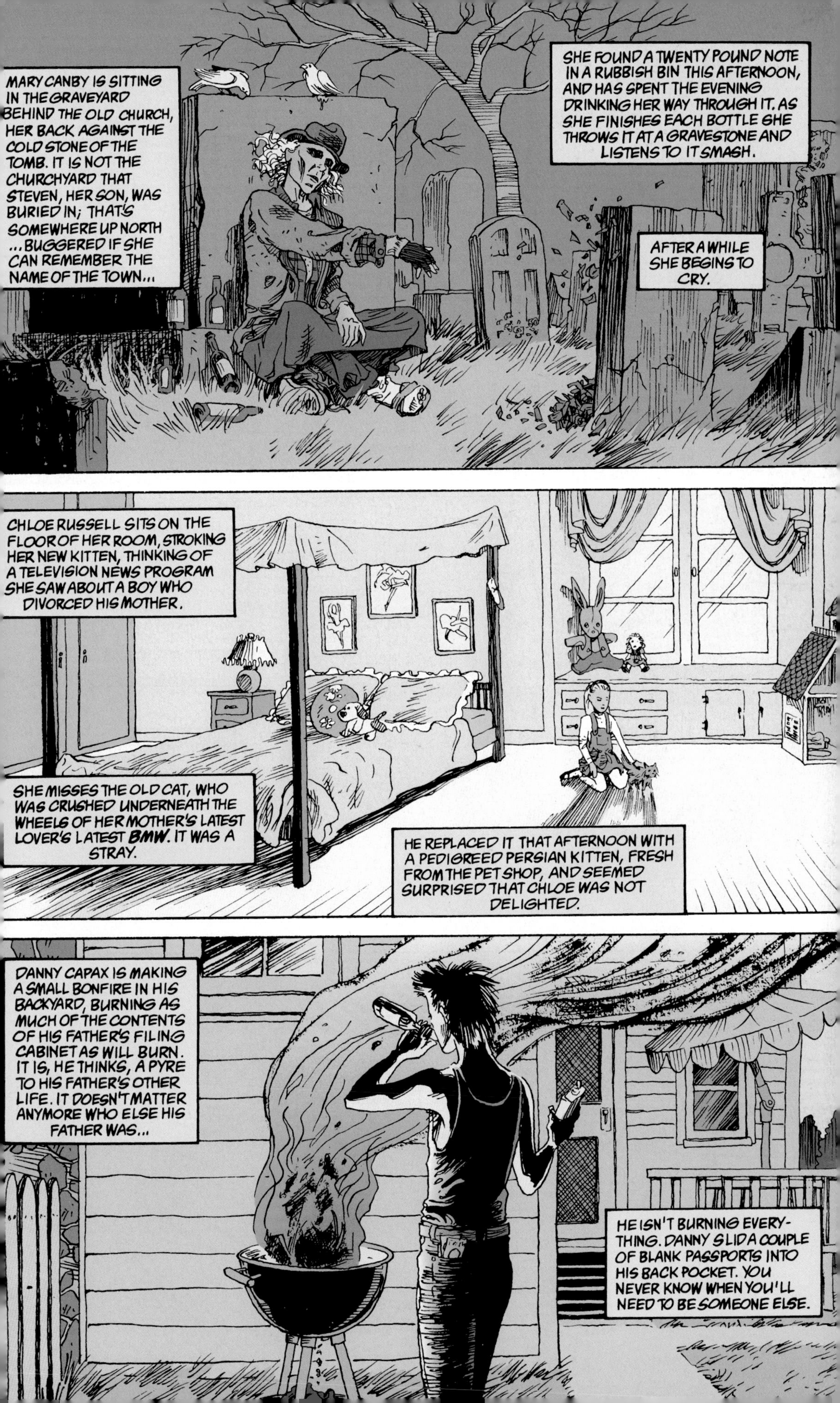
MARY CANBY IS SITTING IN THE GRAVEYARD BEHIND THE OLD CHURCH, HER BACK AGAINST THE COLD STONE OF THE TOMB. IT IS NOT THE CHURCHYARD THAT STEVEN, HER SON, WAS BURIED IN; THAT'S SOMEWHERE UP NORTH ...BUGGERED IF SHE CAN REMEMBER THE NAME OF THE TOWN...
SHE FOUND A TWENTY POUND NOTE IN A RUBBISH BIN THIS AFTERNOON, AND HAS SPENT THE EVENING DRINKING HER WAY THROUGH IT. AS SHE FINISHES EACH BOTTLE SHE THROWS IT AT A GRAVESTONE AND LISTENS TO IT SMASH.
AFTER A WHILE SHE BEGINS TO CRY.
CHLOE RUSSELL SITS ON THE FLOOR OF HER ROOM, STROKING HER NEW KITTEN, THINKING OF A TELEVISION NEWS PROGRAM SHE SAW ABOUT A BOY WHO DIVORCED HIS MOTHER.
SHE MISSES THE OLD CAT, WHO WAS CRUSHED UNDERNEATH THE WHEELS OF HER MOTHER'S LATEST LOVER'S LATEST BMW. IT WAS A STRAY.
HE REPLACED IT THAT AFTERNOON WITH A PEDIGREED PERSIAN KITTEN, FRESH FROM THE PET SHOP, AND SEEMED SURPRISED THAT CHLOE WAS NOT DELIGHTED.
DANNY CAPAX IS MAKING A SMALL BONFIRE IN HIS BACKYARD, BURNING AS MUCH OF THE CONTENTS OF HIS FATHER'S FILING CABINET AS WILL BURN. IT IS, HE THINKS, A PYRE TO HIS FATHER'S OTHER LIFE. IT DOESN'T MATTER ANYMORE WHO ELSE HIS FATHER WAS...
HE ISN'T BURNING EVERYTHING. DANNY SLID A COUPLE OF BLANK PASSPORTS INTO HIS BACK POCKET. YOU NEVER KNOW WHEN YOU'LL NEED TO BE SOMEONE ELSE.

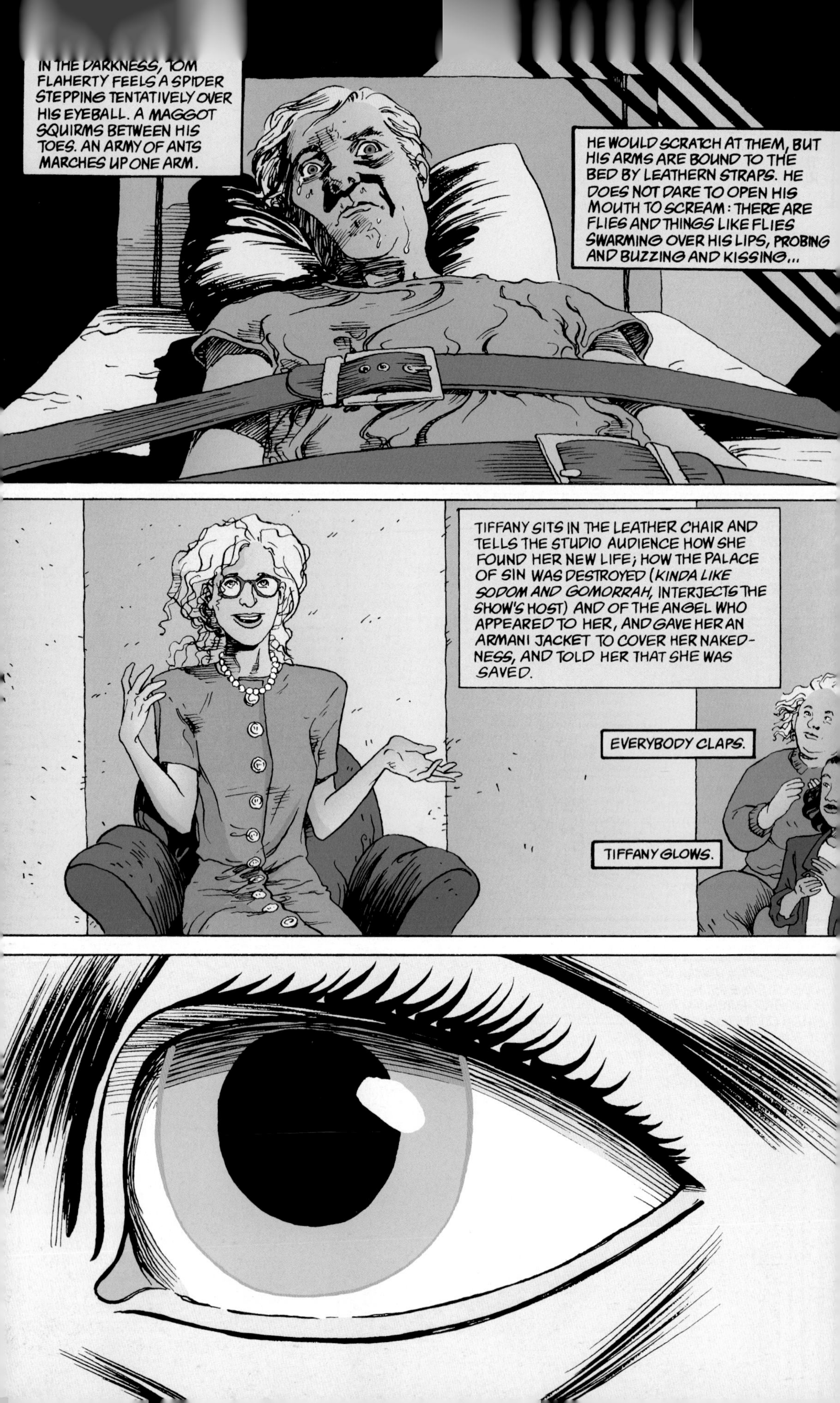
IN THE DARKNESS, TOM FLAHERTY FEELS A SPIDER STEPPING TENTATIVELY OVER HIS EYEBALL. A MAGGOT SQUIRMS BETWEEN HIS TOES. AN ARMY OF ANTS MARCHES UP ONE ARM.
HE WOULD SCRATCH AT THEM, BUT HIS ARMS ARE BOUND TO THE BED BY LEATHERN STRAPS. HE DOES NOT DARE TO OPEN HIS MOUTH TO SCREAM: THERE ARE FLIES AND THINGS LIKE FLIES SWARMING OVER HIS LIPS, PROBING AND BUZZING AND KISSING...
TIFFANY SITS IN THE LEATHER CHAIR AND TELLS THE STUDIO AUDIENCE HOW SHE FOUND HER NEW LIFE; HOW THE PALACE OF SIN WAS DESTROYED (KINDA LIKE SODOM AND GOMORRAH, INTERJECTS THE SHOW'S HOST) AND OF THE ANGEL WHO APPEARED TO HER, AND GAVE HER AN ARMANI JACKET TO COVER HER NAKEDNESS, AND TOLD HER THAT SHE WAS SAVED.
EVERYBODY CLAPS.
TIFFANY GLOWS.

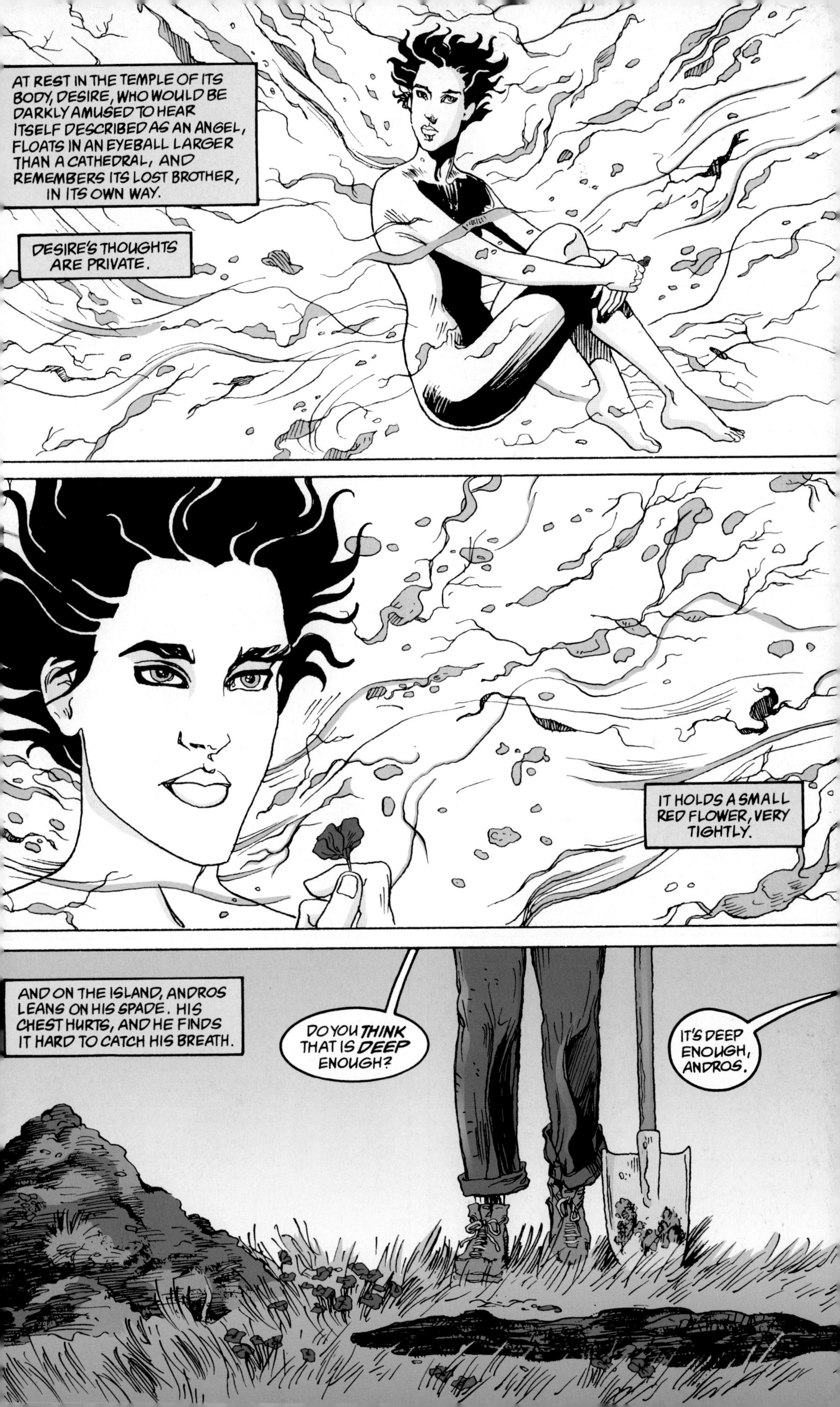

AT REST IN THE TEMPLE OF ITS BODY, DESIRE, WHO WOULD BE DARKLY AMUSED TO HEAR ITSELF DESCRIBED AS AN ANGEL, FLOATS IN AN EYEBALL LARGER THAN A CATHEDRAL, AND REMEMBERS ITS LOST BROTHER, IN ITS OWN WAY.
DESIRE'S THOUGHTS ARE PRIVATE.
IT HOLDS A SMALL RED FLOWER, VERY TIGHTLY.
AND ON THE ISLAND, ANDROS LEANS ON HIS SPADE. HIS CHEST HURTS, AND HE FINDS IT HARD TO CATCH HIS BREATH.
DO YOU *THINK* THAT IS *DEEP* ENOUGH?
IT'S DEEP ENOUGH, ANDROS.

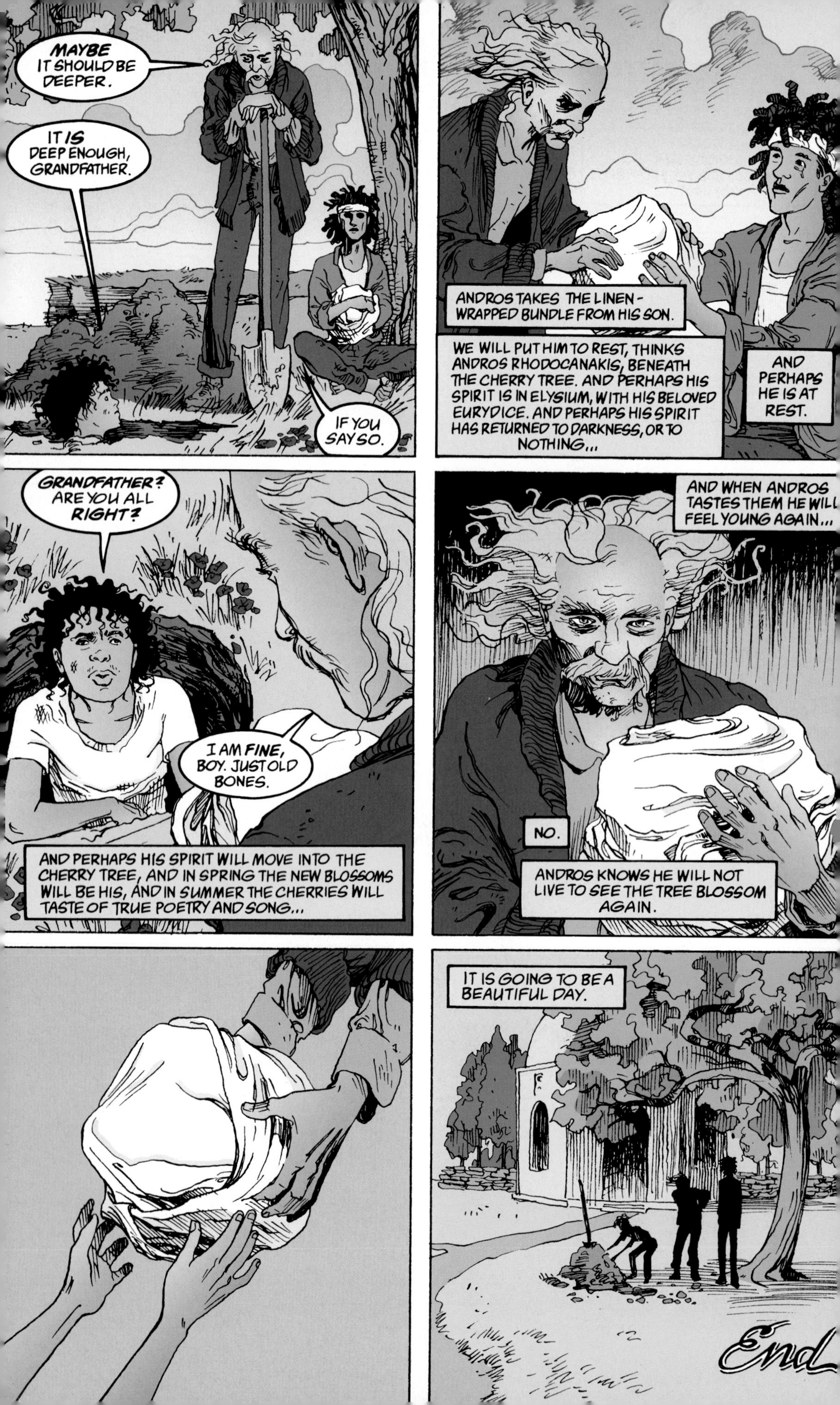
MAYBE IT SHOULD BE DEEPER.
IT IS DEEP ENOUGH, GRANDFATHER.
IF YOU SAY SO.
ANDROS TAKES THE LINEN-WRAPPED BUNDLE FROM HIS SON.
WE WILL PUT HIM TO REST, THINKS ANDROS RHODOCANAKIS, BENEATH THE CHERRY TREE. AND PERHAPS HIS SPIRIT IS IN ELYSIUM, WITH HIS BELOVED EURYDICE. AND PERHAPS HIS SPIRIT HAS RETURNED TO DARKNESS, OR TO NOTHING...
AND PERHAPS HE IS AT REST.
GRANDFATHER? ARE YOU ALL RIGHT?
I AM FINE, BOY. JUST OLD BONES.
AND PERHAPS HIS SPIRIT WILL MOVE INTO THE CHERRY TREE, AND IN SPRING THE NEW BLOSSOMS WILL BE HIS, AND IN SUMMER THE CHERRIES WILL TASTE OF TRUE POETRY AND SONG...
AND WHEN ANDROS TASTES THEM HE WILL FEEL YOUNG AGAIN...
NO.
ANDROS KNOWS HE WILL NOT LIVE TO SEE THE TREE BLOSSOM AGAIN.
IT IS GOING TO BE A BEAUTIFUL DAY.
End

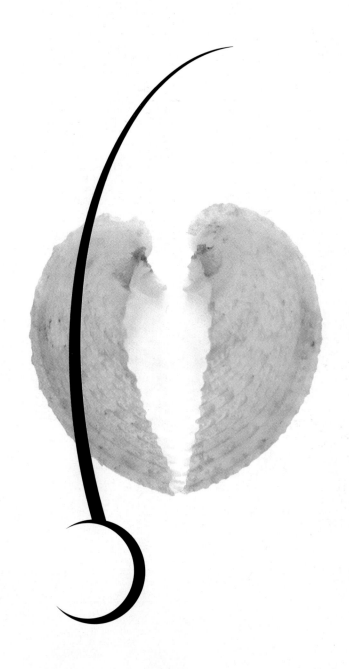

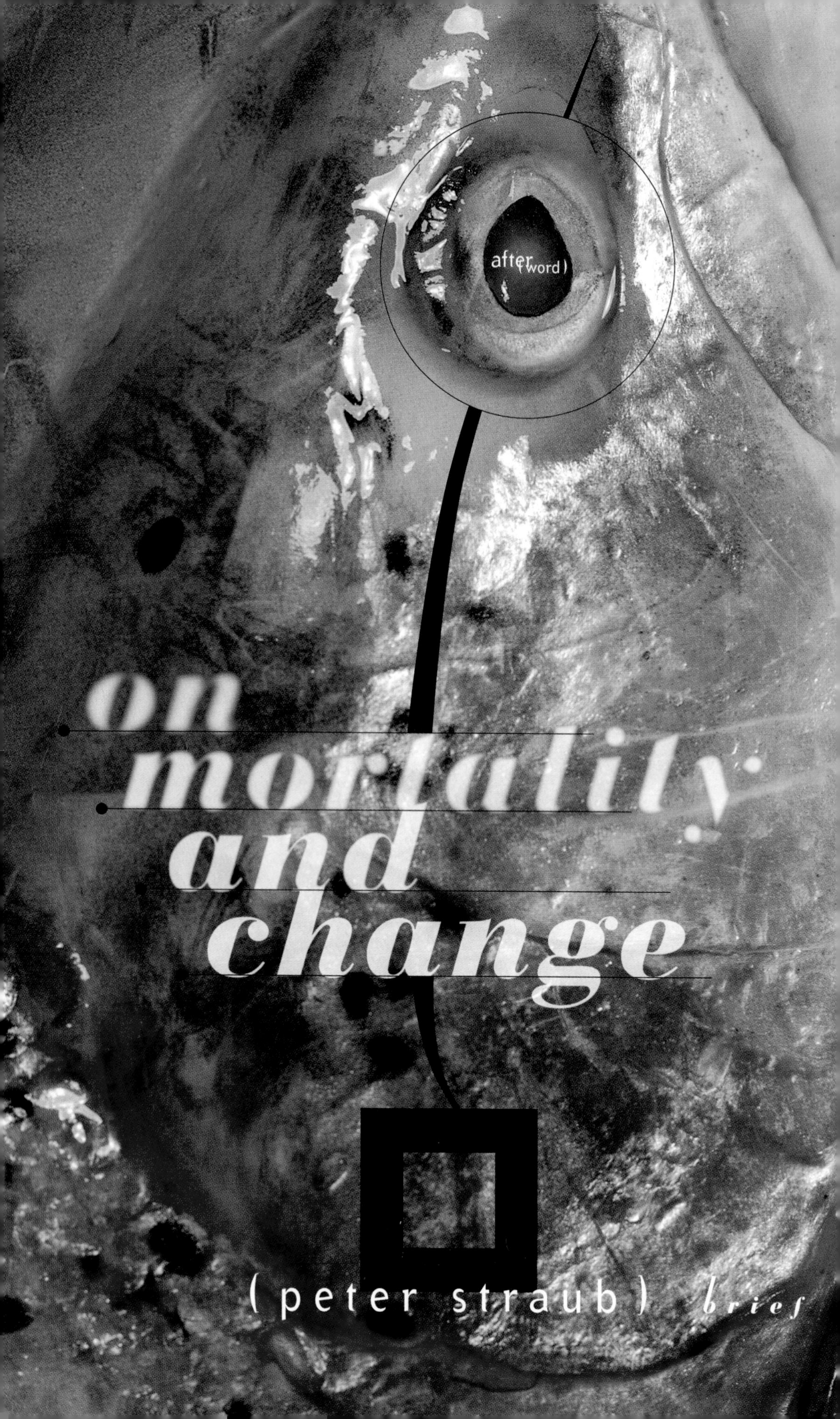
after(word)
on mortality and change
(peter straub)
brief

After being turned down by Despair and Desire, Delirium is finally joined by moping Dream, who feels like getting away from home for a while. Everything that follows takes its character from Delirium. She is the object of universal condescension. Even Destruction's talking dog patronizes her, for, being delirious, she is almost always incapable of following the thread of an ordinary conversation, much less an argument, she speaks in a series of non sequiturs; and her behavior is as giddy and unmediated as a four-year-old's. And like a child, Delirium cherishes excess, spontaneity, grand gestures, color, eccentricity, and excitement. So although it is the search for Destruction that drives the story, it is Delirium who drives the search and in doing so brings these qualities into the story.

In other words, *Brief Lives* is a wild ride, the high point of which takes place in a shabby strip club called Suffragette City as dancing Ishtar turns on the heat to an Iggy Pop record and gives a few louts the opportunity to sample the power of sacred, undebased sexuality before bringing the roof down on them. Before this moment of glorious and insightful power comes an artful skein of characters and incidents, but I will leave the reader to recall them wide-eyed and wondering, and return to my theme.

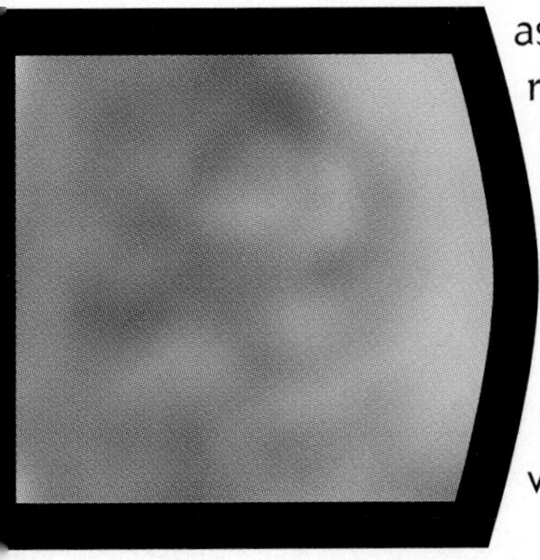

on mortality and change

Delirium's faithfulness and affection, not to mention her willpower, eventually lead the search to a successful conclusion, and Destruction is discovered in his island redoubt. People have been killed, buildings destroyed, lives ruined (poor nasty Officer Flaherty!) and called into question (poor ignorant Danny Capax!) that Delirium and Dream reach their destination. Ordinarily, our traveling pair would be sublimely indifferent to the confusion and suffering they have brought about, and Delirium clearly is unaffected – her own considerable confusion and suffering are quite enough. But Dream confesses that he felt compelled to continue the search in order to honor the death of a specific innocent (poor calculating Ruby!). Destruction points out that his brother's morality seems to have evolved, and Dream coldly denies this suggestion. It would amount to an acknowledgment of change, and he resists change.

The entire search has been conducted in resistance to change. Delirium does not merely want her brother back because she misses him, she wishes to restore the old order. She wants things back the way they used to be. Dream, less naive, merely wants things to remain as they are and assumes that they will do so. He sees Destruction's defection as no more than a shameful abdication of family responsibility. Destruction's response to this charge is a summary of the book's attitude toward change and a challenge to Dream's central attitudes.

In effect, Destruction says that the Endless do not exist. They are merely mythic patterns, and as such do not have the authority to interfere in human lives. The only one of them to survive this epoch in the ongoing story of the universe will be Death, who existed before life began. In time, mortals will cease to honor or accept the idea-patterns represented by the Endless, and another great change will overtake them. Gaiman is preparing us for the end of the Sandman tales, perhaps even for the end of the Sandman mythos itself – for a kind of death.

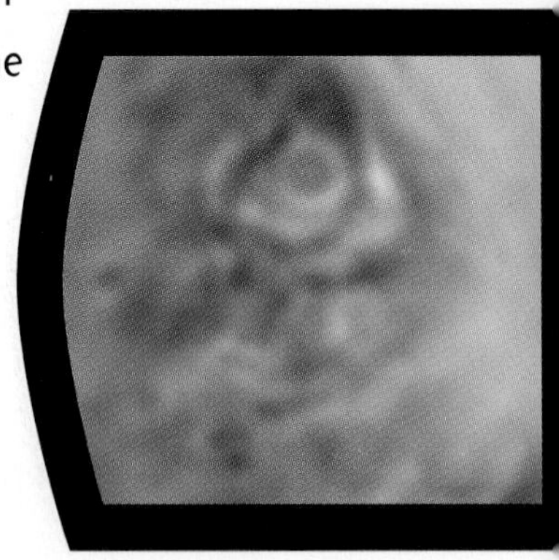

Then, as if inadvertently, Destruction remembers a night – long ago and far away – when Death told him something that he still does not comprehend, that we all, Endless and human beings both, know everything that can be known. All knowledge – it must be assumed, I think, that knowledge is other than fact – exists within us. When he asked her why, then, did people, the Endless, and gods all keep on making ridiculous and painful mistakes, she answered: in order to make the knowledge bearable, we pretend not to possess it.

Dream just ignores this, it doesn't penetrate at all, but Delirium, who has perfectly understood Destruction's first point – that there is no such thing as a one-sided coin, that the believed requires the believer, that beginnings imply endings – understands this one, too. "Not knowing everything is all that makes it okay, sometimes," she says. This is true, it's wise and sad, but it depends for its truth on the coin's other side. Mortal humans possess the secrets known to gods, and these secrets are often painful. To negate the pain, men and gods forget, pretend to forget, then forget to pretend, but the great secret knowledge remains within, ready to be gained again, however partially. We share more than the brevity of life with the Endless.

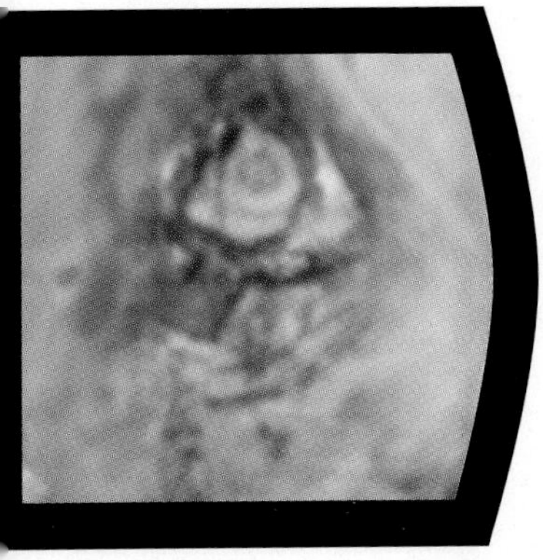

on mortality and change

Finished with what he has to say, Destruction sails off into unknown alien realms, leaving Dream to acknowledge its accuracy by bringing about a great change precisely of the sort described. He must grant to his son, Orpheus, the literal death he had promised him long ago. When that has been accomplished he may return to his realm, so altered by heartache the Gryphon attendant on his door does not recognize him.

All of this action, emotion, and revelation is contained within a frame which contains in haikulike form the values and insights of the larger story.

This frame introduces and concludes the Orpheus story by focusing on his aged attendant, Andros, whose father held the same position, as did his grandfather, and so on, back for thousands of years. These mortals coexist with the divine, in full recognition of what that means. The first and last sentences of Brief Lives are Andros's – that is, they are the words of a man in close proximity to death. Andros begins this long, energetic, brilliant story by saying, "It is, of course, a miracle." The oxymoronic of course is pure Gaiman, anchoring the miraculous in dailiness. He concludes the story by saying the same thing in another way: "It is going to be a beautiful day." The sacred severed head has been buried, deep. All change is change for the worse. All change is change for the better. It's going to be, like every day, a beautiful day.

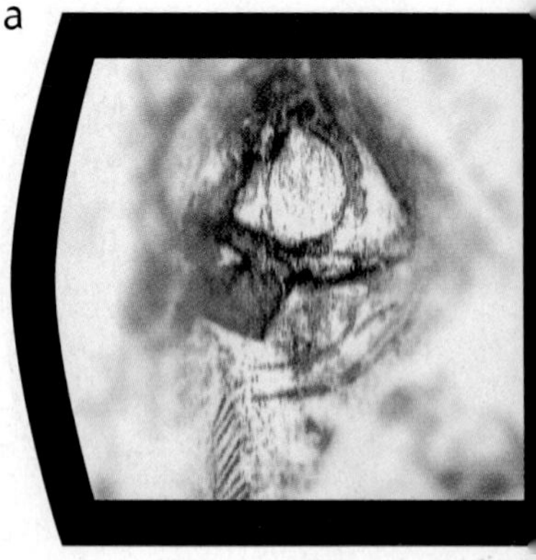

on mortality and change

Neil Gaiman is on a plane all his own. Nobody in his field is better than this. No one has as much range, depth, and command of narrative. Gaiman is a master, and his vast, roomy stories, filled with every possible shade of feeling, are unlike anyone else's.

If

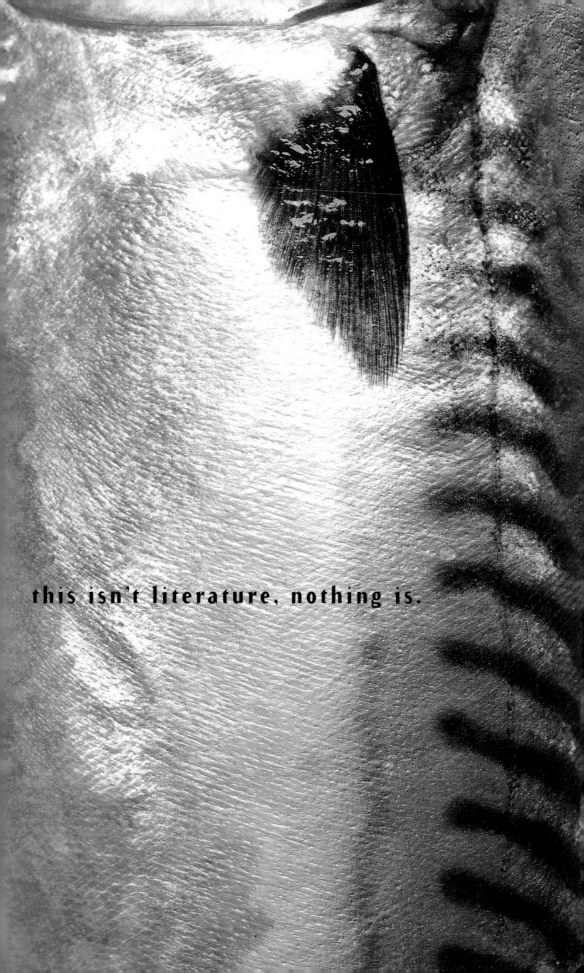

this isn't literature, nothing is.

bio GRAPHIES

RODNEY SPANDREL (b. 1911) -
Looked for love in all the wrong places. Eventually found it where he'd left it.

NEIL GAIMAN (b. 1960) -
his dreams come only true

FISGARD ROSEMARSH (b. 1913) -
Drank too much, but gave freely to those less fortunate than himself.

RORY CHESS (b. 1912) -
Would obliquely refer, from time to t to the single sexual relationship in w he had indulged, in Calcutta, during t winter of 1929, but with whom, and what occurred, he would never say.

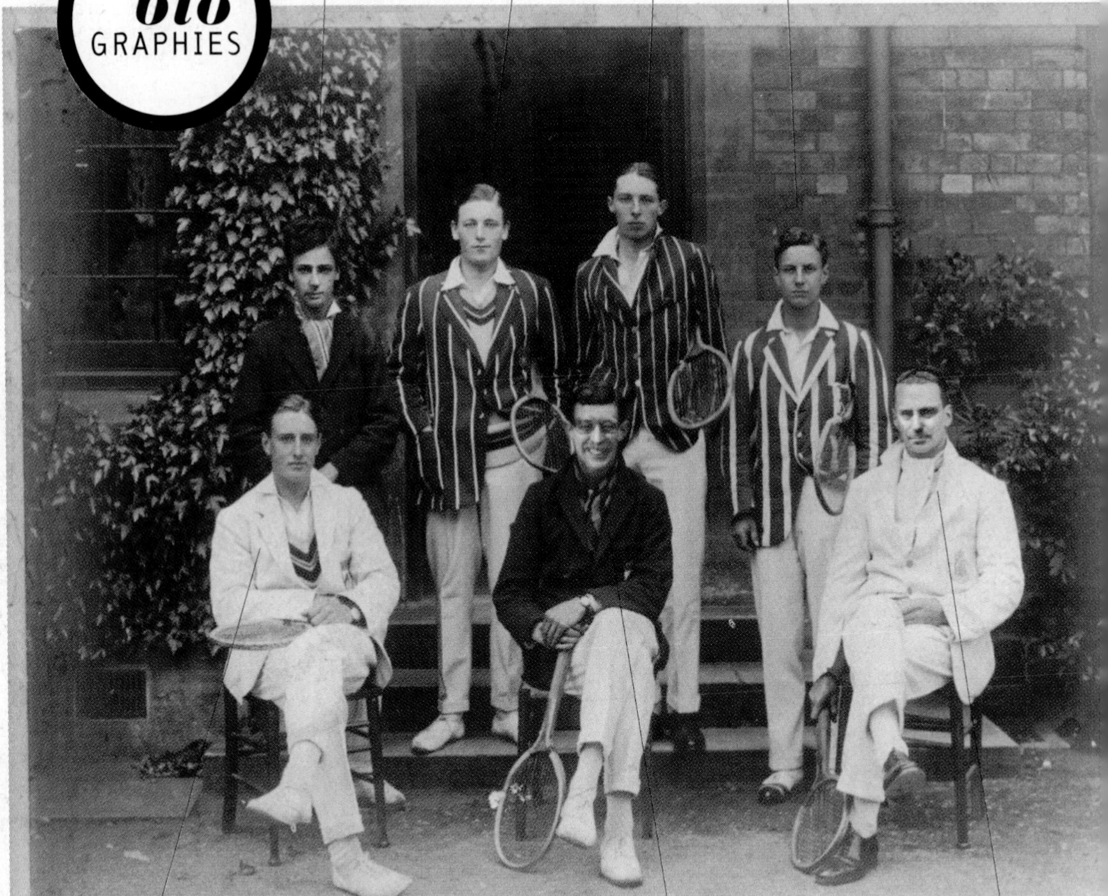

Biographies researched and written by Neil Gaiman. Photographic research by Dave McKean.

BUTTON NELSON (b.1949) -
Wrote a short book about his childhood, to be remembered forever. You have not read it, and you do not know anyone who has.

PETER STRAUB (b. 1943) -
Writes fine, fine novels.

DICK GIORDANO (b. 1932) -
Has retired in order to work more and harder.

VICTORIA SUNSHINE (b. 1947) - Died in 1963 with the reputation of having saved no fewer than twenty-eight lives from water and fire.

JILL THOMPSON (b. 1966) - Is a one-woman episode of *Talk Soup*.

SHELLY ROEBERG (b. 1966) - If only Snow White could tap-dance, she would want to be Shelly Roeberg (currently available in brunette, auburn, platinum, and honey-blonde.)

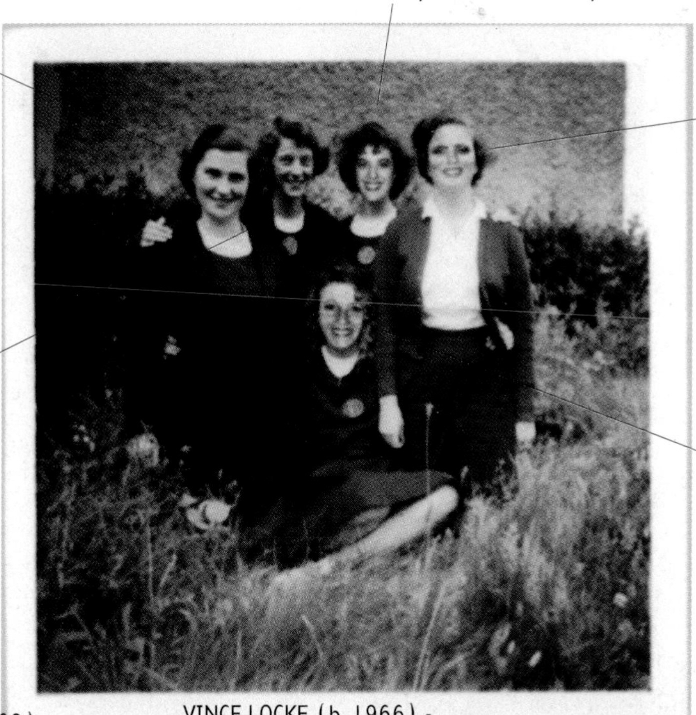

MANDY THURIBLE (b. 1601) - Terribly afraid of kittens.

KAREN BERGER (b. 1958) - Ever so slowly her jurisdiction will spread. She will eventually dominate the entire universe, whether she wishes it or not.

DAVE McKEAN (b. 1963) - Spawned a goblin and is wary of sheep.

VINCE LOCKE (b. 1966) - Is getting married, but still speaks little and listens much.

FRANK L. PRIVETT (b. 84 A.D.) - There are too many places to which he will now never return, but there are a number of places he has yet to visit.

DAEDALUS HOOPER (b. 1914) - Sang sweet, sad songs of quiet lust and madness.

BOB KAHAN (b. 1954) - Makes fine galleries and strange books.

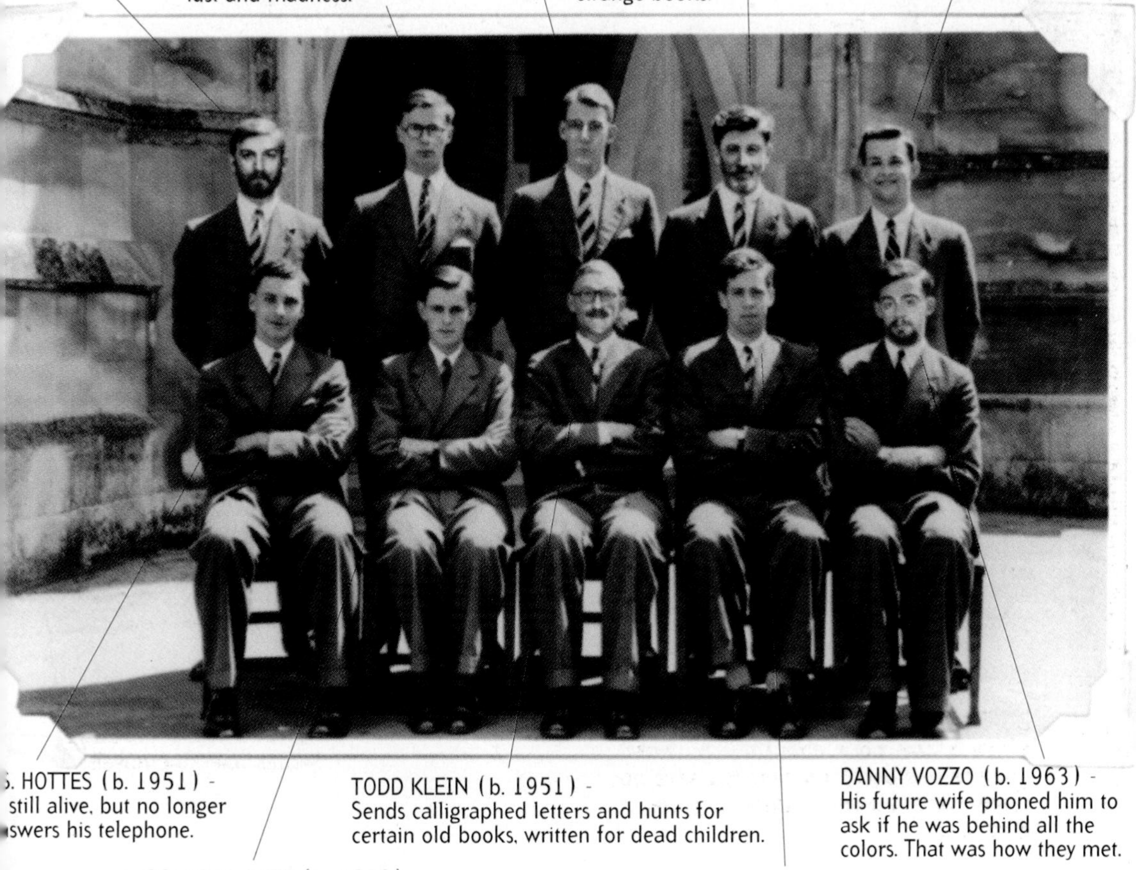

. HOTTES (b. 1951) - still alive, but no longer swers his telephone.

TODD KLEIN (b. 1951) - Sends calligraphed letters and hunts for certain old books, written for dead children.

DANNY VOZZO (b. 1963) - His future wife phoned him to ask if he was behind all the colors. That was how they met.

WOOLMER WHITE (b. 1950) - Not his real name.

JEREMIAH JOHN MAHONEY (b. 1952) - Collects butterflies.

19
46

henry treece

collected poems

The Characters

The man in the mask swings a sword of bright stars
The cloud of his breath is the shroud of the earth.
But the man in the robe from a book reads our fears,
And ticks off the minutes from death until birth.

The woman in white is the mother of hope,
And the twin doves of peace rest on her twin breasts.
But the woman in black, with a knife and a rope,
Is the watcher at gateway, the guardian of ghosts.